Ali Poyraz

TWENTY-ONE YEARS, FOUR MONTHS

The Journal of a Kurdish Political Prisoner

translated into English by
Andrew Penny

Gomidas Institute
London

As the original work was written in Turkish, we have retained the use of the modified Latin alphabet in the English translation. Notably, these include the letters: ş (sh), ç (ch), c (j), ğ (originally a guttural "gh" sound, now a soft sigh in modern Turkish), and ı (similar to the sound "e" in "the"), as well as ü and ö, as used in French. The author also uses the letter "x" to represent "kh," a guttural sound that has been removed from formal Turkish but remains in use in Kurdish.

© 2025 Gomidas Institute. All Rights Reserved.

ISBN 978-1-909382-82-4

For further information please contact:
Gomidas Institute
42 Blythe Rd.
London, W14 0HA
England
Email: *info@gomidas.org*

Translator's Note

Ali Poyraz's book detailing his 21 years and four months in various Turkish prisons gives us an insight into a different world, one of which in the West we know very little. The way the PKK developed from a small cadre-based organisation into the mass movement it became in the early 1990s can be followed in the pages of this book.

The book also introduces us to Kurdish history, a subject which receives a lot less attention than other issues in the Middle East. The last century of Turkish state oppression of the Kurds is not well known, even amongst the Kurds themselves, especially the Kurds who have suffered a century of denial of their very identity and assimilation under the Turkish Republic.

The detailed accounts of the comradeship necessary to overcome the hardships, attacks and torture of the Turkish prison system is the most impressive aspect of the book. It is hard to imagine the discipline required to organise frequent hunger strikes and to ensure that fellow inmates survived the regular attacks and searches carried out by the Turkish authorities.

How anyone managed to survive the ordeals described in this book is something I frequently asked myself while translating.

The events of the 1990s which Ali covers in his journal lend a different angle on current affairs to that which we are used to in the West.

The capture of Abdullah Öcalan in 1999 had a seismic effect on the Kurdish movement. The shattering effect it had on Kurdish political prisoners is reflected in this book.

To sum up, this book is not an easy read, but offers important insights into an often ignored issue.

—Andrew Penny, London
3 Oct. 2024

TWENTY-ONE YEARS, FOUR MONTHS

The Journal of a Kurdish Political Prisoner

IN LIEU OF AN INTRODUCTION
(ORIGINALLY WRITTEN IN 2021)

I spent 21 years and four months in Turkish prisons between 1981 and 2002. As will be seen from the diary I kept, I was taken to several prisons and released in 2002. Looking back, I am sorry to note that Turkey has been transformed into an enormous prison. This has been due to the continuity in the country's disposition towards imprisonment, a practice that now encompasses society at large.

After the military coup of 12 September 1980, prisons, torture, hunger-strikes and death-fasts, as well as unlawful arrests and a system of solitary confinement became commonplace. All colonialist and capitalist countries, first and foremost those in Europe, are in the same state. They are now "modern" prisons for people from Kurdistan and all those who struggle for the working people.

During my time in prison, it was sometimes not possible for me to write or protect what I had written. For this reason, the journal I kept begins in 1994, 13 years into my imprisonment.

Sharing the journal is, first and foremost, a necessity to pay my respects to those comrades who are no longer with us, having joined the caravan of the immortal.

Many friends also rightly pestered me for years to publish my writings.

I would also point out that, rather than being a journal, these writings are like documents from the period in question.

I have related only a small portion of what we experienced in prison in these pages. When I think about it, even I, as someone who lived through those times, find it difficult to believe what I have recorded. On occasions, a pickaxe handle descended on my head and blood splashed onto the ceiling. Another time, they tried to suffocate us with smoke from fires. At other times we were put in underground cells that had been declared uninhabitable and full of sewage. There, while trying to fight off dozens of rats the size of cats, we were gasping for air in the suffocating heat of July in Adana.

During 21 years of incarceration, when I add up the days I was on hunger strikes, long and short, they total at least three years. Is it possible to comprehend a human being going hungry for three years? Yet, it is true. For this reason, it is essential that these experiences are recorded and, most importantly, not be forgotten. It must be known how incredibly strong human willpower and physical endurance can be in the face of unlimited persecution.

I believe that everything that has happened during the struggle, whether in the mountains, in the cities, abroad, or in the prisons, needs to be recorded.

Every period of history has its own experiences and riches.

And when, where, and however they occurs, the battle between good and evil continues.

Those who are on the side of the workers, the people, and what is right are constantly engaged in struggle and will continue to do so.

While transcribing my journal, I found some sections very difficult to read. Many things I had to write again and again. Along with the pain, I felt once again, the warmth and self-sacrifice of those comrades.

One of the most difficult parts was the section on my sisters who were martyred. I rewrote hundreds of pages. When writing about the moment I heard of the death of my sister, comrade, and confidante, Rahşan, my pen gave out. I was virtually transfixed. I slipped once more into the abyss of my sorrow. Dozens of pages later when writing about the death of my little sister, Handan, my pen gave out in the same way. It was incredible, as if the pen had locked, like me. It, too, cried out.

But, despite everything, these things had to be written about.

While rewriting the section I had written in Aydın prison with a typewriter, partly handwritten, I used the same style I had used in prison.

I once again remember with thanks and gratitude all the lovers of freedom who are no longer with us.

IN THEIR MEMORY
APRIL 2019 / JANUARY 2021
ALI POYRAZ / LONDON

IN THE BEGINNING

When going through a difficult process, a person can rely on an idea or a movement. Otherwise, no human being could overcome pain and hardship.

Journals are grains of truth that constitute history.

Until recently, as a people, our awareness of history was weak, and because that history had been distorted, we had no tradition of transmitting our own grains of truth through writing.

However, in the midst of warfare, our people are writing their own poems, novels and, indeed, their history…

From the first day I entered prison, I wanted to keep a journal. But, unfortunately, most of the time, this was not possible. Sometimes a piece of paper or the ink tube of a pen were concealed like a weapon. Sometimes everything we had, including our bodies, were ravaged….

When we look back and recall what we went through, it seems impossible even for us to believe.

Did these things really happen to us? Or were we merely witnesses?

For someone in prison, a "prison journal" is not very appealing. This is because days and events in prison life are restricted and closely resemble each other. Despite this, our outlook on life made us think of this issue as an arena of struggle, shattering the monotony of our existence to a certain extent…

How are our days in prison passing?

What are our fundamental endeavours?

What do we think of ongoing events?

What do we feel?

Even our interesting dreams…

Our ideas and emotions regarding all the above need to be known in particular by those who are outside.

For this reason, I resolved to write after 1994.

Most important of all, how aware were we of internal and external developments, and how did we position ourselves with regard to them?

And our longings and utopias…

This is the reason for endeavouring to write in detail on certain days, if not every day.

E Type Prison / Aydın

AYDIN PRISON

Block 9
28 November 1994

Yesterday, we endeavoured to celebrate the anniversary of the founding of our party, as far as possible, given our circumstances. The enthusiasm and participation was generally good.

The years are flowing by like water.

We're into our 17th year. As preparations had begun in all our blocks ten days earlier, all blocks were ready for 27 November. Everyone got up as usual at 7.30, and there was unusual vitality in the air. All the friends leapt from their beds, saying "Rojbaş" [good morning in Kurdish], and got dressed. In an hour, the necessary tasks had been carried out and breakfast finished. People shaved and put on their best clothes. At 8.30, 38 comrades were lined up in two rows in the exercise yard.

When comrade Mehmet Ayçiçek uttered the word "Rojbaş," we responded heartily. This was followed by the recitation of our vow. Without a change in formation, I changed places with Ayçiçek. After making a four or five-paragraph statement on the importance of 27 November, I invited the comrades to stand in silence for one minute to remember those who had fallen in the name of the revolution in Kurdistan, Turkey, and worldwide. I then read out a two-page declaration. The friends listened intently. I took care to ensure I read correctly with a vibrant voice. Despite this, I tripped up on several words.

After the declaration had been read, all the comrades in single file exchanged greetings in celebration of the anniversary. The event then began. Nihat and Acar carried out the organising in the block. We all sat in the dining hall in a "U" shape. One side had been turned into a stage. The choir came onto the stage and began to sing our folk songs. The line-up of our choir was something to be seen. Hamit, with his tiny body and huge glasses sat at the front playing the saz. The choir was comprised of Şıxo, Nihat, Acar, Şehmus, İhsan, Sincar, and Zeki.

The shortest was Acar, at 1.50, the tallest was Sincar, 1.90 with his bulky frame…

The line-up was reminiscent of a mountain range, with its ups and downs.

After two songs, the message of our prison administration was read out. Then, the soloists and those who were going to recite poems were invited onto the stage, one by one. I recited the first poem, reading the sixth chapter of Adnan Yücel's book, Children of Fire and Sun. This was followed by Mümin reading the seventh chapter with much enthusiasm.

When messages were read from the other blocks, there was huge applause. Those from other political movements delighted us even more. For the first time, I witnessed the struggle in Kurdistan and our party being the subject of such clear and realistic assessments.

Celebrations continued into the afternoon with a quiz. The block was split into four groups. Of course, as in all quizzes, the questions and answers were controversial. As objections were made, the jury tried to calm things down, saying, "Comrades, let the team leaders speak." The questions were mainly internal. In addition to the subjects of prison resistance, conference decisions, and national liberation, there were also questions regarding abilities.

Afterwards, we went out into the exercise yard and lined up for a halay. As always, Ayçiçek led the dance. His smooth movements, once again, added colour to the show.

Once the exercise yard door had closed, the event continued in the blocks. We listened to comrade Acar, who sat on bedding in a corner. He asked for contributions from comrades who had celebrated 27 November before to explain their feelings and excitement, giving priority to those who had been guerrillas. But, for some reason, comrades were shy. Due to their modesty, I guess, they allowed the old guard, the "dinosaurs," to speak.

Comrade Mümin reminisced about the group's early period in Ankara. Those years were recalled with some sadness, affection, and nostalgia.

The companions introduced a new idea. There were small packets wrapped in newspaper in a plastic tub. A packet had been prepared for everyone. 24 notes had been placed on a dish, and everyone took one. In some notes, a song had been written, in others, a memory, while some had the number of a packet. When I chose one, I mumbled that I didn't want a song. Mine had "memory" written on it.

I explained the time in 1979, when I first heard that the party had been founded. At that time in Antep, around 20 friends had gathered in the "Tutluk" neighbourhood, and it was announced that a party had been established. We were delighted, and most of us immediately scrawled the party's name on our palms in order to learn it by heart.

I took care to explain a memory linked to the founding of our party. A few days after hearing the news, I was with a group of around ten friends chatting in a café we frequented in the Nuripazarbaşı neighbourhood of Antep. We noticed an elderly man we did not know sitting at a table nearby. When we realised he was listening to us, we began to whisper amongst ourselves. We were saying: "Is he a policeman or an informer?" At that time, we were suspicious of anyone we didn't know. We decided to speak to the elderly man. A comrade invited him to join us. He came without hesitation. Of course, we exchanged knowing glances as if this proved our suspicions. The comrade said:

Uncle, where are you from?

"I'm from Nizip."

"How are things there?"

"By God, they're good. There are Apocus there."

"Do you know them?"

"Of course I know them. There was one called "Tosun" (Mehmet Ece). The Türkeş supporters [Grey Wolves] killed him in front of Nizip park. After Tosun, all hell broke loose."

"How do you mean?"

"After Tosun's death, they shot the chair of the Grey Wolves, then they shot the new chair... They kept on going."

The elderly man must have realised who we were as he was talking freely and trying to be accepted.

After laughing together, a comrade said, "Uncle, the Apocus have formed a party."

"Really?"

"Yes, really. They are no longer just a group, they have established a party."

"Good, good. From now on, we'll vote for this party."

"No, uncle, it's not that sort of party. It won't take part in elections. It's a clandestine party."

"Now, won't we be able to vote for this party?"

"No, but if you want, you can help it in other ways. For instance, you could assist the Apocus you mentioned with material support. You can invite them to your home and tell them you want to help them."

"Alright. Seeing that they won't contest elections, we'll help them with money."

A few months later, I saw this old man in Nizip and was delighted. The fact that he was Turkish had pleased me even more.

While reminiscing, I was living those days again. Those places, people, and moments passed before my eyes like yesterday.

At that time, the total number of our comrades could have gathered in a corner of that café. But today, there are tens of thousands. Looking at comrades from Cudi, Dersim, Gabar, Sason, and other regions, I am both surprised and pleased.

Especially, children born in those years grew up becoming guerrillas and even commanders directing the war. It is particularly exciting to see 17-year-olds and 70-year-olds in the same ranks.

In brief, the dozens of yesterday have become the millions of today.

We no longer fear loneliness, for we have become a popular movement.

I would really have liked to share the outside world, the mountains, the struggle, with these companions; but still, it is great to be with them under these conditions. Nevertheless, making their acquaintance in prison is indescribably sad. As I look at them and listen, I can feel, in my lungs and my heart, the winds of freedom blowing from our mountains.

Block 9
1 April 1995

Today, all our blocks started to exercise. At 6.45, I woke everyone with Rojbaş. With the excitement of the first day, everyone was ready in a few minutes.

After carrying out our morning tasks, we began to wait in the kitchen downstairs, as the gate to the exercise yard opened at 7. They opened it five minutes late. The deputy governor, the head guard Bekir, and nearly ten prison officers were waiting for us. They were surprised we were all ready. Nedim and I were making for the gate when the head guard asked sternly:

"Ali, haven't you got a pen?"

As I wondered what he wanted with a pen at that time of the morning, I turned to Nedim and said:

"Give me your pen."

As Nedim reached into his inside pocket and brought out one of his three pens, I said:

"Stop! It's April the first today."

It will harm our pride if we let the guards take our pens.

When we went into the exercise yard, we quickly lined up in twos. After comrade Ayçiçek said Rojbaş loudly, he recited the party march. He then said that elderly and sick comrades who were exempt from sporting activities were free to go and allowed two kitchen lookouts from each block to go inside.

We ran for as long as ten minutes. As it had rained the previous night, the surface was slippery. Comrade Ihsan, who was in front of me, slipped over and fell. I tried to prevent him falling, but as he is a bit "plump," I was unable to do so. Although he picked himself up promptly, he was unable to prevent other comrades' laughter.

Despite Ayçiçek telling him he could drop out, he kept going.

When the run ended, we started the exercises, drawing a large circle on the ground. We followed Ayçiçek's movements. As it was the first day, he stopped after 30 minutes. He wants our bodies to slowly get accustomed to the movements. After press-ups, we moved on to free movements. Comrade Osman, who was turning left and right in front of the wall, laughed, saying, "Our exercises are just beginning." After a few exercises, I did some skipping. After working up a sweat, I went for a shower, but I didn't stay long in the shower, as the water was cold. You have to be careful on the first day.

We held a panel discussion on recent developments. The Turkish Republic is continuing the invasion of South Kurdistan it launched in March with 35 thousand troops, 3,000 armoured vehicles, dozens of helicopters and planes, 2,000 officers, 13 generals, and thousands of village guards and special forces.

Despite there not being many clashes, apart from certain points, the mountainous terrain is still hindering their advance.

According to today's newspapers, a Cobra helicopter has been shot down. It was not well publicised, but we learned about it from the report of an officer's funeral.

The day before, the sudden disappearance of five thousand guerrillas in that region created great alarm. They do not conceal their concern that "the area could turn into a quagmire" once they have occupied it.

They have announced that 20 soldiers have died. But according to Kurd-Ha, the figure is more than 500.

If hit-and-run tactics are stepped up, it is certain that Turkish troops will be ravaged. It looks as if our side has learned a lot from the war of '92. The fact they are not engaging in a frontal war demonstrates this.

It is this concern that frightens the Turkish army.

The view emerging from the panel is that the occupation will not last long, and that they will withdraw on account of the international situation, guerrilla attacks, popular resistance in the region, etc.

It is also true that for a long time they have wanted to remain there, but it is also a fact that imperialism does not want the status quo to be upset.

Besides this, it was said that the USA approved of this invasion and that it had proposed different "solutions" to Europe.

At this moment, they have gone more than 50 kilometres beyond the border. It is said that they have occupied an area covering 9,000 square kilometres. But, with this operation, the fact of the matter is their wish to prevent the leap forward the party wants to make in '95 and the announcement of the founding of a Kurdistan parliament.

As many comrades had watched "Siyaset Meydanı" on TV until 3am last night, and many were drowsy in the morning, we let them sleep until noon.

I took a look at the newspapers until 10am. They called us to the kitchen for our ten o'clock tea. As our lot didn't wake people up, we were subject to taunting from the block opposite. We replied, jokingly, that "everything is under control."

As usual, we started collective education at 1.30pm. The 13th block remained outside. We read the leadership reality and fighter's life and freedom section from the February '94 analysis. Some comrades made contributions. Following tea and cigarette breaks, we finished at 4.30.

There was lovely sunshine during our first break. We spent 15 minutes in the sun. It was wonderful.

However, by the time education ended, it was raining. I was angry, again, at the treacherous weather of Aydın and voiced my feelings. It's constantly changing.

Comrade Ferhat said slightly reluctantly, that we should sit down, because we had only just stood up. We had not had the opportunity to relax. There were articles we needed to respond to. Three of us went to block 13. We rapidly read almost a hundred opinions and proposals regarding comrade Fikret. The dominant view was that his self-criticism was sufficient, but that sanctions should be imposed. Taking into consideration our own administration's opinion, we reached agreement on the following points:

* Self-criticism is sufficient.
* Political relationship to be frozen until the annual conference.
* An individual reading programme to be established for educational purposes.

As we were late for the evening meal, we ate late. While other comrades had their tea, we sat down to eat. Despite the soup being cold, it was nice. Comrade Şehmus had made it. It was accompanied by a sour pickle made from Maraş peppers. I gorged on those.

We listened to all the news on the bulletin between 19.00 and 20.00. News items on South Kurdistan had priority.

After 20.00, we kept going. We read a 12-page section on the prisons. After comrade Ferhat had made a summary, we ended the session. We will continue tomorrow. It's midnight. As always, most of the comrades have gone to bed. Six guards came into the block and did a head count. In order to see some comrades who were completely hidden under their blankets, they lifted up the corners gently. They were afraid detainees might react. I will end here and go to bed as we will get up early in the morning.

Block 9
2 April 1995

Comrade Şehmus and I are on duty. Consequently, we didn't attend the exercises. While the comrades were doing their exercises, we swept the block with Koçer from Botan. At 9.00, comrades Celalettin, A. Kaya, Giyasettin, Hamit, Zeki, and Ender from the 4th, 6th and 14th blocks came to visit us.

Conversations continued in the exercise yard in the sun until midday. The comrades were treated to tea and white coffee. Of course, there was more water than milk. For lunch, we had çiğköfte, kneaded by Şehmus Poyraz, and ayran.

Comrade Acar had sent his empty tobacco tin. As I had received the message, I filled the tin. As one of Acar's hands was amputated at the wrist, he has a cigarette-rolling gadget.

We held reciprocal chats with our guests regarding political work. At 13.30, they returned to their blocks. At 14.00, our collective education began and continued until 17.00. Immediately after the evening meal, we were to reassemble and the February instructions of the Party CC [central committee] were to be read out. The session was to continue until 22.00.

Comrade Seyfettin served tea. Half an hour later, he gave each comrade an orange. As everything is restricted, the handing out of oranges immediately changes the atmosphere in the block.

After cleaning the cooker and the ashtrays, I retreated to my bed to read the newspaper.

Block 9
4 April 1995

Today is Tuesday. It was the Turkish left's visiting day. At around 10.00, we received a note from DS [Dev-Sol]. Apparently, the prison authorities wanted to search them as they went to receive visitors. They also wanted them to remove their party rosettes. They refused. In their note, they said they would resist in the event the prison authorities intervene. We passed the notes on to our representatives and to TDKP. Until noon we heard nothing more.

Comrade Sarıkaya came to our block. After sitting for a while, Uncle Xalef cut Sarıkaya's hair. Although he's 67, his haircuts only last five to 10 minutes. Hamdullah laughed, saying:

"Xalo, your customer has deep pockets."

Uncle Xalef said nothing but, clanking his scissors louder, he made his irritation clear.

After the haircut, we returned the scissors and hair-trimmer to the prison administration, as per agreement.

As it's our bath day, we cleaned the sleeping quarters and the dining hall. Straight after the midday meal, we got ready to play football. Meanwhile, we chatted a little with comrade Sarıkaya.

27 people who were to participate in the action were to be removed from the list. Also, because of the large number, it conflicted with the perspective of our prisons centre. The general concern is for it to be successful. But it is clear that, by saying this, an extreme position has been taken. It is wrong to expect the same competence and participation from everyone. Besides, participation is a relative situation.

After playing football, we went to the bathhouse at 14.00. As always, it was noisy and smelly. Again, they cut off the hot water early.

As we were getting dressed, the sound of slogans and slamming doors was heard. Although we had told the guards we were returning to our block, they did not let us out. We were kept locked in the bathhouse for an hour. Although we banged on the door, no one turned up.

We realised they had attacked DS. The fact the guard who opened the door was hastily rearranging his clothing confirmed our conjecture.

There was a visible cloud of dust in the corridor and it was apparent that some people had been dragged along the floor. When we reached the block, we heard the sound of the Dev-Sol members' slogans and banging of doors.

Four comrades who had remained in our block had also banged on doors, thinking the authorities had attacked us. We told them they had done well.

We immediately wrote a note to DS, asking about the situation. We also wrote to the middle blocks. A reply came immediately from DS. They had apparently been attacked in the visiting area. They wrote that doctors had not been called despite two of their comrades having been injured.

Our comrades wrote another note, saying that our blocks should also protest at this situation, and that we should voice this with a collective slogan.

Our representative immediately went to the governor's office to express the fact we did not accept this situation.

DS and TDKP continued to bang the doors and shout slogans for two hours. In particular, the slogan, "Prisoners cannot be left to die," caught our attention.

Before receiving a reply from our block, a proposal came from DS for a collective slogan and joint banging of doors. We reproached comrade Sait Hoca a little because of our being late, as we should have made our position clear before such a proposal was made.

After a few messages were exchanged, agreement was reached. That night, between 20.00 and 21.30 and at 23.30, the whole prison was to shout the slogans:

"Fascist attacks cannot cow us,"

"Human dignity will defeat torture," and

"Down with the fascist administration."

The attack was aimed at all of us, so a joint stand was important.

Just before the exercise yard closed, a note arrived, saying: "It has been decided that exercises will not be engaged in on Thursdays." As we didn't consider it a correct approach, we immediately wrote a reply. We said each block should not do exercises on its visiting day. It is dogmatic to suggest no one should do exercise on the same day. While writing this, I know that some comrades in our administration will misunderstand, but, despite this, it needs to be pointed out.

After the 20.00 news and the slogans, we read the leadership's article in *Özgür Halk* magazine on the new human being. We spent some time on some comrades' questions. We ended without finishing the debate as, at 21.30, the slogans were to be shouted.

While perusing newspapers, there was a midnight head count.

Since I was tired and reading while lying down, I gave up and put the papers on the empty bunk nearby and fell asleep.

Block 9
5 April 1995

Today was visiting day for blocks 8, 9 and 13. All our comrades used to go on Wednesday. As we now number 125 people, we have two days assigned in a week.

As for Thursday, it is blocks 12, 14, 6 and 4. Compared to the situation before, we will be able to have longer, more comfortable visits. Of course, there are also disadvantages. When we all went together, there was the opportunity for 50-60 comrades to see each other. In my opinion, one visiting day is better. It is also better for joint action by families if they are not divided. With two days, it will be more difficult to mobilise families.

The complaints and suggestions of those comrades who were unable to talk at length and "comfortably" with their families were effective in making our point.

As it suited the prison authorities, they also seized the opportunity. Usually, they would stall on even the smallest of our demands for weeks or months.

Close to 20 of the comrades in our block went for a visit. As always, they started calling for them at 09.30. On every visiting day, we get the families to write requests so that five extra comrades can have visitors.

Since our 42-day hunger strike, our visitors are allowed to remain with us until evening. If we wish, they can also stay over lunchtime.

Towards midday, the TDKP representative, Kazım, came by. He said, "When we went for the visit, the DS members were there. They were going to celebrate the anniversary of the founding of their party. The guards wanted to remove the rosettes they had made and put on their collars. The DS members didn't accept this demand and the guards attacked and removed them from the area. We protested by shouting slogans."

The group of guards who carried out the attack was the one that is on duty during the day. They acted like a sort of prison special force.

A doctor went to the block to attend to the injured inmates, saying, "I'll go down to the dining hall and examine your friends." They apparently protested at this by shouting slogans.

It was evident from what he was telling us that they were upset by this. Once again, DS will criticise them for passivity, and they will respond by saying DS are ultra-left.

At 16.00, the comrades came back from their visit. There were no problems.

Today, I wrote a letter to my mother. I also sent a picture I had taken with Nihat. I hadn't written to her for a long time. I couldn't have remained insensitive any longer after the enthusiasm and warmth in her last card. Sentences full of warmth and feeling a comrade had written compelled me to write.

Block 9

17 April 1995

As it's the anniversary of the deaths of Sabahat Karataş and her comrades, DS started a commemoration. Things were normal until noon, when we heard sounds of a rumpus from block 7. The prison authorities had tried to take down a large banner they had hung in the exercise yard, and when they resisted, there was confusion. Two soldiers, who were brought in, took two inmates to solitary. At first we thought they might be Bedrici [supporters of

Bedri Yağan, who opposed the DS leadership],* but then, we heard that they had also taken the others away. We began to bang the doors and shout slogans.

No one had been taken to solitary in Aydın prison for five years. This is a serious development… In protest, we refused the lunchtime and evening meal wagon.

Block 4

31 October 1995

AN OLD GREYBEARD AND A CHILD

In the next few days, there will be a re-organisation of our blocks. Hasan Yağız is one of those who is to leave our block. Last night, as he packed his belongings, he held up an exercise book, saying, "Do you remember this? There's also a note from you." At first, I didn't understand what he meant. I quickly scoured my memory. In June 1993, when we had been in the same block, I had written a few pages. I had forgotten it. When I looked at the exercise book, I realised that he had not read what any comrades had written. Perhaps that was a good thing. But it is interesting that he was not curious and resisted the temptation. Perhaps it is a better feeling to know that comrades had written to him on those white pages without reading them.

The exercise book took me back to the old days. How time flies. Three years in a prison is both a long time and a time that has passed so swiftly. During this time, we have changed blocks three or four times. We have had two indefinite hunger strikes, one that lasted 30 days, and one that lasted 42 days. We've lived through many protests and support actions. Ten-day alternating hunger strikes and a whole series of incidents…

And since then, more than a hundred comrades have come from Buca prison in Izmir to join us here in Aydın. At the moment, we number 181 people, having recently received three groups from Buca of 8, 15, and 20 people. For this reason, we need a new arrangement. At the moment, they are in blocks 2 and 5, but they will need to be taken into our blocks.

Taking the exercise book, I went down to the dining hall with Hasan. After 23.00 is the time of silence. Downstairs, comrade Hüseyin Acar was sitting at a table, perusing an article. From time to time, he teased us.

I had written the following in the exercise book:

---

* While a leading member of the DS (Devrimci Sol) [Revolutionary Left] organisation, Bedri had disagreements and left the organisation. Subsequently, he experienced serious problems with them. Those who acted with him were called 'Bedrici'. —Author

12.06.1993 Aydın.

Dear Hasan,

Real friendship is superior to everything. And, for this reason, when necessary, a friend will face death instead of his friend. For his friend, he will endure all manner of pain and suffering, so that his friend does not have to. Because it is known that fellow companions in a cause will support their companions in struggle.

Meeting one's friends is always a source of excitement and enthusiasm. Even if this encounter is in a prison, it loses nothing in significance. However, the sourness of encounters in prison are felt in the very depths of the heart. But to spite incarceration, one's eyes still sparkle when meeting a friend. Just like when meeting in our mountains, whose peaks stand for freedom.

Perhaps it is like the May flowers enveloping nature, perhaps in the dreams of a guerrilla resting on a tree and observing the dawn, perhaps it is a position during hand to hand fighting. These encounters are like swimming in the sea of immortality. Every stroke brings one closer to the future.

As for the Future, it is FREEDOM.

On the page I began to write was the note stating "unity is strength." This is absolutely true. Today, this strength is being created in our country. And our people are involved in an intense effort to take possession of it and sacrifice everything for its sake. Otherwise, would they have flowed towards tomorrow in uprisings? Would they, who bear the scars of centuries, have embraced the freedom fighters, and more, ushered their own children onto the path towards hope?

The struggle for existence and a free future needs great self-sacrifice and heroism. Today, these have become commonplace in Kurdistan. Everywhere, epic resistance is taking place. Alongside these great and honourable stands is also immorality. But this does not affect our people. On the contrary, it sharpens their resolution for struggle. For it is well known that where there are the honourable actions of those who resist, there will also unfortunately be turncoats, fugitives, and betrayal. For this is what history tells us. I believe that this will always be the case. But, in spite of everything, today, a new history is being written in our country. A new human being is creating a new history. From now on, our people, not others, will write our history. When the word history is mentioned, those shameful feelings will be replaced by honourable days.

My dear friend, I think that wherever there is life, especially where there is struggle, it needs to be written down. Writing in the beautiful, windy Zagros mountains, or in a broad valley, or the onrushing sound of the Munzur river while leaning against an oak tree is the best kind of writing. Writing in an environment that is close to the clouds of freedom would be more profound. However, the difficulties peculiar to each setting should not be forgotten. But for a guerrilla to keep a journal is such an exciting thing. As wonderful as it is writing in the early morning breeze of the forest of freedom, it is at least as wonderful writing in prison.

However much walls may get closer to each other, ideas and yearnings cannot be shuttered. This feeling is the very act of climbing over these thick walls and meeting the heat of struggle. Writing is a feeling, an expression of sustenance. Otherwise, would a guerrilla high up on Ararat mountain continue to write obstinately despite having frozen hands?

Dear Hasan, we are still yet to truly appreciate the value of real comradeship. Not its theoretical side, but in practice. In addition to the positives of being alongside comrades for many years, some things have been lost. While sharing daily life with comrades with whom we have faced death on many occasions, there are also inadequacies from time to time. We may not be able to appreciate a person standing alongside us. Unfortunately, in most cases, we only understand this after the person has been martyred. A delayed value is meaningless.

At the forefront of values that exalt the human being come the attitude that time develops when it is appropriate.

Our white-haired warrior, Uncle Musa [Anter],* would often mention our fundamental values when narrating his 70 years of experience.

If only all our elderly were like Uncle Musa, we would have begun to break the chains that enslave us earlier.

Unfortunately, we have few Uncle Musas. But we are hopeful. For we have Abidins, who make the sign of victory with their tiny fingers

---

* 'Ape Musa' (Musa Anter). In Kurdish 'Ape Musa' means Uncle Musa. He was a prominent Kurdish writer and political figure. He was arrested and tortured numerous times. Many of his articles and books were banned. In spite of this, he did not submit. On 20 September1992 he was murdered by state forces in Diyarbakır. The people of Kurdistan and beyond cherish his memory as 'Ape Musa.' —Author

even under the tracks of tanks. And there are thousands of them. And these small hands play an important role in constructing the future.

In our country, every dawn signals a new spring.

We are again in prison. Face to face with our captivity and beliefs. But we sense the beauty and birth of spring in our country. Walls cannot prevent the freshness of spring reaching us…

We are at the uprisings in Cizre. Alongside us stands an elderly man, endeavouring to stand erect and walk. He holds both hands aloft, making the victory sign with one hand while waving a stick in the other air. It is as if he is expressing his rancour… The surname of another elderly man is Gün [day].

It is a day to remember. The day is flowing from the district to the city. The procession has stopped, it is in Zele [PKK camp in the Zagros mountains]. The camp residents welcome those arriving. Right at the front is a child, but this child says, "I'm a guerrilla." He explains his role is "Keeper of the chickens."

The old man, the child, and the guerrilla come together. Their real duties are just beginning. They are confident. One is elderly and has seen what has been done to his people. One is young and closer to the future. And he has listened to the old people talking about the past. He has got to know himself and his enemy. A community that used to hesitate to express its identity has now risen to its feet in a throng of thousands and is marching. It has taken off to every part of the world, saying, "I too exist."

This is probably the most practical way of expressing freedom. This passion of our people can be nothing other than freedom. Our people are now convinced of the necessity for freedom. We too can easily hear these shouts from behind the thick walls.

Salute those who pour onto the streets for the sake of freedom.

Salute those who defeat the ferocity of nature amongst the peaks of the Zagros with their willpower.

Salute those who call for resistance while enduring torture and summon others to stand up for freedom.

Salute those who set fire to their own bodies with the fire of freedom…

Revolutionary greetings…

I knew about the "keeper of the chickens" from the newspapers. He was 10 or 11. He had a brother of around the same age and they joined the guerrillas together. He was one of those "portable" comrades. I can see him in front of my eyes. One day, he was on a hillock, with an AK47 slung over his shoulder, looking with a steely gaze. That stance both pleases and enthuses those who see it. Thinking of such young comrades makes one more determined. One can see the future in the glint in their eyes.

Three or four months after the interview with him was published in newspapers, a section of an article I am reading in *Özgür Halk* magazine, "A Page from a Guerrilla's Journal" catches my attention. I read it in one breath. I don't want to believe what I am reading. I read it again and again. It was about the martyrdom of that "portable"* guerrilla comrade. He had fallen asleep in a squad tent without extinguishing the stove. When the tent caught fire, the occupants dashed outside. The "portable" was one of those who exited the tent. After a moment of confusion, he made to re-enter the tent, at which point comrades asked, "What are you doing, comrade?" He replied. "I'm going to retrieve the leader's photograph," as he dived into the tent. They were unable to prevent him going back inside.

Unfortunately, he was unable to make his way out. When the little guerrilla was rescued from the tent, he was still holding the half-burnt photo. His last act demonstrated his loyalty to the leader.

This makes all of us think. We should learn lessons from such noble loyalty. He is no longer with us. He touched our hearts with his departure. I will always recall his smile and his steely gaze, just like those guerrillas of the same age who will remember him…

Block 4

1 November 1995, Wednesday

Today we started a hunger strike. It will go on for nine days, three days each alternating. The hunger strike DS started in all prisons has now lasted over 40 days. While it began as a protest against the attack in Buca, it now includes the demand to close Ümraniye prison, as well as other specific demands.

This action is our second support action. A petition was handed in this morning regarding the obscenity written on the floor at the entrance to block 14 during the last search. We made clear the fact we do not accept such insults.

It is a reflection expressed by individuals of the enemy's helplessness. It is crude and vulgar.

---

* Potable ("portatif" in Turkish): A nickname used for young, small and likeable people.

Today, comrade Orhan and I were on duty. Since we were very busy until evening, he had to do all the work.

We had to listen once again to A. Z. about the loathsome things that went on in Kadife Kale. He was informed that he should be honest, open, and serious. Despite our pointing out that he was to do this to solve his problem, what we were told was no different to what we had heard before. He explained the offences and the harm that had been done outside. It is on one's conscience when you think about our honest, self-sacrificing people outside. Now I understand better why some of our people have left and distanced themselves. Our poor people!

Although it is known about outside, in certain areas, the repeated appointment of incompetent characters who create problems again and again drives people mad. It would benefit the struggle and the people if such appointments were not made. I think this is the reason we are failing in the major cities of Turkey. If really serious interventions do not take place, irreversible damage may result.

When I went to drink tea in the dining hall of block 6, I noticed that Xale Xalef looked depressed. He told me in a gasp.

"If I don't take medication and don't have an injection, my blood sugar level will rise. I am already blacking out and feeling giddy."

"Xalo, why aren't you taking your medication, as usual? Your special food is coming."

"No, my food hasn't come. They've put me down for the hunger strike."

"Are you joking? How can they put you down for the hunger strike?"

"Yesterday, comrade Sevkan got me to sign the hunger strike petition."

"Are you sure the petition you signed wasn't the one we wrote to bring a case?"

"No, it was for the hunger strike."

"Xalo, are you sure? Because you shouldn't be going on hunger strike."

"While signing the petition I said this, but the comrade said it wouldn't be a problem, so I signed."

I immediately found the comrade who had written the names on the petition. When he said that he had been told "everyone will be included," he had also got Xalo's signature, I made my displeasure clearly, stating:

"Even if a person cannot think, he should question himself. This comrade is elderly and on medication. He doesn't take part in actions. I'm amazed it didn't occur to you."

We immediately wrote to the prison authorities on behalf of Xalo, informing them that there was an error in the petition. We then took him to the medical room, where he received his injection. Then his food arrived.

When chatting to him, he said, "When they asked me to sign, I looked for you, but couldn't see you anywhere."

That such a thing had happened depressed me, because, if Xalo misses an insulin injection, his sugar level is all over the place. Everyone knows he is old and ill. Despite this, he did not want to offend the comrade and signed the petition.

When his evening meal arrived, he didn't eat it. When we insisted, he said, "Everyone is on hunger strike. How can I eat?" Seeing we were insistent, he took his meal with a piece of bread, sat under the stairs, and ate it there. This touched us. It is a sensitivity that gladdens you.

I went to the doctor yesterday about my knee. He referred me to hospital, to the orthopaedist.

In the evening, comrades Fuat Kav and Kemal Aktaş came to our block. After we sat for a while in our dining hall, we were treated to a glass of lemonade each. Of course, as always, it was well diluted.

It is now 23.40 and I want to sleep.

Block 4
3 November 1995

Towards evening, our block reorganisation took place. They hadn't told us they would do it today. But we had guessed because of the noise that had continued until late last night. They had been repairing block 1/1 opposite block 5 for days.

There was confusion as always when changes are made. Belongings hurriedly packed, beds being rolled up, and the general hustle and bustle…

Once one block was finished, they started on another. They don't all happen at the same time. When requesting which blocks we will move to, we arrange things in communication with each other. We wanted all our blocks to be side by side. In that way, we will be in contact when there are emergencies.

Considering that new comrades might come here, we showed two or three vacancies in each block. We now have another new block.

Xalo, Xalef, Bayram, Hamdin, Baraj Kılıç, Tekmenuray, Fahrettin, and I remain in block 4. Along with the new arrivals, we now number 18.

Eight comrades from the DHP [Revolutionary People's Party] founded in Turkey have moved to block 14. We were curious about them and are glad they have come to our prison and our blocks. I have seen the same joy and yearning in these eight comrades. But I can say that they are a little worried. They have expectations of our "old" structure in the prison. I think they are expecting too much from us. I am concerned about this. I'm afraid they will be disappointed. I hope our environment does not make our comrades feel like this.

The sanctions imposed on A. Z. have been slightly relaxed. He will be able to join the duty rota, take part in social tasks such as joint activities, and comrades will chat with him – because, for a while, nobody was allowed to talk to him.

As we have recently opened blocks 5 and 2, some comrades will have to be separated from each one. Once again we parted ways with comrades with whom we have been together for a long time. Perhaps we will meet again in the same blocks, or call out to each other in new confined spaces.

Our alternating hunger strike is continuing.

Block 4
8 November 1995

The analyses, which were submitted to the party's 5th Victory Congress and we have been studying in collective education for some time now, will be dealt in two groups. The fact we have worked on these for a month has created certain problems. Progress has been slow due to differences in level of understanding. For the second group in particular, more explanation and discussion is necessary.

Moreover, for our block, collective education means a class of 50. Education based on levels of understanding would be better.

Today we covered the themes of "the resentment that should be felt for the enemy; war; human beings; courage; and affection."

Towards evening we read the reports of some recently arrived comrades. In general, they had had duties and responsibilities on the patriot level. Some of them had been more active. As is usually the case in the major cities of Turkey, their demeanour when dealing with the police was deplorable. Very few of them were able to demonstrate natural authority.

It would be better if such work and committees did not take place. Such appointments in the name of the Party, but far from its method, should not take place. At least then the people and our values in those places would not be harmed. And the enemy would not achieve "success."

An update was also made regarding Aziz P. Sanctions had been imposed on him for telling a comrade, "It is also the fault of whoever gave you this task," after a simple disagreement. He had been banned from social activities for ten days. Is it worth being reduced to such a state for the sake of half a bin of hot water? It is our wish that he learns a positive lesson from this. He has also continued to act in a similar way and not kept his promises. In fact, he is to be released soon. In that case, he will not be able to harmonise with anyone. He will be challenging. If he had been in prison for a long time, I would have said his nerves are shot, but he has been inside for less than three years. His reaction is not understandable. He is someone who can throw things and lash out when angry with someone. It is not appropriate and an insult to the other person.

This situation both saddens and angers me. A few days ago, when he visited our block, he said, "Whatever happens from now on, I will not be a problem and will not annoy people." This had pleased me.

As will be understood, when there is a problem in a block, all our blocks are informed. From time to time, when there is a serious incident, the views of all blocks are taken into account when reaching a decision.

Last night, when the doors were shut at 03.00, we slammed the doors and shouted slogans in protest at the arbitrary attitude of the prison authorities. As our ten blocks acted in unison, I'm sure the noise and the slogans were heard in the nearby neighbourhood.

I had another strange dream last night. A dream where you are outside but the location of the dream is a prison.

A place like a seven or eight-storey business quarter. Comrades alongside me were inmates of the prison. Prison officers monitoring the comings and goings between the floors. Between every floor was a section like the one we call the checkpoint. We were sitting in a section when a prison officer handed us an ID and asked us to put it on our collars. I told him, "Tell your superior that none of us will put this ID on our collars. We will not abide by such a rule. Do the best you can." Then, I argued with the prison officers standing in front of the bars. I explained why we refused. The prison officers were from the torture squad. For this reason, the discussion became heated. When one of them told me not to make gestures with my hand, I reacted. I told him he couldn't tell me how to speak.

When I woke up in the morning, I was angry at myself for having such a dream. Neither completely outside, nor completely inside. If the term is appropriate, a freakish situation.

When lying on my bunk at night, I like to read a novel before going to sleep. For a long time I haven't started a novel. When I found a section on "The Secret Prisons of El Salvador," I thought I'd read it in the study section to gain additional information.

It's past 23.00. Most comrades are asleep. Comrades H. Acar and Turan are writing in their bunks.

A cold, quiet night...

Is this because of the prison walls, or the weather? It's not clear, but it is a chilly night...

Block 4
10 November 1995, Friday

Today has a particular significance for the special war regime. This year, as in other years, they held celebrations to "commemorate" their forefathers. It is a day for some to recall the past sadly, while for others to cry. However, one thing is certain, and that is that they themselves do not believe the demagogy they express. They do not want to see the regime that has been decaying for 70 years.

We heard the sound of sirens at 09.05. The sound of sirens in the city reached as far as us.

After the morning soup, we began to wash our block. As it was a cold morning, my feet were frozen even in the plastic shoes worn in Kurdistan. At that moment, I thought of the guerrillas' feet in the winter snow being always frozen. I felt sad.

After washing the block, we went to the bath house in two groups. As always, they cut off the hot water before we had finished bathing. After we complained and shouted, they turned the hot water on again for five minutes. Of course, several comrades were angry and reacted as they left the bath house.

Until lunchtime I sat in the sun for 30 minutes. The sun, which shone on the corner of the exercise yard, warmed our bones. I sat in a way that the rays of the sun would hit my knees, as the pain in my knees has intensified in recent days.

After lunch, I sat to rest on my bed until 13.15, as I wanted to have a nap. But, although I felt drowsy, I was unable to sleep. One feels more tired in such a situation.

At 14.30 we began our collective education. Comrade F. Şahin gave some explanations. The reports of two new arrivals were read out. They made a self-criticism regarding some deficiencies they had experienced outside. Their reports and self-criticism were considered sufficient.

Later on, we heard that the prison authorities were going to exclude us from selecting an extra five people to go to the inter-block visiting area. We forwarded our reaction to this through our representative. This is an insidious approach by the prison authorities.

Comrade M. E. Karatay was released on Wednesday. As he was classed as a deserter, he was taken directly to the military service office. When he came to our block as a guest a few days prior to his release, he explained his aspirations, his joy, and his concerns to us in the exercise yard as it drizzled. He said that despite the party having provided him with all manner of opportunities, he had not understood the value of what he had received, that he had wasted it and not been worthy of it, and that during his eight years in prison he had constantly weighed this up and been able to renew himself thanks to the assistance of comrades. We applauded him as he was released.

He departed saying he would join the struggle. He has accumulated knowledge and experience. But I don't know whether his situation of having been an informer will prove to be a barrier. I hope he overcomes that problem.

We hadn't had anyone released like that for a long time. It happens occasionally in Aydın. This place is just like a well. We "oldies" have got used to it, but new arrivals have also begun to become permanent.

Today, I chatted to comrades Birol and A. Rıza (both from the DHP) while walking back and forth in the exercise yard. They asked me about our past education, structure, composition, open visits, etc. At times we were laughing and at others lamenting. For us, it is very old, but for newcomers, it is possible to see them feel bad as new things come to light.

We talked a bit about urban activities prior to 1980. They were experiencing the exasperation of going to jail without having been able to accomplish anything. This also saddens us. Our expectations were great, and still are.

After the evening meal, we read the leadership's analysis of the South. It was very comprehensive. An evaluation that examines many aspects relating to the region and the world. We also learned about our own position there.

A full list of the comrades in our blocks at the present time:

Block 2: Welat Çetinkaya, Mehmet Tören, Ali Budak, Nihat Kanat, Ali Kaya, Bahittin Şahin, Muhittin Dolaşir, Ahmet Cerenbeli, M. Ali Aslan, Mustafa Karadağ, Ömer Üzüm, Orhan Durak, Mehmet Ayçiçek, A. Rahman Akın, Hasan Yagız, Mehmet Yıldız, Ender Kantaroğlu.

Block 4: Suphi Bal, Esat Turan, Fahrettin Şahin, Hamdin Demirkıran, Hasan Baraj Kılıç, Halef Özer (Xalo Xalef), Hüseyin Acar, Ramazan Tunç, Bayram Ekelek, Salih Yılmaz, Kadir Öztunç, Şirin Tekmanuray, Erşat Güden, İ. Halil Turan, Harun Gül, M. Emin Gökdemir, M. Tahir Doğan, Ali Poyraz.

Block 6: İzzettin Öztunç, Kenan Ayaz, Tekin İrez, Nejat Özcan, Sakıp Hazman, Şamil Batmaz, Hasan Kasım, Mehmet Sevdan, Ferit Kolcu, Sinan Gür, Yusuf Karakuş, Mehmet Eryılmaz, Ferhan Bulut, Selahattin Mete, Zülküf Sanır, Feyzi Gün, Ömer Akıncı.

Block 14: M. Şahin Doğan, A. Rıza Çelik, Uğur Tuncer, Aşkın Tuncer, Şenol Bilgen, Mustafa Tacer, Selamı Uzunmehmet, Birol Çalen (all 8 from DHP), Kemal Aktaş, Orhan Boz, Muhittin Tacer, Orhan İvdil, Hamit Coşkun, Cemal Yılmaz, Hüseyin Öztürk, Tahir Yalçın, Fuat Kav, Azrail Özer.

Block 12: Zeki Alpboğa, İlhami Gülmez, Cesim Soylu, Şehmus Demir, Sabri Yavuz, Mehdi Öztürk, Aziz Poyraz, Mesut Gülmez, Metin Gümüş, A. Selam Arık, İlhan Dayan, Turan Genç, Sabri Kavak, Fırat Elbir, Emrah Temel, M. Şirin Gümüş, M. Nuri Ekinci, Sadi Kaya.

Block 8: M. Sait Üçlü, Bilal Ülkü, Zeki Aksoy, Ethem Kışkır, Kenan Şen, Yusuf Oktay, Celalettin Delibaş, Aziz Tunçtürk, Çeknaz Ekrem, M. Salih Öncü, Süleyman Aytaç, Latif Kara, Şehmus Poyraz, Behrem Akkurt, Musa Gül, İbrahim Özmen, Arif Ekren, Nesim Konma, Bekir Orak.

Block 9: Bedrettin Çaylak, Aydın Bor, Cemal Ağcakaya, Hamit Okay, Cahit Karaaslan, Mehmet Tokay, Aydın Ardal, Mustafa Ağcakaya, Zeki Acar, Cemal Günsel, Seyfettin Dağ, Mümin Ağcakaya, Mahmut Aktaş, Şemsettin Gözcü, Alattin Aktaş, H. İbrahim Özcan, Nedim Aslan, Hamdullah Kıran, Mehmet Tari, Cemal Kılıç, Cömert Bozkurt.

Block 13: Remzi Özçelik, Nasır Yaşa, Heyet Kaya, Hasan Zan, Yusuf Onat, A. Asker Bingöl, Davut Aslan, İzzet Eker, Rıza Aslan, Burhan İlik, Mehmet Kartal, Şenol Hantekin, Ferhan Korkut, Ahmet Güzel, Ahmet Ertaş, Recep Nur Cengiz.

Block 1/1: Mustafa Sarıkaya, İbrahim Elbir, Yaşar Elbir, Musa Turan (Koçer), İhsan Çelebi, Rıza Tan, Yaşar Eroğlu, Zeki Karatay, M. Emin Çetin, İbrahim Karakoç, Selahattin İllere, Kenan Eğer, Rıdvan Yüksel, Ramazan Taş, Ahmet Aksoy, Mehmet Bidav, Selahattin Aşan, Halil Kurt, Halil Bulan, Süleyman Tunç, Özcan Erdem, Hasan Karataş, Mehmet Alper.

Block 5: Celal Salgut, Müslüm Uğur, Lezgin Çulduz, Sabri Keve, Vehbi Koç, Davut Kaya, Osman Demir, Adem Bulan, Halil Yaşar, Salman Aktaş, Alaattin Kurt, A. Celil Durak, Yavuz Mavuk, A. Kadir Aksoy.

At this moment in Aydın, our total number of comrades is 182.

Block 4
13 November 1995, Monday

Our panel that had continued for three days ended towards 15.00 this afternoon. The subject: the role of the big cities, the practices of the enemy, developing Kurdish structures, its effect on personality, its effects on the struggle and the prisons and what needs to be done.

It had been planned to last two days, but went on into the third day. Although there was lots of repetition, it was good as a reminder.

Despite some favourable foundations in all areas, it has unfortunately not been possible to channel them into the struggle in the way intended. Hence, lots of values and opportunities have been squandered.

In fact, these factors should have been made the enemy's worst nightmare. He should have faced obstructions at every step he took. Even at home, he should have been unable to sleep. He should have been able to feel the heat of conflict in a ghastly way in the house of colonialism, so that he understood the reality of war and realised his own inhumanity.

There were six speakers on the panel. The listeners contributed by asking questions. Although my occasional interventions led to polemics, there were no obvious deficiencies.

From now on, our visits will end at 4:30. As for the doors to the exercise yards, they will open 30 minutes later in the morning. Apparently, it's a winter thing. Since they had communicated it to our representatives, we did not object.

Comrades Soydan Akay, M. Zeki Deniz, A. Aziz Özdemir, Bedrettin Özgür and Ömer Kılıç have been brought here from Buca prison.

Also, M. Omaç, who was thrown out of our environment six months ago, has returned to block 8. He was happy to be leaving, but when he found it difficult there, he began to make requests. You feel both anger and pity. People shouldn't reduce themselves to such a miserable state.

Immediately after the panel, a search was carried out. It was due. For the first time soldiers didn't search us or our belongings. That was the agreement. Prison guards will do the searching while soldiers provide security.

As always, our belongings were strewn all over the place. Every fortnight, a war of nerves. As they suffer on mount Cudi, they mess up our possessions. While we get annoyed, we also laugh.

Block 4
15 November 1995, Wednesday

Yesterday, I had another interesting dream. As always, I was outside, but there were prison procedures. Soldiers were raiding houses, I was fleeing. There was a situation of conflict. I was at a place like the deep hollow near the old bus station in Antep. There were some columns and sections. A few taxis were waiting on one side. Students and civilians were seated at tables around the columns. The civilians were travellers. One was holding a book, a file, and a piece of paper on top of them. There were notes on the paper. The book was written in prison by comrade Şamil about his arrest and the period of 1981. It had a black cover, like the way we bind books here. A comrade said, "There's been a hitch. You promote the book." I said "Okay." When I picked up the book, I took a quick look at the notes. The first thing that caught my attention in the long sentences was the importance of our struggle for other peoples, China, Mao, Russia, Lenin, guerrillas, etc.

I stood up and asked them to gather at certain tables. I told them to sit in a way that they could see me. Meanwhile, the police were approaching. I put on a bold face and began to explain in a loud, clear voice why the book had been written and its aim. I pointed out the importance of our struggle for other peoples. I followed that by mentioning the importance we attached to peace and brotherhood with other peoples.

The police intervened. As they tried to catch me, I continued to speak, moving left and right to avoid being caught. After a while, they trapped me in a corner. They rained bullets at me. I was hit and fell to the ground. I wasn't dead, but I couldn't speak. I didn't want them to shoot anymore. My clothes were soaked in blood. One of them caught me by the leg and began to drag me, thinking I was dead. One person knew I was alive, but didn't say anything.

I realised he was trying to ensure I was treated in another place. They didn't want to treat me, as they were scared. In my dream I realised the person carrying out the treatment was me. That is, both the wounded person and the carer was me...

I woke up four or five times, despite not sleeping until 02.15. After reading an article about A. Z., I couldn't sleep. It distresses me to think of the baseness and shameful behaviour that goes on in our name.

Today, a meeting was held regarding general life and regulations, for the benefit of the newcomers. Comrade Delil explained things in broad detail. The newcomers said it was good. I hope that is the case...

Yesterday in the dining hall, while walking back and forth with Emin Gökdemir, Hamdin and Şirin, the conversation returned to bartering. Comrade Emin explained something that happened to him when he was young. My head ached from laughing. In the old days, peddlers would go from village to village on horses or donkeys buying plastic, wool, wheat, etc., and selling porcelain, trinkets, and sweetmeats. When Emin approached the peddler, some dried figs caught his eye. As he had nothing to exchange, Emin took off one pair of his plastic shoes and offered them to the peddler. The peddler accepted the shoes, exchanging them for the figs. Emin and the other children enjoyed the figs. When he got home, his father asked Emin where his shoes were. Emin replied, naturally, "I gave them to the peddler; in return I got figs, which we ate." His father replied in the same tone, "Come in and close the door." Once inside, comrade Emin received a good beating.

Amongst the laughter, one said, "You really suffered," to which Emin replied, "You ain't kidding. I will never forget those figs."

Just now I wrote to my cousin, Yaşar. I haven't had a letter from him in months. I was annoyed. I assume he's suffering from depression.

It's now 00.30. It's just started raining. It had been cold for ten days. The rain will break the cold.

From outside the prison, the barking of the Alsatian guard dogs can be heard. The only things breaking the silence are the dogs' barking and the sound of rain. For a moment, it reminded me of the rural areas and the guerrillas.

Oh, the mountains... Will I be able to meet you again? Will I be able to drink my fill of that cold, fresh water? Will I be able to breathe that clean, cool air? I cannot know. But I have never lost touch with the mountains. When I close my eyes and take a deep breath, I always feel I'm in those mountains and forests and breathe more deeply. In spite of this, when I look at our reality, and this cruel enemy, those mountains seem so unattainable. We will be held for many more long years. I know this, but I cannot stop breathing that mountain air. This is my connection. If I don't die and get out one day, I want to climb those rugged peaks of Cudi. Even though it will be arduous, when I reach the highest point, I will watch the two sides of the "border" in the moonlight. I will observe the amazing view as far as the eye can see and fix the image in my memory. I will definitely see that peak that recognises no border. Just as behind the high prison walls I close my eyes and breathe in its air, I will draw that air into my lungs.

Block 4
16 November 1995

The conditions here directly affect my dreams. In this respect, dreams generally reflect people's state of mind and certain reactions. For this reason I record as many as possible, if not all, of the different dreams in my journal, as I want comrades who read this in the future to be able to study our feelings and state of mind. I believe that even our dreams are a subject of research, as they reflect our conditions. I hope that certain dreams I have cited will be made the subject of study by psychologists who feel the need to do so.

Despite going to sleep late last night, I again had a strange dream. We were in the Nuripazarbaşı neighbourhood of Antep. The old days of our neighbourhood. We were in the street in front of our street. As far as I can recall, it was called "Şehit Şemsi" street.

We were outside, but again, prison regulations were being applied. It was being said that 80 to 100 prisoners had been transferred to where we were.

We entered the long street to welcome the newcomers. We lined up on both sides, forming a corridor. The street was lined with paving blocks, as it used to be. The comrades were walking up the street. I had halted in front of Koçero's house and saying "Welcome" to the newcomers, who had only recently been arrested. There were all kinds of people of all ages and we were delighted to welcome new comrades. While shaking hands, there were short questions and answers. Their bags and cases were in their hands. There was a transfer atmosphere and the confusion of a transfer was dominating the street. When one was asked, "Were there any possessions that were not handed over by the authorities?" the answer was reproachful, "They didn't even give us our most basic things. They didn't even give us our pound shop white board." One of them was holding a telephone, a desk telephone. When I looked closely, it looked like a plastic toy.

I awoke in the morning to the duty comrade's "Rojbaş hevalno" but had trouble getting up. I could feel the pain in my lungs from my back. Usually, I get up before the "Rojbaş." Realising there was only 5-10 minutes until breakfast, I immediately had a shave at the upstairs basin. After the meal, the upper corridor door between block 4 and blocks 6 and 14 opened and comings and goings commenced.

As there is no collective education today, I sat down to finish the book I'm reading, Resisting Palestine. I am taking notes as it is our study topic. After the evening meal, while drinking tea, we heard the sound of doors being banged. We moved quickly to the door and the windows. On hearing the slogan, "The dignity of humanity will defeat torture," we started to strike the doors and shout slogans. We subsequently learned that the reason for the argument and slogan was an inmate whose release was due but had not been released.

Block 4
17 November 1995, Friday

Today was our day to go to the bath house.

By noon, I had finished my notes on the book. I have acquired lots of new information about Palestine. I once again learned of the betrayal of states in the region that appear to be friends of the Palestinian people and cursed them. I gather that two comrades quarrelled while playing chess and swore at each other. As this was not the first time such an incident had occurred, comrades are dealing with it. Such things do not usually happen in our environment, and are definitely not tolerated. Of these comrades, B. İ. is a relatively recent arrival. I'm sorry he has behaved like this. He is young, but despite having a good understanding, as well as having been in the guerrilla environment, he has been banned from all cultural and sporting activities for a week on account of his ill-discipline and ignoring of warnings. Since all the comrades in the block took this decision, there is no question of objecting to it.

As for S. Ü., he is a real problem. I believe he is responsible for the recent incident. He has had lots of problems. Each time, it is said that he does not know the party sufficiently and his behaviour is glossed over. He has insistently rejected becoming a revolutionary. He has constantly put his individuality first. He has received the same sanction. But I do not believe he will learn lessons from this. He has repeated this behaviour in every block he has been.

I did the laundry with comrade Emin and hung it out to dry. Soon after, it started to drizzle. As we had done the washing, it was either going to rain, snow, or stones were to fall from the sky.

Last night, in my dreams, I was again in the same house. A wooden house with a garden of bare soil. When I was about to leave the house, a small child asked for money. I checked my pockets but didn't have any money. I was sorry I couldn't give him anything. His innocent face caught my attention. Meanwhile, a comrade came and gave the child some money. After leaving the house, police and soldiers began to chase us. After some great effort, I managed to turn the pursuers into statues by staring at them…

Today, I began reading F. Bulut's book, Lessons of the Intifada. I have realised how little I knew about the intifada. The unseen organisation of the intifada was truly amazing. Incredible control and initiative…

Block 4
18 November 1995

We all awoke at the sound of "Rojbaş." As comrades Ramazan and Bayram were on duty, they had got up early. Those who are on duty get up an hour earlier and make preparations.

While getting dressed on my bunk, I looked at the exercise yard. It was dry. It had not rained overnight. Our clothes were dry.

At breakfast, we had "sirikli torak" (dry cottage cheese with garlic). But it was very salty. Little of it was eaten. When someone said, "People from Botan don't make it like this," comrade H. Acar said, "What? Ask me about it. Since salt is cheaper than torak, they put a lot of salt in it to make it heavier." This led to laughter.

We listened to ideas regarding the proposed decision about comrade Dilok. He had been sent from Europe to the Aegean in 1991. On account of certain relationships that we could not approve of, he had been removed from activities. He had even become more vulnerable to being arrested. When this situation emerged in Buca, he had rejected it and not behaved honestly. On coming to Aydın in 1993, this issue had been addressed, but due to the absence of concrete evidence, it had been closed. We had had similar impressions, but they were not sufficient. He had merely been sanctioned for three months on account of talking during police interrogation. On this topic, our prison centre had no different information. But during the period of evaluation of the Aegean region process, comrades had made a proposal that was rejected. Every time, he went onto the defensive, saying, "Efforts are being made to discredit me." Subsequently, when a lady in another prison explained everything, his contact was immediately suspended. Initially, he again chose to reject everything, before making an admission. Since his sanctions had been in place for a year, it had been proposed that they be lifted. But it was necessary for him to write a self-criticism report. During the year of sanctions, he had only been allowed to take part in collective education. I think, during this time, he has really tried. Let's see how it is reflected in his report.

Around 10 others coming from the Aegean region had been subjected to sanctions. Since most of them are troubled and have not opened up, they are causing us problems. A proposal had been made to throw out some of those involved in the Aegean process, but inside, this cannot be done in all circumstances. Some of them are personalities you would not even pass the time of day with outside.

And we were wondering, "Why are we suffering such blows in the big cities?" Whereas, in fact, there is no need even for the enemy with characters such as them.

In spite of all this, our people around here are truly self-sacrificing.

On this evening's news, the MHP announced it was to have an electoral alliance with the DYP. As the Constitutional Court had rejected the request to lift the regional electoral threshold, low-life Türkeş made his announcement an hour before the Court decision was announced. It is obvious he had received intelligence.

The special war has lost its bearings.

Block 4
19 November 1995

Today, nine of us went as guests to blocks 8-12. It was our first visit after the Conference. There were comrades there we hadn't seen for ages. They were delighted to see us.

Half the people in the block were new. Most of the new arrivals were young. It is pleasing to see young comrades, but unfortunately, they don't look dynamic. 12 September 1980 fascism is aging our people before their time, particularly in the big cities. It's really ruining them. It's draining them and throwing them to one side.

The comrades made us watery coffee with milk. As a meal, we had çiğ köfte, a feast.

The comrades were generally enthusiastic. I chatted to two comrades. I knew about their latest situations. I expressed my concern and reaction. They said they would bear it in mind.

We have paused collective education on account of preparations for 27 November. Apart from things like choir, folk dancing, and theatre, comrades will continue their individual work. They will not be idle. Such a system was introduced to organise a celebration worthy of the importance of the day. In the evening, all blocks will continue collective work. Certain articles from publications and analyses will be read and studied.

These days, I am thinking of using the daylight hours in a useful way. I am thinking of at least finishing the periodicals, as there is little other free time. Tomorrow, I will write to comrades Nihat and Tören, asking them to get working on our study project.

Comrade Şehmus Yüksel has returned from Buca prison. They said his stomach was deformed and advised him to have an operation. As he has had a stomach operation before, he refused.

Block 4
21 November 1995

Yesterday, comrades from blocks 5 and 1/1 moved to blocks 7-15. Their blocks have been exchanged with Dev-Sol (DS). For better communication between our blocks, they are now all in the same row.

Early in the morning, comrade Fuat came to our door. After initial surprise Hamdullah and I went with him. We sorted through Az's jury proposals. 15 people suggested he receive "a heavy penalty," while 55 people thought "he should be thrown out of the environment and ostracised." It was suggested there should be absolutely no dialogue with him as his approach to our relationships has been like that towards a commodity.

Towards noon, while chatting to comrade Şamil, I pointed out that we had made an operational error regarding Az. Reopening a closed case based on the same reasons is not correct, either legally or operationally. It is necessary not to act emotionally. If there is a deficiency, an objection can be written and sent to the administration. If the problems in the Aegean region are to be addressed, then the files on all of them should be reviewed. While those who, when outside, committed worse blunders in a superior position are saying "let's condemn this," it is important not to make a mistake regarding procedures. I reluctantly wrote a report and, in spite of abhorring his practices outside, we have to take our operational process as a basis of action. This is fundamental in all circumstances.

I followed this by reading three comrades' self-criticisms. The block structure had handed all three warnings and reprimands. When going upstairs to the dorm, they had left some articles downstairs that shouldn't have been left there. Prison guards had found them and taken them away. A typical case of irresponsibility, when you think how difficult it is to get the most basic material inside.

Tonight, I will again go to bed late, as I'm going to continue taking notes from publications.

As comrade Sakıp is our guest today, he will also work late.

Tiny sores have appeared on Xalo Xalef's feet. We linked this to his diabetes. And to his age... Today his right eye was bloodshot and the area around the eye was purple. To tell the truth, Xalo is disturbing me. Things are not going well. He must also have realised that, as he takes care not to miss a namaz. I don't want anything to happen to him. He is our most elderly inmate. I also have a good dialogue with him. I can say it is a formal but warm dialogue. He says, "There are two old guerrillas here, me and Poyraz." Of course, when he says this, he runs the risk of argument. He considers me to be from the same generation as him. If that's how he feels, no problem. After all, "the old generation" is something else. More resilient than the "nylon youth." Especially if he has a gun in his hand. And, of course, if he has got himself behind a boulder, he thinks he can take on an army.

Block 4

23 November 1995, Thursday

I've still not finished taking notes from the publications for my research topic. But I can say I've broken the back of it.

The weather has begun to get really cold. It has snowed in many provinces. It's raining here, but it's still cold. It's a dry cold. Like it's going to snow. On coming out from under the blanket, you can't keep warm.

Today we received an update on E. Karatay. As he was released, he was taken directly to do his military service. Despite all his efforts, they didn't give him leave. They only allowed him to see his family for an hour under police supervision. They took him to Sarıkamış. Since he had deserted with his rifle before joining the struggle, he was arrested and taken to a military prison. He was tried for killing many soldiers and officials and then released, and now, years later, he is arrested for taking a weapon. What a paradox. First he will serve his sentence, then he will be made to do his military service. An absolute comedy. Again, if he is determined, he could flee once more and reach the mountains. That is, if he's not murdered in the meantime. The enemy does not cast you aside until he has squeezed you almost to death. Karatay knows this from his prison experiences in particular.

Today I wrote four postcards for Uncle Xalef.

Before our night tea, I chatted to comrade Erşat from Mardin while striding back and forth in the four or five yard space under the stairs. As he had suffered so much, as soon as I mentioned his ordeal, he poured out his woes. "If only I had run into old comrades outside," he lamented. In the area where he lived along the Aegean, he had not had contact with our people. He complains that, despite being economically comfortable and having a good circle, he was unable to take advantage of it. As soon as he met comrades, they made him a member of HADEP* and put him on the management committee. In this way, they had proffered him to the police before he could accomplish anything. When you hear these things, you get angry. This approach demonstrates another reason why we have been unable to get a toehold in the big cities of Turkey. Whereas, were such relationships different, more permanent channels could be established. Let him remain at his work, but don't involve him in legal activities. In this way, thousands could be reached and all sorts of activities could be carried out.

He told a story. Like Aziz Nesin, "We laugh at our lamentable state."

There was an elderly man in a village in Mardin province. Since there were arrests and widespread torture in the region after the fascist military coup of 12 September, there was fierce reaction against the state. After the beginning of the armed struggle on 15 August 1984, there was great jubilation there. They told the elderly man, "Every Apocu has an AK47. The armed struggle has begun. You get one too." As the elderly man didn't have any money, he went to the nearest town and sold his only cow and bought a nice gun. He then secreted it in the village, saying it would come in handy one day. In 1993, when the leader said, "We had to start the armed struggle; if the state takes a [positive] step, we are ready for peace," some people went to see the elderly man, saying, "You sold your cow and bought a gun. Look, now the Apocular are giving up their weapons." The old man replied, "That's definitely a lie. Is such a thing possible? I know they won't give up their arms. It's not possible, I sold my cow. And even if Apo gives up his gun, I will not, after what the enemy has done."

---

* Halkın Demokrasi Partisi, HADEP): People's Democracy Party. —Author

The old man was right. He sold his most valued possession, his cow. On that, what can politics say?

After some hesitation, comrade Erşat said, "If you manage to get out of prison, I request that you come and see me. May old comrades come. Whatever you say, I am here." I laughed, saying, "They won't release me. Even if I do come one day, I'll make you sell your cow!"

"By God, I'll sell it, just come."

As the conversation on how work should be carried out in the big cities changed direction, laughter gave way to sadness. It is very difficult to clean up the damage caused in these areas. "If only such a comrade had been there, things would have been different," he lamented.

At the 10pm tea, the name of martyr Şıho Dirlik came up. Naturally, the tragedy endured by the family was mentioned. It was a real tragedy. After his father had died, his elder brother, comrade Mehmet Dirlik, was a teacher in 1977. He was beaten to death in a village in Solhan district and secretly buried next to a stream. He suffered this fate after intervening in a fight between two villagers. When his corpse was found months later, it was brought to Pazarcık. Comrades arranged his grave. Later, I think his elder sister hanged herself. His younger brother was sitting on a wall, watching a football match in middle-school, when a ball struck him on the head. After suffering for a time, he also died. Only Şıho was left. Prior to 1980, he too took part in party activities. After some searching and with pressure from the family, he went to Europe. While his mother and friends were thinking, "We've saved Şıho," he realised he couldn't hack it in Europe and returned to the country. While he was in the rural area of Pazarcık with comrades, his family in the village thought he was in Europe. His mother found out months later. Mother Xate's only concern was to save her only remaining child.

When I was in the countryside around Pazarcık, I stayed with comrade Ş. Dirlik for a while.

About a month later, in May 1981, after a comrade's family reached agreement with soldiers who had actually tricked them, he was captured. As always, of course, the Turkish soldiers didn't keep their promise, and the family's son was charged and put on trial facing a death sentence. He broke down and suffered from depression in prison.

After comrade Ş. Dirlik had spent eight years in prison, he was released from Eskişehir Special Type prison. He went straight to the Mahsum Korkmaz Academy. Taking into account his slipped disc, he was sent to participate in activities in Europe. During this time, we heard from him on several occasions.

He later returned to the camp in the Middle East.

Following the damage caused by Terzi Cemal,* he was sent to the South West. A short time later, a clash broke out. The enemy surrounded a large group on Nurhak mountain. Most of them were new recruits. They succeeded in getting most of them away to safety, Those fighters who were surrounded, numbering 18, including comrade Ş. Dirlik, were massacred by the enemy using chemical weapons.

We were shocked when we heard about this. We were very upset. Just when we thought his mother would be grief-stricken, we heard from comrades that "Mother Xatun is fine, she has become active, saying, 'All the fighters are like my Şıxom. I have devoted my life to this cause.'"

His mother's resolution delighted us. We were really pleased for her.

One more of the families in Kurdistan that need a novel written about them. As time passes, the number of families that will have novels and stories written about them increases rapidly. New generations will in the main undertake this task. But it will be more meaningful if these stories were written while the iron is hot, as there is a difference between what is written during the heat of conflict and what is written under normal conditions. In order to reflect this heat, joy, enthusiasm, pain, grief, and difficulty, the writing needs to take place in an environment where that spirit is dominant. Consequently, the best novels are written during periods when incidents occur.

Today, we learned that agent Bilen Çiftçi, who fled our environment in Buca prison and took refuge with the enemy, has taken part in operations, particularly in Antalya. A person doesn't know what to say. Comrades gave him a second chance, despite his talking under interrogation, but at the first opportunity he returned to his real self. When his brother deserted from the guerrillas in Dersim for the second time, he ran to the prison authorities.

Both incidents show that in giving people "a chance," we are overreaching ourselves. Unfortunately, the resulting cost is very serious.

For two days the TV news have shown Turkish PM Çiller at a press conference in front of the UK Prime Minister's residence with UK Prime Minister Major. Our people were protesting when Çiller was speaking. They were waving red flags. There were also Greek Cypriots protesting. I think it was a joint protest.

---

* "Terzi Cemal" (Ali Ömürcan). A PKK cadre in the first period after the founding of the organisation. After many guerrillas in the region under his control had been captured and killed, he was taken to the PKK camp in the Bekaa valley and tried. He admitted all accusations levelled at him. —Author

As the 24 December elections approach and there is turmoil amongst the main parties, Çiller has gone on tour in Europe. Contacts prior to the Customs Union. But as always, one of the subjects on the agenda in bilateral talks is our struggle. As MED-TV got a licence from a British institution, Çiller said at the talks that this TV has caused serious problems for Turkey. Major said they would not be able to intervene in a legal channel, but that if there was appropriate evidence, they would be able to apply to a higher body and assist.

There is no need to point out the contribution of the TV channel to our struggle. We feel we are missing out as we cannot watch the channel here in prison. As a radio station has yet to be established, we are trying to follow developments while lagging behind. I gather that our TV broadcasts for six hours a day, but it will be extended to 24 hours a day. And then there will be no need for a satellite dish. Maybe then we will be able to watch it.

Block 4

24 November 1995, Friday

Today, comrades Abbas Yasak and Şükrü Topkan came from Buca. They've been allocated to our block. Comrade Şükrü was in Mersin E-Type prison in 1983. I saw him a few times. He was on trial with the Adana group. I heard then that his wife had behaved in a more consistent and astute way. He was released in 1984 after 40 of us were exiled to Antep E-Type. 12 years later we meet in Aydın E-Type prison. He considers this period one of "lost years." Although in recent years he has carried out various duties in Antalya province, he could in fact have been a lot more useful. But I gather that individual and family concerns have prevented this. The consequence of not leaving the big cities is to meet up in an E-Type. On saying, "You left, wandered around, then returned," it was as if I was criticising him with this simple sentence. He seemed to confirm this with a wry grin.

Today, photographs were taken for 27 November. Four photos each were to be taken. The posing took about half an hour. As always there was confusion. I had a photo taken with Uncle Xalef. But this only encouraged him. It was as if he was going to be in every shot. I restrained him. In fact, on the way down, when I'd warned him about not having more than 4 pictures, he had said, "No, no, four is too many, three will be enough."

As the camera got hot, the guard left, leaving the photo-session half finished. He will come on another day.

At around 23.00, I had retreated to my bunk, when comrade Ramazan, who was downstairs, summoned comrade Fahrettin. On hearing the sound of the peep-hole opening, I changed my mind about undressing and went downstairs. The Dev-Sol representative was at the peep-hole. Their comrade, Ümit Doğan Gönül, had fallen ill and been martyred on the way to hospital. The representative was going from block to block, informing them. Meanwhile, DS slogans began to be heard.

After half an hour, all our blocks began to shout:

"Martyrs are immortal!"

"Down with the special war!"

"Long live the fraternity of peoples!"

We followed this by banging on the doors for 2 minutes.

After the sound of slogans and clanging of doors had broken the silence of the night, the sound of the mechanism of the on-duty soldiers' guns was heard. They made sure we heard by tugging the trigger hard.

All these noises disappeared into the darkness of the night.

Ümit had previously been a DS representative. He was a friendly young comrade in his twenties.

We repeated the slogans and banging of doors at 01.00.

Block 4

25 November 1995, Saturday

Although it was our block's turn to welcome guests, we didn't do so. 8-12 block went to offer their condolences to Dev-Sol. I was expecting this in the evening. Again, I was pleased.

We held a minute's silence at 15.00.

This was followed by the entire prison shouting:

"Martyrs of the revolution are immortal!"

"Long live the fraternity of peoples!"

"Ümit Doğan Gönül is immortal!"

"Martyrs are immortal!"

We repeated the slogans three times, then banged on the doors.

The walls of the prison shook.

If the prison authorities had taken him to hospital earlier, he might have still been alive. This is why we have to make our protest.

The implemented policy is clear. Even in a potentially fatal situation, they make you wait for a few hours. This is another way of killing you. Anything can be expected from them. They carry out their animosity well and consciously.

Our slogans and door protest were repeated four times during the day.

Comrade Erşat has taken three tablets on account of severe pain in a molar. Despite this, the pain has persisted. It is plain from his face that he is in pain. As tomorrow is Sunday, he will probably have to suffer for a few more days.

Block 4
26 November 1995, Sunday

During the morning roll call, we demanded that comrade Erşat be taken to a doctor urgently. The head guard hummed and hawed as we persisted. They left the block, saying, "We'll see." Towards noon, they took him to the sick bay and removed the tooth. They can do it if they want to.

Comrade Dilok's report was read out to the group. On the recommendation of the administration, the general structure approved it. In such situations, the general structure does not tend to make decisions different to the administration. His self-criticism report was more comprehensive than previous ones. He opened up on many things he had not previously expanded on. This was good for a new start, as if had he continued for long, he would have been worn out. He supported the report with quotes. In summary: he became acquainted with comrades in 1977, during his time as a student he took on some duties, during that period he was influenced by his feudal and petit bourgeois milieu, and following the arrests after the military coup of 12 September he lost contact. At this time, he experienced some alienation on account of his aspirations and was engaged. However, his family did not accept this and he suffered an economic embargo. For a time, he worked in Antep, then, when he found things difficult, he returned to his village, where he married another woman his family had picked. He then went to Europe, where he again made contact with comrades. After being involved in activities, he returned to the country by his own volition, being appointed to a supervising position in the Aegean region. However, he explained that he did not wield his influence in a correct manner, causing harm with goals that agents could not achieve, that this was treachery, that he had ruined values, and that he was arrested at a time when he had not been able to represent the party, and that he had talked to the police to a degree that amounted to betrayal. He added that, when he came to the prison, he had not reflected on the reality of the situation, that he had concealed it and that, when doubts were raised about him, he had rejected them, calling them a "conspiracy," going on the counter-attack and pointing out the weaknesses of his accusers, and in this way becoming a conspirator himself.

As can be understood, he has really caused Buca and us some trouble. If he weren't in Aydın, he might not have been persuaded. But as everything has been revealed and he wasn't in a position to reject it, he was convinced.

As for the period of sanction, he states, "It was like shock therapy for me." He adds that, from now on, he will concentrate on service to the people and the party and apologises to the people and the party. "I will strive to serve the people and the party," he says.

He will now continue on his way without sanction. I hope he will prove worthy of the opportunity and trust. It is entirely in his hands.

It was pointed out that we need to make preparations for tomorrow's party celebration. We all had a shave in the evening. In order to celebrate tomorrow in the appropriate way, comrades have been preparing for several days.

Before sleep, I wrote a letter to Şahsürek.

Block 4
27 November 1995, Monday
THE GLIMMER OF BEAUTIFUL TOMORROWS

We have celebrated another day of historic importance for our people and our party. As a matter of fact it is necessary to celebrate this day with increasing enthusiasm every day and every hour, not just once a year. As for this, it is possible by representing the party in a correct manner in whatever area.

It is difficult to express the significance of this day. A historic turning point and settling of accounts is concealed within this day. The more realistic shaping of the understanding that halted the downward slide and decay in our history coincided with this day.

History has now condemned the idea that the founding congress of the party in the village of Fis in Lice* was merely an ordinary meeting. The developments of today were formulated with that first step.

We have celebrated another founding anniversary in prison. Our party has entered its 18th year. All comrades believe that the new period will develop more successfully and comprehensively.

---

* Lice is a district of Diyarbakır (Amed). Amed is an ancient city established on the banks of the Tigris river. It is the capital of Kurdistan. It has been a key city for many civilisations and empires. Epic resistance has taken place there on many occasions. Many Kurdish resistance fighters and leaders have been executed there. Following the military coup of 1980, the "No.5 E-Type prison" earned notoriety as the place where Kurdish prisoners suffered horrendous torture. The brave resistance of the prisoners and their political defence in military courts revealed what was going on. A total of 73 prisoners died as a result of repression and torture in this prison, and hundreds were left with permanent disabilities. Thousands more caught incurable diseases. —Author

We are in prison for another anniversary. The only thing we know is that, when we celebrate this day here, our comrades will also celebrate it in the mountains and cities with the same feelings. Even if we are unaware of and distant from each other, the excitement of knowing we will have similar celebrations at the same moment is limitless. Undoubtedly, to breathe the mountain air that smells of freedom, to feel the joy created by viewing the mountains, forests, and horizon without obstacle, to dance with nature in an immense space, and to passionately embrace it — is magnificent.

The high walls that surround us only allow us a limited view of the sky. But we experience what is beyond these thick, high walls without seeing it…

The eyes of guerrillas sat on the edge of a mountain watching like an eagles, are our eyes, their hearts are our hearts, their joy is our joy. Our hearts are there, their hearts are here…

And for this reason, comradeship is held higher than fraternity.

And for this reason, when facing death, one will not retreat.

November is, climatically, a cold month, but for us, it has a warmth that takes us to the future. It is with this belief and enthusiasm that we prepared, like children preparing for a festival…

At 07.00, with the call of "Rojbaş," all comrades leapt from their beds and began to get dressed.

Comrade Esat and I had got up at 06.00, as we are on duty today, and carried out the necessary cleaning, etc.

At 08.30, our block (4-6 and 14) were lined up in three rows in the exercise yard of block 6. After comrade Fahrettin had briefly explained the meaning and importance of the day, he invited us to take part in a one-minute silence. He then read out a statement. In places, he stuttered from excitement. We followed this by reciting the Ey Şoreşger [Hey revolutionary] march. And all blocks shouted slogans in unison:

"Down with the special war!"

"Long live the fraternity of peoples!"

"Long live leader Apo!"

"Long live 27 November!"

All the tables and benches had been taken into the exercise yard. Our 12-member choir began to sing songs to the assembled crowd. During the first song, there was a problem with harmony, but it was quickly resolved. They had been preparing for a month. All the members of the choir wore red check shirts, black trousers, and black shoes. They also wore waistcoats. It was a pleasing sight. Comrade Hüseyin was the choirmaster.

When there was a break in the songs, DHP member Mahmut was called to read the first message. He was excited. Emphasis was on the party's importance for the country, region, and the Middle East.

They put on a sketch. While a "doctor" rummaged through medicines in a box on a table, a "patient" came in holding his back, saying:

"Comrade doctor, how's it going?"

"Fine thanks. How are you?"

"By God, I'm not well."

"Why, what's up?"

"My coccyx is hurting, I can't walk, it's playing havoc with me."

After looking closely at him and smiling, the doctor put his hand on the patient's shoulder, saying:

"I know your problem, but I won't say."

"Comrade, please tell me, I beg you. "

"OK, if you insist. How long have you lived in the big city?"

The patient looked at the sky, mumbling the number of years.

"It's been more than 20 years."

"And how long have you been in contact with the party?"

"Allah, Allah! My coccyx is aching, what's that got to do with the big city and the party?"

"It's connected, I assure you. Because you have had difficulty understanding the party, it hurts."

"What's that got to do with it?"

"Before the party commenced the struggle, they didn't consider the Kurds to be human, saying 'they have tails'. You see, the party removed your tail. Your pain is due to this. There's no need to take tablets or anything like that." The patient angrily leaves the stage as the doctor tells him "the only medication you need is the PARTY and ITS LIFE."

After a few more songs, we had a tea break. We drank the tea where we were sitting.

After the break, a "wolf and lamb" play was put on. Six or seven sheep bleated their way onto the stage. (Although they looked more like wolves than sheep). The shepherd was trying to direct them by making sounds. The shepherd acted well. Alongside him was a small dog. After gathering the sheep in a cluster, he looked around and began to dance with his dog. He then threw some objects and the dog caught them in the air. When the shepherd lay down, the dog became his pillow. Comrade Zülküf set a rhythm on his saz, sending a signal to the wolf, who stood on one leg and hopped. After circling the flock, he attacked a sheep. When there was a racket, he fled. When the shepherd woke up, he saw that the flock had been scattered. On seeing the dying sheep, he let out a cry. The sheep trembled and died in the shepherd's arms. The shepherd chased the dog, swearing at it, and kicking and hitting it. Then the shepherd again gathered the flock as if nothing had happened and lay in wait. As the sound of the music rose, the wolf appeared once more. Just as it was about to attack another sheep, the shepherd went on the attack. As the wolf thrashed about on the ground, the dog strutted around. As the shepherd took the wolf and left with the flock, applause broke out.

I recited Cigerxwin's poem, "You're a revolutionary," that he wrote in 1981. I chose it especially because he explains revolutionary and guerrilla tactics. I also made a short explanation, saying, "This aspect of the poet is not well known. He didn't see today's Kurdish guerrillas, but he discussed today and its guerrillas in his poem of previous years."

This was followed by a sketch featuring a man who visits a patriotic home after spending long years in prison. When there is a knock at the door, the man of the house opens it and says:

"You can take your shoes off here."

"No, I won't take them off."

"But comrade, it will be more comfortable if you do."

"No, we don't take our shoes off unless the detector goes off."

The owner of the house looks at the guest in amazement.

"What detector, comrade? What are you talking about?"

"The guest smiles bashfully."

"Ah! For a moment I thought I was back in prison."

After a moment's hesitation the guest asks:

"How is your health?"

"I hurt my back at work and went to the hospital."

"On the way to the hospital, did the soldiers create problems?"

"What problem, comrade?"

"Whoops! Again I was back in prison."

Just when the room is deep in conversation, there is a knock at the door and the guest leaps to his feet and moves towards the door.

"Is there a search?"

"Hey! What search? It's only our relatives."

We laughed out loud at this sketch. Since there were not many comrades who had been in prison for long years, I turned to comrade Şamil and said it was just as well we were not likely to get out soon, as we would embarrass ourselves. At this, others started to laugh at us. When there was a break, I went straight to block 4. Uncle Xalef was at the door. I asked him:

"What are you doing at the door?"

"When I saw there was no one at the door, I thought I would keep watch. If you like, you can do it."

"No, Xalo, as there is a celebration today, we're not keeping watch."

I smiled as I said this. It pleased me to see that, despite his 66 years and his health problems, he was aware. He was like a "guerrilla," ready with the zip of his parka done up. Of course, an "old" guerrilla…

I went with Xalo to the exercise yard of block 6.

Our six-man folklore group performed new dances and figures. The efforts of comrade Ayçiçek were immediately evident. They put on a professional show.

When comrade H. Acar was to recite Nuri Dersimi's "Address to Kurdish Youth," 60 of us got to our feet.* As he began to read the first sentences, everything was normal. As he progressed, the excitement rose. His voice changed and the veins in his neck bulged. Despite his short stature and his amputated arm, he looked bigger. After a while, he couldn't prevent himself trembling. He was shaking like a leaf and his voice was also affected…

When he reached the last section and said "vengeance," we accompanied him by repeating the word vengeance in unison. Everyone shouted at the tops of their voices. It was quite a sound. A moment when emotions and anger were intensified…

When the address ended, it was clear that most comrades had been profoundly affected. For many of them, it was a new experience. And most were hearing about these painful incidents for the first time. The address strikingly expresses what the Turkish army did during the Dersim Massacre of 1937, its treachery, and the state into which they brought human beings.

---

* Nuri Dersimi. A renowned Kurdish intellectual and activist. While studying medicine in Istanbul in 1911 he was also involved in politics. He played an active role in the launching of many Kurdish publications and associations. He participated in many endeavours for the independence of Kurdistan. In 1920-21 he was actively involved in the Koçgiri rebellion that was a response to oppression and depredation. After the massacres of Kurds in Koçgiri, he moved on to Sivas and Dersim. During the 1937-38 Dersim revolt, he acted in unison with the Kurdish leader of the resistance, Seyit Rıza. When the revolt was bloodily suppressed by the state, he went to Rojava. He confronted all manner of oppression without submitting to his foes. He wrote of his experiences in his book, *Hatıratlarım* [My memoirs]. His 'Address to Kurdish Youth' in this book is a call for 'vengeance.' He died in Aleppo in 1973 yearning for his homeland. —Author

It is a bitter scream about what was done to the Kurdish people. His bequest to Kurdish youth, calling for these deeds not to be forgotten, and for people to definitely be brought to account.

Despite his being one of the educated Kurds, the fact they could not provide a contemporary leadership during this uprising, and the fact that they were defeated and forced to live in exile, can be felt in that bitter scream.

I would have loved these people to have seen today's struggle and guerrillas. The last words of those who walked proudly to the gallows during those rebellions:

"Long live independent Kurdistan!"

"Down with Turkish tyranny!"

"May our grandchildren not disappoint us, and may they take revenge for us."

I would have loved for those who witnessed the rebellions and survived—forced to live in poverty in exile, burdened by the bitterness of being unable to do anything, and whose last words were "Kurdistan" or "Dersim"—to have seen their ARGK guerrilla grandchildren. I would have loved for them to witness the step-by-step liberation of an independent, free Kurdistan, the bequest of the martyrs.

I'm sure this would have been the greatest happiness for them.

While reading this text in prison, we once again commemorated them.

I have witnessed many times the excitement that comrades feel when this oration is read out. Just like a foaming wave. Like a mass of water returning time after time, relentlessly crashing into the breakwater…

We had a break in the celebrations for lunch. We had chicken and rice cooked by comrades, and ayran. It had been prepared especially from the communal kitty. During the meal, no one spoke. The comrades heartily ate the rice topped with chicken in front of them.

A poem, Statelessness and Yearning, written by comrade Delil, was performed as a play. Mainly comrades from the fraternal party, DHP, were involved. It explained fleeing the country, alienation, degradation, self-questioning, and a yearning for homeland.

This was followed by two more sketches. In the first, an elderly mother visits her son in prison. In the visiting booth, the mother talks of the family and her children in the traditional Kurdish way, while her son, in his 20s, talks of imperialism, colonialism, internationalism, cosmopolitanism, etc. Of course, the mother stares in bewilderment.

As for the second sketch, it dealt with two villagers with adjoining lands continually trying to extend the boundaries of their own land without their neighbour's knowledge. The sketch discussed the craftiness of villagers—their quarrels, being taken to the gendarmerie station where the commander takes money from both of them, then sends them off. Following this, the guerrillas get involved and resolve the issue peacefully.

Towards evening, we all took part in the halay. As the song was sung by everyone, it was extraordinarily loud. After the second song, the dust loosened by the dancers' feet striking the concrete surface had covered everything. We were all sweating.

Sixty souls stood up to perform the halay
Their hearts were all beating violently
Birth was being celebrated
In prison
Amidst torture
Even if in ambush
Hands linked together
At every step approaching tomorrow
What is shaken is not the concrete of the prison
It is the decay of centuries
Sixty souls stood up to perform the halay
A gleam in their eyes
The gleam of victory
Of freedom
Of a better tomorrow
The enthusiasm of today
Existed in hearts there years ago at its birth
When they first experienced this joy
There were but a handful of them
The few of yesterday
Are now the multitude of stars today
The life of stars is long
As long as that of sand on the beach
Stars that confront the darkness
That live for thousands of years
They are different from each other
Those who want to see the Pole star

Who want to get to know it
That seek it in every corner of the world
And when they find it stand up for a halay
Its enthusiasm will be something else
In prison
In the mountains
Or in the city

I felt tired in the evening on account of the day's activities.

After the evening news on TV, conversations began in the dining hall. How and where we had heard about the founding of the party, and the particular characteristics of that period were once again explained.

The comrades generally listened to us "oldies." I don't like the term "old," but it has been in use in our environment in recent years.

It is meaningless to compare today's conditions and possibilities with those of the past. It would be like comparing an ant and a mountain. The level and dimensions the struggle has reached are gigantic. In the old days, comrades staying in large areas knew each other. They would travel from province to province just to recruit or make contact with one person. Now, masses are seeking party workers. Putting the regions to one side, in the prisons new comrades are arriving before we are able to get acquainted with the existing ones. But can there be a better feeling than being side by side in the struggle with 17 and 67-year-olds? There are now people from every class and tendency in our ranks. Besides the advantages, there are also disadvantages to this.

When you look at the possibilities today, you see the real power of the people in practice. For those of us who have spent long years inside, this is our greatest yearning.

In the period before 1984, when the withdrawal to the Palestinian region took place, we used to think, "If we hear the war has begun, we will know we have not left anything undone." Today, those days are far in the past. Our war is at its highest level. There is no longer a concern about using too many bullets in an action. Hundreds of bullets are now used in a single action. This inevitably makes us sad. But, apart from the waste, even just thinking about the possibilities provided by our people delights those of us who are in prison.

When comrades are sitting and chatting, random62ents and situations come to mind. Although most of these thoughts are not revealed, they lead to feelings that are difficult to describe. I'm thinking, how many of the comrades I met are still outside in the combat environment? And it's not clear how many of them are intact. To just think of those heroic, courageous comrades who have dedicated themselves to the people, is by itself sufficient reason for the war and for life.

At 22.00, during the conversations, glasses of cola and nuts were distributed.

After completing daily tasks, I retired to my bed at midnight. Most comrades were already asleep. Although today was a search day for the prison authorities, they didn't come on account of the celebration. Our representative had asked them not to come. That was in accordance with our most recent agreement. Still, we had anticipated that they might come, as the enemy is unpredictable. But they didn't turn up and our celebration was not disrupted. It will continue tomorrow.

Block 4
28 November 1995, Tuesday
TO BEDRAN ÖNEN

At nine in the morning, we continued from where we had left off. We were in the dining hall of block 6 for the painting competition to commemorate martyr Haki KARER.* There were three prizes and an honourable mention being offered. The prize giving ceremony took place in a very formal atmosphere.

After comrade Kemal had made a short introduction, he called the recipient of the prize and the person who was to present it. This was a first for us. It was an innovation worthy of the occasion.

Comrade Uğur asked me to present the poetry prize. I wasn't expecting it. As I took my place to applause, I thought of the words I would use. When presenting the diary wrapped in a newspaper, I said, "Having the task and responsibility of perpetuating this important day is a wonderful duty. Perpetuating this day everywhere and working towards this goal pleases me, and I wish it to continue so."

The fact the comrade was from the DHP increased my delight. The comrade said, "I know my involvement has been insufficient. I felt I had a responsibility to take part in this competition in memory of the martyr,

---

* Haki KARER: He was an internationalist revolutionary from the Black Sea region of Turkey and one of the nucleus of the first PKK cadres in Ankara. At that time, he was one of the few people who said, "The peoples of Turkey cannot be free unless Kurdistan is free." He was killed by state civilian forces that considered him "the group's leader" in Antep on 18 May 1977. He made important contributions to the current struggle of the Kurds. —Author

comrade Haki. This prize, which has been deemed worthy of such an important day, will enhance my efforts."

Comrade Şamil said, regarding his prize-winning work, Birth, "I tried to reflect the party's innocence and purity in the picture. I believe this is still the case. I would also like, with your permission, to give this prize to Orhan, our youngest comrade, for his contributions." Great applause rang out. Comrade Orhan was joyful, surprised, and embarrassed. After congratulating the comrade, he turned to us, saying, "I don't know what to say about being seen as worthy of such a prize. This will motivate me."

Comrade Şamil had also participated in the story-reminiscence competition. He had explained the 1981 period and his arrest. What took place in four-person groups, conversations, the martyrdom of two comrades, and the wounding of two others during their arrest and the aftermath was explained in the book.

This work won first prize. When accepting the diary and pen, he said, "The period I describe was important, because it was our duty to write about our martyred comrades and the party. I feel relieved to have written, but I realise that my responsibility has increased. As this book has been written as a critique, there are lessons that may be learned. This prize is in two parts. With your permission, I would like to give it to comrades Poyraz and Fuat, with whom I have spent long years."

Again the applause brought the house down. I was really embarrassed, to tell the truth. After congratulating the comrade and glancing at the audience, I said, "It is pleasing that the comrade is sharing the prize with us. It is even more meaningful in that it is both the day our party was founded and on account of a competition to commemorate martyred comrade Haki KARER. It increases our responsibility and I will strive harder in the upcoming period. And I accept this prize on behalf of the structure." I noticed while speaking that some comrades were visibly moved. Subsequently, some comrades said, "For the first time in prison, we experienced such a wonderful moment that we were moved to tears."

This was followed by a pantomime-type sketch performed by a single person. He is being shot under a wall. Every time he gets up, he is shot again. Finally, he struggles to his feet and, thrusting his fist into the air, cries out at the top of his voice, "Ser-kef-tin, Ser-kef-tin [Victory, Victory]" and remains standing.

The competition included all our blocks in the prison. There were a total of 20 prizes.

While singing continued, our representative, comrade Sarıkaya, came to our block. He said that comrade Bedran Önen had been martyred in Buca prison. For a moment, the whys and hows disappeared in the silence of the sea of sadness.

We paused the celebration.

> *Every day news of martyrs*
> *One*
> *Then another one*
> *Falling in the redness of the struggle*
> *But not dying*
> *Living on with thousands*
> *They say:*
> *It's always the good ones who die in the struggle*
> *And the innocent, too*
> *Our hearts have not turned to stone*
> *Our tear ducts have not dried up*
> *Yet still, we do not cry*
> *Because we are in struggle*
> *Once again we are martyrs.*
> *How many more martyrs?*
> *How many more BEDRANS? Who knows?*
> *It is not known and will remain unknown.*
> *But what is certain is that there will be more BEDRANS.*

I saw the tears of comrade Tekin, who was standing next to me during the minute's silence, hit the concrete floor. They fell like large raindrops. I gather he was his childhood friend. They had deliberately not treated him in prison. This is another way of killing...

The whole prison concluded the day by shouting the slogans:

"BEDRAN ÖNENS are immortal!"

"Long live the fraternity of peoples!"

"Down with the special war!"

Block 4
29 November 1995, Wednesday

The things we had left half done yesterday were continued today. The Diyarbakir character "Qırıx" [tough guy] was to be animated. But before the performance, comrades were warned not to use the words or manner of speaking in the performance in daily life. This warning led to some smiles. Comrade Zülküf was the performer. He had scraped his hair and beard really short and drawn deep scars on his head and face. He had blackened his eyebrows with shoe polish. With his trousers and waistcoat, he resembled a real "Xançepek Qırıxı."*

He explained his quarrels with his friends, his conversations, his pursuit of his girl, the way he sat in Ramazan's café, his discussions and dialogue with "political bro," and when he was unable to stand seeing plain clothes police abducting a female student, he intervened, ending up in the police station where he cringed with embarrassment.

It was very well received. The performance was followed by a volleyball match. The celebration was into its third day. For the first time, we are celebrating 27 November in such an extensive and comprehensive way. In the afternoon, they came to conduct a search. As usual, they left everything in disarray.

Today, comrade H. Acar was taken ill. We sent him to the sick bay. They gave him an injection, he had a temperature. He was shivering in his bunk. He said, "This time it's gone on longer. I think I'm getting old. I've taken to my bed." We were demoralised. He got up at night. He looked weary, but appeared to have got over it.

Block 4

1 December 1995, Friday

This morning, I had difficulty getting up, as I hadn't slept much. I went to bed at midnight, then woke up at 02.00. I looked through publications until 03.30. When guards came to close the block door at this time, I went downstairs to the dining hall. When they carry out searches every night, one of us is there as an observer. First, they close the doors of all the blocks. Then, they come back to carry out their search. In fact, they could do the search when they close the door. They do it in this way to cause discomfort. I had to wait in the dining hall for 50 minutes. Two administrators, four head guards and 10 guards came to carry out the search. One of the head guards looked around, then said:

"Why are you still up?"

"Because of this arbitrary and unnecessary thing that you're doing, that's why."

"You inmates wanted it like this."

---

* "Xançepek Kırıkları": A person who is looked down on and oppressed by the system, but does not submit and is a gruff, impoverished type who does not abide by the rules. The name derives from the "Xançepek" neighbourhood of Diyarbakır. They have their own amusing, particular form of language and way of life. They represent a distinct personality type in Diyarbakır provincial culture. —Author

"No. We said let's have an observer when you carry out a search. We didn't say close the doors, then come back an hour later for the search. What's the point of that? You could search when you close the doors."

"That's up to you. If you don't want to, you don't have to wait. You can go to bed."

As I moved towards the stairs, I said, "If necessary, we'll wait until morning. But we also know how to resolve this problem," adding, "There's no need for you to make up new rules."

When I went to bed, I couldn't sleep for an hour out of irritation. It didn't help that a comrade was snoring like a tractor.

In a dream, I am standing in the block, dealing with an aching tooth. When I put my hand in my mouth, two molars come out. One looks sound, but the other seems decayed. I look at the corner of the tooth while explaining something to comrade Erşat. In a second dream, I am in another prison but the comrades from Aydın are there. An official comes and tells me that I and Fuat Kav are to be transferred. Before leaving, we have breakfast in another block. But where we are eating, there is a sheet placed on the ground on the side of a street. Comrades are sitting on both sides, both eating and chatting.

We go to the office, but that also looks like a dining hall. While the paperwork is being carried out, I remember that I haven't taken my money and address book with me. I'm thinking, "In the place I'm going, I won't be able to write to necessary places." I tell the authorities:

"I've left my money and address book in the block. I need to get them."

Comrade Fuat, on seeing me arguing with the official, says:

"What are you going to do with money on the way?"

"Comrade Fuat, you can't be transferred without having money."

"It's alright. I've got some as a precaution so that we're not in need of them…"

When they insisted that guards could get my things, I said, "The guards can't find them," so they sent two soldiers with me to the block. We were meant to be going to the block, but we went out into the street. We were walking towards Yavuzlar in the Karayılan neighbourhood of Antep. One of the soldiers was close to me. The other went into a grocer's. When he was 10 to 15 paces away, I started to run. I was not handcuffed. I ran and was sure the soldier would not be able to catch me. He was shouting and chasing me. I tried to increase the distance between us. I went into the lower road, below Çamlık, where I spent my childhood. I turned into another street. In reality, there was no such street there, but I have seen it in previous dreams. I remember its width and even its paving stones. A person in the street said, "This road leads to the parliament building." I notice that a little ahead the street was covered with a dome-like structure. It reminded me of the Urfa tunnel. I realised that it was the Syria gate. In front of the gate, I encountered President S. Demirel. Moving along the tunnel, I saw the Syrian ambassador praying. I tried to hear what he was mumbling. Amidst the prayer, he said, "I know you are here. Our great leader knows what you have said when and where." Going further along the tunnel, I encountered a small soldier. He was holding a rifle that resembled a G-3, but was shorter. I lunged and grabbed the gun. I couldn't see his face properly as the hood on his parka was covering it. After hitting him in the face a few times with the rifle butt, fragments of stone started to fall from it. Surprised, I mumbled, "This bloody technology makes fake everything," and I woke up to the sound of my own voice. For some reason, I recalled the soldier who went to the grocer's before I got up.

This morning, we went to the bath house. Again, they cut off the hot water early.

As I hadn't slept well at night and due to relaxing after a bath, I had a snooze from 12.30 to 13.00. Of course, it is necessary to inform the duty comrade of such a thing. Normally, no comrade sleeps during the day. And there's not really time for it.

While completing the photo session, comrade Sarıkaya arrived and I had a photo taken with him.

I told him that we didn't accept the night searches and the waiting, and that it was necessary to speak to the prison authorities.

In the evening, we read an interview the Leadership had given to a Russian newspaper.

Tomorrow we restart the educational activities we have paused for a few days. As it is time for three of us to prepare an article, we will not take part. Tören, Nihat and I will prioritise the article.

Block 4
3 December 1995

Yesterday, I received a short note from comrade Tören. His determination to start the article was reflected in the note. I hope this determination continues. It should, and as long as there is not a hitch, we will finish the article this time. He also said he had sent a fax on our behalf, as comrade Cerenbeli's mother has gone into hospital for an operation.

Mother Fatma had a serious operation on her head when we were outside. Sometimes she would mention her pain. I'm sorry she is having another operation. We are concerned. She has done a lot for us. In Antep, she did not abandon us under the worst conditions. While certain comrades fled to

Europe during the military coup, she did not hesitate to be a mother to us. I cannot forget how she sold the bracelets on her arms for us. Those valuable ornaments, which she would not sell for her family, she sold for us. Her only concern was that we would survive. Now, at this moment, I want her to survive, because we owe her a debt. We have promised to give her gold back after the revolution. May nothing happen to our self-sacrificing mother.

The "Doomsday ball" we use to exchange messages between blocks got stuck on the roof the other day, on the roof, near block 9, and the comrades were unable to dislodge it. The prison authorities retrieved it. There are apparently documents with names, the subject of an investigation. Despite this, the authorities handed over the note. We were surprised. Still, we received self-criticisms from two comrades who were involved in the note-sending for carelessness…

Today, six comrades came to visit us from block 9-13. They had also wanted to bring comrade Mahmut, but he didn't come. He is a veteran comrade whom we respect. But, from time to time, he has a problem getting on with "young" comrades. His non-arrival is partly due to his embarrassment and partly due to a clandestine attitude.

I had expected old man Cemal to come, but they didn't bring him. To cheer him up, I sent my greetings and a single cigarette. He loves cigarettes…

I have written part of the El Salvador section of the article we are jointly preparing, but I am unable to concentrate as I would like. Interruptions are not good and discomfit me. I will try to concentrate better.

Yesterday, we received a card from comrades Nimet and Ömer. It was sent to Acar and me. Ömer has been transferred from Bartın to Bursa prison. The move will be good for him.

Block 4
4 December 1995

As an analysis of comrade Tolhildan's personality was taking place in education today, I took part in it. He said:

> I met the comrades at the end of 1977. And I assess the period from then until now as one in which I was an opponent of the party most of the time. While my family was in the village, I went to school in Maraş. During that period, there was a Turkish left that was identical to Kemalism. This was mainly on the basis of defending Kemalism against the fascists. I was expelled from school for getting into fights. This led to disappointment, as the dominant logic was that studying guaranteed one's future. During this time of confusion, I became acquainted with the comrades. It

was not an ideological choice, but I was aware that I had met with humanisation. I liked the comrades who represented the movement. The feeling to reciprocate developed as they valued us. The interest shown by comrade Kemal Pir in a very difficult situation created the feeling that colonialism could be destroyed. Comrade Kemal was staying in a room without a door or a window. The walls hadn't even been plastered. It had no stove. Instead of a door and window, sacking had been hung up. The room was freezing. And, apart from a mattress, the room was empty. When I went into the room, Kemal Pir was shivering like a leaf. Despite this, his enthusiasm was not diminished. It was this belief and determination that developed the feeling in us that colonialism could be destroyed. After some education, we became patriots. The more we become Marxist-Leninist, the more patriotic we become. But we were unable to make much progress in developing patriotism. While still in the development stage, I took on responsibilities in Maraş city. I was inadequate, but there was an amateur spirit, enthusiasm, and loyalty. This lasted until the Maraş Massacre. I saw during the Maraş incidents how the people could resist. The view developed that revenge must be taken for what was done to the people. After that, I gave more importance to action rather than theory, but I was unable to combine revenge with revolutionary integrity. I was in the Pazarcık area until I was arrested. My practice there was far from representing the party. I was pleased that people were talking about me in an exaggerated way. In the middle of 1980, the party criticized our practice, saying, loyalty to the party, not a person, should be developed. My exaggerated personality prevented me seeing my reality. Now, when I evaluate myself, I see the situation was not very consistent or conscious. Also, the fact that I approached things in an exaggerated way discomfits me. I was too fond of myself. This brought with it a lack of confidence in the people. My personality conflicted with our line. I was arrested in this state. I thought they would kill me straight away. I wasn't expecting the torture to go on for so long. At first, I accepted responsibility for everything in order not to cause harm to anyone else. This brought weakness with it. During interrogation, I was unable to represent the party. The enemy won a victory through me. For long years in prison, I have felt low because of this. For five years I couldn't lift my head. But I didn't leave the environment or the comrades. The discipline taught me by the party necessitated this. When I entered prison I said, "I won't take part, but you build the organisation." I told the comrades, "However you want, I will behave in that way in court." I participated in the resistance that took place. In 1986, I was admitted to political relations. As time passed, my self-confidence grew. But this led, in time, to slackening. My old weaknesses reappeared. By comparing certain responsible comrades to myself and raising this in the environment, I caused the organisation to be weakened. In social life, my relationships were too familiar. After being transferred from Eskişehir to Aydın, I gave up the hunger strike on the 41st day. Despite hearing two comrades had been martyred, I said, "There's no need to persist with the action." I once again entered a period of faint-heartedness. I subsequently left the environment of the comrades. Defeat in the elections in Nicaragua seemed like the defeat of the revolution in Kurdistan.

After months had passed, the comrades called me to their environment. Following the 1991 prison resistance conference, I began to accuse past administrations of wrongdoing instead of blaming myself. I said comrades and administrations that tried to impose a little order to life were "narrow-minded." In fact, this was me wanting to be myself. I said many rules were "a fashion, arbitrary." Sometimes I am secretly pleased to be in prison, as I know that if I took on a duty outside, I would cause harm. Sometimes, exactly opposite thoughts develop.

He also explained at length how in the past he had been the "bogeyman" mothers use to silence crying children.

I do not want to comment on how much he expanded on certain subjects or how sincere he was. But to even put himself forward for analysis and scrutiny is positive and takes courage. We should give him the opportunity to prove how sincere he is in practice.

After education, the reports of two comrades who came from the Aegean region were read out. Their practice outside, under interrogation and in prison, has been a disgrace. There is nothing positive about it. But since they have come into our environment, we cannot abandon them to the enemy. After certain restrictions, they will remain normally in our milieu.

In a letter that arrived today, I learned that some of our villagers have gone to Europe. I don't know what to say. For years they moved from Gürün Bozhüyük to Istanbul. They vacated the village. Now, from 10-year-olds to 60-year-olds, they are moving to another continent. They are doing their utmost to go as far away as possible from the country. They don't understand, unfortunately, that this is an insidious state policy. After our fellow villager Hüseyin İNAN's execution, the village was slowly evacuated through a subtle state policy. The state of this Kurdish and Alevi village that is a dot on the map is worthy of study. I am saying nothing about those who have to remain there. But those who leave will find it very hard in the place they go. For they have no idea what they will encounter. Leaving their roots seems easy. We will in future suffer the trauma of what today seems attractive about foreign realms, and although it will be late, comprehend it.

Block 4

10 December 1995

As the elections of 24 December are approaching, we have been debating possible outcomes over the last two days. There are views that dismiss it, and others that have well-intentioned expectations. The view I have espoused in block 6 and here is as follows: it is necessary not to see the early election as separate from the war in Kurdistan. Governments that have followed the special war regime similarly stagnate in a short time. The Republic of Turkey is experiencing this in every field.

Possible developments will be determined by election results. This election, in spite of all the traps, obstructions, and the fact that millions of voters will not be able to cast votes on account of being forced out of their homes will signify either an approval or rejection of the dirty war that has been waged for 10 years. If the Labour, Peace and Freedom Platform set up by HADEP is successful, it could be the first step to a face-off type situation in Turkey. In this respect, this election is very important.

Since the majority of HADEP's voter base will not be able to cast their vote, the party may not be able to exceed the ten per cent threshold. If the people displaced in Turkey have been able to register, then that problem will have been resolved.

Even if the threshold is not exceeded, every vote cast for HADEP signifies opposition to the dirty war. As far as being on the side of the people is concerned, every vote counts.

It is striking that, unlike in previous elections, most of the candidates put up in Kurdistan have not been rejected. In previous elections, candidates were not even allowed into their electoral areas. They were even attacked by groups escorted by police. All these attacks did not help the state. It was the PKK that gained in strength. The Kurds, whose very existence has been denied and who have been slaughtered for 70 years, have established a fighting force. There are no methods the state has not used or tried to implement against them.

Europe and the US say, "Resolve the Kurdish question." They also accept there will not be a solution without the PKK.

The existing parliament and parties do not have the capacity to resolve the Kurdish question. If HADEP enters parliament, then partial steps may be taken. They may become indirect interlocutors.

A possible RP government is disturbing some circles. The votes HADEP wins will weaken the RP. If it doesn't pass the threshold, its votes will automatically switch to the RP, according to electoral law. This risk exists. The fact that hard-line bureaucrats are standing as candidates for the DYP at a time the war has been intensified is interesting. They are now more active and effective in their posts. When they are elected as deputies, most of them will be there for show only. I wonder if the idea is to get rid of some of them. Nowhere in the world have so many police officers and bureaucrats been candidates for a ruling party in a single election. We need to be watchful.

Our party may announce a ceasefire before the election.

Another possibility is that if the state attempts to inflict another blow, HADEP may boycott the election.

It is clear that the elected government will not consist of only one party. The chances of there being a coalition are high.

Whoever becomes the government, they will be unable to resolve the Kurdish question. They won't resolve it.

Recent events, such as certain fascist businessmen mumbling about resolution, the TV programme Siyaset Meydanı being in Diyarbakir, permission being given for a democracy conference in Diyarbakir, German MPs talking to soldiers, our candidates not being harassed, ANAP's attempts to promote Korkut Özal and meetings with writer Yaşar Kemal should not be considered separately. They should not be assessed in isolation from the election.

Block 4
11 December 1995

As I went downstairs for breakfast, comrade Sevdan said, "The TV said, while going through the newspaper headlines, that the party was going to announce a ceasefire." As I had mentioned this the previous evening, he particularly wanted to inform me.

As newspapers reach us two or three days late, we will learn the details later.

The photographs we took have arrived. I noticed straight away that the "old" comrades had got older and thinner. I said to comrade Acar, "I was going to say something, but I have changed my mind so as not to upset you." I knew he would insist. "I won't be upset. Tell me," he said. "I noticed you had got older in the pictures," I said. From where he was sitting, he thought for a moment, and then said, smiling, "No, not got old, we just haven't lost weight." When we were alone, he said, "What you said was like a lance in the heart. How will I sleep tonight?" How we laughed.

We were both young when we were arrested. We couldn't keep still. We were on fire. All the comrades arrested then were young. Over time, their hair has gone grey or fallen out. Illnesses have begun. Still, that generation is sound and hearty…

Block 4

12 December 1995

Today we listened to the Leader's vibrant voice speaking on MED radio. I felt that the loudspeaker on the radio was shaking. The leader was speaking and we were listening in prison. Both his voice and on our radio. A fantastic feeling and great joy. All comrades were listening, without a sound, as if they were erasing years of longing. It was possible to feel the gale coming from smiling eyes and the depths of hearts.

He mentioned the historical and topical aspects of our ceasefire with the KDP. He stressed that uniting the forces in Kurdistan will benefit the people and that it is necessary to ensure this step doesn't remain limited to a ceasefire, but is transformed into a political-democratic step. He said that Barzani and the KDP administrators would be able to rely on it, that we had not set any conditions, that we did not see the people of the South as separate from our revolution, but adding that no one should tell us to leave here. I received a letter from Yaşar. I was surprised. It means he has recovered from his depression. He's not working, but his wife has a job. He is supposedly a toiler and an intellectual…

On the evening news, we heard that 14 inmates had been injured during incidents that broke out in Ümraniye prison. The incidents are still continuing. I assume they have tried again to take away rights.

Because of this situation DS shouted slogans at 23.00.

Block 4

6 January 1996

Comrades A. Boztepe, B. Elden, U. F. Süvarioğulları, M. Birkan, Y. Gül, H. Ulusoy from Buca prison and Comrades Y. Gülcan, E. Teker, İ. Eker and F. Yaşlı from Bayrampaşa prison have been brought here.

The comrades are young and dynamic. Despite being only 18-20 years old, they are very respectful. The party manner of those who have come from Bayrampaşa is immediately obvious.

Today, some comrades came to visit us from block 9.13. There is apparently an outbreak of flu in their blocks. Nur Cengiz has got pneumonia. I'm sorry, as his lungs are not good.

In my dream last night (again a dream with a mixture of prison and outside), we are outside in a tent but conducting a prison conference with 50-60 of the comrades here. Suddenly, a large group of guards descends on the tent. As I am sitting at the entrance, I start an argument with the head guard. We're shouting at each other. We state that we don't accept such entrances. They say they will undertake a search. I snatch a sheet of white paper that the head guard had taken from a coffee table in front of me. The sheet of paper changes hands a few times. Eventually, I become annoyed and say, "Are you blind? It's not a blank sheet of paper." They threaten to torture us. I shake my forefinger at the guards, shouting, "It's up to you, but every time you hit me, my resentment will increase." The tent is in a neighbourhood. On leaving the tent, a chase begins. There are half-finished buildings in the area. I remember this place from previous dreams. They are unable to catch me. I jump from one building to another. I gain strength by putting one foot on the corner of a building. Sometimes, when under pressure, I use my arms like wings. There are builders in some of the buildings. They cannot catch me.

In another dream, I am sitting with a friend close to Hoşgör neighbourhood, next to Çamlık in our own neighbourhood, typing. We are sitting on the road between Çamlık and the houses. We are right next to the barbed wire. Of course, Çamlık is still just as it was 15 years ago. At one stage, the comrades called us for tea. We went to the Kıbrıs neighbourhood behind Çamlık for tea. Just like in prison, they call us for tea when it is ready. I say to my comrade beside me that it will be good if nothing happens to the typewriter here.

I am surprised that I saw such detail of Çamlık in my dream.

Yesterday, I received a card and letter from auntie Aley in the Kıbrıs neighbourhood. It surprised me that she wrote for the first time after 15 years. I gather she has only recently learned my address. Soon I will learn about her. I remember the treats she used to bring us as a child.

Block 4
12 January 1996

Today, another 10 comrades were brought here from Buca. There are now more than two hundred of us here.

And Supi Bal was transferred to Ceyhan.

Block 4
16 January 1996

While walking back and forth in the exercise yard of block 6 this afternoon, two comrades came over and said, "They are calling you urgently to block 2." I ran there to be told by comrade Tören that Cerenbeli is being released. This was followed by Cerenbeli saying in a strange, excited voice, "I'm going." At that moment, I could only say, "I wish you success."

He is being released after exactly 14 years and seven months. It's a weird situation. They are now releasing people who at one time they wanted to speedily try and execute by separating our files from the main 6th army one. It was 1984. They began to try Metin Uluca, Hasan Şerik, Ahmet Cerenbelli, and me separately, but "specially," in a military court. They were ill-intentioned. Then, when things didn't go as they had hoped, they again added us to the main trial. Şerik and Metin were released in 1991 and Ceren today.

It's a really paradox and difficult to explain. The three comrades were tried with me to the first degree.

Block 4
18 January 1996

Today, I went for a visit. When I heard what had happened to Ceren on his first night outside, I was upset. We have become completely alienated from the outside world.

As his time to be released had come, they gave him a document valid for 24 hours to serve as an ID. The police left him outside the city. He had no choice but to walk back to the city. As he didn't have an ID, he couldn't go to a hotel. He sat in a café at the bus station all night. In the morning, he saw some visitors on their way to the prison. They told a patriot to take him home with him, but he said, "I can't. My cover has been blown." But they could have taken him somewhere else. This is the attitude of a degraded, cowering Kurdish individual who is running from himself, whereas Ceren is a Turk who has served 15 years in jail for the Kurds. The families had no choice but to bring Ceren with them on the visit. A day later, there he was. We were flabbergasted. Once visiting is over, the families will take him to

Izmir. For the night he spent at the bus station, he said, "It cost me a million, I don't understand how it happened." The families were apparently laughing at him as he had forgotten how to spend money. It's clear we are all going to find this difficult.

Block 4
30 January 1996

I have finished my section of our study-research, typed up, and sent it to my "partners." It is longer than I expected, covering 55 large pages. If comrades Nihat and Tören's section also turns out to be long, it will be somewhat large. They will arrange the final format. I hope it is finished on time.

Block 4
18 February 1996

Today is Sunday. I will not say, as Nazım [Hikmet] did, "Today is Sunday. For the first time, they took me out into the sun. I rested my back against the wall."

We do not have either the time or the opportunity to sit facing the sun.

Today, eight comrades from block 7-15 came to visit us. After a chat, folk songs were sung in the dining hall of block 6.

It is being said that E. Karatay has gone to the academy. If he has gone, a comprehensive analysis and research will be undertaken about him. It's not definite that he's gone, as there are various claims being made.

As it's a religious holiday, there was a closed visit today. When we realised they were not allowing anyone in except for immediate relatives, the comrades protested and returned to the blocks. At 12.45, all our blocks shouted the slogan:

"Our right to visits cannot be obstructed!"

We also shouted, "Down with the fascist administration!" While shouting, "Our right to visits cannot be obstructed!" I thought, "They're certainly obstructing it." It seemed strange to shout such slogans. We definitely wouldn't have shouted such a slogan seven or eight years ago.

Tomorrow is our visiting day. Let's see what happens.

This is a conscious policy of the administration. The fact that we have withdrawn and, in particular, our education seriously troubles them. They also know that we have our conferences in these months.

There might be attacks in the coming days.

There is a flu outbreak in our block. Around 20 comrades have chills. We have halted the two hour education sessions in the evenings. Comrades who wish may go to bed early. They won't have to wait until sleeping time at 23.45.

Block 4
21 February 1996

Comrades Tören and Nihat sent me the article towards evening. 105 large pages. The fact it came today surprised and pleased me. A few days ago Nihat had sent me a note mentioning comrade Tören's procrastination. I wrote a vitriolic note back, saying, "If you're not going to concentrate, send it to me, I'll write it." So I wasn't expecting it to come today. I was surprised.

In the note he had attached, Nihat said he had been joking. It would be naïve to think that comrade Tören had nothing to do with this. I immediately wrote a note in return, expressing my pleasure that they had completed it early.

The article commission will check it, then Tören and Nihat, who have said they would type it up, will complete the task. One couldn't ask for more.

Block 4
26 February 1996

In prison, one finds writing some things to be very difficult. One of these is recounting dreams. Despite this, I am continuing to record them. I believe that it is necessary to do this, even if only in a limited way. I think it reflects our psychology, even if that seems nonsense to some people. It may be data for researchers in the future.

We were in a place that resembled the outside world. But as always, a prison exercise yard. A bit of Eskişehir L-type, a bit of E-type. In order to send a note to the neighbouring block, we threw a "guide ball." There was no reply. After waiting a while, we began to get annoyed. If there was no reply, we wouldn't throw the ball. This is the rule. Three or four of us went up onto the roof. We were walking on the tiles. It was daytime. When we got above the E-type corridor, we saw two guide balls on the first part. We wanted to take them, but changed our minds, as we thought the guards would see us. Meanwhile, comrade Hamdin had found a bulb. Just at that moment, the guards came onto the roof. The comrade stated, "They cause problems if there's a bulb missing in the bloc" and handed the guards the bulb. There was a deep fissure between the roof and the wall. It extended a long way down. Perhaps more than a hundred metres. We made our way down a narrow pipe, like a cable pipe. We went down one at a time. Meanwhile, we joked with each other, saying, "As we're holding on with our arms, our muscles will develop fast." As we descended into the fissure, the guards did not intervene. As we neared the bottom, we saw a settlement. It was as if we were birds seeing a city from far above. We descended to a wide, busy street. We stopped in front of a large closed door. We could see through the window. There were bars on the window like in prison. Before going into the room, I said I was going to the toilet. They directed me to a place at the end of the street. And they gave me some loose change. Three comrades gave me a total of 60TL. I tried to give some of it back, saying, "It's too much." But they said, "It'll only just be enough." I was really surprised and said, "In the old days, you could have bought a house with this money." Meanwhile, a two and a half TL coin came into my hand. I stared at it in amazement. As for the comrades, they were surprised at my amazement. Some of those in the room had AK 47s. Naturally, it attracted our interest. They looked quite natural about it. At that moment, I woke up.

Today I received a letter from Yaşar. He had spoken to my mother on the phone. He writes that she is to have another operation. I didn't understand why he wanted to tell me this. I haven't heard from my mother for months. Yaşar had also not written for a year. It's strange.

Despite it being winter, they cut off our water for six or seven hours today. They do it deliberately, as they wish.

Block 4
3 March 1996

Last night, I again shouted out in my sleep. Everyone was woken up. They told me in the morning. In fact, I did wake up at one stage. A few comrades were awake, but I didn't understand what had happened. They had been woken up by my voice. Comrade Acar said he had felt demoralised at that moment, saying, "I rebelled against prison. As I felt sad, I went downstairs in the middle of the night for a cigarette." It was clear from the lines of his face that he was sad. I generally shout in my sleep when I am particularly stressed. I generally feel weary the following day.

Block 4
7 March 1996

While looking through the daily newspapers this morning, comrade Cemal arrived with a syrup bottle in his hand. He had filled it with water from the tap. The water was cloudy and in it was a worm, six or seven centimetres in length. It was still alive. Our water is muddy, oily, and sometimes runs cloudy, but this was the first time we had witnessed this. It is impossible not to be flabbergasted. They don't clean the tank out of their hatred for the inmates. Who knows how many years of filth there is at the bottom of the tank. We have to drink this water. Many comrades have caught intestinal infections and typhoid from drinking it. They do it deliberately.

They're going to show a sample of the water to the doctor, but we know it won't do any good. We don't expect anything to be done.

Block 4
10 March 1996

They are going to resolve the absence of a government that has gone on for three months with a coalition of the DYP and ANAP. Mehmet Ağar, who is responsible for the slaughter of thousands of people, has been made Minister of Justice. He shouldn't be made a minister. But at this time, Turkey needs people like him. For days, the press has been focusing on the prisons for no reason. They are preparing the ground for new attacks.

The new cabinet consists mainly of fascists. Eight of the 35 ministers are former police chiefs.

This government is entirely a war government. Everyone agrees about this. It looks as though the coming period will be action-packed. It appears that prisons will be on the agenda. They may open the Eskişehir basements and transfer certain comrades there. They may introduce restrictions in all the prisons. The fact they often mention our organised structure and education in prisons is a sign of this.

We are doing what we can to prepare for new attacks and restrictions.

Block 4
17 March 1996

Today is the day I was captured.

It's been exactly 15 years.

Is it possible to forget that day? 15 years…

It's such a long time. Just like endless roads…

And, as close as it is endless and distant, it's as if it happened only yesterday…

It could be called the paradox of pain.

All night, until dawn, we made our way over the mountain. There were three of us. And only two weapons: one a pistol, the other a semi-automatic rifle. That's all…

We were to meet up with comrade BESE ANUŞ's group. When we reached the rendezvous point, they were not there. On the bank of a small stream were three poplar trees. We found a note the comrades had written in a hollow we had identified previously. In crooked letters on a small piece of paper were the words, "Let's meet on the side you've come from." However, it had taken us a whole night to walk from there, and crossing the surging Aksu river had been difficult.

Since we didn't travel during the day, we went to the top of a hill and began to wait. Less than an hour had passed when we began to hear the high-pitched whine of the Reo vehicles used by soldiers. We weren't to know that, at that moment, they had arrived at our rendezvous point. We also didn't know that the group with which we were planning to meet had been captured and that comrade Bese Anuş had been martyred. Comrade Bese was the first woman martyr in our party's history.

From the top of the hill, we secretly watched the soldiers. When they couldn't find anything, they began to widen their circle. Realising they were heading in our direction, we moved towards the other side of the hill.

Until noon, we made slow progress through water and snow. At one point, some Turkish fascists from Kısık village saw us from far off. Despite being the poorest village in the area, they immediately telephoned the soldiers and told them which way we were going. Just before noon, as we reached a clump of poplars, around 100 soldiers and 30 to 40 fascist villagers with sawn-off shotguns encircled us. They began raining bullets down on us from a crescent. The sound of gunfire resounded.

As a result, comrade Ali CİNKILIÇ and a patriotic Kurdish villager, Salman CENGIZ, who was with us, were martyred, while the wounded İmam Güler and I were captured alive. We were met with violent brutality from the first moment, and we were to wish for death.

They had shot to kill and they were going to do a job on those who had survived.

How long were those moments and every minute of the following days…

As a result, exactly 15 years as a captive…

There is an account to be settled
Vengeance to be taken
We have reason to live and fight
Young people
Who fell while still only 17 or 18
Endless torture…
Every day
Every youth
Every, each one…
Shame on those who don't hold those accountable
For 15 years I am nurturing my rage
To break down the walls of the prison
And destroy the oppression

Block 4
22 March 1996

We celebrated Newroz as well as we possibly could. Yesterday, the day passed in celebration. Despite it being our day for visits, we returned early from the visiting area. The number of visitors was small, anyway.

As always, we began by standing in silence, reading out a statement, and the "Hey Revolutionary" march. Although we had not had the opportunity to do much preparation, it was stirring. All the comrades were enthusiastic and in good spirits.

In the morning, four representative comrades came. They also watched our theatre. They read out their messages and departed.

The day was packed with things such as sketches, folk dancing, poems, messages, and group dances.

Prizes were awarded to projects in a competition to commemorate comrade Mazlum Doğan. My diary records that they gave me a shirt for being third in the "27 November celebrations section."

The celebration continued in the evening in the block.

Although it was just the one day, we were all tired.

Throughout the day, we watched the news at every opportunity. The fact that thousands of people had gathered to celebrate Newroz and display the party flag in many places in Kurdistan, Turkey, and Europe, despite it not being permitted, pleased us greatly. The celebration in Zeytinburnu in Istanbul was particularly radical. The police did not intervene but arrested some people as the crowd dispersed.

The mass attendance in public places in accordance with the leader's call was the best response to the special war regime.

Block 4
24 March 1996

Today, an indefinite hunger strike began in Bayrampaşa prison. They announced that they were protesting at repression in prisons, the targeting of Bayrampaşa, and the appointment of Mehmet Ağar as Justice Minister. It appears the protest will spread. I assume the comrades will feign to do one thing and then do something else. It may be a tactic appropriate to the period. Perhaps they do not want certain prisons to be in the forefront.

We in Aydın have been caught unawares, as we have only just finished preparations for the conference.

Three people have arrived from Elazığ prison. A. Aslan has come to our block. The other two opted to stay in the "non-aligned" block.

It is the first time we have received people from Elazığ prison. Interesting. I gather they carry out torture at every opportunity there. They don't allow *Demokraci* newspaper. Despite everything, it is still good to be in Kurdistan. At least they are near their families.

I hope this comrade is not disappointed. When newcomers feel like that, it upsets us.

Block 4
27 March 1996

While in block 4, we were busy writing, while comrades were panicking, wanting to send comrade Hazbin to block 6. We were curious why they should call for a medical student, so we rushed out into the exercise yard of block 6.

Comrade İ. Eker slipped while playing football due to it drizzling and hit his head on the concrete. He was lying on his back on the ground. His eyes were open but there was no reaction. We massaged him a little, but there was still no reaction. Four guards came with a stretcher, saying, "There's no doctor in the sick bay, but let's still take him there." I was angry and said, "If there's no doctor, don't take him and just leave him there." Because they could do such underhand things in these situations. They said, "We will phone for a doctor" and took the comrade to the sick bay.

He was taken to hospital. On the way back to prison, he regained consciousness. When he realised he was handcuffed, he presumed there had been an attack on the block. He learned the truth from us when he returned.

It's despicable to handcuff an unconscious person. He couldn't stand up when we took him into the block. His head was spinning and he was extremely tired. We were really scared when he fell. It could have been a lot worse. It saddened us all the more as he is only in his 20s. He was very unfortunate. Now, he is resting. It will be better for him to be in the block.

Block 4
29 March 1996

According to a joint statement by some Turkish left movements, a one-day refusal to attend roll call and a three-day practical obstruction protest will take place in all prisons. The DS representative dropped into our block. They have started a hunger strike today. They are not going to attend roll call this evening. Due to the harshness of the prison authorities here, there may be a rumpus at the midnight roll call. Fundamentally, they are protesting the appointment of M. Ağar as Minister.

For about a month now, Turkey has been deploying troops on the border with South Kurdistan. From time to time, planes are carrying out bombing raids. In a statement they issued yesterday, they called it "an operation to prevent the PKK's spring offensive."

They are targeting the areas where our party is based in the South and spring preparations. But they also know they will not be able to prevent it.

Just as in the South, peace has been made with local forces, and a conference and congress with all Kurdish groups is on the agenda. This is what our comrades are involved in.

There are serious developments going on. In Europe, first and foremost Germany, the attitude towards us is hardening. They are developing hypocritical policies according to the balance of forces and developments in the Middle East.

The imperialists wish to encircle our struggle. But there is a situation they have forgotten and are disregarding. The reality of our struggle will demonstrate this to them.

Today, a card came from my mother. She hadn't written for 10 months. Perhaps she couldn't find anyone to write for her. Her address has changed. She wrote that she may return soon. She misses being at the prison gate and seeing us. She's had another operation. In every line of the card, it is possible to see "Kurdish Zeynep." She is, after all, an old lefty…

Block 4
30 March 1996

The comrades in Bayrampaşa have ended their hunger strike. It means it was a week-long one to send a warning. Mehmet Ağar as Justice Minister has again uttered threats against the prisons. If we can't prevent Ağar's intentions, shame on us. Whatever he does he should regret it. His one and only target is the organised structure within the prisons. They will target our very lives to achieve this. However, even if they put us in single cells, even if they torture us every day and seize everything we have, they will not be able to succeed. Our struggle in this arena will triumph.

The guerrillas, who are our essence and our guarantee, are continuing to stoke the flames of freedom in all parts of the country. No longer will they be able to force us to surrender as they did in the past. They will not be able to succeed.

Wasn't this the greatest yearning of those who turned their own bodies into burning torches?

It is not us who are being exhausted, it is the enemy.

Until our conference ends we have doubled the number of night lookouts to four.

It would have been good if I could have concentrated for ten days. I don't know if I will be able to find the opportunity. These days, both us and the general agenda are hectic.

Today, from what we understood from the television, it appears the leader said use violence against the German police. This has apparently shocked the German police. The Germans say, "Suicide actions in particular would worry us." The German state opposes our struggle everywhere. It is one of the countries that sells the most weapons to Turkey. Also, when in the past the Turkish army carried out massacres of Kurds during uprisings, there were German officers alongside them. The Germans absolutely deserve it, but it might well be news fabricated by the Turkish press.

Block 4

17 April 1996

After 15 days of hectic activity, we have completed our conference, in spite of some forced intervals. We assessed our work over the year and made our plans for the New Year. The fact that we have 183 comrades in all our blocks stretched us, as some work was centralised. This naturally took time. Despite this, it was a success.

We are sure the next year will be tough.

These days, the Turkish army is carrying out large scale operations in close to 20 areas of Kurdistan. They say they have lost 40 soldiers in the last ten days. This is an admission that a larger number have died. 27 died in clashes around "Ape Musa Camp" alone. They are saying it is "the largest losses we have suffered up to now."

Block 4

19April 1996

Today, we commenced a three-day hunger strike to protest at the treatment of comrades in detention centres.

Xalo Xalef has been ill for a few days now. Today we sent him to hospital on a stretcher. They kept him in. His condition is getting progressively worse. He didn't sleep all night. It's obvious he's in a bad way.

We sent some things to the hospital.

As we do every year in spring, we are going to make changes in our blocks. We sent a list to the prison administration today. They had told us, "Don't make it too long."

After all the education and experience, I become irritated when certain comrades were uncomfortable with the proposed changes of place and made suggestions. It is not correct to place personal concern above the general will.

I am due to go to block 8-12. Although it's my old block, there are not many comrades remaining from that time.

We have no vacant spaces in our blocks. If just one more comes, we will have problems with the authorities.

Block 4
22 April 1996

Late in the evening a guard came, saying, "However much bread you've got in the block, hand it over as there are transfers coming from Diyarbakir." In this way, we learned that our number was rising. They have been put in block 1. We will have to take this into consideration when organising our blocks. We will speak to the prosecutor and try to open an empty block above us on the third floor. But I don't think the authorities will accept it. They have left all the blocks empty on the third floor and keep guards there 24 hours a day. If they make it difficult for us, we can tell the TDKP comrades that we can place them in block 3 with the new arrivals in block 1. As they only have one block, it won't be a problem for them. But for us, it is important. If they stay in block 1, we will have a communication problem.

Our number has gone up to 219. We have to evaluate the conditions well and help our new comrades.

Block 4
25 April 1996

We sent a telegram to Xalo Xalef's family to inform them he was in hospital, but it was returned saying they could not be found at the address. It's not good. If we could have informed them, they would have taken an interest in him.

Yesterday, when comrade Tari was on the way to hospital, he resisted an intrusive search carried out by soldiers. As arguments dragged on, he asked to return to the block. When a guard tried to prevent this, he punched him. When I heard this, I was very annoyed. There is no point in behaving irresponsibly during this period. How many times have such individual outbursts taken place? It's a situation that needs to be addressed.

Despite clashes in various parts of Kurdistan, the party's ceasefire is holding. This persistence is having a positive effect on Western Europe.

Today I noticed in a daily newspaper that ERNK's European spokesperson has asked Austria to mediate between the PKK and the Turkish government. It looks as if our side is going to launch a new process. This is a serious proposal. It will become clear in the coming period.

Block 4
27 April 1996

They refused to open up a block on the third floor. The prosecutor will be spoken to.

We have changed the list three or four times on account of the administration's negative attitude. They've turned it into a jigsaw puzzle.

We have rearranged our visiting days and made block changes.

Xalo came back from hospital with a bag of medication. Although he is a little better, he is moaning from the pain. As it is a religious holiday, they didn't want to keep him in hospital.

Block 4
1 May 1996

It's been 110 years since imperialism's bloody attack on tens of thousands of American proletarians demanding an eight-hour working day on the streets of Chicago.

After these incidents, the words of four proletarian leaders who were executed turned into the footsteps of millions of workers who were to take ownership of May Day.

We were unable to do much preparation, as we have been very busy, but we did have our shaves last night. We started the day with a minute's silence and the May Day march. All the blocks sent each other messages. At lunch time, we all congregated around the TV set. In many places the police had attacked the crowds. In Kadıköy, Istanbul, the police opened fire, killing three people and wounding many others.

We continued our activities in the afternoon. The comrades had organised a multi-cast pantomime. The theme was like that of a film. Turkey, feudal lords, security officials, intellectual youth, the proletariat, the peasantry, bourgeois leftists, and guerrillas – all types were represented.

The show went down well. The handing of sickles and scythes to those fickle types who abandoned the masses when the going got tough, and then became prominent after the revolution, finally sending them off to toil. It was applauded enthusiastically.

The way the guerrillas convinced the people after long exertion and merged with them was also explained well.

After the play, Mustafa, who is of Georgian origin, danced the horon to applause. It was nice.

This was followed by a volleyball match to commemorate May Day. It was watched by everyone and our team won after a competitive game. We completed our activities with a halay.

Between 19.00 and 20.30, we scoured all the channels for news. In Istanbul, in particular, many organisations had put on a display of strength. In some places, things had got out of control. It was noticeable that, although DS "youth corps" all wore the same outfits, they didn't cover their faces. The HADEP contingent made up a large proportion of the crowd. A seven or eight-metre poster of the leader caught the eye. This is the first time our lot has done this in Turkish provinces. And they were active. The same was true in Izmir.

This is an actual reflection of the revolutionary wave in Turkish cities.

Block 4

2 May 1996

Prime Minister M. Yılmaz said, on calling an emergency cabinet meeting, "What took place in Istanbul was a programme for an uprising." And the first statements after the meeting concerned, "Ending prisons being nests for education and a review of police laws."

They want to enact some laws during this confusion. The first places they will attack are the prisons. They are preparing the ground.

Today was our visiting day. As it is a religious holiday and children were allowed onto our side. It was a good change for young children.

We had entertainment in the evening in our block. After the singing of songs and the reciting of poems, the comrades running the commune distributed a piece of fruit to everyone. This was a most joyful moment. If it had been outside, these people would not have even looked at the fruit on the table, but here it is precious. We sometimes go months without seeing fruit.

Block 5

3 May 1996

The prison authorities are not definitely saying "no way," but they are stalling on the issue of a change of block. They want to prevent some of our internal activities by dragging things out.

We made a proposal regarding the Istanbul martyrs to the Turkish left groups. At 18.00, the whole prison shouted:

"The May Day martyrs are immortal!"

"Martyrs are immortal!"

If there is no snag, I will go to visit block 8-12 tomorrow. It will be good prior to block changes.

Block 4
4 May 1996

When the communicating door opened, the comrades said we were to meet in block 9-13 instead of 8. To tell the truth, I objected. We were meeting there for the third time in a month. It's pointless to persist.

We have to deal with comrade Tari's behaviour. Firstly, our administration provided information. In particular, it is unacceptable for someone who used to be in the administration to behave in such an irresponsible way, for him to not listen to our representatives alongside the guards, and to reject the criticisms made in the block.

Fuat and I were harsh, reminding people of the process observed, saying we had spoken to him for the final time about this, and that he needed to pull himself together and respect the will of the block. Despite our well-intentioned approach, he spoke in a provocative manner. I was surprised. He is doing the things he previously criticised in others. He is attempting to avoid responsibility by claiming, "There is a special campaign against me."

For 20 days, he has not uttered a word during education, undertaken no practical tasks, and not been serious. These alone are offences. His attitude was enough to be a provocation. The decision was taken to exclude him from relations with the structure for one month. At the end of the month, if he is not self-critical, his position will be reassessed.

Despite there being a forum today, we were able to participate in the afternoon session. The subject was, "The reasons for the Israel-Turkey agreement and the current period." It will continue tomorrow.

Comrades who received life sentences will be released this year. Being released after 15 years inside is a strange situation. They will be going out into a new world. Those going out have problems in all areas of life. It needs great determination to overcome it.

At this moment, it is 2 o'clock in the morning. I am writing at a table. As most comrades are snoring, it is like a symphony orchestra.

The weather has really warmed up.

They are still dragging out the block changes. We are face to face with an authority that uses the special war intensively. They express their animosity openly. They even record on the computer who visits other blocks, apparently… They are trying to monitor our every step.

For a few days, I have been reading George Orwell's 1984 (Big Brothers). I finished it today. In essence, it is an anti-socialist book. It explains how technology and government enslave people, make them a monotype, and turn them into robots, alienated and cut off from their past. The government and society he recounts has no place for creativity and warm human relations. He describes a petrified type of human being, whereas the essence of socialism is the human being. In short, a book and critique of a turncoat "socialist." Nevertheless, some critics say, "This book describes the Britain in which he lived."

Block 4
5 May 1996

After writing my journal and reading the *Demokrasi* and *Evrensel* newspapers, I went to bed at 03.45.

In a dream, there was a crowd in a street I had seen in a previous dream. They said there was a young woman in a house with a pistol who wanted to commit suicide. I immediately took a Smith-Wesson pistol, loaded it, and entered the house. I was going to intervene to prevent someone committing suicide. The young woman was in the bathroom. When she saw me, she pointed her gun towards me and warned me not to approach. In a swift movement, I took the gun from her, and on shouting, "Committing suicide won't solve anything. You have to live in order to struggle," she gave up resisting. Meanwhile, her sister, who resembled her, appeared. They didn't explain the reason for attempting suicide and I didn't ask. After chatting for some time, I woke up feeling angry.

As Aziz P. is being released tomorrow, he came to visit our block. He made a short speech. He said he would respond to the values he had received. Let's see if he will honour his word, as a promise inside is different to one made outside. I hope he keeps his promise.

In the evening education, we read a section of the article, "What is debate?" We will continue tomorrow.

As it is now a lot warmer, we removed all five panes of glass in the block.

It must be the football that has made the pain in my knee worse. Although some comrades say it is down to "getting old," in my opinion, it is a joint infection.

Block 8
6 May 1996

Just when we had begun to say they wouldn't change the blocks, this morning they told us they were going to do it. But again, they created problems. When they started going block to block and calling one name at a time, we reacted and argued with them. They searched our belongings in the corridor and took everyone to the block to which they had been assigned. Those who were coming and going said farewell to each other.

At this moment, I am in block 8 and on the bunk I had three years ago. The bottom one next to the window. The layout of the bunks has not been changed. The cards I had stuck on the cupboard at the end of the bunks were still there. I was surprised but pleased.

Some young comrades who were leaving block 8 reproached me, saying, "You're coming, but sending us away."

The first thing I noticed was that the air here was hot and stuffy compared to 4, 6, and 14.

I chatted to the comrades all day.

Today is the 24th anniversary of Deniz and his comrades' execution.

Today, the guerrillas in Kurdistan represent those heroes who courageously faced death on the gallows.

Every day we are in chains increases our passion for freedom.

Today, in captivity, we are breathing the air of a free tomorrow in a free country.

Block 8
7 May 1996

Our exercise and education activities will restart on Thursday. In this way, all the activities which we had halted will have begun. We started by organising the education groups. We need to re-establish discipline in daily life.

Today, I received a letter and four pictures from my sister Fatoş. I hadn't heard from her for months. She had written four letters but they didn't reach me. They deliberately don't give them to us. One part of the letter and two photos were from comrade Kenan.

According to the TV news, Turkey has again carried out an operation into South Kurdistan. The chief of staff and several generals are in Kurdistan at the moment. If the weather warms up a little, the course of the operation will change. "If we hadn't carried out an operation, the PKK were going to establish a liberated area," says the special war regime.

US President Clinton said, "The PKK is an influential organisation in South Kurdistan." This contains new messages for the new period.

Block 8
9 May 1996

Aziz Poyraz's cousin came to visit me. I wasn't really expecting him. Aziz embarrassed me. The fact that he listened with interest to what we were saying also pleased me.

Three comrades have been brought here from Antep and two from Buca.

The newspapers report that the Eskişehir basements have been reopened. Those recently detained are being taken there. In order to break their will, they are not permitting them to gather strength. They want to cow them into submission. They are using a very dangerous technique, but still, they won't succeed.

Block 8
13 May 1996

An alternating hunger strike in Amed prison has been turned into a limitless one. They have already been worn down. There may be some martyrdoms soon.

Their families are continuing an alternating hunger strike in Amed city. As usual, mothers, in particular, are not abandoning their sons.

A limitless hunger strike has begun in Bursa prison to support Amed prison. It is clear that this will spread to all prisons. That's fine, psychologically, we are prepared. For two months now, since prisons came onto the agenda, we have been sharpening our sensitivity.

Block 8
16 May 1996

Two sick comrades were taken from the blocks, purportedly to go to hospital, but on the way out, they protested at the insults they suffered and returned to the blocks. It is a dilemma to go to the hospital or not, as sometimes they handcuff you to a bed in a cell in the basement. Sometimes, the place is right next to the morgue.

Previously, a comrade who was taken to hospital went on hunger strike after they tortured him there.

Today we argued with the duty guard at the door. They cannot tolerate things going to and fro between blocks. I assume this is a harbinger of a new policy.

Otherwise, a door guard cannot take such an individual decision. It has to be up to the authorities.

The protest has spread to other prisons. We are trying to receive more sound news.

We held our weekly general meeting today. Apart from certain practical shortcomings there are no problems.

Block 8
17 May 1996

All blocks shouted the slogans:
"Repression cannot cow us!"

"Down with the fascist administration!"

This was to protest at the oppression that took place on the way to the hospital.

We also wrote a petition to the administration. As part of the protest, we rejected the midday meal cart. We prepared food using our own resources.

We appointed comrade C. Delibaş to replace Sarıkaya as representative.

Enquiries have been made outside about two newcomers. "Do whatever those inside propose" was the reply. One will be removed from the environment, the other will be retained under observation. We are particularly angry at those who caused such harm in the Aegean region and are concealing it.

With regard to the limitless hunger strike, we will clarify our position with meetings in all blocks.

The administration has been spoken to about the comrade who was beaten on his way to hospital and brought back without being treated. It was made clear that we will definitely not accept such things.

Block 8
18 May 1996

We held a commemoration today, as it is the anniversary of the martyring of Haki Karer and the Four. This date is also our Martyrs' Commemoration Day.

We started at 09.00 with a minute's silence. This was followed by our and the DHP's messages being read out. Then, the following slogans were shouted:

"Martyrs are immortal!"

"The Hakis, Halils and the Four are immortal!"

"Down with the dirty special war!"

"The revival has succeeded, now for the liberation!"

"Long live Leader Apo!"

As our numbers in the prison have swollen, our joint slogans are quite effective. And, as they were in unison, there was nice harmonisation. I wasn't expecting it to be that good.

We followed this by starting collective conversations in the exercise yard. But I had to get up a few times. It was necessary to have an exchange of views on various topics. Bursa's decision on a limitless hunger strike was published in *Demokrasi* newspaper. In this way, the suspense has been overcome. Naturally, we discussed this between ourselves. The general opinion was to do it in a few rounds.

We started our education today with an hour-long Kurdish lesson. It is our painful reality that we don't know the grammar of our mother tongue. We will have two lessons a week.

Yes, today is 18 May. From Kaypakkaya until today, the spark lit by Haki, Halil, their comrades and the Four has turned into a roaring fire. I would really have liked these comrades to have seen today, where the people have risen everywhere.

The May martyrs have inspired all our people by bringing the heat of May to today. All the pain of those difficult days is now giving its fruits, its fruits of revolution.

Block 8
19 May 1996

Comrades in blocks 7 and 15 will begin the first round of hunger strikes tomorrow. There will be five rounds of five-day actions. When our last block completes its action, if it is still continuing, 20 comrades will start a limitless hunger strike. The blocks will also continue in an alternating way. At this stage, each prison will also raise its own particular problems.

As the canteen is closed today, we sent all our cheese and other foodstuffs to those comrades who are starting their action tomorrow.

A statement was made to the general structure regarding what needed attention during the hunger strike in order for disciplined and coordinated action to take place.

A temporary commission was established to deal with petitions and press statements during the action.

Block 8
30 May 1996

The first day of the hunger strike.

We got up early and had the breakfast prepared by comrades. We signed the petitions and started our action.

Apart from the two comrades who arrived recently, all the comrades in our block are taking part.

It is possible to see and feel the enthusiasm for the action in all the comrades.

Before visiting began, we wrote a hurried note proposing that on account of recent developments, we have to go on a limitless hunger strike at an earlier date. If we act according to the plan, we will be late.

Taking the attack in Amed prison into consideration, we have to bring our action forward.

After a short correspondence, it has been clarified that 18 comrades in our block will start a limitless hunger strike tomorrow. The other comrades will continue the alternating action.

In four days' time, 20 comrades in blocks 6, 14 and 4 will start a limitless hunger strike.

We altered our petitions and signed them. We will send them tomorrow.

The comrades going on limitless hunger strike are as follows:

S. İldere, E. Teker, Y. Gül, C. Ağcakaya, A. K. Aksoy, C. Polat, İ. Dayan, S. Öncü, A. Poyraz, Ö. Akıncı, İ. Gülmez, M. Konma, D. Keklik, Z. Alpboğa, S. Çelik, Ş. Demir, S. Yavuz, B. Akkurt.

When we made the announcement to comrades, some of them proposed taking part. An appropriate reply was given. Some were insistent, while others were sad not to be amongst the 18.

I believe all comrades will successfully complete the action. However, it is not possible to include everyone all at once in the limitless action. We have to think ahead. We also have to consider the possibility that the enemy could carry out all kinds of assaults and we need to deploy our forces appropriately.

All the comrades are now deemed "old." However, it is still necessary for certain comrades to gain experience through action.

It is good that our limitless action has coincided with our visiting day.

The attack is continuing in Amed prison. It was on the BBC evening news. 19 comrades were injured in the attack and were taken forcibly to hospital. The blocks were raided and ransacked and two comrades set themselves alight in protest. They are said to be in a serious condition.

They had decided not to go to hospitals or courts (DGM-State Security Court) on account of the oppression and insults they suffered on the way. When attempts were made to transfer some comrades, they set up barricades.

It is a serious and extensive attack. They particularly want to topple Amed prison. They want to defeat it. This attack is also an assault on the morale-boosting influence of Amed prison.

Our stance will be harsher than ever. We will demonstrate this to the special war regime and to M. Ağar…

We will oppose all manner of attacks with our belief and our bare hands. We promise our martyrs, our Leader, our people, and our guerrillas, whose hearts are beating for us amongst the mountain peaks, who are our moral commanders, that we will use our chests as shields to confront all manner of attacks, and endeavour to be worthy of them.

Today at 13.00 and 18.00 the whole prison shouted the slogans:

"Long live our Amed resistance!"

"Repression cannot cow us!"

"Resistance is life!"

Block 8
31 May 1996

The second day of the hunger strike.

I got up at 07.50. By the time I had washed my face, they had come for a roll call. There were a whole herd of them. The fact they had a senior manager with them was an indication a search was to take place today.

I cleaned my teeth and went out into the exercise yard. At 10.00, when we heard the thud of boots, we prepared for a search. Towards noon, it was our turn. As usual, they made lots of noise, scattered belongings, and left. It's as if they gain satisfaction from this.

Meanwhile, we read the individual report of a new comrade. As there are no objections, it was decided he should go to 6-14. We said our farewells and he left.

Most of the comrades who are not involved in the limitless action made objections again. We explained the situation. It's pleasing that the comrades are putting themselves forward. It's a lovely feeling to be able to say, "Let me bear the pain instead of my comrade"…

I read M. Ağar's statement where he says, "I won't make any concessions to them." In fact, this is an expression of his fear. He is emboldening himself. Just like the special war regime that is being defeated in war…

Block 8
1 June 1996

The third day of the hunger strike.

The 17 comrades who were taken to hospital after the attack on Amed prison have been sent to Antep Special Type Prison. They were transferred on the 35th day of their hunger strike. Similar to our being sent to Aydın from Eskişehir.

This transfer is definitely part of the attempt to defeat Amed. I hope the comrades there were prepared for such a development. Otherwise, it will be extremely difficult for the remaining comrades. The necessity of transforming our action into a limitless one is becoming clearer. Today, I began to read the book on barracks culture. On reading about the massacres and the Kemalist personality that was created, you feel revulsion again and again.

Our administration is involved in internal correspondence regarding topics such as the cessation of exercise during the action, carrying out education within the blocks based on a selected source and planning new rounds in the event the action continues.

In the upcoming days, we will have a forum on "The consequences of the ceasefire and the latest domestic and foreign relations of Turkey."

Yesterday, two people came from Konya. We read their briefings. According to what they have written, one became an informer while outside and was subsequently arrested. The other messed with our contacts outside. It is not possible for us to accept unethical behaviour in our circle. Both of them will stay in the environment for now, but will not be involved in political relations.

We can't help but be surprised.

We are now scared to read/ask about a person's briefing report. This is too much. People should have a conscience. However ill-intentioned a person is, they should not play around with the party's name and the people's resources.

Have a heart!...

Following an instruction from the Ministry of Justice, they are no longer providing us with salt, sugar and tea during hunger strikes. Previously, they would sometimes give us these instead of food. Now we are buying them. That is, they are now selling us what is our right. They want to weaken our action in this way.

Even so, we are consuming six glasses of liquid a day.

We have removed those on the limitless action from the duty roster, as it is tiring.

Block 8
2 June 1996

The fourth day of the hunger strike.

They have sent the two comrades who set fire to themselves in protest at the attack in Amed to Antep, torturing them on the way. They've been put in solitary. Brutality and savagery. It demonstrates that they have no trace of humanity.

From what we've heard, the inmates' families in Antep have turned their action into a death fast.

Even though we're on a protest, we, as individuals, have to make use of our time in a productive way. In the near future, we might not be able to do that. We have no time to lose.

Comrade Aziz had a fit of coughing today. His whole body is shaking. In addition to being asthmatic and bronchial, he has also had an allergy diagnosis. When he has an attack of coughing, we feel uneasy. The way he coughs is as if his internal organs are going to split.

There is nothing worse in prison than going down with a serious illness, becoming bedridden or, worse, losing your mind. In such situations, death is preferable.

The state tries to act in a very dirty and underhanded way by depriving you of resources. It uses everything against you. In this respect, the fundamental solution is not to be taken prisoner by the enemy. And even if you are captured, it is essential to remain mentally and physically healthy.

What we have gone through has taught us this.

Block 8
3 June 1996

The fifth day of the action.

Comrade Sabri's statement in *Demokrasi* newspaper is an indication of the broadening of the action.

There are four political demands and four demands relating to the prisons. The political demands are:

* Recognition of POW status.
* A response to the PKK's unilateral ceasefire.
* Allowing delegations to freely carry out investigations of evacuated and destroyed villages and migration in Kurdistan.
* Compliance with the Geneva Convention.

As for the prisons, the demands are as follows:

* An end to repression in prisons, first and foremost Amed prison, and acceptance of prisoner demands.
* The creation of humane conditions in prisons.
* The halting of forced transfers.
* Ending the obstruction of the right to mount a defence in courts.

At the present time, the action has gone beyond Amed and become a general one.

Efforts are being made to benefit in the best possible way from the conditions Turkey finds itself in and the effect created by the existing action.

We have intense days ahead of us.

> *We are in unequal conditions.*
> *Our hands are bare,*
> *Our hearts are equipped,*
> *They are beating in time with the guerrillas in the mountains,*
> *Their pin has been removed and they are ready to explode.*

Whereas they have cudgels, truncheons and bayonets,
Trained dogs,
And eyes that darken the tomorrows,
They, who have no tomorrow, who fear us today
Attack us ferociously.
By the time they understand their mistake, it will be too late.

Today was our bath day. I didn't stay in very long.

Comrade İzzet dropped in to see us. As he is the barber, he is able to go round the blocks. We were pleased to see him, as he was pleased to see us.

In order to protest at a comrade being tortured on his arrival at the prison, we, all the movements here, have written a petition. Everyone signed the joint text. It will be sent to official bodies. Petitions have also been written to certain embassies on behalf of a group of comrades.

Since our block has completed the fifth day of the hunger strike, 21 comrades have gone to block 8, while those of us on limitless have come to block 12. We only brought essentials with us.

When they had their evening meal and went out into the exercise yard, it was not possible to look at any of them. Since we are on hunger strike, eating demoralises them. We can see that some of them are on the verge of tears.

At 21.00, we hear the sound of folk songs from the neighbouring block. As blocks 6-14 are starting a hunger strike tomorrow, they were organising entertainment this evening. After hearing the noise, we summoned comrade Şehmus to our block with his saz. Suddenly the sound of songs was heard in our block, too. Comrades in the opposite block came to the windows and began to accompany us. After a few poems, it turned into chatting.

Comrades asked me to talk about the past. For a moment, I didn't know where or how to start. I recalled the harsh conditions of the time, the arduous actions, and the lovely people. If I had to summarise, the current actions are luxurious compared to those past ones. But, let it be like this…

I explained to the comrades our transfer to Eskişehir and the resistance of January 1988. That was one of the harshest times in the period at Eskişehir. They tried to force us to wear a uniform, and when we refused, they tortured us and put us in solitary cells. We were left in our underpants. We shivered in the January cold. But, despite that, we refused to wear prison uniforms. They set fire to the depot containing mattresses at the entrance to the cells. We could all have died in the dense smoke…

Towards midnight, we ended the chatting.

Block 8
4 June 1996

The sixth day of the action. Towards morning, I couldn't sleep properly. I woke up numerous times. Every time I tried to get back to sleep, it was more difficult. I think it's the change of place that's caused it.

At 03.30, when the guards came to close the block doors, they hesitated for a moment, when they didn't see anyone downstairs. I assume they asked the guards on watch on the top floor opposite, as "OK, shut the blocks" was heard on a walkie-talkie.

From where I was sleeping, when I raised my head slightly, my eyes met those of comrade Kadir in the block opposite. Despite the exercise yard being between us, I could tell from his gestures that he was asking me why I wasn't asleep.

I woke up at about 08.00. Most of the comrades were still asleep.

Today, blocks 4, 6, and 14 started a hunger strike. 20 comrades also started a limitless action. They are:

Ş. Batmaz, S. Uzunmehmet, F. Bulut, Ş. Topkan, U. Tuncer, Ş. Bilgen, C. Yılmaz, R. Turan, V. Doğru, A. R. Akın, G. Gün, H. Korkut, H. Olsoy, C. Karaasalan, Ç. Ekren, U. F. Suvarioğulları, İ. Çelebi, S. Akay, C. Keskin, B. Elden.

A telegram arrived from the Antep Special-Type Prison. It explained that there was no death fast there, but that 50 comrades were involved in a limitless action.

We reminded comrades that those on limitless should not move around too much.

We sent a comrade who was poorly to the sick bay. When he explained the doctor's attitude, I was annoyed. He's not a doctor, he's a prison creature and opportunist. Normally, sick comrades are given an appointment three or four months later, but when we start an action, they immediately bring it forward and want to send us away, even though they know we don't go to hospital during protest actions. They clean up the list in this way and demoralise people.

The enemy carries out its enmity perfectly. On many topics, they are more aware than us. They seize upon even the slightest opportunity. Otherwise, this state would not be able to survive, given all the crises.

There is no visible discomfort amongst the comrades involved in the action. Morale is good. During the day, they are reading from time to time, sleeping and doing a little walking back and forth.

Comrades not involved in the action gave our block a good wash. By noon, it had dried. Laundry was also done for some comrades. Thanks for that.

Block 8

5 June 1996

The seventh day of the hunger strike.

There is once again a bulletin of comrade Sabri's. I assume they have started late in order to extend the action over a period.

Our families' action is continuing in accordance with their resources. I think they will liven it up in future.

As for other news, children held a march in Izmir. They shouted for peace and said, "We will not abandon our elder brothers, fathers, and siblings. We support them." We laughed as we read about it. For sure, it was more radical than lots of protests.

The children's action recalls the streets of Cizre in 1990. The first thing that comes to mind are tanks from oil-tanker trucks being dragged into the street to make barricades, collective efforts. Even with armoured vehicles, they couldn't do anything. They confronted the enemy, practically facing death. Unforgettable scenes.

When it comes to support for the prisons, the mothers and children are the first that spring to mind. They've never abandoned us, whatever the circumstances. In all our actions, they have also wasted away drop by drop, second, by second along with us. They have also shared the pain of our torture. They have enthused with us after the actions. They run excitedly to the prison gate and the visitors' cabins. It's possible to see the joy and surprise in their eyes every time.

And it is especially worth seeing them tremble after long protest actions, as if they are gratifying years of yearning.

Another comrade has come from Malatya.

In the afternoon, we read comrade Ferhat's self-criticism and the opinions of the block structure. I was very angry with the current situation. In an environment where people are setting themselves alight, when tens of thousands are involved in protests against the enemy, it is unacceptable that he should stand up and say, "I'm leaving our blocks." Let this be the last. He must pull himself together. There is nowhere else to go and he knows he couldn't hack it there, anyway. I was also annoyed that he got someone else to write his report. It is abstract and far from reflecting reality. Despite this, he will be given another chance to sort himself out.

The comrade who represents the DHP dropped by. He told us about the meeting with the prosecutor. The approach of the authorities is to go on the defensive and delay. They are trying to get us used to the existing situation.

Towards evening, on comrade Aziz saying, "I'm having a haemorrhage," we immediately notified the authorities. He didn't look at all well. The symptoms were bleeding in the stomach. I told him to eat a bit of ice. They summoned him urgently to go to hospital. After emptying our pockets, we sent him with some money. But an hour later, they brought him back. They had given him painkillers. They had also carried out a blood test. He had also said, "I'm bleeding" yesterday. But he thought it was the effect of the previous hunger strike and not dwelt on it. We had said that it might be caused by his severe cough of the last month.

The bourgeois press is maintaining its lack of interest in the prison actions. Amed is now in its 40th day. The "Mehmetçik Press" is performing its duty very well.

Today, comrade Şehmus, who is on the limitless action, is not well. He's feeling cold. On seeing him shivering under two blankets, despite it being hot, I said he had a fever. He's got a constant headache. When he said, "My stomach is fine," I was pleased, as on a limitless hunger strike, a healthy stomach is good. Otherwise, it's a pain in the neck. He has a weak constitution. I think he's got a chill.

After 22.00, I noticed comrades were shaving, so I too had a shave. When I cleaned my teeth and washed my feet with cold water, I felt better.

While walking slowly back and forth in the exercise yard, comrade Hamit came over to me and said, "Eating after completing the five-day action seemed like I was a scab, as if I was a thief," adding, "I know it was the decision." I sense this is the feeling amongst all the comrades in the opposite block who are not involved in the action. When they see us, their embarrassment increases. We try not to be visible during mealtimes, but we can perceive this constant feeling of our comrades.

Block 8

6 June 1996

The eighth day of the action.

While waiting for the newspapers this morning, we formed a small cluster in the exercise yard.

Bursa has turned its two-day protest into a five-day alternating one. For several days, they have been saying, "We will escalate it," but the present situation is insufficient, as news of martyrs in Amed could come at any time.

At noon, they called me to the visiting area. Ali Yıldırım had come. "He is imposing himself, go and see him," they said. I am pleased he was released and has come to see me. We informed him about our action. After he had been transferred from Aydın, he had been at six or seven different prisons and suffered during all the transfers. His morale seemed to be good. He wanted to go outside to reach comrades, but we were not in a position to assist him. It's a bad situation.

During the visit, we gave four bundles of clothes to TAY-DER (Association of Prisoners' Families), saying, "Distribute them to families in need."

Most of the families had recently ended hunger strikes. Some were just about to start new rounds. They were all enthusiastic. In Izmir, eighty family members are on hunger strike. It's encouraging news for us. Such support is good for our morale.

According to the MED-TV news, there are prison support actions in many countries, from Europe all the way to Africa and America.

The visiting area was crowded. We had the opportunity to see lots of comrades. The best solidarity messages are passed on in these areas. As it is tiring, when I was about to leave towards 15.00, I said to comrade Tören, "Meet you on the barricades." His eyes sparkled. Hearing the words "resistance" and "barricades," he gets carried away.

In the last two weeks, our visitors have brought us lots of tea and sugar. They bring us all the things they find. Just as they do for the guerrillas, they don't eat, drink, or open them, instead bringing them to us. To think of anything apart from being worthy of this self-sacrifice, to have other calculations, is shameful. Anyone with a scrap of humanity left will respond positively to these efforts, will not be ungrateful or allow anyone else to be so.

Today Mesut Yılmaz submitted his government's resignation. He did this after yesterday's censure motion. This means the government is going to hobble on. It is not possible for any party or government to survive the war in Kurdistan. Perhaps they want to bring the Refah Party, regarding which they keep saying its vote has increased, into government in order to erode its vote. Because their policies are all state patented. "Deep structures" determine everything in Turkey, not parties or individuals. The RP is anyway a party of the system. What will emerge is its real face. The masses will see it.

In any case, in every "innovation" and every crisis our struggle will emerge stronger. Reality has proved this.

Block 12
7 June 1996

The ninth day of the hunger strike.

We have learned that most of what we heard during the visit was true.

A three-person investigation committee has been set up on account of certain problems continuing in one of our blocks, before and after a conference. In that case, all the comrades will be asked to submit reports. Their observations and testimony will be examined. If different unknown problems emerge, the investigation will be deepened. Perceptions that contradict the party will be clarified. Perhaps it's not the right time, but it will be good to be clarified. It keeps happening and troubles us.

The investigation committee will present its report and findings to our administration. We reminded them that while dealing with the problem that concern the party, the struggle should be paramount.

I edited the administration text in the form of analysis, but I was not happy with it as I was unable to concentrate as I wished.

Although we are involved in an action, the regular fortnightly meeting of the administration will still be held. We will try to avoid disruption unless there is a very serious situation.

On the evening news, Star TV mentioned the hunger strikes, the demands, and the actions by families. It surprised us to see such a discussion on the channel. It listed nearly all our demands:

"Transfer or servitude?"

"Search or raid?"

"Hospital or delayed death?"

The use of such expressions was good for public opinion.

Families have issued press statements and taken actions in three places in Istanbul. At Bayrampaşa, 80 relatives of prisoners, including Ercan Kanar, were detained.

While he was being dragged away by police, E. Kanar wagged his finger at the police, saying, "This regulation of the Justice Ministry will be revoked."

This scene reminded me of Hatip Dicle.

These kinds of attacks and interventions by these cretins leads to increasing public support. They don't realise this.

Comrades who are not involved in the action washed the exercise yard towards evening. They used lots of water to try to ensure it is cool at night.

Since the windows of the Malta (the main corridor running through the middle of the prison) open onto our exercise yard, they open them at night, especially so that the noise from the corridor reaches us. Guards shout and holler in an attempt to get on our nerves. They drag benches and shout to each other at late hours. Of course, this is not done without the knowledge of the prison authorities. They are particularly trying to prevent those on hunger strike from getting a good night's sleep. It is a war of attrition.

The more we ask them to stop, the more they do it.

As we are in financial difficulty, I have written a letter to my sister, Fatoş. I will post it on Monday.

For a few days now, my halitosis has been horrible. My stomach has also begun to send signals. Sometimes, there is burning and nausea. I will have to take care not to stand up for too long.

Some comrades involved in the action have diarrhoea. This is not good, as it will increase weight loss.

Block 12

8 June 1996

The tenth day of the action.

In the newspaper today, there is a picture of the families' action in Izmir. In the foreground is a mother of 75. She is holding both hands in the air and making the victory sign. "Three of my children are in prison, but I am taking action for all prisoners. They are all my children. We want peace," she said.

This kind of news demonstrates the level our people have reached. Our mothers who perhaps before the struggle were unable to express themselves are now making political statements.

This is the greatest happiness for us. This situation of our elderly is a mirror of the dynamic section of the people. It is an indication of how the party has put down roots amongst the people.

I had just sat down to type in the dining hall of block 12 this evening, when they summoned me, as two comrades had arrived from Amed prison.

One of them, a young man, MK, immediately drew attention to himself with his height and slimness. His shirt was torn in several places. It was obvious he had suffered an attack. He also had bruising around his eyes. He had been on the road for five days. Eight of them set off from Amed. When they went to Elazığ, where they were to pick up another prioner, they were all taken out of the vehicle and tortured. Of course, the comrades responded with slogans.

They suffered during the journey. Even when they went to the toilet, their handcuffs were not removed. The soldiers stopped at a few places to drink alcohol. They demonstrated their yobbishness.

This behaviour demonstrates their attitude to the people of Kurdistan.

The other comrade, A. T., had a deep mark on his wrist caused by the handcuffs. It was almost down to the bone.

As for R. K., who came from Amasya, he paid for his own transfer. He paid 20 million to endure such a journey. He is someone who visited us before being arrested. While he could have been much more useful, he made a basic error and was collared. I am annoyed with him. He didn't understand us sufficiently at that time. Now, as he gets to know the enemy, he will understand us, but it's futile.

We notified the prison administration that we did not accept what was done to the comrades and asked for them to be taken to a doctor. They tried to delay, but we reminded them constantly, and forced them to take them to the sick bay. But when they returned, we learned that they had taken advantage of the comrades' naivety by charging them 1,800,000 lira for medication. I was very angry. It is daylight robbery. In fact, it is forbidden to sell medication in the sick bay. Of course, they always cover up what they have done.

Moreover, apart from selling medication, despite the doctor seeing the comrades' bruises, he didn't give them a report. These doctors, who have taken the Hippocratic oath, have always tried to conceal torture. Especially those doctors who have worked in prisons for a long time. They act just like counter guerrillas. If this wasn't the case, would they have given comrades who had been on hunger strike for 35 days in Amed prison, "Safe to be transferred" reports?

Court reports have documented the fact that, on many occasions, torture has taken place under the supervision of doctors. The public knows this. Unfortunately, such doctors exist.

While speaking through the wall with the neighbouring block, Uncle Xalef came over. His voice was clear and joyful. They had told him I was on the limitless action. "May God be your helper, may He give you strength, may success be yours," he said. Of course, when speaking in his good Kurdish, he also mentioned the Leader.

While chatting in the evening, comrades mentioned the Aegean and Mediterranean regions. What they said are things that drive you mad. While it is possible to organise and bring hundreds of people into the struggle, someone who is meant to be "in charge," gathered together elected representatives in the villages and spokesmen for bourgeois parties and endeavoured to give them "perspective." Of course, the police soon heard about it, and it was immediately ended.

He followed a typical peasant method.

Despite such a way of working, when they come amongst us, they praise themselves to the skies. They assume we won't hear about them.

Using the name of the party and the people, the people have been humiliated in that region. If they hadn't had the authority of the party, no one would have passed the time of day with them. And, of course, it is the enemy that benefits the most. They watch the damage being done, then swoop.

Today, comrades in blocks 4, 6, and 14 completed their five-day hunger strikes. But 20 amongst them are continuing on a limitless action.

It's the 45th day in Amed prison.

The action is continuing in all areas with the participation of new groups.

Block 12
9 June 1996

The eleventh day of the action.

A new bulletin has been sent on behalf of all prison administrative committees to our newspaper. There are the names of two comrades from our prison.

The policy of not going to court or hospital now includes all prisons.

Today we read F.'s report and the evaluations of comrades in his block.

In order for him to focus, he will be excluded from political relations for 15 days. During this time, he will scrutinise himself. He has stayed at Zele camp, been a platoon commander in the South-West province, and was later arrested during activities in Istanbul. He was unable to courageously express his reality.

I don't think there will be an outcome, but I hope I'm wrong.

On account of the ongoing action, we will shout slogans at certain times on Wednesday and Thursday.

There is now a visible emaciation of the comrades. Some comrades are finding it difficult to drink tea. This will increase in the coming days.

In the morning, we argued with guards at the windows of the corridor that overlook our exercise yard. They are raging. They are experiencing the helplessness of being unable to torture us.

However many lowlife there are around here, they've all been made guards. I believe the prison corridors are where they are most "free."

Block 12
10 June 1996

The twelfth day of the hunger strike.

At around 01.30, we heard a scream. As there was a cacophony of voices, we couldn't understand what was going on. We dashed over to the windows and four or five comrades shouted the slogan, "Long Live Leader Apo!" We asked them to wake up the comrades who were asleep. I was ready, as I hadn't undressed. Those comrades who were in their pyjamas quickly got dressed. The comrades in the opposite block also came to the windows.

We sent a comrade downstairs to listen at the door.

The blocks were shouting to each other, asking what had happened. The comrades in 7-15 said, "We will speak later." I was annoyed that they didn't share it with us.

We guessed that, "A new transfer has arrived. They asked for a representative, but when the prison administration tried to force the block into accepting the transfer, slogans were shouted."

We went back to bed, concerned and apprehensive.

I awoke at 08.00, as I was curious about the incident during the night. Soon, an explanatory note arrived.

Comrade K in 7-15 said he would go on watch. After everyone had gone to bed, he went downstairs to the dining hall, put a blanket on the floor, spread newspapers and wound them around his body, poured oil over himself, and set himself alight. When the smoke reached the sleeping area, a comrade woke up but did not intervene, thinking that it "might be organised." But when the comrade in charge woke up, he started pouring water over him. As the water splashed over him, K. started to shout slogans. As some comrades awoke to the sound, they thought "we're under attack" and joined in shouting slogans. This was what we had heard during the night.

When the guards wanted to enter the block, the comrades had not allowed them in. "The comrade set himself alight to protest at the repression and in support of the hunger strike. As we knew he would not receive treatment in hospital, we won't hand him over to you. We will look after him," they told the guards. This was what the comrade wanted, we gathered.

Comrade K. had cried until morning. I don't know whether that was because his action was unsuccessful or due to his state of mind.

Such actions, if not organised, can take place if there is a need for them, but they are not appropriate when there is organisation. The best place to make a self-sacrifice is within organisation, otherwise the chance of success is slim.

However, I must say that setting oneself alight in any circumstances needs courage and willpower.

In the newspaper there is a statement regarding the health of some comrades.

Some comrades asked, "Why do we only drink six glasses of sugary water a day? Why don't we drink more?" We held a short meeting about this, during which we made a statement regarding political, ethical, programmatic points and self-control, self-denial, and control of willpower.

Towards noon, I had a tepid bath. I felt really relaxed.

We read what comrades in the block thought about two comrades and their own reports. It is unacceptable that even in these conditions there is a lack of trust in comrades and the imposition of individuality. Every comrade who cannot integrate with the structure has bouts of depression.

Towards evening, we held our second regular meeting. We addressed our general shortcomings. I have to write down the conclusions. Naturally, it's tiring during this period.

I have a slight ache in my right kidney. I think it's down to the infection I got during the October resistance in Eskişehir prison. There's nothing else for it but to be careful that it doesn't trouble me more in the future.

Block 12
11 June 1996

The thirteenth day of the hunger strike.

The foreign guests at HABITAT II have been added to our families' action. I gather they will lend their support every day during the summit. Turkey is making a fool of itself. It doesn't need us. It is exposing itself better than we do.

S. A. has said he wishes to leave the environment. We told them not to admit him to education. After a few hours had passed, we asked him again. Although he was hesitant, he repeated his wish to leave. He said he couldn't even harmonise himself with the environment in the social sphere, that he was a burden, that there were problems every day, and that, as he had lost his self-confidence and belief in himself, he wanted to leave for a while. We didn't comment on whether his attitude was correct or not, we just listened. But we pointed out that his departure was an escape. Consequently, no period could be given and he shouldn't deceive himself or us.

To be fair, he is not wrong. We are fed up with him. Everything he says, every behaviour is a problem in the environment. He can't say two words to anyone without arguing. Despite this, tolerance has been shown to him, but he is now damaging the environment.

I have sent two comrades' introductory articles to the comrades. I observed once again our people's wounded state, their low self-esteem, and their alienation, their inability to adapt to harsh conditions, and their being a soft touch for the enemy…

A letter arrived from Cerenbelli. He is still waiting and complaining he has not been able to make contact. It is possible to understand from his lines that he is suffering. Such comrades should not be kept waiting. It can be wearing and dangerous. I'm annoyed with him. How can you let yourself get like that outside? He's had to ask us for help.

A person should leave no stone unturned in that city. Then they will find a contact. It's not as hard as it used to be. Whichever stone you lift up, you will reach our comrades.

I've just written to him and sent two addresses…

Two hours sitting at a typewriter today tired me out.

Comrades are visibly getting thinner. Smokers are being given 15 cigarettes per day, but it's not enough. They are destroying themselves.

So far, no one has cut out sugar, but that will start in the coming days. The fact that it is very hot during the day is exhausting. Moreover, the reality is that nutrition was insufficient before the action.

Block 12
12 June 1996

The fourteenth day of the hunger strike.

Despite the fact we are on hunger strike, in general, our lives are continuing to be regular and in accordance with rules. Continuity is fundamental in organisational relationships, and on this basis, life is continuing in an orderly way. This is one of the most important factors in what distinguishes and embellishes our life from that of the special war.

Until lunchtime, we spoke to the new arrivals. We told them that it was necessary for them to take responsibility, that we wouldn't readdress past shortcomings or weaknesses, that we grounded our work here, but despite that, they shouldn't let themselves go, that the best settling of accounts was the "first" one. And we wished them success in the "new period."

From now on, we will shout the following slogans twice a week on our visiting days (Wednesday and Thursday) at 11.00, 14.00 and 23.30:

"Long live our prisoner of war action!"

"Down with the special war!"

"Resistance is Life!"

"Long live Leader Apo!"

As the last two slogans are harmonised, the whole prison was shaking. All our blocks were in unison…

Yesterday, two people came from the Aydın human rights association (IHD). They called the Dev-Sol representative and comrade Celalettin from our side. Since it wasn't considered a serious initiative, the comrades came back. I assume the prosecutor is testing the water. As far as we know, the Aydın IHD is a bit different, a bit more passive…

In the coming days, lawyers are going to send a delegation. It could be good for winning over public opinion.

Today, the police attacked a demonstration by our families in Taksim Square in Istanbul and detained everyone.

After the doors had closed, comrade Abdulkadir sang the Halabja lament, accompanied by comrade Şehmus Demir on the saz. I was standing, listening in silence. Whenever I hear this song, the image of that town of ours after being bombed with chemical weapons is revived in my memory. I think of an elderly Kurd crouched on a rock witnessing that terrible human tragedy, singing the lament and crying. When that song is sung, especially when comrade Abdulkadir sings it, it is impossible not to remember that terrible day.

> *Today a Kurd's every moment is HALABJA*
> *Bombs*
> *Napalm*
> *Fire and death rains down*
> *Efforts to destroy humanity*
> *As the world looks away*
> *Every breath becomes death*
> *For babies in arms*
> *And babies in the womb*
> *The tears of those who survive turn into blood*
> *In every lament for Halabja*
> *They relive that death.*

Block 12
13 June 1996

The fifteenth day of the hunger strike.

There is an appeal on behalf of HADEP in *Demokrasi* newspaper. The party spokesperson said, "Turn the limitless hunger strikes into alternating ones until a government is formed. There is no political interlocutor at the moment. You can later review the situation."

It is not a good idea to debate this at the moment. It is not clear whether this is an "approved" statement. The hunger strike in Amed prison is in its 50th day. It is not realistic to have such a change when the action is at its peak.

Yesterday in Aydın, 40 family members started a hunger strike. Families from the Aydın area.

Shortly after waking up this morning, guards and soldiers barged in with a manager. We reacted, saying they shouldn't come in on a visiting day. As always, they shrugged off responsibility and repeated their misconduct. The manager once again showed how temperamental he was.

We argued with them, as they made a mess of our block. The soldiers should not be touching our things, only acting as observers.

Those comrades who were called to receive visitors during the raid protested by not going.

In the afternoon, I read a book. As it's very hot, I had my first cold shower of this hunger strike and washed my clothes.

The DS representative came to our block. We chatted for a while. They have got ten of theirs to end the action. Those who are not on a limitless are going to continue with an alternating hunger strike.

In Manisa, families have started a hunger strike. In Izmir, actions are continuing at four locations.

At 22.00, a manager, guards and a doctor came to our block. We explained our general ailments and reiterated the fact we would not accept treatment.

Block 12
14 June 1996

The sixteenth day of the hunger strike.

It was a hectic day. Firstly, conversations were had with a few comrades who are becoming a problem. When it was comrade K.'s turn, we found it very difficult. Despite his personality being analysed and his making a self-criticism 20 days ago, he forgot and failed to attend morning education without permission. When care is taken not to pressurise him too much on account of his problems, he takes advantage and tries to evade responsibility with inconsistent explanations. When we were unable to convince him, he said he wouldn't speak to people here.

We told him we would evaluate his situation and inform him later. The longer he fails to review himself, he will continue to have problems. Whatever we do, it will be difficult for him.

The notification from the central administration was read out to the structure. It explained that, since the existing situation started, there has been a political vacuum and efforts are being made to avoid martyrdom in Antep and Amed prisons. The actions there will continue in an alternating form.

Until Antep and Amed halt their action, we will not make any changes. To suddenly end the action at this stage has created disappointment in us.

Towards evening, five representatives held their regular weekly meeting in our block. After chatting with them for a while, I left them to it.

While I was typing at the typewriter, comrade Ömer said to other comrades, "Comrade Ali's face has darkened." To which I replied, "It's due to being irritated, not hungry," to laughter.

Today we read R.'s report and self-criticism.

There are some comrades who, whether it be with the guerrillas or here, despite constantly becoming involved in investigations and sanctions on account of their way of talking and stubbornness, do not abandon their conduct and continue to be obstinate. They are a pain in the neck for the party and the people. It's a pity, a great pity…

Turkey has once again entered South Kurdistan, both from land and air. Officially, they are saying, "5,000 troops entered," but it is clear there are more.

It is an attempt to distract from new developments, as in yesterday's newspaper, the headline was, "PKK holds its 4th National Conference." This operation, first and foremost, is connected to these developments.

It is also apparent that the attempt on the life of the Leader has been timed to coincide with this period.

The calculations and attacks are comprehensive.

They are directly targeting the revolution.

Block 12
15 June 1996

The seventeenth day of the hunger strike.

We have ended the limitless hunger strike. We wrote a petition to the prosecutor, saying we would end the action at 17.00 and continue as an alternating one, block by block.

We had intended to wait for Antep and Amed, but when we learned from *Demokrasi* newspaper that the action there had been transformed into an alternating one, there was no point in waiting.

Most of the comrades hadn't imagined we would end the action. Swords had been drawn from their scabbards to settle accounts with fascist M. Ağar and the special war. This resolution was evident in everyone. Even if our form of action changes, there are some things we will not accept. However, ending the action at this stage may adversely affect future actions. Hence, it is necessary to be careful. This afternoon, we passed our order for the canteen to the representative. Normally, they don't take orders on Saturday. We will get milk, potatoes, yogurt, and some crackers. We reminded the comrades that we should be careful in the first few days.

The doctor did not visit after the end of the action, although there could have been a need for him. But we didn't ask for a doctor or a diet. We didn't expect him.

After the meal, we read the reports of two comrades whose sanctions have ended.

Their hesitant and inconsistent attitude troubles us. This also prevents them getting organised and adversely affects their morale.

Our lot and German organisations have held a big demonstration in the German city of Hamburg. The BBC said 40,000 people had marched. It was shown on the evening news on Channel 7. The marchers were very lively. Party flags and posters of the leader were carried. A large area was jam-packed. When the "Ey Raqip" march was played, I got goose bumps. People's eyes were smiling as they shouted, carried away on a wave of emotion. A mood of closeness, from seven to 70, was reflected. The crowd was flowing from the square into the streets. It was a real mass of colour. And in this sea of colour, the main colours were green, red, and yellow.

You can see the revolution in the enthusiasm of this crowd. I'm sure that German parties could not attract such crowds.

On seeing this picture, I once again rebelled against the prisons. One day, we will destroy these dilapidated prisons. We won't go out of the doors. We will break down the walls into small pieces and leave. And we will vanish in that flood of humanity. We will go to the future in the depths of that sea of colour. While marching in that huge cortège of people, we will shout until we run out of breath.

We will also raise our fists in the air.

Just like children.

Just like those elderly people.

Just like the Kurdish mothers who are marching at the front.

Because we are part of them…

After 22.00, an entertainment programme began. Almost all of us sang folk songs accompanied by comrade Şehmus's saz to applause…

In songs, we saluted the revolutionary action of the working class all over Turkey on 15 and 16 June 1970.

Block 12
16 June 1996

The comrades in Antep have turned their action into an alternating one. As for Diyarbakır, they have got the first group to end their action after certain demands were accepted. Talks are continuing. For it to be happening in this way in Diyarbakır, in particular, is good. Otherwise, it would have been really demoralising. Emotional ruptures at such moments are profound.

Block 12
17 June 1996

Süleyman, who is staying with us, was insisting on leaving, as he cannot adapt to the environment. A decision was announced to exclude him from all social activities for two weeks so that he can think and concentrate. Despite most comrades saying, "Let him go," we said, "Let's give him another chance. Perhaps we can save him." He must have been positively affected, as he said, "Thinking of the enemy's approach, I have changed my mind and will stay." We said we would help him, but before an hour had passed, he said, "Even if 15 months pass, my mind won't change. Let the structure take a decision about me." Just when we were trying to assist him, for him to act like this made me really angry. We told him to immediately pack up his things and go. At that moment, I acknowledged that the comrades who said, "Let's throw him out," were right.

In general, we do not approve of anyone leaving the environment. We do our utmost to keep them. However, it is pointless after a certain point, as they begin to cause harm. Then, efforts to win such individuals over have no effect, as they shuts themselves off. Again you feel bad, as everyone who leaves our environment finds themselves with bigger problems. It's a shame!

Block 12
18 June 1996

The fifth day of block 7-15 is over. Tomorrow it's the turn of 9-13.

We have been in meetings all day. Certain comrades' problems were dealt with.

It was explained emphatically that unorganised behaviour cannot be accepted in the environment. Some comrades carelessly tried to find a justification instead of making a self-criticism. Knowing they are insincere is a more demoralising situation.

At the root of many problems is a failure to collectivise and imposing individuality on the environment.

As the situation of certain comrades is serious, we did not take a block decision. Action will be taken based on the opinion of our general prison structure.

While the position of a comrade was being discussed, I saw that person nodding off as I spoke. I was offended. "Does this comrade care what we are saying about him?" I asked myself. I cut short what I had to say as the wind had been taken out of my sails. After I had finished speaking, I sufficed with telling the comrade, "Get up and throw water over your face." There was no need to say anything more.

Comrades' attendance at the meeting was good.

For the first time since ending the hunger strike, we ate from the lunchtime wagon. Comrades had cooked chicken the previous evening. It didn't agree with me, as I threw up during the night. I was sick to my stomach. Other comrades were also affected.

Block 12
20 June 1996

We read our general administration's 13-page instruction regarding the block units as a unit. The general shortcomings of units and topics that should be taken into consideration in the coming period were explained. After reading it, I repeated some emphasised points. These are to exert efforts to work on the potential in the groups, prepare backup for every individual, to take ownership of problems when necessary, implement proper manner of speaking, oratory, formality, military life, playing a vanguard role and a rules-based life in all spheres, take care that this is properly implemented in our environment, comradeship relations and solidarity, affection/respect, natural responsibility, being planned, dealing with the essence of problems rather than secondary ones, behaving collectively rather than as individuals, balancing flexibility and strictness, implementing instructions and having confidence in yourself, ending intellectual laziness, attaching more importance to administration and coordination, relying on reciprocal trust in individual relationships, following individual education programmes, bringing through more young educators, being more conscientious in the selection of comrades to present seminars and forums, making proposals for new seminars, forums and leaflets, having a stronger dialogue with the structure and, in addition, to being more receptive to criticism, maintaining enthusiasm and high morale.

This was followed by sitting down with block educator comrades to remind them of the points requiring attention.

After the educators, a debate was held with the structure after reading out the evaluation of the recent action. This will be particularly useful in order to create unanimity regarding the enemy's policies, the latest state of the war, and attacks on the prisons.

Then, the meeting records of Meta from Amed were read out. He experiences lack of harmony in all spheres. All rules and those with duties seem meaningless to him. Although he appears to be quite radical, he has trouble with collective work and tries to remain outside it. Finally, when his attitude reached the level of insult, his block administration and eight or nine comrades held a meeting. Once more, he was not persuaded and he said, "Even if this movement's central administration comes, I won't be persuaded." In spite of the structure proposing he be thrown out, we did not agree. We said, let him stay in the environment without any right to have his say on any activity.

Even if they are exhausted, we generally prefer not to send people away from the environment. Our perspective is, "Even if there is only one hair left, rescue is the watchword."

Block 12
21 June 1996

I read out the instruction from our prisons' coordination. They criticised us, saying, "You are acting harshly towards those who avoid participation in the collective environment." I think they are contradicting their own attitude. I proposed to the administration that it should be dwelt upon and read out to the general structure.

The decision regarding comrade S. has arrived. He cannot manage to free himself from the past, linking all the problems he has to that period. Rather than hold himself responsible for his reactions, he blames comrades. He has let himself go and not reviewed his experiences, and this has worn him out. The decision of the general structure is:

1. A one month period to be granted for him to focus.

2. He should receive 15 days of special education.

3. At the end of the period, he is to write a self-criticism report to be submitted to the structure for approval.

Towards evening, comrade Celalettin dropped by to give us some news. A delegation from Aydın HADEP, ÖDP, Emek Party and the Human Rights Association has visited the prison and met representatives. But we don't believe that they will be effective or that notice will be taken of them. For them to take an interest is sufficient for us, as it is good support as regards developing public opinion.

Comrade Salih Öncü has been ill since ending the hunger strike. He cannot eat anything on account of stomach pain and is vomiting. I think he has gastritis. Such things are worse for the body than a hunger strike.

Block 12
22 June 1996

The 6-14 blocks came to see us. We sat down and chatted all together.

After football yesterday, comrade F. Suvarioğulları collapsed. His blood pressure was up to 21. He was rushed to hospital. It's unbelievable. It's fortunate that he didn't have a brain haemorrhage. Despite the fact he's only 21, he has pains in his heart, kidneys, and back. He is also worn out from the hunger strike. When we don't include such comrades in actions, they react.

We reviewed the weekly reports. No weeks go by without problems.

For the first time since the hunger strike, I played football this afternoon. I'm quite tired. It is hot, but I think we are now "over the hill."

Block 12
23 June 1996

At 18.00 we finished the seminar we had started yesterday. During education, we sensed the smell of smoke. The waste-paper bin downstairs had caught fire. I assume someone put a cigarette butt in it without first extinguishing it. The seminar was on "seeing the reality of the enemy."

Tomorrow is our block's turn to participate in the alternating action. But comrades who were involved in the limitless hunger strike will not participate, as they need to recover. There is no point in them straining their bodies too much.

I typed up the short story I have written. It took up five large pages. I took particular care not to exceed the limit of the magazine we produce in the prison. The subject is about a guerrilla comrade's resistance to certain difficulties he experiences. Every moment, every day, every journey of a guerrilla is really a story, a novel. To see, feel, and write about these things is a lovely sensation. This is also sharing.

Today HADEP held its second annual congress in Ankara. We watched it on TV. There was a really enthusiastic crowd. Certain symbols and the leader's picture caught the eye. The prosecutor intervened on the pretext of the Turkish flag being lowered and replaced with symbols of the struggle. I gather they are going to open a case to close down the party. The bourgeois press is dwelling on this in particular. I think the lowering of the flag was not pre-planned or organised.

Block 12
24 June 1996

The HADEP congress went on until 04.00. Murat Bozlak was re-elected. 200-300 people waited until the closing statement was read out. That is, self-sacrificing people waited until dawn.

Despite it being said in the closing statement that the lowering of the flag was not approved of, Murat Bozlak and 33 party executives were arrested as they left. Our people waiting outside made their disapproval clear by whistling and ululating. The police were ready and attacked ferociously. The shrieks of our people as they fled were heart-rending.

They cannot even tolerate ululating.

They fear our voices, because fascism fears sound.

During the day, the party's central office was raided and all documents were taken to the DGM [State Security Court].

These scenes are also indications of a general attack. Around the same time, a bomb was thrown into the HADEP building in Izmir. One person was injured. A vehicle returning from the congress was stopped by ten men on their way back to Elbistan and raked with gunfire. Three delegates died and one was taken to hospital with serious injuries. One of those who died was the former district chair of the Elbistan branch.

The vehicle had been followed from Ankara. On the news, they were said to be "the group that lowered the flag at the congress." It is blatantly obvious it was an attack and massacre by the deep state.

In the coming period, they may close down HADEP and bring an election onto the agenda. A good trick and plan to exclude them from the election…

An entirely new agenda has been created. And all the pro-government media is making provocative broadcasts along the same lines. They are provoking the conservative section of the population. It looks as if the war will come to the boil in the days ahead. They want to put a brake on domestic and external support for HADEP with these attacks.

Block 12
25 June 1996

From 09.00 until 18.00, we read the general instruction from our prisons' coordination. We once again emphasised the points we had identified. I am tired from being on my feet the whole day. There was criticism of certain understandings, critiques, and "Aydın prison ways." We also read the section of the 4th National Congress relating to prisons. There were also assessments approved by the leader of the latest actions, demands, etc.

Comrade Murat went to block 6-14. Comrade Muhittin Tacer arrived in his place. A few other comrades' places were also changed. But the changing of certain comrades' positions doesn't sit well with me, as problems are not resolved by a change of position. It is always more realistic to resolve problems in situ with the interlocutors. This method is not one of resolution, but of farming out. It is something we condemn.

On the TV, there was news of eight people being arrested with a whole arsenal including bombs, five flame throwers, AK 47s, etc. They were apparently arrested on the eve of carrying out an action. You are devastated when you see this much equipment.

They go to such lengths to take the materials to the city and then get arrested. It's such a pity! With such an amount of materials, the place could have been turned upside down and great damage could have been visited upon the enemy. The wasting of these values is absolutely a crime against humanity.

Block 12
26 June 1996

The flexibility granted to those comrades who left the unlimited hunger strike ended today. We began as a block to read the monthly culture/art/political magazine, *Arjin,* that we have produced in the prison. We read it together and discussed certain sections.

When the evening meal arrived, I was at the typewriter. A comrade came over to me, saying, "Comrade İlhami Dayan is not himself, have a look." I asked what had happened. He replied in some surprise, "He fell while playing football and the back of his head hit the concrete. He doesn't remember what happened." I immediately went upstairs to the sleeping area. He was standing fully dressed in front of the bunks with his head leaning on the upper bunk. When I asked him what was going on, instead of replying, he asked me what had happened. I asked him some questions, trying to get him to talk, but he was not himself. He didn't even remember having a cold shower after falling. I immediately asked them to bring some ice. Despite asking several blocks, they were unable to find any. I was somewhat annoyed and went to the fridge and opened the ice box. I scraped the layer of frost off, put it in a bowl, and went back upstairs. Comrade İlhami is young. Even though he says he's fine, I made him lie face down on the lower bunk while I moved the ice around the back of his head for about five minutes. Meanwhile, when he mumbled, "Aren't we on an action... why did Zeki hit me?" I knew he was not himself. After remaining with him for a while, we dispersed after he said, "I'm fine."

Block 12
27 June 1996

Aziz Poyraz came to see me. I found him a bit more civilian-like and noticed he had put on weight.

Due to the racket in the visiting area, I found it hard to hear.

After 21.00, I kneaded çiğ köfte while comrades sang folk songs. A change like this immediately alters the atmosphere in the block. For a moment, everything is forgotten.

Block 12
28 June 1996

At around 09.00, comrade Celalettin dropped by. He gave us a short update. I took some notes, as I will need to write my ideas and proposals to Fuat later.

All the DHP comrades have proposed going to Bursa prison. They said it would be better for their political relationships. They thought this way before coming to Aydın.

It is necessary for our meetings to be made more practical, in line with decisions of the 4th National Congress. In order to prevent wasting time, it is necessary to limit the length of speeches and announcements during meetings and education. I pointed out that there was no problem about our issuing an announcement regarding the 14 July Death Fast martyrs, but as there is to be a central announcement for all prisons, it is not necessary.

I proposed that those comrades whose period of sanction is ending should be readmitted to relations and that those who were showing progress amongst the others should be reviewed by the administration after block meetings.

We were on our toes today expecting a search. While walking back and forth in the exercise yard with two comrades, around 14.00, we noticed one of the corridor windows being silently closed. They don't want us to notice movement in the corridor.

When we went to the door of block 8, we saw it had been opened. We alerted the comrades in block 12 who were having an education session that a search was happening.

As usual, they ransacked the place. It's a routine action to upset us.

Today is the 5th day of block 8's action. Tomorrow two blocks will start together. Justice Minister M. Ağar has sent an instruction to prisons after meeting a group of prisoners' families.

From now on, we gather, prisoners' hair will be cut with scissors, not an electronic device. Those who have a special diet report from the prison doctor will receive food from outside.

Legal action will be taken against personnel who mistreat prisoners.

Behaviour that conflicts with human values will be avoided and those that need treatment will receive it...

Entirely crocodile tears. But it is a reality that M. Ağar has said from the beginning, "I will not make concessions to prisoners." Even meeting our families was backing down. Otherwise he wouldn't have eaten humble pie.

People have been on hunger strike for two months. And he says he's showing his "human" side.

We heard on TV that a 40-metre tunnel had been discovered in the block where our comrades are in Çankırı prison. We were amazed. It was only three or four metres away from completion. It was probably exposed from an outside connection.

Kemal Aktaş, Mehmet Tören, and I had written a petition requesting a transfer to that prison. We were the most surprised that a tunnel had been found there. Of course, we had no prior knowledge of it.

When we turned the radio on, we heard the leader speaking on BBC. They'd taken a clip from MED TV. The leader's voice was echoing. He had taken part in the programme by telephone. "The lowering of the flag at the HADEP congress was a provocation. As a party, we had no knowledge of it. Again, I apologise if there were people using our name who did it. My character also does not accept such behaviour," he said. He used harsh words about MHP statements.

Efforts were made to use the flag incident and put the party in a difficult position. The special war utilised it very well. They hung up flags all over many cities. It was as if they had just remembered their flag. Our visitors told us that even sheds that dogs wouldn't sleep in had been decked out with Turkish flags.

Today, the Refah and True Path parties reached agreement on forming a new government. After receiving the approval of Çankaya, they announced their cabinet. Necmettin Erbakan, Prime Minister; Tansu Çiller, Deputy PM; Mehmet Ağar, Interior Minister; Tayan, Minister of Defence; M. Sağlam, Education; Ş. Kazan, Justice Minister.

The most "appropriate" of these is the Interior Minister. It is in keeping with their character to have a murdering policeman at the head of a police state...

The tableau is a perfect special war office construction.

Police and soldiers have shared the cabinet and made a few useful "Kurdish" idiots accessories as ministers.

The system wants to try out the Refah Party. By hindering its rise in this way, they want to bring it under control.

A great potential mass of voters will distance itself from the Refah Party when it sees it is no different from the other parties of the system. It was Kurdish votes that lifted the Refah Party.

If it is not closed down, HADEP's votes will increase in the coming period.

While the war continues in Kurdistan, no government has a chance of success.

Turkey, which yesterday entered South Kurdistan by land and air with a large force, announced today that it had withdrawn. They are training their troops. They are also carrying out hit and run-type operations and trying to keep topical coverage about security and a buffer zone.

Around a thousand Kurds held a protest in front of the Turkish consulate in Urmiye, Iran, lowering the flag, on account of Turkey bombing civilian areas. The nationalist press is enraged. They are overdoing the lowering of the Turkish flag to incite people while not mentioning the bombing of civilian areas.

It is now 02.00 in the morning. I will continue to read until 03.00.

Comrade Salih is also still awake. He looks a little better. He has had a rough week. He is still really thin and pale. He no longer vomits after eating. He is also reading something. He lost a lot of weight during the limitless action. Despite that, he still wanted to take part in the alternating action. I got annoyed with him. It's just as well we didn't allow him to take part. I think he now realises I was right. Although I was angry, his desire to be alongside comrades during the action is heartening. The wish to be alongside one's comrades whatever the circumstances has made us strong.

Block 8

30 June 1996

Today as the block education committee was meeting to discuss articles written in the block, I needed to get involved in the education. There were certain reductions in specific dimensions.

After a break, we read the assessments of Zeki and comrade Ka. In particular, comrade Zeki's knowingly concealing the situation came in for criticism. And, as this is a serious offence, the decision was taken to remove him from the block unit for 20 days. As for the other comrade, he will write his report. Comrade Zeki has fallen victim to his emotiveness and cronyism. I hope that in future he will not allow this to happen.

We heard on the TV news that in Dersim city, a woman bound a bomb around her body and detonated it in front of a row of soldiers engaged in a flag ceremony. The official death toll is five with 30 wounded. There must definitely be more fatalities…

The identity of the perpetrator is not known, but this is the first time with us that such an action has taken place. In our struggle, "firsts" have always opened the way for development. Otherwise, without strong willpower and belief, such a self-sacrificing action cannot be carried out.

Block 8
1 July 1996

We have begun preparations. We have made arrangements between blocks 8 and 12. When one comrade said, "Let me stay where I am, the opposite side seems like a dungeon to me," I told him he shouldn't think like that.

It is difficult to understand some characteristics of our people. After all that has happened and so much education, there can still be hesitation over certain matters. A lack of awareness when someone says something like, "If he's there, count me out," can occur. In fact, people should no longer stoop to such things. We cannot forget we are in prison. It's not always possible for us to find people after our own heart.

While we were collectively reading *Demokrasi* newspaper this morning, comrade Celalettin dropped by.

Two comrades in Amed prison are now on a de facto death fast as they cannot obtain sugared water. A group of our families has had a meeting with the new Justice Minister, Ş. Kazan. The families were pleased with the meeting. The minister apparently said, "I will send a delegation to Eskişehir to carry out an inspection. If necessary, we'll close it." Just like in 1991, they will pretend to be democratic, while stirring up war.

According to a statement by the DEM agency, the self-sacrificing action in Dersim was carried out by a Kurdish woman, Zeynep Kınacı (ZİLAN). It is said she had personal approval from the leader...

We gather that a similar action was supposed to have taken place in Amed 15 days ago. However, the police realised what was to happen and killed the comrade a short distance from the target. There was nothing in the media. They concealed it.

For a woman to carry out a successful suicide attack is of historical importance and is a first in the region.

Firsts in history always have a special place. It is necessary for us to appreciate this spiritually and physically in our very bones and to lower our heads in respect.

The action has had a shock effect on the Turkish front. It's certain they will be shocked further.

Today, I read the minutes of block 2's meeting. They completely glossed over everything. There were lots of shortcomings in the language used. It reflects certain approaches that have become chronic.

Tomorrow is our turn to go on hunger strike.

According to the Turkish news, MED TV's broadcasts will end tomorrow. As far as we know, the contract is for ten years. You never know with the

Turkish state. They've almost sold Turkey in order to get the channel shut down.

The party may set up another channel, as TV broadcasts have a positive effect on the people.

Today, I received a telegram from Nihat and a letter from my sister, Fatoş. They hadn't received my letters. The baseness of colonialism.

Nihat's mother came from Germany to visit him. She brought news, things, and money from my mother. My mum has embarrassed me. The fact she is constantly thinking about us pleases me/us.

Fatoş mentioned my sister Rahşan and elder brother Hüseyin. As far as I can understand, they are in a hot, hectic area. To get news of them is, likewise, pleasing.

> *They are in the mountains,*
> *I'm in prison*
> *In their hands are Kalashnikovs,*
> *On my wrists are chains.*
> *They are free*
> *While I am a captive.*
> *But my brain is free!*
> *My heart is free.*
> *Just like those in the mountains.*
> *Just like those who have spread their wings towards freedom.*

Block 8
2 July 1996

We started the block meeting this morning. After the block unit report was read out, criticisms regarding the report were accepted. In general, the criticisms were appropriate, but some were views of the individuals themselves.

At 10.00, we stood in silence for comrade Zilan and a statement was read out. Then these slogans were shouted:

"Comrade Zilan is immortal!"

"We are Zilan, we are a bomb exploding in the midst of the enemy!"

"We have succeeded with the revival, now it's the turn of liberation!"

"Down with the special war!"

"Long live President Apo!"

All the blocks shouted in unison.

The enthusiasm of the action and its morale resounded between the walls, reaching mount Spil, and from there to the Taurus mountains.

When we moved on to individual reports at the meeting, we had problems with some comrades. There were discussions on subjects such as not realising your own shortcomings, not organising yourself, conservative attitudes, and not adapting to the structure by reflecting Turkish left understandings from which they had come.

In the afternoon, comrade Cesim dropped by. He gave us information regarding theatre and the commemoration of 14 July.

At 16.00 and 23.30, we repeated the shouting of slogans.

MED-TV broadcasts have been interrupted. The company unilaterally cancelled the licence. Our side made an agreement with a Polish company, but they cancelled it on the same day. In this situation, Turkey is saying, "Cancel unilaterally, we will cover your losses, and pay you extra. If necessary, we will pay for the frequency, but not use it."

The special war is doing its utmost.

Today on the BBC, after leader Apo said, "We will extend the ceasefire for a time in order to examine the actions of the Erbakan government," he commented on comrade Zilan's action, saying, "This action of our comrade was a reaction of the people. If these actions continue, Turkey will lose two or three years."

There are now programmes about comrade Zilan on TV. She was a nurse. Her husband had been captured wounded in our cause. MED-TV broadcast her voice accompanied by footage of guerrillas. "I am sacrificing myself for my people and my country," she said. It is said she used 30 kilos of TNT.

Block 8
3 July 1996

Although we were in session throughout the day, we couldn't complete our meeting today, either. Five or six people were left. In general, participation was low. The usual people spoke.

The structure laid into certain comrades. Focus centred on failure to participate and reluctance to make criticisms in order to avoid confronting problems. Our structure misses nothing, but, unfortunately, it is not always possible to transform this into organised power.

The alternating action is continuing. Tomorrow it is the turn of blocks 1 and 2.

Today, one of our representatives, comrade Aşkın, dropped by.

DS and the Platform have decided to start a death fast. They have started off centrally.

MED-TV broadcast for an hour. They will continue like this temporarily.

Today the bourgeois TV channels broadcast an interview with comrade Zilan's elder brother. He made some vile statements. A real lowlife…

Last night, I woke up several times. It was quite hot. Sometimes, it's intolerable. I was annoyed. In my dream, I was outside, in a familiar place, but I don't know where. While wandering around at one point, I passed in front of a platform that resembled an official ceremony. There was a stand that was full, but behind it was empty.

I saw a comrade's mother amongst the crowd. She was in the stand. When I went towards the back of the stand, I saw Süleyman Demirel fall towards the back. There was a bullet hole in his head. There was blood on the concrete. I thought there might be a rumpus, so I hurriedly left the scene. While walking along the street, I noticed military vehicles going by. I went to the outskirts of town. There were a few comrades there, including Aşkın from the DHP and Ali Rıza. We had a chat and I talked about camouflage. I realised the place I wished to go was the İslahiye district of Antep.

We were walking, passing places that were a mix of hospital and streets. The places were ones I have seen in previous dreams.

Block 8
10 July 1996

The action in Amed prison has ended as a result of the demands being met after prolonged talks. The statement said, "We thank the families and friends outside and the prisons for their support. We are ending our action, but our five-day support actions will continue to support the actions in other prisons."

The new justice minister has announced that the circulars sent out by M. Ağar in May have all been revoked.

If we look at the essence of the matter, not much will change. The "special" prisons will remain open. They won't take new detainees to Buca and Bayrampaşa.

After the "new" government won its vote of confidence, it wants to pull the wool over people's eyes with such an announcement. "Once a month visits with children" is part of this pretence.

The actions of the Turkish left are continuing, and three members of prisoners' families have started a death fast.

During this action, our families outside have worked well.

Comrades have been preparing for the 14 July commemoration for about a week.

For the first time since starting the action, we attended the philosophy class today. Once again, we are going to devote two days a week to philosophy.

It's very hot. Afternoons and early evening are particularly stifling. It's so hot that after you come out of the shower you start sweating again straight away.

A situation has attracted our attention.

Apart from the initial bulletin, there has been nothing about comrade Zilan's action. There has been little coverage in our press. The impression may be created that the action is not being owned. However, even if it is said to be "a premature action," responsibility for it was still taken by the leader.

It is now 02.50. Just now, a mouse shot out from the corner of the cupboards. After watching it for a while, I saw it go between two cupboards. I immediately went downstairs and picked up a broom and a mat. Meanwhile, comrade A. Kadir, who was reading a book downstairs, followed me.

He took the broom from me and waited in the middle of the room. Suddenly, saying, "Aha, aha," we went into action. The mouse tried to escape into the corner, then scurried out under the corridor door. A. Gaffur said, "If we had killed it, it would have been a great action. We could have hung it on the door first thing in the morning to surprise the comrades," laughing. In fact, his heavy build was the reason the mouse escaped.

Although we have all kinds of insects here, we rarely encounter mice. Five years ago, we saw one in block 13. Comrade Gezgör was scared of it and panicked, which we found most amusing.

We put cloth under the corridor door to stop it getting back in.

Compared to the rats the size of cats we have seen in certain prisons and sometimes even had to live with, these mice are quite cute, but still it wouldn't be good if they multiplied.

Two days ago İ. Özmen, and today comrade Hamit Tokay were released.

Hamit sent a message to all the blocks. Two releases, two attitudes…

I have never thought it appropriate to comment on those who leave prison, as the most unexpected person can adopt a positive attitude outside. His behaviour inside and the words spoken are not a criterion. The only yardstick is the practice outside. But the way a person walks, even one word, can expose more or less what a person will do once he's outside. A single word, just as it can be reassuring, can also cause worry.

The man who was formerly responsible for Turkey in our party did not depart leaving a sound impression. But then, you never know. I hope I will be mistaken…

Block 8
14 July 1996, Sunday

The 14th of July 1982 has a very important place in the history of our struggle. The death fast of 14 July, during a period when our party was involved in a withdrawal, gained respite for the revolution in the specific setting of Diyarbakır prison, and shocked the enemy.

It also broke the atmosphere of submission in Diyarbakır prison.

We were preparing for days in order to commemorate Hayri, Kemal, Akif and Ali, to reflect the fact we are their followers and to be worthy of this day.

When I woke up in the morning, comrade A. Gaffur was up, standing tall with his burly frame of nearly two metres. "Comrade, get up, we'll only just make it in time," he said. After telling him it was still early, I went back to sleep, as it was only 06.30.

When I went down into the exercise yard, Kadir and Yusuf had already washed the concrete surface. After the morning roll call, we immediately prepared the theatre stage from cloth. We had made the stage, curtain, cells and other decorations all from the prison's dirty bedding, washing lines, and benches.

At 09.00, after comrade Kemal had called us to stand for a minute's silence, he read out our prison administration's statement. Then, while Selami was reading out the DHP statement, I was summoned to the door. "Later," I said and remained in the line. The whole block was lined up in three rows. However, when they said, "Prison governor," I moved towards the door. In the corridor I saw that seven members of Dev Sol and a comrade from the MLKP had arrived with musical instruments. As I was shaking hands with them, the deputy governor, M. Ceylan, shook the walkie-talkie in his hand, saying:

"Lower the curtains in the exercise yard."

"We have a play, we can't!"

"It's not on, because the curtains make it impossible for inspection."

"Guards are looking from the top and the opposite window. What do you mean, it can't be inspected?"

"No way!"

"We won't lower the curtains. Only after the play has been performed."

"So when does it begin?"

"We will start after chatting to our guests."

"Have your celebration later. Let them start the play first."

"Don't give us a time or a period. Whenever we start, that's when we'll raise the curtains," I said, leaving the door.

The fact he had summoned me by name had demoralised me a little. If it hadn't been a special day with guests, I wouldn't have given him the time of day. Summoning me by name instead of the person in charge of the block is a message: "We know who you are."

While the guests waited in a corner of the exercise yard, we sang the "Hey Revolutionary" march and shouted the following slogans:

"Down with the special war!"

"Resistance is life!"

"The 14 July martyrs are immortal!"

"Long live leader Apo!"

The fact the guests waited in this way depressed me. In fact, I had spoken to the comrades and asked them to pay attention to courtesy. The continuation of dogmatic, old understandings depresses me. We should have read it out before they arrived, or not made them wait in this way.

Comrade A. Gaffur was directing the choir. After a few songs, he invited the DS choir. This was followed by both movements' messages being read out. The DS message was, as always, a dry slogan, but careful and thoughtful language was used. As for the MLKP's, it was more mature and political.

The guest choir presented a colourful concert.

Next, the stage was opened. The first scene featured captain Esat Oktay, the commander of Diyarbakır prison, striding back and forth, speaking. He mentioned his "special" methods, his successful duties, special activities in Cyprus, and his determination to break people.

In the second scene, Kemal Pir, M. Hayri Durmuş, and Akif Yılmaz were chatting in a cell. Kemal says to Hayri:

"Doctor, doctor, the action of the Four was majestic and appropriate. We should have done something like this before. We are late, very late…"

In short, the play focused on the circumstances of 14 July 1982, the importance of Diyarbakır prison, torture in the harshest of conditions, torture during journeys to and from court, attacks in the court room, efforts made to break them using hunger and torture, their determination in the later days of the death fast, and dialogues between them and with soldiers.

It lasted about an hour.

At lunchtime, we ate the meal we had prepared in the exercise yard.

The guests said they had been profoundly affected by the play and departed.

As evening began, we concluded with the vow of Nuri Dersimi. As we recited the vow together in unison, I once again had goose bumps.

At night, we listened to the memories of those comrades who had known the July Martyrs. Their common points were their characteristics of maturity, resistance, and acting in a constructive way with comrades, in addition to their loyalty to the people and the party.

We believe that our comrades outside also commemorate 14 July. For the resistance spirit of 14 July has become concretised in the guerrillas and the sacred uprising of the people.

This is what loyalty to the July martyrs and the values means. This is immortality.

In a statement in *Demokrasi* newspaper, it was announced that in all prisons comrades will begin an alternating five-day action in support of the Turkish left's death fast action.

The Turkish left and the prison authorities are making reciprocal strident statements. Despite this, I think the action will be called off soon, as around 160 people are on the verge of death.

The action has reached an impasse on the demand that Eskişehir prison be closed.

Block 8
17 July 1996

There is a picture in *Hürriyet* newspaper of a new group arrested in Izmir. On the table in front of them are a lot of publications and technical equipment. Ş. Poyraz, M. E. Karatay, and 13 others have been arrested. According to the news item, the whole Aegean Regional Committee has been arrested.

Naturally, we are demoralised. It's unacceptable that Karatay, who had been arrested many times before, disintegrated under interrogation, and had many problems, was still put in charge of the Aegean. As for Şehmus, he was put in charge of military matters. First and foremost, the person who appointed these exposed characters is guilty. When we heard that M. Emin had been appointed, we immediately wrote a note to the prison coordination expressing our concerns. We openly expressed our reaction, as they themselves had made the appointment. Today, it has become evident how right we were to be concerned. I wish we had been mistaken.

It's a great shame for these values, the people, and relationships. While trying to get things done, the people and the party are suffering.

It is absolutely crucial that all aspects of this matter are investigated. For someone in charge to send a message to prison asking for contacts is by itself sufficient to arouse doubt. How is it possible for someone who has been at the academy, who had a role there, to end up in such a situation?

Block 8
18 July 1996

Today is Thursday. Our visiting day.

Until noon, I read a piece written for 15 August. I didn't find it appropriate.

I was called to the visiting area at lunchtime… I met the father of comrade Ö. Akıncı. It is possible to see in his face the tribulations and suffering of the years. Despite being elderly, his heart and brain are like a fountain-head of enthusiasm. As he spoke, he got excited like a young person and sometimes was unable to control his language. A real man of the people. If there were three people like that outside, they would create a great mass for the organisation.

The police have arrested him a few times. "When they swore at me, I swore back. I didn't accept what they said. It's surprising that young people don't resist. It is those old resisting comrades that are in my heart," he explained.

Despite his daughter, grandchildren, and son being in the visiting cabin, he didn't give them a chance to speak. At the end, he said, "We will succeed," angrily.

It's impossible not to admire such people. To chat to such people and listen to them in the midst of so many adverse situations is comforting and increases one's loyalty to the people.

I was delighted to meet him.

Since it is our block's turn to go on hunger strike tomorrow, we had entertainment until midnight. Time flew by with poetry, songs, and chatter. Perhaps the hunger strike will be over before our five days are up, as there are reports that Eskişehir prison is being emptied.

According to what we have heard, M. Emin is being driven round in a vehicle by the police. It's apparent that he has once again disintegrated under interrogation. It's impossible not to be depressed. Is history repeating itself once again?

At 01.00, I was woken up by a commotion. When I realised the doors were being banged, I jumped out of bed and hurriedly got dressed.

I said to the lookouts, "Wake up the comrades immediately."

The comrades were shouting to other blocks under the door, trying to find out what was going on. The whole prison had got up in a moment. Apparently a comrade in block 1 had been taken ill. He had been taken to hospital, but brought back without being treated. The comrades had refused to take him back into the block and sent him to the sick bay. In spite of the insistence of our representatives, they were not allowed to go to block 1. The sick comrade may be Eryılmaz.

In such situations in prison you are helpless to do anything. Your comrade is alongside you suffering and your hands are tied. The one thing you can do is become enraged and gradually eat your heart out. Again and again, you experience the frustration of not being able to do anything. Your anger is directed more at those who are outside, but are not calling someone to account. The enemy's rule is the same everywhere. And in opposition to it is resistance…

Block 8
19 July 1996

The first day of our hunger strike.

As for the death fast, it is in its 61st day. There may be deaths at any moment.

The representatives' meeting today will be in our block. First, comrade Cesim arrived, followed by the others… After having a short chat with them, I left. After a short meeting, five of them came out into the exercise yard. They wanted to chat to comrades.

Kemal from the TDKP is very thin. The veins in his arms are prominent. Their action is in its 30th day. They went on hunger strike in support of the other groups. They have to continue. Kemal complained about the inexperience of the other groups.

Meanwhile, we learned that the comrade who was taken ill last night was Eryılmaz. He had a muscle spasm. At first, they thought it was a heart attack.

He had a cardiograph and was then brought back. When those in the block wanted to see a representative before taking him back, all hell broke loose. For the sound of moaning from the sick bay could be heard in the block. Eventually, at 04.00, comrade Celalettin was taken to the sick bay to speak to the comrade.

When the manager said, "You are using this just to create a noise," Celalettin replied, "We don't need this. Our guerrilla comrades in the mountains are making a noise. That's enough for us," then returned to the block.

Block 8
20 July 1996

The second day.

As always, I woke up at 06.00. Remembering we were on hunger strike, I went back to sleep, saying I would sleep in the cool air.

At around 08.00, when a comrade on lookout brought me a note, I had to wake up. Doing the necessary cleaning, I went into the exercise yard. Four of five comrades from block 12 were up. After striding back and forth for a while, I went back inside and began to read the minutes of block 9. It took until nearly noon. Reading the meeting minutes takes quite a long time, what with the reports, assessments, and proposals. And if you have to take notes on each topic and write your opinion, well, good luck…

Boris was a wonderful PM.

Block 8
21 July 1996
IF WE FORGET THE ZILANS, WE WILL FORGET OUR HUMANITY

The third day.

Last night, I was on lookout between 01.30 and 03.30. During that time, I wrote a letter to my mother.

The expected news came from Ümraniye prison. The death fast has given its first martyr. He was only 25 years old. If I'm not mistaken, his name is Aygün Uğur, of TİKKO. His family and some lawyers are outside the prison. We watched it on the news. Watching it, your hair stands on end. His mother and a few young people were hugging each other and crying. As for the father, he shouted that he was a human being and a worker, and that he was going to go on a death fast.

According to what the lawyers said, there may be more deaths at any moment. Today is the 63rd day. Critical days. Poor conditions in the jail increase the risk of death. The next few days will be key.

He who is patient and develops the superior manoeuvre will win.

But even if the action is ended today, there may be more martyrs. Physically, they are at the point of no return. Most of them will suffer lasting damage and they will have to live with the pain of this damage for the rest of their lives.

Tonight, in some districts of Istanbul in particular, there may be protest actions such as occupations, demonstrations, and Molotov cocktails thrown.

According to what we have heard, his comrades in the block did not hand over the body, saying, "We will have a ceremony."

The Turkish left may act emotionally and embark on over-hasty actions. The consequences of such actions in prison will be grave.

At around 21.00, comrade Delil called us over by banging on the wall of the neighbouring block. As always, we began to speak though the walls. Comrades from the Turkish left in Aydın prison have apparently taken the decision to set up barricades. All our blocks will be informed and asked to be watchful.

At midnight, the sound of slogans was heard. Although it was the time for roll call, the guards were naturally unable to enter the blocks. In such situations, if no agreement is reached, they knock down the walls and attack. They attack in such a savage way that dozens of gas canisters can be fired into a single block.

Today K. Aktaş, M. Ağcakaya, and M. Tören have written petitions requesting to go to Çankırı. I don't think they'll be taken there. They don't easily transfer people from here to prisons where the political-organisational component is weak. Of course, you never know. It will be fortuitous if it happens.

Today we had visitors from blocks 7-15 and 6. Although we sometimes speak to comrade Sarıkaya through the walls, we still miss our comrades. The 10 centimetres of wall between us is thin, but the concrete can separate us for years. These walls need to be destroyed.

We had a short meeting with Sarıkaya, as we are going through a sensitive period. We have to be ready for anything at all times.

While speaking to comrades Celal and Aziz last night, they discussed the Zilan massacre [a massacre of Kurds by the Turkish army in 1930].*

It is impossible not to be depressed. Despite 70 years having passed, you are horrified as you listen. Every part of it could be the subject of a novel.

People [in Zilan] were herded into a gully just because they were Kurdish and raked with gunfire from machine guns. The soil there is still black from the blood of people who were massacred. Grass still does not grow in that area. Only one child survived from the community that was slaughtered. He didn't leave the area. A month later, when Kurdish fighters in the mountains came to the area, they saw the child. Thinking others had survived, they followed the child without revealing themselves.

---

* Zilan Massacre (Zilan Katliamı): In July 1930 in the Erciş district of Van province, tens of thousands of Kurds were slaughtered in the Zilan valley. The massacre, perpetrated by the 7th and 9th divisions of the Turkish army included the use of aircraft and continued on for days. Groups of civilians were rounded up and slaughtered. Not one case was opened against those responsible for this crime against humanity. This genocide was so massive that even after nearly a hundred years, mass graves containing human bones are still being found. —Author

The child went through the bushes and towards a pile of bodies. To the amazement of those watching, he made his way between the putrefying bodies and began to suck on his mother's breast.

Those watching angrily grasped the child and took him away from that place, but they could not control him. He threw himself on the ground. Eventually, they realised the child was scared of them. It was normal for him to fear creatures called humans, as those who had carried out the massacre resembled humans...

When the massacre began, some women, who had been unable to take their babies with them as they fled, had left them at the well. And 25 years later, some mothers who returned ran towards that well, looking helplessly with the hope that they might see the babies they had left there a quarter of a century earlier.

And the heart-breaking thing is that some people there threw stones at these mothers.

Moreover, while fleeing in a group, at certain places some mothers covered their babies' mouths with their hands to prevent them crying so that Turkish soldiers would not hear them, thus silencing them forever. For a mother to kill her own child, part of herself, in order to save others, is an indescribable horror.

Dozens of similar incidents...

When the elderly people who witnessed the Zilan massacre recount the incident, they and their listeners still break down in tears. It is certainly not enough to describe Zilan as savagery and a tragedy.

Today, the guerrillas are taking revenge for the massacres of Zilan, Dersim, Ararat, Kochgiri, and many other massacres in Kurdistan.

Today the guerrillas are taking revenge for the babies left abandoned at wells.

And for this reason, the people are embracing the guerrillas.

And for this reason, the people of the Zilan region still refuse to become state village guards [*korucu*s].

Because that savagery has not been forgotten.

Because that betrayal has not been forgotten.

Because the Zilan stream flowing blood-red has not been forgotten.

And the wish for vengeance was concealed in those anguished hearts.

It is these anguished hearts that today take the guerrillas, their real children, under their wing.

Massacres like that in Zilan are too multi-dimensional to be explained. This is why so many laments are sung and so many tears are shed for it.

If we forget massacres such as Zilan, we will forget our humanity.

Block 8
22 July 1996

The fourth day.

Today comrade Sabri and I were on duty in the block. After we had done the general cleaning in the morning, we prepared a watery lemonade and gave everyone a glass.

There was an announcement from our central prisons administration in *Demokrasi* newspaper today. It was said that because the death fast of the Turkish left has now reached a critical stage, groups of fifteen in Bursa, Çankırı, Istanbul, Aydın, Ceyhan and Bartın prisons had started an indefinite hunger strike in support, while in other prisons five-day alternating hunger strikes would continue.

Every block in Aydın has proposed, "Let us begin first." Consequently, a decision was made selecting blocks 4, 6, and 14. Tomorrow, 15 comrades will start. They are Kenan Şen, Orhan İvdil, Lezgin Çulduz, Nejat Özcan, Aşkın Tuncel, Bahattin Şahin, F. Oktay, A. Uçar, Harun Gül, Bayram Ekerek, Orhan Boz, A. Rıza Çelik, Z. Deniz, Sait Üçlü, Muhittin Tacer.

We read the minutes of the meeting in his block regarding the situation of E. It has been read in every block for the purpose of both information and education.

Almost all comrades made assessments and criticism regarding his stance, life, and attitudes. But his response was both disrespectful and insulting. A pain in the neck character who refuses to become part of the party while being within it. Despite having made many mistakes and committed many offences for which he has been sanctioned, he has an incorrigible personality. This has led to reactions around him. The majority in his block have proposed the freezing of his organisational status. In order for it to be more democratic, proposals have been received from all comrades in the prison after the minutes were read. The dominant view is for his relationships to be frozen while remaining with us.

From watching the news on TV, it seems there have been night time protests and the use of Molotov cocktails in many places in Istanbul and in Buca district of Izmir. This is good for the morale of the prison resistance and the families.

The Health Minister has made a statement, hinting that those on death fast might be forcibly treated.

D-Sol's barricade action in Bursa prison is continuing. The exercise yard door is open and they are not attending roll call.

Block 8
23 July 1996

The fifth day.

Our block has ended its action. From now on a limitless action will continue with 15 people.

News of the second martyrdom of the death fast has come from Bayrampaşa, on the 65th day of the action. He is Altan Berdan Kerimgil of D-Sol.

20 people are also in a grave condition.

Protests are taking place everywhere. There have been many incidents, particularly in Istanbul. Footage of soldiers attacking protesters and mothers has appeared on TV.

Justice Minister Ş. Kazan made a statement today using a vile expression. He claimed people are forced into joining the death fast and that they have no control in the prisons…

Although he says, "I will make no concessions," this is an expression of the fact they are under pressure and of their helplessness. Otherwise, he wouldn't have spoken like this in parliament.

Even many bourgeois parties are saying, "This issue cannot be dealt with ideologically, resolve the humanitarian demands."

With this action, the real face of the Refah Party, is becoming a bit more apparent.

Comrade Celalettin came to see us.

The DS members here are continuing their barricade protest. They went for a visit, but three of them are in critical condition. It's reached sixty days here, too.

Block 8
24 July 1996

On the 66th day, news of Dr. İlginç ÖZKESKIN's martyrdom has emerged.

It's easy to say, but to live death in every breath for 66 days… Everyone can stand up to death for a moment, but to gradually wither away second by second in such a marathon and stride towards death is not something everyone can do. Only those with strong willpower can manage this.

Officials from the Justice Ministry are meeting representatives from Bayrampaşa prison. Meanwhile, the Justice Minister is issuing threatening statements. They are pressurising them to abandon the action. If you're that determined, why are you letting talks take place?

In Ankara, around a thousand people marched towards the Ministry, whereas in Istanbul around 70 banks and other buildings were damaged by Molotov cocktails. In one demonstration, a municipal bus was burnt.

Writer Orhan Pamuk, Zülfü Livaneli, and Yaşar Kemal have issued a joint statement criticising measures taken in the prisons and asking for the inmates' humanitarian demands to be accepted.

There is also positive reaction in international public opinion. The French Foreign Minister has called on Turkey to end the death fasts.

I chatted with comrade Muhittin until lunchtime. I mainly listened to him. Then, I drew his attention to his mistakes and advised him not to look outside and to comrades for all the problems. Only in this way will he overcome the fantasies in his head. Otherwise, he will continue to reach different conclusions to every word and action. It will only heighten his stress and cause depression. Sometimes, listening to someone at length relaxes people.

Today, we repeated once again the shouting of slogans three times.

Block 8
25 July 1996
THE DAYS ARE HEAVY WITH NEWS OF DEATHS

At around 11.00, the silence in the main corridor caught our attention. We realised that metal cylinders were being carried. We notified all the blocks, asking them to be on alert. We tapped on the wall to speak to Sait hodja and they told us there had been a martyrdom in Aydın, too. Dev-Sol's representative told us before informing the authorities. As today is our visiting day, he asked for the families to make phone calls to certain places.

I gather the martyr here is Müjdat YANAT.

Meanwhile, the prison authorities sensed what was happening and made secret preparations to intervene. Consequently, they were late with the visits. We demonstrated our annoyance from the door.

We have been demoralised by the martyrdom.

A decision has been taken for the entire prison to shout slogans at 13.00, 15.00 and 23.00.

On the 12.00 news, we learned that Hüseyin Demircioğlu of the MLKP had died in Ankara closed prison, and that Ali Ayata of TİKKO had died in Bursa prison on the 67th day.

The sixth martyr, but dozens of other people are also on the verge of death.

After a minute's silence for six comrades at 23.00, the whole prison shouted slogans:

"Down with the Special War!"

"The Martyrs of the Revolution are Immortal!"
"The Müjdats are Immortal!"
"Long Live the Fraternity of Peoples!"
Our blocks then added the slogan:
"Long Live Leader Apo!"

Comrades held a minute's silence in the visiting area and made a statement. The families were apparently really affected. There was an emotional atmosphere. Our families are more emotional and sensitive on this subject. They are really on edge.

The days are full of news of death
Those becoming immortal on the way to death
On a long journey
Those who fight against death with every breath
Who gasp as they waste away
Who stare down death after sixty days
Putting up barricades against death in their twenties
Who look with hope towards the future
With pride
Smiling as they take their final breath
Greeting life with a "hello"
Who plant the seeds of resistance for the future
The seeds of yesterday
The fruits of today
The resistance seeds of tomorrow…

Block 8
26 July 1996

On the evening news we heard that Tahsin Yazıcı in Bayrampaşa and Ayşe İdil Ekmen in Çanakkale had been martyred.

Those who are in the first group to join the action are in a grave condition. The number of deaths may rise.

The National Security Council (MGK) are persisting with their classic policy of issuing veiled accusations.

The Justice Minister spouted more nonsense. "There are weapons in the prisons. Some places we can't enter. They have forced some ex-informers to go on death fast. If they don't hand over those who are in a serious condition for treatment, we will retrieve them using force, etc."

They want to reduce the positive reaction of public opinion.

Today we attended education together as two blocks. We read the article, "To take your own manner as a basis." We tried to discuss it. Some comrades adopted a defensive attitude when talking about themselves. It was as if everyone was relying on seeing problems outside themselves. Of course, these approaches were criticised.

Despite today being a search day, they didn't turn up. The authorities are lying in wait. We are, too…

Block 8
27 July 1996

IT IS FUNDAMENTAL TO LIVE HONOURABLY IN ALL CIRCUMSTANCES

Last night, I only just lasted until 23.45. I don't remember what happened after my head touched the pillow. Is it because of the heat, from thinking too much, or being too busy, I don't know, but these days sleep is tiring me.

In the afternoon, I saw the notice in the newspaper from three comrades in the name of our prisons' coordination. "If deaths continue as a result of the death fast, as PKK prisoners we will be more active by turning our limitless hunger strike into a death fast."

I immediately wrote a note to Fuat and the others, reminding them that we would need to make preparations here.

The news of every death explodes like a bomb in our hearts.

With the martyrdom of Hicabi Küçük and Yemlihan Kaya of the TİKB and Osman Akgün of Dev Sol in Istanbul, the number of deaths has reached 11.

More deaths may occur at any minute. Even worse, there may be mass fatalities. The point of no return has been passed. Most of them cannot even take water. The body will not accept it.

Today, they didn't give us the *Demokrasi* newspaper, saying, "It hadn't arrived at the outlet." Either there was an article about us or the paper has been closed down.

In the afternoon, I wrote another note to the other comrades in the administration, pointing out the necessity of preparing ourselves for an enhanced form of action as we cannot remain silent as the deaths rise, given the profound and multi-dimensional nature of the orientation.

We have received a note from F. and R., who are in a different block from ours. They wish to re-join the environment. They say they cannot remain in their current environment and are constantly experiencing problems. They mentioned Şerzat as an example. Some of those who have problems in our environment and go there recognise no boundaries. I gather he sent a congratulatory fax to Ş. Kazan on becoming Minister. Whatever he hoped to gain from that…

Even if someone is not in the PKK or a revolutionary, they should not do such a treacherous thing. A person who leaves the organised environment also moves away from human values. By the time they realise this, it is too late. While with us, it may seem attractive, but things may not work out as planned.

I am sure that after experiencing the situation there, they will better understand the purity of an organised environment.

I get angry with people who, when with us here, do not understand the value of comradeship.

As there is a commune in the organised environment, individuality and selfishness have been reduced to a minimum. Money received by individuals is spent mutually. Consequently, there is complete equality. Those who are in a poor economic situation are not made to feel this. Everything is used equally, from clothes to soap, tea, and fruit. If one person is depressed or ill, everyone in the block feels it. In the event of an attack, everyone tries to defend the others by putting their head above the parapet. This, naturally, further strengthens comradeship ties.

Ideological unity is also implemented in full in life. Of course, there are also difficult aspects of life in an organised environment. There are a series of rules, from morning group exercise to collective education, collective meals, collective individual education, and the times of getting up and going to bed. In an organised environment, nobody insults another.

A guard or a soldier also acts more carefully towards those in an organised environment. But those who leave us to go to an outside block, thinking it will be more "comfortable" are usually disappointed on the first day and feel regret. They have disputes with others over basic issues and experience all sorts of problems, including daily humiliation by guards.

The great majority of those who have left us have later wanted to return. Their situations are assessed and some are accepted. If their conduct there has been bad, or if they have insulted or committed a crime against the movement or the people, they are not re-admitted. Even if they go to another prison, first they will write a report and will not be admitted until the administration there has consulted the organisation in the place from which they have come. Most of them leave without thinking of the consequences and waste themselves. And they cannot rid themselves of their depression. Many of them also have problems with their families.

In spite of everything, you still feel sorry for them.

On the 23.00 news on TV, it was reported that agreement has been reached with those on death fast. It's very probably true. We will learn the details tomorrow. But even if they end it at this moment, there will continue to be deaths. Some of them are in a vegetative state. It reported that some have been unconscious for days, others have lost their memories and are having difficulty speaking.

While the agreement was being made, well-known people like Yaşar Kemal, Z. Livaneli, H. Ergün, Eşber Yağmurdereli and others were present, along with the prison prosecutor and brigade commander…

Block 8

28 July 1996

The action ended last night. The negotiations continued for 10 hours. A fax was sent from Bayrampaşa prison to all prisons where actions were taking place regarding the ending of the protest. Here, too, it ended during the night. They took the fax around the blocks. The fax included the signature of our representative in Bayrampaşa, Ferhan.

Proposals were received regarding what should be done in the existing situation. Since the protest is over, a date for returning to the normal programme will be fixed.

Today, we went as guests to block 7-15. After a short chat with comrades in the exercise yard, we went to a silent place with Delil. He expressed the view that, "It would have been better if we had ended the action after the news from the internal coordination." He knows that even if we had waited, the outcome would not have been different. I pointed out there was no need to do that.

We sat down with Delil and comrade S. He was insistent on being transferred to another prison. He is having problems as the comrades have not approved it. We told him that his mistakes and fallacies will not change by going to another prison, that he should stay here and focus on himself, that his obsession with a transfer is an escape from his reality, and that he should stay here and make a contribution. He blames every adverse situation on the block administration. We explained that it was not ethical to accuse the administration over every incident.

It is necessary to seek what is lost in the place where it is lost.

After meeting with a few other comrades, we returned to our block to hear the news from Bursa that Hidayet CAN from the TDKP-L has been martyred. He departed this life on the way to hospital.

The number of martyrs has reached 12.

Block 8
29 July 1996

At 10.00 in the morning, they came to raid the blocks. Slogans were chanted in block 6-14, where they remained arbitrarily for two hours. We immediately dashed into the exercise yard and joined in the slogans. All at once, the slogans,

"Down with the Fascist Authorities!", "End the Arbitrary Searches!", and "Fascist Repression Will Not Cow Us!" rang out around the prison.

Meanwhile, deputy governor M. Ceylan left his walkie-talkie in block 6 in an attempt to create a provocation, claiming, "They took it from me." Naturally, the comrades in block 6-14 reacted and handed it back.

When the meal wagon arrived, we noticed the food was covered in ants. When we informed the guards, they didn't take the food away. After some debate, they had to take it when we said, "If you don't take it back, we will tip it under the door."

H. Zan, in spite of all our efforts to persuade him, has again written a petition to the prison authorities, asking to leave our environment. Although he has said, "I will go" numerous times, we have tried to manage things, saying, "He's one of the people." But there is no point at this stage in insisting so much. It's not possible to keep someone in this environment against their will. Once he has gone, he will regret it, like the others, but by then it will have no meaning.

Today, we had a seminar on the concept of the family. As it was limited to one day, we didn't have much debate. Although it's a familiar topic, it was good to have a discussion given the participation.

In the evening, some comrades did folk dancing, and we all joined in.

Block 8
30 July 1996

It was the Turkish left's visiting day. They asked for some pots from our blocks. We sent them over, saying, "They must need them." A short while later, they sent them back full of food. We gather some democratic mass organisations outside had sent the food.

After a three-month break, we restarted collective exercise. The exercise yard was once again a sea of colour.

Our comrades in Erzurum and Maraş are in the 50th day of their limitless hunger strike. It hasn't really been covered in the press. We have a base of support in Erzurum, but not much in Maraş. In both places, there is a special policy of repression being applied. They want to enforce submission with rules.

It's necessary to offer active support for both prisons without delay.

The deadline to apply for the 15 August competition has been extended until 5 August. A proposal was made for articles that couldn't be completed.

There have been forest fires raging in the Aegean coastal region for a few days. In some places, they are threatening residential areas. The fact they have occurred at the same time in certain areas raises the possibility that they are the result of actions. At first glance, your heart bleeds, but what can you do? Our country, Kurdistan, is being burnt every day. Napalm is raining down and causing death on a daily basis. There are hardly any forests left in our country. They particularly want to destroy them.

Comrade Vakit came to our block to cut our hair. His shortness and plumpness was reminiscent of İzzet.

The prison authorities have gradually stopped the to and fro of letters. If they had done it suddenly, there would have been a reaction, but they have drawn it out, getting us used to it. This is an insidious tactic of the policy of rehabilitation. Silently habituating, bit by bit…

We will react and not accept this.

Block 8

2 August 1996

AT ALL TIMES WE ARE EYE TO EYE WITH THE MURDERERS

At this moment, I both want to write a lot, and to write absolutely nothing…

It is not possible to put down on paper the anger and yearning I feel rising inside me.

To write about today means to come face to face with the innocent faces of comrades Hüseyin Hüsnü Eroğlu and Mehmet Yalçınkaya.

It was exactly seven years ago. And I have once again experienced that day, the 2nd of August 1989.

Sometimes I have gone quiet feeling sad,

Sometimes I have wanted to spit venom.

Sometimes my blood has run cold.

Sometimes, when I have read about what the two comrades encountered during their "journey," my eyes have welled up.

Every time I have contained myself with difficulty.

The fact we are now alive is by sheer chance. But still, in the last seven years, I have asked myself countless times.

Why Mehmet and Hüseyin? Why?

And I am asking, shouting, WHY?

Yes! Today is the 2nd of August. And those beautiful people, not just today, are in our hearts and consciousness every day, every hour, and every minute.

They are living with us. They are alongside us always, in resistance, in life, and in the struggle to grasp the future.

The commemoration began with a minute's silence at 09.00. As I read the memorial, I once again lived through that day and them. My eye was on the text while my thoughts were in the past.

Following the memorial we shouted slogans.

"The Martyrs of the Revolution are Immortal!"
"The Hüseyins and Mehmets are Immortal!"
"Down With the Special War!"
"Resistance is Life!"
"Long Live Leader Apo!"

This was followed by two blocks reading aloud the leaflet devoted to the two comrades. The final section was about the journey. Just listening to those moments was horrendous. Although I have been through it before and read it many times, I was still incredibly affected.

Yes, they attained martyrdom. But our pain and suffering is continuing to get worse.

Those who murdered them are still in post here. They are impatient to carry out new massacres.

At every moment, we come eye to eye with the murderers. And apart from reacting inside, we can do nothing.

In the section on the journey, I couldn't look at the comrades who were brave enough to listen to the sentences about both comrades losing consciousness. I sensed it. The sobs of some comrades had knotted in their throats, while the tears of others were silently trickling down their cheeks.

There was a profound silence and this silence was a kind of rebellion.

They had initially attacked our blocks in Eskişehir Special Type Prison on the pretext of two tunnels having been discovered. Despite these tunnels not having been found in our blocks, we were the first target, as always, being Kurds. All the rights we had gained through resistance were taken away and new rules imposed. As we refused to accept these new rules, torture began. On the 35th day of the first hunger strike on 2 August 1989, our death journey began.

The transfer vehicles stopped for breaks many times under the hot sun, the intention being to slaughter us through heat and lack of water. Following the long journey, some comrades were semi-conscious on arrival at Aydın Special Type Prison. Hundreds of prison guards and soldiers awaited us at the entrance and commenced intensive physical torture in order to force us to abandon the hunger strike and impose certain arbitrary new rules.

In spite of the long journey, they didn't take us inside immediately. We continued to be held in the vehicles, exhausted and dehydrated.

They took us in two by two and attacked us like carrion crows. On the one hand, they were hitting us with clubs and truncheons, while on the other putting our hair through machines. We were in the air one moment, the next on the ground.

Sweat, blood, exhaustion, and brutality were all mixed up.

We have no idea how many hours later the last people were taken out of the vehicles. As we refused to accept the impositions, we were flung, four or five at a time, into single cells. The soldiers and prison guards were lined up on both sides of the long corridor of the E-Type prison leading from the governor's office to the cells, bringing down their clubs on our heads.

Days later we learned what had happened.

Hüseyin and Mehmet had been slaughtered at the entrance. 150 of us sustained injuries. Dozens could have died. The wounds of many of us had not healed months later. And, as for two deep wounds in our souls, they were to bleed as long as we lived.

Despite all this torture, they were unable to break our action. All the organisations in the prison continued with their resistance.

Outside, our families' wonderful support action and mass solidarity protests in cities all over Turkey and Kurdistan provided us with support. A large group of relatives pitched a tent outside Aydın prison, staying there for a month. We were aware that the conditions endured by the families were worse than ours.

Still, they didn't abandon us. In the same way, many administrators from the Human Rights Association (IHD) exerted great efforts. Many human rights activists, first and foremost Hüsnü Öndül, who had supported us for years, and others, such as then MP Kamil Ateşoğulları, took many initiatives on our behalf and visited us on many occasions.

At a time when we were considering turning the hunger strike into a death fast, on the fifty-second day, the prison authorities agreed to meet our representatives and, after long negotiations, agreement was reached, and the action ended.

When we heard the ululations and applause of the family activists outside, the prison reverberating between the bars of our cells, we felt the real success.

Yes, they are not actually physically with us, but they are with us and the guerrillas marching shoulder to shoulder towards tomorrow. And without complaining, devotedly protecting their comrades…

Mehmet Yalçınkaya

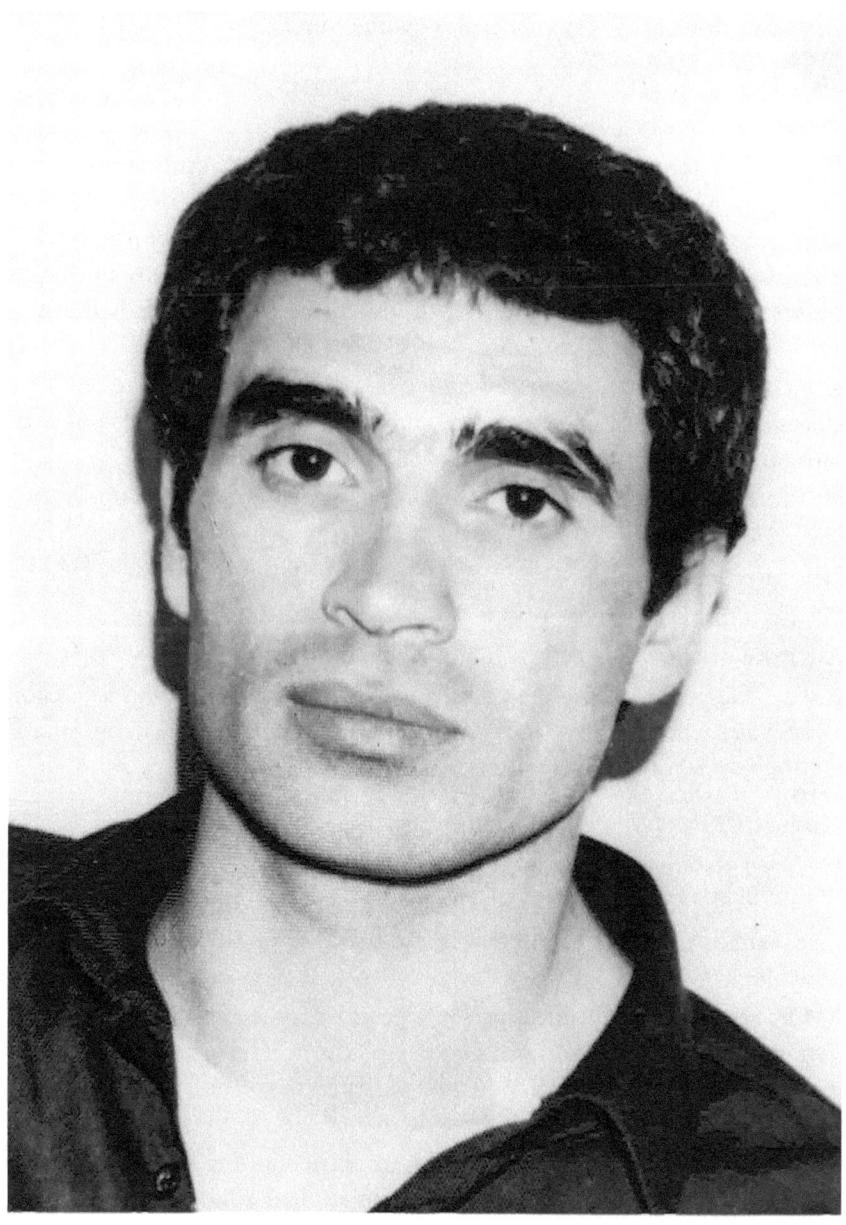

Hüseyin Hüsnü Eroğlu

We will not forget them!
Because they,
Are closer to us than we are,
Just as they are closer to tomorrow than we are.

Block 8
6 August 1996

It's really interesting. Although I have not been thinking about it, last night, in my dream, we were being exiled to Eskişehir prison. Since we already know the place, the architectural structure was no surprise to us. As we knew it was cold there, we wore white cotton long johns under our trousers. Comrade Kemal said, "Just right for Eskişehir. This is the most useful thing about the commune," at which we all laughed.

For a moment, we understood we were in a different prison. The block was like a single storey tea house. Since our choir was singing folksongs, the guards and a deputy governor with a walkie-talkie shouted:

"It's forbidden. You can't sing folk songs and marches in a group."

"Why?"

"It's forbidden."

"Is this a ministry ban or yours?"

After the discussion became fraught, they left.

I said, "Comrades, since they don't want us to sing folk songs as a choir, let's sing as a whole block," and we all sang the "Hey Revolutionary" march.

Block 8
7 August 1996

We read the assessment regarding block 9-13. It will be read in all our blocks for the purpose of education. It is 47 pages of comprehensive analysis in the form of a summary. There was also a section on the role of individuals in the block.

Mert's attitude was not healthy. He argued with the committee and didn't listen in order to create confusion on the platform. He wished to distort the agenda by making a polemic. When he persisted in spite of warnings, he was thrown out of the meeting.

It is necessary to address this situation in particular. He is not an unaware person. It is unacceptable for someone who studied at an academy outside, and who had a high level position in the Aegean and Marmara region, as well as the Aydın prison administration. It is a situation that is not in harmony with party ethics. When you're an administrator, enforce the rules; when you're removed, do the exact opposite. Prevent and oppose discipline and the rules, and argue about everything. This is unacceptable. He damages his prestige by vulgarising himself.

When I see the state he is in, I feel sad for me/us. It is evident that it was a mistake for us to bring him to prominence, saying he was "young," and to give him more responsibility than was warranted. We made a mistake. What he is doing now is absolutely a special war tactic. He is frittering away his political life. It's a shame…

Block 8
13 August 1996

Towards evening, a guard opened the small loophole under the block door and said, "From now on there will be no guest visits between blocks or of representatives."

We immediately informed the comrades on the administration.

This is a central decision. Further restrictions will come. They will introduce these at different times and in different ways in each prison. In this way, they will try to prevent prisons adopting a joint stance. They will start by selecting a few pilot areas.

They have immediately taken a measure against us in this period when we have been using the inter-block visits to meet our organisational needs.

They are carefully watching our every step, our every move, and reaching a conclusion. The special war never relaxes. Many approaches are developed centrally.

Block 8
15 August 1996

At nine in the morning, we assembled in the exercise yard and started the day with a minute's silence. Our celebratory statement and that of the DHP regarding the day were read out.

As always on the occasion of a celebration, everyone had had a shave and put on their new clothes.

After the "Ey Raqip" anthem, slogans were shouted.

"Long Live the 15 August Launch!"
"Long Live the PKK!"
"Long Live the ERNK!"
"Long Live the ARGK!"
"Down With the Special War!"
"Long Live Leader Apo!"

As today is our visiting day, we postponed the rest of our celebration to another day. Those of our blocks that do not have visitors will continue.

Towards 11.00, I was summoned to the visiting area. Most of the arrivals were known visitors. After going round all the cabins to say hello, I addressed them, saying, "Friends, will you please listen to me?" Immediately, the hubbub subsided. I continued, "As you know, today is the anniversary of August 15th. In 1984, the first blow of the armed struggle was struck in Eruh and Şemdinli under the command of Comrade Agit. With this "first bullet" fired at the enemy, it was announced to the world that the resistance in Kurdistan was not over and had officially reached the phase of the armed struggle. The enemy was in a state of shock when it lost control of those two districts against a handful of guerrillas. This shock caused an even larger tremor in the central government in Ankara. With this action, at the very time when they were saying, "We've broken the resistance of the Kurds," the guerrilla movement began in Kurdistan. This first shot was a reply to the massacres that had been perpetrated in Kurdistan in the past, the savage torture in the prisons, and the tyranny inflicted on our people. I invite you to join in a minute's silence in respect for all martyrs of the world revolution in the person of our heroes." Once again, there was absolute silence.

For a moment, the guards in the visiting area hesitated. When they realised we were taking no notice of them, they did not intervene.

We celebrated our and each other's festival. For now, 15 August is one of our most important days.

While in the visiting area, we heard that comrade Tören's request to be transferred to Çankırı had been rejected. The Ministry had apparently not considered it appropriate. Comrade Zeki had also come to the visiting area. We were a bit surprised to see him there when it wasn't his day for visitors, saying:

"What's up, why are you here today?"

"I don't know, my visitors got permission to come."

When he wanted to speak to me, I realised he had organised it himself, but I paid no heed to him.

When I saw that he was quite upset at what was being said, I decided to listen to him until the end. He said he had not been given enough functions in the block where he had been placed, that he had been said to be ideologically-politically insufficient, he had been overlooked and was, consequently, seeking a transfer to another prison. He was rather stressed. He was mistaken on some issues, but he was not wrong about everything. Unfortunately, some "intellectual" type comrades have such attitudes. I said that in spite of everything, leaving was not a solution, and that he should remain here and wage a struggle against attitudes he considered erroneous. He didn't oppose what I said, but made no comment.

Block 8
17 August 1996

As we had postponed the 15 August celebrations until today, we did not get up for morning exercises. At 09.00, we assembled in the exercise yard. The stage had been prepared. After the choir had sung a few folk songs, the nine-person folk dance group put on its costumes and we took to the stage. After our first dance, messages from our other blocks and other organisations were read out. Some solos were also intermingled. With short sketches, the atmosphere livened up. After a quiz between groups, we performed a collective halay.

In the evening, after the doors had been closed, we continued in the format of reminiscence-conversation. With fruit and some nuts being distributed to everyone, it was a different night. Under these conditions, we cannot always find fruit so that, when there is an apple, it becomes like a ceremony. A pleasant atmosphere was created.

The Hakis, Mazlums, Kemals, Hayris and Zilans were present in every moment today. We were together with them and the guerrillas. Although they are not amongst us, we feel their presence at every moment. Just as we feel the presence of the guerrillas, our guarantee of life…

Block 8
18 August 1996

Today, our month-long voluntary giving up smoking campaign began. It's a joint decision we take at the conference we hold every year. It's voluntary, but generally, people feel the necessity of participating. To not participate is perceived as a lack of willpower. The aim here is both to demonstrate the strength of willpower and to make economic savings. For every addicted comrade is given ten cigarettes a day. This is a serious burden on the communal budget, such that more is spent on cigarettes than food. When the conditions of our nourishment are taken into consideration, this sort of campaign gains importance.

Of the 40 people in our block, only four are not taking part. These comrades will find it difficult during the campaign, as they will not be able to smoke everywhere, as that will draw attention to themselves.

We collectively read the central commune's article on the campaign. We reiterated the willpower issues that need to be observed, as this is a matter of a struggle of will for the individual. To demonstrate weakness on this matter will open the door to other weaknesses. For, in the past, comrades who didn't give their name during months of interrogation by police and soldiers showed weakness in prison on the subject of cigarettes. A comrade who experiences this will constantly feel low.

Anticipating that the restrictions on rights introduced by the prison authorities will continue, we have made some preparations. These are:

Externally:

1. Our representatives will write petitions to meet with the prosecutor.
2. Petitions bearing the signatures of all comrades will be sent to the prosecutor, ministry, and Prime Minister's office.
3. Our families will issue a press statement. On Wednesday and Thursday, they will go as a group to the prosecutor.
4. We will ask the prisons monitoring committee to come to Aydın.
5. In addition to the democratic mass organisations being aware of the situation, they will be asked to send delegations.
6. Steps will be taken to ensure all the families are aware of the situation. Efforts will be made to ensure it is not limited to just a few certain families.
7. A group of families will meet the prison authorities and ask for representatives to be consulted.

Internally:

1. At certain times, the doors will be banged, and slogans shouted.
2. Three days a week, on visiting days, the entire prison will particularly shout the slogans, "Down with Fascism!", "Repression cannot cow us!", "End the isolation!".
3. On 21 August, when the guards enter the first block for morning roll call, they will be met with a slogan in the exercise yard.
4. Regarding relationships with the prison authorities, at every opportunity the intercession of representatives will be asked for.
5. For the first two days before the representatives come, no block will accept the meal wagon.
6. On certain days, 15 comrades in every block will write petitions to the prison governor requesting a meeting. If representatives are not being accepted as interlocutors, 15 comrades from every block will listen to the problems and demands.
7. In order to go as guests to visit other blocks on Saturdays and Sundays, block 6 will write a petition.

In today's *Hürriyet* newspaper, the ministry's latest instructions were discussed. Sporting activities have apparently been banned. From now on, the prison authorities will organise the composition of blocks, not the inmates.

We were expecting restrictions and bans to continue.

Today, morning soup was a strange şehriye. They must have put something in it as everyone was weary and exhausted throughout the day. People seemed to be half asleep. This is a rare occurrence. Consequently, the decision was taken that, in all our blocks, those who wished could go to bed at 22.00.

Block 8
21 August 1996

When I woke up this morning, my wristwatch was missing. I must have felt unwell and taken it off in my sleep.

Until noon, I both kept watch at the lower door and prepared for the seminar, "ESCAPING THE ENVIRONMENT, FLEEING TO THE ENEMY."

We always have a comrade on watch at the entry door. On the other side of the door, a guard waits. Two separate understandings and two separate worlds on either side of the door.

In the afternoon, I attended the philosophy class. Due to the debate, it went on until 5pm. Following that, we attended the Kurdish class for an hour.

They said they would close the exercise yard door early this evening. We went out at that time and took a stand for 10-15 minutes. We decided to insist on our representatives being present. Of course, we took the precaution of leaving a look-out in the dormitory and one in the dining hall, as you can't trust the enemy. They might take something, or "leave something," or if we stay outside for a long time, we might feel a need. It's even necessary to take precautions in case they shut the exercise yard door on us.

As they waited a long time in the other blocks, it was late by the time they reached our block.

Today was visiting day. For the first time, they allowed in stew that families had brought for us. For the special war to do this, when introducing restrictions in all areas, this is an insidious step. It is clear what the purpose of this "flexible" approach is. They want to ignore our main demands by distracting us with economic or basic issues. This is a reflection of the depth of steps taken regarding the prisons.

The clashes that have broken out again between the PUK and the KDP are continuing. I think this time imperialism and Turkey are using Talabani a little. I assume that recent meetings between the PKK and KDP have upset them.

It is a step against Iran-Syria-PKK having similar views on certain points. Also, steps towards the establishment of institutions in South Kurdistan has led to fears that "the foundations of a Kurdish state are being set down." Even those who appear to be supporting the Kurds do not want the Kurds to establish their own institutions. The one thing they want is for the Kurds to be fighters of their colonising states, not of their own country. If this is not happening, they incite conflict between Kurdish groups. Historically, that is what they have always done, but the PKK has demolished all these calculations. This time, the plan of the colonialist states will not work.

Block 8

22 August 1996

In the first block the guards entered in a herd to carry out a roll call, they were confronted with slogans. All the blocks that heard the noise joined in with the slogans. For a moment, the whole prison reverberated.

When they came to our block, the same thing happened. The anger of the guards could be seen in their eyes, but they looked on and didn't say a word before leaving.

While in the visiting area, the time for slogans arrived, and we joined in from there. There was a large crowd of visitors. There was a really different atmosphere. It was a good sensation to feel their support.

When I looked out of the window of the visiting area, I saw comrade Celalettin in the exercise yard of block 1. We held a short meeting through the bars. I gather the prosecutor phoned the prison governor. The governor said he would resolve the problems on Monday and meet the representatives. When comrade Celalettin said, "I need to go round the blocks to speak to comrades," they gave him permission to go round our blocks.

After the meeting on Monday, we will review our action plan.

Today, the soldiers who are the party's prisoners appeared on TV. Their way of speaking has changed. That was the first thing I noticed.

Block 8

26 August 1996

As I was unable to finish it last night, I was typing up the section of the 4th UKK on prisons until 9 this morning. As we read the conference analysis, we realise once again how heavy our responsibilities are. If we can respond to the expectations of the party, many problems will resolve themselves.

Although today is our bath day, we had to sit together until noon, as there were documents and minutes we had to read.

The section on comrade Serho was striking. We had presented his latest practice with a briefing to his block, as his situation is no longer acceptable. As a result of a narrowing of his thinking and his insufficiencies, he has created scenarios in his head. In addition to not seeing his own responsibility, his explanation to the structure is provocative…

With a typical Kemalist logic, he says, "Apres moi le deluge." He is trying to claim lack of organisation justifies confusing the structure. I am angry with myself for offering him individual support in the past. I was very naïve and hasty. He didn't deserve such value and party authority.

I was even more surprised when I saw the assessments and proposals of his block comrades. Despite a large majority of them saying, "His practice is a crime," they only proposed a one-week sanction. A worrying and opportunistic approach. Even in less serious situations, they propose sterner sanctions. These double standards further demoralised me. People should be more principled.

The representative comrade has met the prosecutor. He said, "If I accept your demands, I will be at variance with the ministry's circular, and they will put me on trial." As the other representatives had not been called, the comrade left without discussion. It was good that he took a stand, because they want to weaken us through distraction and demagogy.

Block 8
28 August 1996

Despite it not being our visiting day today, I was called for a visit. I realised there were people who had obtained permission to come. I had a quick shave and went there. Comrade Ibrahim was there with his daughter-in-law. His nervousness and shyness was immediately apparent. He is receiving physical treatment. He also reflected his tendency, albeit indirectly. We repeated that we could not approve him for the legal sphere. The fact there is a vacancy cannot be justification. Furthermore, the police are sure to be monitoring him at this time.

As I hadn't seen lots of the comrades for a long time, I stayed there until the end of the visiting period. It was a good "open visit."

Block 8
29 August 1996

Today, comrade Aziz, who had only just been released from here, came to visit. The visiting area was more crowded than yesterday. To see Aziz's enthusiasm and eagerness was pleasing. He was in the legal sphere, and it is clear he is doing all he can.

Since I felt tired after yesterday, I returned to the block at around 15.00.

When a group of families asked for a meeting with the authorities, they were a bit obstructive. After we intervened, they accepted. I gather the latter demanded representatives be accepted as interlocutors, and that solutions be found to problems.

As always, the efforts of a few conscious families.

For two days now, the television channels are showing lots of footage of captured soldiers in coverage of the delegation going to the ZAP camp.

The delegation led by Fetullah Erbaş was met with a military ceremony in the guerrilla area. It was shown on the screen.

The majority of the large guerrilla group were women. The uniforms and weapons of all of them were spotless. They all looked keen and active. Comrade Duran Kalkan said, "We won't release the captured soldiers as an official interlocutor delegation has not come," but I am led to understand that they will be released on 1 September, World Peace Day.

There were two mothers of soldiers on the delegation. There was lots of footage of them embracing their sons and them sobbing. They used it…

In a word, it was heart-breaking.

Comrade Duran seemed to have lost weight. Comrade Rıza Altun was alongside him. When the delegation left, the two mothers stayed behind. They said they wouldn't abandon their children. The comrades must have given permission, as no one objected.

The Turkish press reacted, using headlines like, "The PKK's game" and "They used the delegation."

Block 8
1 September 1996

Our 15-day protest action programme ended today. Today, we read through the second 15-day programme. Apart from some diversification in the section on internal and external, it is almost the same. Additionally:

* Going to the sick bay collectively,
* Protesting visiting,
* Not placing the meal wagons in the corridor,
* Blocks to request a meeting with the governor with the same demand at every hour; in the event of his not turning up, ten minutes of banging the doors;
* Banging the doors for ten minutes at midnight;
* Opening the grilles of the blocks on the way to the bath house;

* Drawing curtains over the windows of the block at certain times in order to prevent the guards seeing inside (this irritates them a lot).

Block 8
3 September 1996

On the way to the bath house yesterday, we moved towards the grilles. The guards and the prison authorities were unprepared. With a perfect guerrilla tactic, the corridors were "occupied." The grilles of blocks 2, 3 and 9, and all the windows looking on to the exercise yard of block 2 were opened. Once the guards had got over their surprise, there was a brief argument and scuffle. As our action had been successful, we didn't stay long in the corridor.

They had taken precautions before block 9-13 went to the bath house. We were all vigilant. We heard a melee and shouting in the corridor. When they opened the grille of our block, the guards intervened and attempted to close it. As I tried to stop it being closed from the inside, my fingers were between the slats and I almost lost the ends of my fingers.

After the comrades had gone into their blocks, the guards broke a window looking onto the exercise yard of block 2 in their anger. I expect they will make us pay for it.

Block 8
4 September 1996

As grilles have been targeted on the way back from the bath house, the authorities have taken steps. But today, as block 6-14 were on the way, they changed tactics and made a move. The guards were taken by surprise. They must have been very annoyed, as we could hear them grumbling in the corridor.

After things had calmed down a little, when the next group were on their way for a bath, they tried to get to the grilles. They [the prisoners] were roughed up, as the guards had taken more precautions. All the blocks protested when they heard the assault, by banging on the doors. The walls of the whole prison shook.

A cloud of dust covered everything.

Today, they didn't take anyone to the sick bay, as 250 people had written a petition requesting to see a doctor. The authorities expressed their disquiet about this, which means it is effective.

According to our prisons internal coordination, there are similar restrictions in eight or nine other prisons. In their message, they say, "Avoid limitless hunger strikes and continue with effective peaceful protests. In the event of restrictions continuing, we will develop a general stance."

In the coming period, our active-resistance stance will be prioritised.

Yesterday, Akın Birdal from the Human Rights Association was remanded in custody for "aiding and abetting" the PKK. They have again made a blunder. This state enjoys exposing and humiliating itself. They are using his visit to the camp to meet the captured soldiers as an excuse.

The humanitarian sector, in particular, will react to this. It is clear that Turkey will have a hard time.

There are very serious developments in South Kurdistan. Several states have made active interventions there.

Initially, Iranian forces carried out attacks on the KDP. And, of course, at that time, there were clashes between the KDP and the PUK. Iraqi forces that saw Iran carry out an operation in support of the PUK entered Erbil, after a six-year absence, with the KDP. The PUK's influence was broken, Talabani's wife and politburo members were arrested. After the city had fallen, Iraqi forces withdrew.

In another development, the US bombed Iraqi cities, mentioning this situation as a justification.

Meanwhile, leader Apo said on BBC yesterday that we did not accept intervention by any state, making a strong appeal to Barzani and Talabani. He said that, in the event attacks and clashes did not stop, we would move into action.

Talabani welcomed this appeal.

As for Turkey, it is preparing to enter the South…

The history of the Kurds is unfortunately being repeated. Whenever the Kurds have achieved some power, and whenever external conditions are favourable, an environment of conflict is created by mobilising some Kurds for internal treachery. That is what is happening today. In the South, steps are being taken towards establishing a state. There are efforts being made for national unity under the leadership of our party. The PKK's influence there, and its steps towards national unity, was the only pretext.

In this period, such internal conflict and bombs raining down will do us a lot of harm.

In the last three days, the special war has talked about the deaths of soldiers. It is said that 10 soldiers are dying a day.

This news may be the reason for the attack on the South.

On account of the complicated relations in the Middle East, it is not clear who is supporting whom, and who is clashing with whom. There are so many contradictions and misleading images. The just struggle of peoples will defeat these dirty relations.

These days, there is a general atmosphere of intolerance and insensitivity amongst comrades. The increase in these attitudes both pains and angers me. Outbursts can occur over the most trifling things. There may be various reasons for it, but there is a pervading tension. If it cannot be overcome, it may lead to serious consequences. It is a situation that is unbecoming for comrades sharing prison conditions. A normally quiet comrade may suddenly react in an excessive way. Sometimes, the body rebels against the conditions.

Block 8
6 September 1996

The fact we are banging the doors every hour on the hour must have discomfited the authorities, as they have summoned comrade Celalettin and the other representatives. I gather they met with the governor for close to an hour. He changed his tune a little, saying, "The restrictions are not ours" etc. During the meeting, a note was placed on the governor's desk, one sentence of which read, "They will no longer bang the doors." After the governor had read the note, he ended the meeting.

They are simply idiots. Normally, the doors were to have been banged until three in the morning. When it was sensed that the authorities were making certain proactive preparations, the doors were not banged at that hour. Most probably, the guards listened to this change in the blocks and immediately reported it to the governor. They assumed we had completely ended the action.

In order to show them they were wrong, all the prison doors began to be beaten at 18.00. They immediately summoned all the representatives. While the governor apparently behaved more cautiously with the older representatives, he used a more threatening tone when addressing the new comrades. He mentioned soldiers in an effort to intimidate them, although the new comrades are more strident and impatient. The governor is once again mistaken.

After the meeting, comrade Celalettin was permitted to go round all the blocks. He informed all of our blocks.

Block 8
10 September 1996

THE DILEMMA THAT KURDS EXPERIENCE DURING EVERY PERIOD

Today, the KDP took control of Suleimani province. Fierce clashes with the PUK are continuing. Suleimani was Talabani's headquarters. Seeing an exodus of armed Peshmerga heading towards the Iranian border is irritating.

People shouldn't be so eager to fight their brothers. As the PUK peshmerga come under pressure, they are moving towards Iran.

The tragedy of the Kurds...

Once again, they are destroying each other.

Once again, Kurds are becoming refugees in their own lands.

It is being said that Barzani has reached agreement with Iraq on the subject of autonomy.

Once Talabani has been liquidated or weakened, the KDP will attack the PKK.

It is the Kurds' ages-old dilemma.

If the two groups hadn't clashed, and if they had acted in unison, all the conditions existed for the establishment of a state in the South.

It is being said that Talabani has taken refuge in Iran. The Turkish special war channels are gleefully presenting this news.

Today, we completed our regular meeting evaluation. Our 45-day routine programme has been clarified. During this period, what the blocks will do is planned. This arranges everything, from the time we get up in the morning until the sleeping time at night. Although, throughout the year from conference to conference, it is clear what is to be done as a goal, this is all clarified in 45-day segments. That is, we do not spend our time idly in prison as assumed outside. Activities that appear difficult keep us fit both physically and as regards morale.

Block 8
14 September 1996
THE LAST LETTER FROM THE IMMORTAL HANDAN

Our forum based on the latest developments in South Kurdistan has begun. I don't know how long the assessments and debates will go on for.

Out of necessity, a proposal to make the sleeping time earlier at 23.00 was put to the structure for approval. As it will enable people to go to bed an hour earlier, I think a large majority will be in favour.

After Y. had withdrawn from all activities, a narrow platform was made in his block, and he rested there. Without elaborating on the real problems, he brushed it aside, saying, "That's it for me." The minutes of the meeting were presented with explanations to his block structure. No one approved of his attitude. The majority view is, "This attitude is unacceptable, when his past is taken into consideration, this is a betrayal. It is not acceptable for him to withdraw while people are making a decision about him."

Since before being arrested he held a leading position in the Aegean region, and when in Buca prison also held a high position there, his situation was referred to our entire prison structure. The majority were of the opinion that "it should be passed on to the prisons' internal coordination and may a decision be taken accordingly."

Our structure here will in no way accept a person's arbitrary attitude, haughtiness, and certainly not feudal superiority, whatever his position. To have a position with us means to be like one of those in the structure and be more self-sacrificing. As long as you strive, you will earn respect.

Ideas and proposals of the general structure regarding the stance we should adopt towards the prison authorities' latest restrictions were received.

The proposal for coordinated and simultaneous actions with other prisons was prominent...

There is an envelope I have stuck between the pages of my journal. It catches my eye every time I open it, ... But I don't open the envelope, because I recall the contents very well. The "examined" stamp on the envelope is always showing. There are two letters in the envelope written at different times. Along with a little personality analysis and self-criticism is a note informing an elder brother, a comrade...

I know the writer very well, although we were unable to spend much time together. I remember when she was little, and her birth in Antep (I think it was 1977). First, she was a sister, the beloved little sister. Then a comrade...

I don't remember the history of her comradeship. As soon as she began to talk, she knew us and the safe house. She grew up in the natural atmosphere of these relations. Later on, she was a regular visitor. Her life was built between the home and the prison. But it was not humdrum. As she became acquainted with free people and free life, she matured early and new subjects began to enter her field of interest.

I last saw her during the open visit in May 1990. She came with her older sister, Rahşan. It was like a farewell visit...

I didn't see her again. But I have the hope that we will meet again in a free environment. Just as she said.

There are dozens of other letters she wrote. But these two letters I have carefully preserved have a different importance. They have more of a spiritual value. In the first, she wrote about her urban activities, in the second she wrote during the days she was to go to the mountain peaks, the inaccessible peaks where falcons soar, in the country for which she had yearned.

Both letters had been written in a graph notebook. I received the first letter when I was in block 6 three years ago.

14 July 1993, Istanbul.

My dear brother,

I haven't been able to write to you for a long time. I don't know how to begin. For five months I haven't read your warm sentences. I read the letter you sent to a comrade, but the sweet sentences full of yearning you wrote to me are something else. Even if we haven't written to each other, I have thought about you and what you wrote. It's not possible for me to forget those sincere sentences. It is now 2 o'clock in the morning and I can't sleep. My memories of the times we shared came back to me, so I thought I would write a few lines to my dear brother. We shared a lot. We had a lovely friendship. And this friendship will continue. Even if at the moment we cannot share our joy and our sadness, I still feel you are always beside me. In the same way I will be beside you.

At the moment I am working with the relatives in the city (she is talking about the fraternal party, the Revolutionary People's Party, in Istanbul). But this is not the place I want to be. I will go to see my big brother and big sister (she means the rural area and the guerrillas). My decision is final. Here does not meet my wishes. I've worked here for five months, but it's not right for me.

My dear, like in the past, I'm writing to musical accompaniment. My health is good. I rang mum and spoke to her. I know you won't fail to write to her. I hope that one day we will meet and drink tea together. This will definitely happen. My dear, in future, I might not be able to write to you. I won't have the opportunity. But you will always be in my thoughts.

I saw your recent photo with a beard. You looked like dad. For me, you have a lot in common. I love both of you. And you are both precious to me and I won't forget you. The affection and loyalty I feel for him I also feel for you.

My dear, I am concluding my letter. I kiss you on your cheeks. Look after yourself. It has made me happy to write to you. I kiss you on your cheeks. Love, Handan.

I have written 30 June 1994 on the envelope containing the second letter. I gather she was only able to post it after carrying it with her for three weeks. After mentioning being extremely attached to some people, others' treachery and the shock that it created, she wrote that she would no longer be able to write and that our mother had gone to Britain. And also, "I'm going to Rahşan, perhaps I'll see my elder brother too. Look after yourself well. I send lots of hugs. Keep my love. I will carry your love in my heart.... With all my love, Handan."

This was her last letter. Perhaps she wrote, but it didn't reach me.

What a coincidence. Today I mention Handan, on the day we read the magazine article about comrades Hüseyin Hüsnü Eroğlu and Mehmet Yalçınkaya, who were martyred at the entrance here in 1989. I again descended into the passages of the past. Sometimes I grieved, sometimes I felt sad. It was as if they were both alongside me.

Immediately after they were martyred, prisoners' families went to comrade Yalçınkaya's grave in his village in Halfeti. His family were very pleased.

Everyone gathered around the grave. I think Handan was around 12 years old. As she was the youngest there, she got them to stand up for a minute's silence. Then she said, "Comrade Mehmet, we will continue your struggle. We will carry your gun. You may rest. I give you my word, comrade."

The people there were really affected. From the grave they went to an apple tree Mehmet had planted. There they listened to the family talk about Yalçınkaya. They looked lovingly at the tree, as the comrade's love and effort had gone into giving it life.

Yes, she kept her promise to the comrade. She took up his gun. She was small, but her ambition was large.

She chose the place where she would be happiest. Her happiness is also my happiness. I don't know if she is alive at this moment, but the one thing I do know is that our mother has not given up on her. I gather she has gone as far as applying to the party for her to be taken from the conflict zone to Europe. I understand her as a mother. I don't know what their answer was, but I know that Handan would not accept it. She made her choice three years ago. When Rahşan left, she said, "I want to go too. I have studied as much as her. I'm more active." At that time, I put it down to childish jealousy. I was wrong...

I believe that, as she wrote, she has taken our love with her to that beautiful land.

Block 8
18 September 1996

Our protests at the removal of rights are continuing. We walked back and forth in the exercise yard in every block, creating difficulties for them when they came to conduct the morning roll call. They found it very hard in the first block with everyone walking at the same time. By the time they got to us, they were well prepared. They came into the exercise yard with close to a hundred guards. They swiftly divided the exercise yard into five or six parts and did a count while preventing people moving from section to section. We made it difficult for them and responded verbally. They left without escalating the situation. It was amusing. There were nearly three guards to every prisoner.

When it was the turn of block 4, we heard the sound of slogans. At the same moment, the slogan, "Human Dignity will Defeat Torture" was heard from all blocks. When some comrades started striking the doors in an uncontrolled way, we stopped them, as we didn't want the noise to drown out the sound of the slogans.

At the same time, we were trying to understand what was happening in the main corridor. It was full of guards. They had roughed up some comrades in block 4. A representative comrade had immediately intervened.

Today, two comrades from block 7-15 were due to go out to get binding for a book, but they were prevented from doing so. They are responding to our protest stance.

The news some comrades have been called to see their lawyers has spread from block to block. The first thing that occurs to us is that someone has been sent into exile. When we heard five lawyers had arrived, they were met and spoken to.

In the afternoon, comrade Celalettin came to our block. A wave of satisfaction formed in the structure. It was a result obtained through resistance. He gave us a brief update and left. We heard there was a large crowd of visitors waiting and that, with the attack on block 4 and our refusal to go to the visiting area, things had been difficult for the authorities.

This awareness demonstrated by all the comrades is pleasing…

After lunch, we held a short meeting with the block structure. After providing an update, we reminded comrades to be calm, to avoid individualistic issues, abide by the established programme, and be careful about arguments with guards at the doors. The two-page instruction send by our prison administration drawing attention to organisation was also read out.

Comrades can be excitable and panicky. In the morning situation, even a barricade was proposed. This is not our form of action. Besides, if you build a barricade, what will be the outcome?

We learned that our visitors are a large group. Our Izmir prison families' association had arranged five or six vehicles and filled them. Our not going to the visiting area last week has created a certain awareness. Coming in such numbers will also have an effect on the prison authorities.

I gather that when visiting ended at 17.00, some families reacted and did not want to leave. After some tension, comrades vacated the area.

We learned that three or four comrades in block 4 were injured by truncheon blows. It was a calculated assault. They tested us. If there hadn't been such a reaction, they would have escalated measures. As our reaction and that of the families was so strong, they took a step back. Of course it is temporary. Restrictions will emerge in a different form.

When they came to close the exercise yard door in the evening, we all went out into the exercise yard, except the look-outs. While five or six comrades who had been selected spoke to the officer in charge, the rest of us continued walking back and forth. Such delaying tactics will be employed in all blocks. 30 minutes later, we began to go inside. As I passed the door, the head guard looked me in the eyes and said, "Ali, you're lagging behind." This was a clear signal. I replied, "The comrades are doing what's necessary," as I went inside.

We entertained ourselves in the evening. The sound of applause and folk songs came from the blocks.

At 23.30, the sound of a slogan was heard. This was followed by a banging on the doors. The prison was shaking.

At the moment it is 03.30. Soon, the guards will come and close the dining hall door. They are continuing to do a search at every closure. We have a comrade on look-out. Today Hasan Kasım will be there. He has tied his trainers tightly and is waiting. Apart from us, everyone is asleep. The block is silent.

It's gradually cooling down as dawn approaches. When I awoke at 01.00, I was sweating.

Today, I read a 25-page essay. Az wrote it. After detailing his life story at length, he says he can't remain with us. I gather he won't return to the block after going for a visit. He doesn't want his degenerate relationships touched. He is known to have been involved with three or four women. When he became entangled with one outside and the comrades asked him to end it, he made such a choice.

What a meaningless life preference. A single attachment... And this attachment has enslaved both you and her. For the sake of a basic attachment escaping from the reality of the people and the opportunity to become human.

On reading the banalities he had written, I was angry with myself. We had opposed the comrades who at the outset had said, "Let's not have him amongst us," adding he was incorrigible. Thinking we could win him over, we embarked on a vain expectation.

I immediately wrote a note suggesting measures be taken, as people who leave our environment in this way are open to all manner of exploitation. "I will not bow my head to the enemy in any circumstances" is an empty boast.

Both run to the enemy and say you won't surrender to him. This is not realistic, it is self-deception.

Today, the most serious development outside was the raid on MED-TV. Its broadcasts have been halted. Close to 60 people were arrested. A broad operation centred on Belgium and Britain was carried out. Many associations were also raided. It will be difficult, but they will restart broadcasts.

Block 8

20 September 1996

We submitted a collective complaint concerning the prison governors and the prosecutor.

The representatives also wrote one for a meeting…

Block 8

21 September 1996

As they didn't allow one of our blocks to go to another block for sporting activities, we shouted slogans and banged the doors at 09.00. Immediately before the midnight roll call, we put out all the lights. In a moment, everywhere was pitch black. Naturally, as it was the first time we had carried out such a protest, we began to wait. Everyone was dressed and alert. After 30 minutes had passed, around 100 guards came in. They had torches and a ladder. They scaled the ladder and switched on the lights. Then, they carried out a roll call and left in silence.

They had come well prepared.

When we went downstairs, we saw they had hurled the sandals all over the place. They had also broken a stool in the opposite block. They took out their anger on our possessions, although they seemed not to be treating the protest seriously. This is a nullifying tactic. A classic special war tactic…

Block 8

23 September 1996

There was a large notice in *Demokrasi* today, jointly signed by all the political movements, including ours. After explaining what has been going on, there was a demand for an end to restrictions and for the state/ministries to abide by agreements, as well as a warning of a three-day hunger strike involving all political prisoners beginning on 27 September. As all movements will take part, it means there will be around 15,000 prisoners on hunger strike at the same time. A serious stance and the presage of more comprehensive actions.

S. K., who had left our environment, has written a request to the prison authorities to return. When the guards forwarded it to us, we said, "Pass it on to the representative comrade." They allowed comrade Celalettin to speak to him this afternoon. He's apparently in a wretched state. He said, "I've come to my senses. I regret it." We said, "It's early, let him remain there and comprehend his situation." Before he went, we told him 20 times, but he insisted on leaving. This is what self-humiliation is. It is also not safe to take him back if we are unsure.

Block 8
25 September 1996
THE SLAUGHTER OF 10 PRISONERS IN THE CORRIDOR

Last night, after 22.00, when we heard slogans being shouted and doors banged in the DS block, we realised there had been an attack somewhere. About half an hour later, the comrades in block 9-13 told us: "We heard on the TV there has been an attack in Diyarbakır prison. Seven martyrs and 12 comrades seriously injured." We immediately passed on the news to other comrades in the administration. The other blocks had not yet heard about it.

While searching through all the TV channels, we came across a programme about MED-TV on 32nd Day. We were very pleased to be able to watch it. It was as if the studio had been covered in an electronic web. Being unable to watch MED-TV is very depressing.

We have learned the number of martyrs is eight. They wanted to transfer 14 comrades to Antep. When the comrades refused to go, they were savagely attacked. All the comrades killed had their heads smashed in with cudgels. And in the main corridor. Even after the 12 September military coup, not so many people were killed in prisons in a single attack. As the special war is helpless against the guerrillas, it is striking out in the prisons. The fact it happened in Diyarbakır is also significant. With this attack, a message is being sent to the party, the people, and prisoners. The intention of this attack is to break the Diyarbakır effect.

At 10.00, a minute's silence was observed in all our blocks, and, after a statement was read out, the following slogans were shouted:

"The Amed Martyrs are Immortal!"

"Long Live our Amed Resistance!"

"Down with the Special War!"

"Long Live Leader Apo!"

Towards evening, the number of those who died reached 10. The situation of those who were seriously injured is critical.

At 15.00, 18.00, and 23.00, slogans were shouted and doors banged.

All our blocks held night meetings. The agenda was the Diyarbakır attack. All the comrades have a heightened awareness.

The fact that so many comrades were slaughtered in a single attack is a sign that there will be similar attacks in the coming period.

Today, none of our blocks engaged in sporting activities. A sense of grief and silent anger is present.

As far as we have been able to establish, the names of those who died are as follows:

Rıdvan BULUT
Erkan PERİŞAN
Hakkı TEKİN
Cemal ÇAM
Nimet ÇAKMAK
Ahmet ÇELİK
Mehmet ASLAN
Kadir DEMİR
Edip DİREKÇİ
M. Sabri GÜMÜŞ

Block 8
27 September 1996

THEY EVEN SLAUGHTER PRISONERS ON THE WAY TO HOSPITAL

The first day.

We have started a hunger strike in protest at the attack.

Details of the attack in Diyarbakır have begun to arrive.

When the comrades were on their way to the visiting area, they were initially subjected to a verbal attack and subsequently to a physical attack from the block housing turncoats. It was obviously a set-up. The authorities were ready for it. That is clear from the way things developed.

On their return from the visiting area, the comrades were corralled and locked in between two gangs. After being kept waiting for five hours, they were told they were to be transferred. On rejecting this, the doors were opened and both gangs attacked them. They attacked with pickaxe handles and rifle butts, taking aim at the head. Some of the victims also had knife wounds on their bodies.

It was definitely an attack intending to cause fatalities.

According to *Demokrasi* newspaper, an eye-witness said, "They brought three people to the hospital. We took two gravely wounded people into the emergency section. When we went to get the third person, the police and soldiers said, 'He died in the vehicle,' but he was not seriously injured."

The fact that comrades were slaughtered in front of the hospital demonstrates the extent and indifference of the attack.

And, of course, the real face of our enemy…

DS has removed its barricade. They have ended it centrally.

After the 30th of this month, all prisons will refuse to go for visits, to hospitals, and to courts for a week. Since there are around 12 thousand of us, the extent of this is clear. In particular, the court protest will be effective.

It has been announced that the governor of Diyarbakır prison and five guards have been suspended. It's just deception and misleading. Everyone knows that the order for such an attack came from way above the governor. It was a central decision. The dimensions of the attack prove that.

The reason for the recent hectic days here has become clear. Before there were no ordinary prisoners here. They have begun to bring them in a few at a time. I think they will put them in the blocks near the kitchen.

Most of the comrades slept today as there were no compulsory activities such as sport or education. It was as if they had been longing to sleep…

Block 8
28 September 1996

The second day.

In news today, it is said that all PKK prisoners have begun a limitless hunger strike. The main demands are:

1. That international organisations go to Diyarbakır to investigate and establish those responsible.
2. An end to torture, provocations, and coersion of prisoners into become informers. Turncoats should be moved away from blocks close to our blocks.
3. Conditions in prisons to be made appropriate to human dignity.
4. An end to the arbitrary transfer of prisoners whose trials are in progress.

During the action, no one will go to court.

After reading the notice, there was some correspondence with the administration. We will take part in turn in groups.

Comrades who smoke will be given rolled cigarettes during the hunger strike, as tobacco makes it more difficult.

Last night, in a dream, my brother Cemal came to visit me. But we were outside. There was a road below the old garages in Antep. There was a minibus stop before the turn off to the Akyol police station. Right next to it was a café, bakery, grocery shop, etc. As we walked along the pavement, we were discussing how he travelled to visit me. We turned right and sat on a bench, (It's interesting that the bench was like the ones we have in prison).

Meanwhile, I said to Cemal, "You wouldn't decide to visit me just like that. Or did mum send you money for the fare?"

Cemal smiled bashfully.

"Yes, she sent 25 marks, and told me to visit Ali."

"25 marks is 1,500,000. Is that enough? (I don't know what rate I am using to calculate the amount)."

"No, it's not enough. It costs twice as much."

The quirkiness of our dreams… It's normal for dreams in prison to be like this. Cemal is in Izmit and I'm in Aydın prison, but the scene is Antep of 16 years ago…

According to the TV news, three comrades in Bayrampaşa prison in Istanbul, one of them a woman, set fire to themselves in protest at the massacre in Diyarbakır. They were taken to hospital.

Block 8
29 September 1996

The third day. The programme here has been finalised. All comrades in blocks 7-15 and 9-13, apart from the sick, elderly and those who won't be able to do it, will turn the action into a limitless one.

The instruction regarding the manner of life and activity during the action was read out.

Our other blocks ended their hunger strike towards evening. They will lend support in the future in sequence.

After the evening meal, we did halay collectively in the exercise yard. Then, folk songs were sung. But there was sadness in all the songs. A sadness wishing to be sent afar. If there was a breeze, that would do it…

Our folk songs have been moulded by pain and sadness, just like the lives of Kurds. When they are sung, they carry you far away. As if to say, "I don't belong here." Like a lost human being chained in his own lands. But it is still put into words.

Today I took my blanket and jacket into the exercise yard to air them.

Despite not sleeping until four in the morning, I still had a dream. We had gone to one of the summer cinemas in Antep. It was in the garden of the old people's home. The cinema was familiar, but the place was different. That was our neighbourhood. There was no cinema in that garden. When I was a child, we used to have picnics there. The rows of seats in the cinema began to fill up fast. Apart from lots of families, A.z. from here was there. I recalled his problems and had to force myself to say hello to him.

As I was tussling with someone outside the cinema, I woke up. I was annoyed. I felt stressed and couldn't get to sleep again. I don't remember how I eventually dropped off.

The dreams I have at different times are similar. Even the places I'm in are usually the same places.

Block 8

30 September 1996

We sent collective petitions to several places to protest at the Diyarbakır massacre.

Being Monday, they carried out a search. We were expecting it. After the search, they took away an oven and two pans. I assume they did it to incite us. We didn't get wound up, as we have more serious things to think about.

In the afternoon, we gave the place a good wash. Following this, we left the block for a bath. As we went along the corridor, we realised there were people in the isolation cells, so we opened the grilles and said hello to them. They were ordinary offenders. The authorities must have warned them about conversing with us, as they were reluctant to speak to us. When the guards intervened, we didn't persist and closed the grilles. On the way back from the bath house, we noticed that the prisoners had been removed from the isolation cells.

At around 22.00, they told us that two comrades had been taken ill in block 7. One was on hunger strike. They asked us because of our stance of not going to hospital. It was said he should go to the sick bay.

Comrade R. T. has a kidney stone. As he's on hunger strike, he didn't allow intervention. He needs to have an injection. After some correspondence through notes, he was told, "If you want, have an injection. If necessary, you can give up the action."

It is not possible to agree with this, as emotions are getting in the way. Even being on a hunger strike is a risk. These risks are ordinary events.

Today, we learned about the Diyarbakır attack by reading an article written by a comrade who lived through it.

It's difficult to find the words to describe what happened.

People were openly threatened and pressured to become informers. Comrades were dragged to the visiting area and slaughtered. They were hit on the head and back in particular. Pieces of flesh were scattered to left and right.

Some comrades were killed after signals were given by guards. They were specially selected. Only two of the 30 people attacked agreed to become informers. All the other comrades put up a heroic resistance.

The attack definitely had external connections.

In a note sent to our block, we were asked if comrade SG had come. As the comrade is elderly, he had apparently got angry at some things. They had not been able to calm him down. When he started shouting and swearing, they said, "Either shut up or shove off." He then left the block, shouting and hollering.

I felt sad. How can you show the door to an elderly person? You have to manage the situation.

I gather he returned to the block a few hours later.

As comrade B. Orak's brother was arrested ten days ago in Amed with 10 or 11 patriots and then murdered and his body dumped, we sent the family a fax today. But the authorities sent it back to us, saying it was "suspicious." First, they arrest our people, then they torture them, fire bullets in their heads and dump them, and then they don't allow us to even share our pain.

WE MUST NOT FORGET...

Block 8
2 October 1996

We didn't go to the visiting area. DS also joined the protest. There must have been only a few visitors, as not much food arrived.

At 11.00 and 13.00, the entire prison shouted the slogans:

"The Amed Martyrs are Immortal!"

"Massacres will not Intimidate Us!"

"End the Isolation Measures!"

There have been barricades in the Çanakkale prison for three days. Comrades from the Turkish left have put a barricade in the corridor. Naturally, our lot are trapped. In the event of an attack, they will be the first target.

I have finished the short story I had begun and given it to the comrades to examine.

Block 8
5 October 1996

Many prisons have begun a limitless hunger strike according to *Demokrasi* newspaper. But it still hasn't mentioned Aydın.

In a statement from the ARGK in the Amed region, comrade Dr. Süleyman said, "To protest at the murder of defenceless civilians in the middle of the street and the slaughter of ten people in Diyarbakır, guerrillas will take action in all regions, and this will be more intensive in the Amed region."

Knowing there is a force outside that can issue such a statement is sufficient for us. If the enemy wishes, it can slaughter all of us in the prisons as a consequence of its impotence. Thousands of guerrillas who are full of energy and have vowed vengeance are always with us.

I woke up in the middle of the night with a cough. I think I have got a chill on the lungs again. After a dry cough, I bring up phlegm.

In my dream, I was arguing with people from DS. The ones on remand here were all there. We were in a weird place in Antep. It looked a bit like the old municipal passage, a bit like Antep's narrow streets, and was similar to the Ünaldı neighbourhood. I don't know if it's due to recent developments, but some DS members have mentioned their problems to us. I tell them it's better if they resolve their problems amongst themselves. When I ask them, "Is the administration mode of your organisation by committee?" they respond, "In the representation mode." Later, I see them lower down Karaçomak Baba Street, where our house is. They knock on the doors one by one. It's interesting. They are knocking on the doors with their shoes. I take a shoe and tell them, "If you hit the door with the heel, it makes more noise."

I'm asking them to do it just as we bang the doors in prison…

Block 8
7 October 1996
"THE KURDS SHOULD TAKE THEIR RIGHTFUL PLACE UNDER THE MIDDLE EASTERN SUN"

We notified who was to take part in the second group of hunger strikers, and we sent those who were to take part extra food on their last day. It's good for morale and they also deserve it.

The prison authorities have introduced new restrictions. People will apparently be taken one at a time to see lawyers. The lawyer of two comrades came, but when they were told "one at a time," they refused to go. It's reminiscent of the "savagery" time during the military coup period. At this stage, it is important for us to put our demands on the agenda. Tomorrow, we will submit them to our general structure for approval.

Today, Y. expressed the wish to end his political ties following a basic everyday problem that occurred in the block. His block raised the issue. Naturally, from that moment on, his existing situation was frozen as a precaution. Close to half of those in his block say, "Let him be thrown out of the environment," while the others say, "Let him be spoken to again and efforts made to persuade him." As in such situations, winning people over is the first option, he is being spoken to one last time on a narrow platform. Since efforts were made to protect him, despite more serious criticisms being made, he must have been persuaded, as he condemned his attitude. He will remain in the environment with his political ties severed. As he requested, after the action, he will go to a different block. But if he makes any more demands, he will be directly dismissed from the environment.

At a press conference during Erbakan's visit to Libya, Gaddafi said, "The Kurds should take their rightful place under the Middle Eastern sun." On this account, some parts of the Turkish press are raging against him. They cannot stomach such open support for the struggle of the Kurds.

I think they are using this to undermine the Refah Party and Erbakan, as they have used him as much as they are able.

Last night, I was woken up many times by my cough. Even the comrades were disturbed. I noticed that. Once I start coughing, it doesn't stop.

Today, I started to draw the 17 million my mother sent. If you have money with the office, they give it to you once a week.

Block 8
8 October 1996

This morning, while reading the *ARJIN* magazine we create here, we heard a shout from the corridor and immediately paused.

Soldiers wearing helmets and guards were swarming about, where the ordinary prisoners are being held. A short while later came the sound of metal doors being sawn. It appears they had set up a barricade. This was followed by their being tortured and stuffed into cells. From the corridor came the shout of "prison murderers." We immediately contacted the other blocks and suggested, "Let's shout slogans, let's not remain silent." Our administration did not approve our requests, saying, "We are involved in a protest action, we don't know what happened, it could be a provocation." We're not used to remaining silent at such moments, and it is hard to accept.

When we arrived at this prison, the same thing happened to us. They lined up on both sides of the corridor and attacked those passing. While walking between them, the blows rained down from the batons.

Although we don't know the actual reason, they may not have accepted certain restrictions imposed by the authorities.

Comrade Celalettin asked the authorities and they said, "It was just a fight." Towards evening, comrade Kemal went to the sick bay for an injection and saw six or seven prisoners who were injured.

Remaining silent has demoralised many comrades. In any event, it was necessary to support the ordinary inmates. Although they may not be organised, and their actions might just be a flare up, we shouldn't leave them on their own.

Our notice appeared in *Demokrasi* today. It was the size of a book cover under pictures of the ten comrades who were slaughtered in Amed. It was published in the name of comrades Şamil, Celalettin and Sait. It was well worth the ten million we paid for it…

Block 8

9 October 1996

IT IS HOW YOU LIVED THAT IS IMPORTANT, NOT HOW LONG YOU LIVED

I commemorate Che with respect and gratitude. He is alive today in our struggle.

According to *Hürriyet* newspaper, there are 48 injured prisoners. They injured the entire block in the attack. The attack was comprehensive and designed to destroy their willpower, to subdue them.

The prison authorities called comrade Celalettin to inform him that Istanbul and Bursa had ended their action. He replied, "We have no knowledge of that, and we have our own specific problems here." It will be necessary for us to evaluate the situation and adopt a stance.

This morning, as a voluntary group, we started to study a source on 'strategic-tactical leadership.'" We will strive as much as possible to have this education every day.

Today, I saw comrade Sarıkaya from the grille, and we had a short chat. I was really pleased.

Block 8

10 October 1996

Vedat Aydemir, who was one of the comrades who set themselves alight in Bayrampaşa prison, was martyred yesterday. After having a minute's silence at 10.30, we shouted slogans:

"Vedats don't die!"

"The Amed Martyrs are Immortal!"

"Long Live our Limitless Hunger Resistance!"

"Down With the Special War!"

"Long Live Leader Apo!"

A few hours later, we heard that comrade Hamdullah Şengüller had also been martyred.

It is difficult to know what they felt and thought before the action, but they both achieved the desired outcome.

They wanted it, and they attained it.

Wanting something is the key to succeeding.

Today, in *Demokrasi* newspaper, it was announced that the action has been ended in Bayrampaşa as agreement has been reached. The terms accepted are listed in a long article. It seems the main problems have been resolved. It looks better than Aydın's old status.

On reading the announcement, I immediately wrote a note, asking for it to be circulated and for no hasty decision to be taken.

As the prison authorities are really concerned, they summoned comrade Celalettin again today. He said, "We won't end our action until our specific demands here are met." The authorities are trying to achieve a fait accompli. They won't be able to resist for long, as the ministry has told them to achieve a resolution. Conditions favour us. There is also strong public opinion in our favour outside.

The injured ordinary prisoners wrote us a note telling us about the attack. The fact we didn't respond with slogans hurt us again.

When comrade Şehmus's mother came to visit, she was verbally attacked by a female guard. It's the second time it's happened. Naturally, we reacted. In order not to remain silent, we immediately summoned the governor. One of the assistant governors came. When we saw he wasn't serious, we demanded to see the governor himself. When they saw our stance, they summoned comrade Celalettin to the governor's office. They didn't want things to escalate, since there were apparently inspectors in the office at the time.

When they promised it wouldn't happen again, we backed down.

Block 8

11 October 1996

We sent a collective petition bearing the signatures of all comrades to the Aydın prosecutor's office detailing our specific problems.

At 10.00 in the morning, we held a minute's silence for comrade Hamdullah and shouted slogans.

A delegation from the ministry told our representatives in the governor's office, "End the action, we will sort things out." The comrades said we would not be able to accept such delay and lack of certainty.

In a statement, the Minister of Justice mentioned four-person cells. This indicates that they will not abide by the latest agreement. Their dishonesty no longer surprises us.

We were asked about our view on the comrades on hunger strike moving to blocks 7 and 9. I wrote that it wasn't appropriate. There is no need for it at the moment. There's no point in turning everything upside down.

Block 8
14 October 1996
"A THREE THOUSAND-YEAR-OLD SCREAM IS CONCEALED IN MY CHILD'S CRADLE"

A small item of news in the paper.

I read it quickly. Nuray Şen, who has had an accident in a private car, is seriously injured. The place, Aksaray.

She has damage to her spinal cord. I doubt it was an accident, as Nuray is an activist. And she loves her country.

As much as being a mother, she is also a good comrade. They have arrested her many times, but they haven't been able to intimidate her. She has made no concessions. We heard her name after her husband, Mehmet Şen, (a member of the National Congress of Kurdistan) was murdered. For a while, she corresponded with us. Then she went to Europe. However, she always talked of the beauty of her country and its life and wanted to return to the most active area.

Suddenly, we saw her on a legal platform. The last we heard, she was the chair of the MKM (Mesopotamia Culture Centre). We could see her efforts and contribution even from here. I know she has a son who is a guerrilla. They've taken her to a hospital in Ankara. Only a small news item, but the pain is considerable. We will be deprived of her writings, her poems, and her warm greetings. Perhaps she will not be able to say, "The 3,000-year-old scream concealed in my child's cradle," again. But she will always be in our hearts and our consciousness.

Block 8
16 October 1996

The action, with our specific demands, is continuing. We have updated the programme. The third group will not start for now. It will wait as a reserve force to react to possible situations/developments.

If the children who come with the families are allowed into our side, we will go to the visiting area. If they don't accept this, we will protest, as they want to restrict this right of ours. What is wrong with the children staying on our side during the visit under their supervision?

My mother telephoned Saadet's family, who live in Aydın, and asked after us. Comrade Yusuf informed us of this with a note.

Block 8
17 October 1996

I was called for a visit in the first group. Aziz P. had arrived. He passed on a verbal message from the Leader. He thanked all the prisoners for the action and sent his greetings. He also made a criticism of Aydın regarding the failure to secure centralisation and overcome personality problems, as well as develop creative, confident personality. As it is not in writing, it is more of a generalisation. I don't know what can be done or what different measures may be taken.

Following the visit, we took the comrades who are on hunger strike into blocks 7-15 and 9-13.

As for those in these blocks who are not involved in the action, they were moved to block 6-14. The fact that the authorities only agreed to the change of blocks on the 20th day is a sign that the action will go on for some time.

There are no serious health problems amongst the comrades on hunger strike. At the moment, they are fine.

Block 8
18 October 1996

The blocks that are not involved in the action will read the *Özgür Halk* and *Arjin* magazines until lunchtime.

We will act in accordance with the new planning.

The prosecutor also came for the search today. He talked nonsense, saying, "You have no problems. Why are you continuing the action?" If they weren't in difficulty, they wouldn't come.

I received a letter from my mother. She included a Kurdish poem. She reminded me of Mustafa Gezgör. She liked him, and, of course, his poems…

Block 8
23 October 1996

Last night, I wrote a letter to my mother. The final sentences she had written took me back in time. I mentioned Gezgör to her. I'm sure she will cry her eyes out when she receives the letter.

Despite our action here being in its 27th day, they have still not made a serious approach. Even the prison doctor is not coming. The governor's office occasionally sends an indirect message. For us, this is meaningless.

Today was visiting day for the other blocks. They didn't allow some of the children in. They only allowed in those who are up to ten years old. I sent two notes pointing out that we shouldn't accept this. Delil, from our administration, also said he wouldn't accept it, but the majority were of the opposite view. It stuck in my craw, but we went along with it. They are introducing new restrictions and rules bit by bit.

In a dream last night, I was again both inside and outside. I was in Antep, a place that has had a profound effect on me. We were in the famous main road that goes through the Nuri Pazarbaşı neighbourhood. The houses, empty plots of land, and pavements were as they used to be. But the first thing I noticed about people there was the fact there were some comrades from prison amongst the people. Our prison structure was there. Although we were outside, the prison rules were in place. I was near Çamlık at the end of the road. I was chatting to a few comrades in front of the Rauf family house where İlhan and Memo were killed in a shoot-out with police in June 1976. I was saying to them, "Again, two comrades from each block will be on look-out." Every part of the neighbourhood was like a block. Mehmet Özkan said, "In the newspaper it says there will be one person on look-out in each block." I insisted that there had been a misunderstanding, that it should be two people. What if there is a raid on the block in the lower part of the neighbourhood, how would the look-out let them know here? Özkan seemed to be persuaded.

The administration was comprised of comrades in the same prison. I asked after comrade Fuat but couldn't find him. I walked towards the tea houses. When I reached the Kalender's grocery store, I chanced upon Şamil. He also said, "There should be two people."

The road was crowded. It was daytime and hectic. A municipal bus passes by. The residents of the neighbourhood are the same. It is as if 15 years ago is frozen in time. But I knew there were no buildings from that time, the reality was different. The only difference was that comrades from the prison caught my attention.

These are places where I passed my childhood and, to an extent, my years as a young man.

Today, we sent two comrades to each block to assist those who are on hunger strike with their needs, as at this stage, they are finding it difficult.

The exercise yard was closed at 18.00…

Block 8
25 October 1996
A FEDAI IN ADANA: LEYLA KAPLAN

Today, Zilan once again exploded amongst the enemy in Adana. She drew out the pin of the bomb amidst the police in the entrance of the riot police HQ in Adana. She'd wrapped the bomb around her body. And was amongst them…

We watched the evening news. The police were crying their eyes out at the scene.

The person who carried out the action was only seventeen.

Leyla KAPLAN.

Still very young.

It is an object lesson in incredible loyalty, belief, self-sacrifice, and courage to decide and carry out such an action.

Yes, a girl of only 17. The heroism of a girl, who until yesterday had no say in what went on in her house, is difficult to put into words…

To attempt this is absolutely the result of becoming free. Someone who is not utterly determined could not carry out such an action.

To march on towards such an action – despite knowing you will also be destroyed – and then to pull out the pin is not something everyone can do. Those who do not devote themselves to their people and struggle cannot even imagine such an action.

To even understand such actions requires honesty and determination.

Her choice of 25 October was also conscious and significant.

EVERY ZİLAN IS AN HONOUR

A bomb fell.
Wave after wave from Çukurova
To the fortress of the snakes,
To the rocks of Anavarza,
To the Taurus mountains,
From the Taurus to the four winds
Who could have known the successors of Zilan.
A Kurdish girl,
Just 17.
Both far from her beloved people and land, and very near.
Her name is Leyla KAPLAN.
A Kurdish girl,
A Zilan
Her ancestors in Zilan,
Were torn apart in the nooks and crannies of mountains,
Next to springs.
Today their grandchildren have memorised the name Zilan.
Every Zilan is a bomb,
Every Kurdish girl a Zilan,

First in Dersim,
Then in Çukurova,
Zilans pulled out the pin.
And advanced on the enemy.
Every Zilan an honour,
Seeds for tomorrow,
An elixir of life
For the life of tomorrow.
A name for new-born children,
Fear for the enemy,
The latest Zilan
That is, LEYLA's shredded body.
No, no, not a corpse,
A shredded mass.
They take revenge from it
They expose it,
By dragging it along the ground.
Out of their fear,
Their confusion,
Otherwise they wouldn't cry their eyes out
And tear out their hair.
Every Kurdish girl is a ZİLAN,
A LEYLA,
And more,
There are more…
Pins to be pulled out,
Lives to be sacrificed
There is a vow of vengeance!
Those who today drag our corpses,
While crying at the same time,
Will cry more,
Because there are ZİLANS who will bomb
Their bodies,
Their hearts,
Their brains.
ZİLANS

Taking the revenge of the Kurds for the Zilan massacre,
That of Leş glen,
And others that are not known.
Of today,
Tomorrow,
Of freedom,
And the essence of the new human being,
The representative of herself.
The "Black Shirts" will cry!
They will drag the corpses of Zilans.
In pain,
In fear,
In panic,
They will see that Zilans have multiplied and turned into bombs.
Yesterday in Dersim,
Today in Çukurova.
Tomorrow in city A,
At point A,
As the struggle continues
History will always remember.
Dersim Zilan
Çukurova Leyla KAPLAN
And times will follow each other
Until a free and independent country is created.

Block 8
27 October 1996

At 11.00 in the morning, we held a minute's silence for comrade Leyla and shouted slogans:

"Leylas are Immortal!"
"Leyla and Zilan are our Honour!"
"Down with the Special War!"
"Long Live Leader Apo!"

We finished the forum that has been going for two days. It dealt with "Libya trip and latest developments in South Kurdistan."

It has begun to get really chilly. We sent our blankets to the comrades on hunger strike. It's just as well, because even we have started to feel cold.

Comrades Ethem and Özcan are poorly. On informing the prison authorities, they said, "Let's take them to hospital." We told our comrades, "Don't request it, but if they take you, don't object."

Our exercise yard door was closed at 17.00. They are slowly implementing the restrictions.

We have heard that Şehmus Yüksel's elder brother, Bayram, has been martyred. We wrote a note, asking comrades to forward it. Despite our suffering losses every day, it is still hard to pass on such news. I gather on hearing the news, he accepted it naturally. But he said it might be Mehmet, not Bayram, as he was apparently separated from the group after a clash in Dersim and froze in heavy snow. It happened seven months after he joined. The fact it took so long to be notified is probably due to it not being possible to establish his identity.

Every death is heart-breaking, but this kind of martyrdom is even harder to bear…

If they don't yet know, we will forward the news to the family at an appropriate time.

Block 8
28 October 1996

Groups that are not on hunger strike today wrote a joint petition to the prosecutor and the Ministry of Justice requesting that our problems be resolved.

Demokrasi wrote about our action as it has been going for a month.

There is not a word from the Ministry…

Today, comrade Cesim spoke to the prison authorities. At first, they wouldn't agree, but after persisting, they summoned him. He told them that the reason for the action was due to the arbitrariness of the prison authorities and their fascist attitudes. The governor apparently batted it away with his customary complacency.

In a dream last night, I was once again outside, but comrades from prison were there. We were in an area as wide as a city, but everywhere there were building sites. You couldn't move for iron and cables. People were jumping over these construction sites, from one to the other. There were places I have seen in previous dreams. There were all manner of plants, flowers, and fruit between the iron and the cables. As some were artificial, they had been hung up left and right. I paid attention to some of them, straightening them out.

I was being chased over and amongst these building sites, but they couldn't catch me. While escaping, I was flying from time to time. Just when they were about to grab my feet, I would soar up into the sky.

Later, I remember, we were in an enclosed space. It was a cell, like a well. I went downstairs to the lower level. It was clearly dangerous. There was a wooden door that separated us from another section. The door was old and unpainted. They were hitting the other side of the door with a mallet. I said to those with me, "The fascists are hitting the door. Soon it will break and they'll attack us." While trying to take steps, I woke up.

In the evening, I read articles typed from the latest edition of *Özgür Halk* magazine. These were letters from comrades who had set themselves alight in Bayrampaşa and statements made by the ERNK representation in Europe, the ARGK HQ, and Amed Command. There was also the leader's latest assessment regarding the recent period. There were very angry, but optimistic expressions.

In all the articles, there was praise and support for the latest prison resistance.

Block 8
29 October 1996
A FEDAI IN SİVAS: GÜLER ORTAÇ

Despite all the measures taken to prevent suicide attacks, they are helpless to do so.

Now all our people are bombs…

This morning, two men and a woman wearing a veil were taken from a village minibus arriving in Sivas city and put in a police car. When getting out in front of the market police station, the female comrade detonated the bomb she was wearing, resulting in six dead and 15 wounded.

The vehicle turned into a tangle of steel and pieces of human flesh stuck to nearby buildings.

The comrade's name is Güler Ortaç from Batman. At one time, she was with Zilan, in Şemdin Sakık's group.

In Amed, a male comrade was arrested before carrying out an action. He had apparently made a bomb from rocket shells. If it had exploded, there would have been a major loss of life. It's a mystery how he was arrested.

The Turkish state is in utter panic.

Block 8
1 November 1996

Today is the 36th day of our hunger strike, and the authorities have still not made a move. The number of comrades who are poorly is rising. Comrades Remzi, Sarıkaya, A. Kaya, Özcan, and Harun are not well. Sarıkaya has a heart problem. I think his heart is strained by his weight loss. Last night, I gather, he vomited. His stomach upsets have increased. The comrades wanted to inform the authorities, but he intervened to stop them.

Comrades' illnesses have demoralised me. I am particularly concerned about Sarıkaya. I am also angry, as he has been on hunger strike numerous times. His constitution is not good, and he also smokes.

Yesterday, as comrades went for a visit during a search, we took out their valuables with them. A spectacle case caught my attention. I opened it and there were pens inside. It belonged to ET. Two of them were pens that had previously gone missing from communal property. I showed them to comrades responsible for the commune, and they recognised them.

As such things don't happen in our environment, I was demoralised. It is the first time I have encountered such a situation.

Meaning to speak to him, I put the case with the pens in my cupboard. When we summoned him, I opened the spectacle case and found one pen was missing. The fact he had dared to do such a thing made me angry. As far as our circle is concerned, such a thing is terrible. We went to his cupboard and found the pen there.

I asked him:

"Comrade, where did you get these pens?"

"They're from Buca prison, comrade."

"Comrade, let's be honest. Are you sure?"

When he persisted, I asked him how the pen I had put in my cupboard had found its way to his cupboard. "I don't know," he said. But it was obvious he was lying. He was avoiding looking us in the eye. I asked him again, abruptly. I was also upset that he had been reduced to such a state. We gave him half an hour to think it over. We couldn't put up with it any longer. When we sat down again, he cringed and admitted what he had done. But, he said, "If possible, don't tell the others."

For someone to lower himself to such a level over such a basic matter is, in a word, disgraceful.

The system has, unfortunately, destroyed our people's sense of shame. It's a great pity.

He had only recently made a self-criticism after an analysis of his character was made.

The special war ruins people in this way. It hollows them out.

When I think about this, my temples ache.

Today comrade Aziz went to hospital to have a tooth extracted. He learned that M. Polat from DS had been released yesterday. He'd done 15 years…

Despite being from DS, he received a 15-year sentence in our case, from the Adana group.

Block 8
2 November 1996

The 37th day of the action.

Yesterday evening, four lawyers came to the prison. Two weren't allowed in. They spoke to comrades Şamil, Sait, and Celalettin. After the meeting, they will visit the prosecutor. If they don't receive a positive reply, I gather they will contact to international institutions.

Today we learned from Ege TV that our family group held a protest in Konak, Izmir. It wasn't a big demonstration. When certain aware families wished to issue a press statement, they were attacked by the police. The police were kicking and hitting the people in the head with truncheons as they were being dragged along the ground. They were especially targeting the heads. Seeing the footage of our mothers being kicked enraged us. But we are helpless to do anything. This fact affects us profoundly.

Ferhat, Doğan, and Feyzullah from block 6 have been taken to the sick bay. They were told they would be taken to hospital if need be. Even if they refuse treatment, the authorities may want to take them. It would be useful as regards public opinion. Our action will continue in this form. Additionally, we will start ten-day hunger strikes in groups. The first group from block 2 will begin on 4 November.

Today, we watched some footage on TV of the leader's meeting with Talabani. It was new for us. The leader looked smart and young. He was dressed in sporty clothes and was cheerful. Some of the comrades around him were familiar.

Block 8
4 November 1996

Two comrades from each block went to the blocks involved in action to assist. In the afternoon, I went to block 9-13. Apart from a few comrades, everyone is fine.

They took Ali Kaya to hospital last night. The action is reaching a critical stage. The authorities have begun to panic, as there are certain to be more people becoming unwell.

Block 8
5 November 1996

Today is the 40th day of the action.

Demokrasi gave a lot of space to our action and demands, as 40 days of hunger strike for people living in harsh conditions for years, is a serious situation. First and foremost, the prison authorities know that many comrades' health conditions are not good.

Block 8
6 November 1996

Today and tomorrow we won't go for visits. Celalettin went to inform the families. When he told them that 85 people were on unlimited hunger strike, 17 people had begun a ten-day action, and that they will stay outside the prison. The visitors heard the sound of slogans and doors being banged from inside and responded by hollering loudly. They reacted to the authorities by shouting at the same moment, as if a button had been pressed. At the same moment, when comrade M. Tören went up to the window of block 1 overlooking the visiting cabins and shouted, "Why did you come, to collect the dead bodies? Go and create public opinion," the reaction of the families reached a crescendo.

We can understand from the blocks that the mothers in particular are badly affected.

Since a considerable public opinion has developed, the minister of justice made a statement, saying, "We will soon end the actions in Aydın and Amasya." He issued such a statement because he is under quite a bit of pressure.

Comrade A. Kaya is still in hospital. I gather he is in critical condition. 30 comrades have fallen ill, and the number is rising every day…

Block 8
7 November 1996

Our shouting of slogans and banging on the doors continued today.

Our notice appeared in *Demokrasi* newspaper. There was a long article on prisons in general and on us. At the moment there are limitless hunger strikes going on in 11 prisons.

Bursa has begun a hunger strike in support of the actions. That's good, but a delayed step. When the death threshold has been reached…

The article said A. Kaya, who is in hospital, has agreed to treatment. If that's the case, it means he has given up the action. As far as we know he is continuing the action. If the article is wrong and A. Kaya has read it, the effect will be very bad. If it's true, he won't be able to pull himself together again.

We heard soldiers have been deployed outside the prison.

At around eight in the evening, I heard noises in the corridor and pricked up my ears. I made out the words, "Stomach bleeding… A. Aktaş" from the guards' conversation.

Aktaş had been quite poorly in recent days. He was looking older, but his morale was good. I hope there is nothing serious with him and the other comrades.

In recent days, we had temporarily stopped compulsory daytime education on account of the flu outbreak. As it was a pretext for over-relaxing, we have ended it. It's no longer necessary.

This demonstrates that we still haven't internalised certain things and have not been able to make it a way of life. The slightest hiatus can lead to an immediate resting on our laurels.

Block 8
8 November 1996
THE FAMILIES' GRUELING WAIT AT THE PRISON GATES

There are 14 comrades in hospital. They are A. Kaya, H. Acar, A. Aktaş, A. Ertaş, A. Bor, Ö. Erdem, M. Sarıkaya, O. Güzel, R. Özçelik, B. Akbay, F. Aksu, D. Aslan, F. Başakçı, D. Baltacı, K. Oktay.

It was good that they all went together, as it's hard to be on hunger strike on your own in hospital.

Another group of lawyers came today. One will remain with the families outside Aydın prison, one will go to Istanbul, and one to Ankara.

There are around 100 family members outside the prison. They are not leaving.

The news item about comrade A. Kaya was apparently wrong.

The lawyers also spoke to the comrades in hospital and received information about them.

This period is very important and sensitive for Turkey. It is also a very risky period.

At around eight in the evening, comrade M. Pelin from the adjacent block called out. He explained that the delegation of lawyers that visited had met the Minister of Justice, Ş. Kazan, following an initiative by the human rights association, but that the minister had not been sincere, and after ten minutes had displayed an attitude far from being serious and courteous, saying, "I'm going to pray." In fact, there are dozens of prisoners on the brink of death in 11 prisons. This cannot be considered separately from the policies of the RP and special war.

At 00.30, comrades Celalettin, Cesim, and Aşkın came to our block. They were going round all the blocks. They passed on information regarding the meetings with lawyers, prosecutor, and governor. They have said there is no way our main demand for representatives to go round the blocks or weekly inter-block sporting activities will happen. The aim is to impose the isolation of the 12 September military period. It is not possible for us to accept this.

Comrade A. Bor is in a critical condition and we were asked whether we should get him to end his hunger strike. He is apparently having difficulty speaking. I said, "To get him to end the action in these circumstances would lead to the action dragging on. It would weaken his resolve. If he can go on for a few days, then let him continue." But, I added that if he is in critical condition, he could go to hospital and use his initiative. The decision is entirely up to him.

Families are continuing to wait at the gates. They are well aware that a critical stage has been reached. It is hard to stay at the gates in this cold. It provides us with fortitude to know that our families, that confront everything, are waiting outside the gates.

It is also difficult for comrades who are not on hunger strike. They are emotionally affected. They also want to join in. It is hard not to acknowledge that they are right, however much we tell them that it is impossible for all of us to go on a limitless hunger strike. It is terrible to stand by and watch as dozens of comrades edge second by second closer to death. It is impossible not to be affected. But again, for us, it is fundamental to do what is logical, correct, and organised.

Block 8
9 November 1996
CRITICAL DAY FOR THE PROTEST

The TGRT channel showed footage of our families at the prison gates in its morning news. There were as many as 200 people there. The numbers are constantly increasing. This is great and emboldens us. They spoke to several mothers. Comrade Umut's mother also spoke. They were all angry and concerned about their children. Some of them said, "If anything happens to our children in there, we will set ourselves alight."

Apparently, Ceyhan and Bayrampaşa have begun solidarity actions. It is difficult to understand why Bayrampaşa waited so long.

After the representatives had been round the blocks, they took comrade Cesim to see the comrades in hospital. They had put them all in rooms in the basement. None of them are accepting treatment. I gather they are in good spirits.

Comrades had said, "The final say belongs to those in hospital," adding, "The majority are in prison. They are the ones to decide."

As it's the 44th day, the opinion of the general structure is important. They are in favour of continuing the action, as every new restriction that is introduced in this prison will subsequently be introduced in other prisons. We're in a very difficult situation. We are trying not to suffer fatalities, while also not taking a backward step. We have to act very carefully and politically.

We will wait until Tuesday. On the 50th day of the hunger strike, the first group will end it, while the others will continue with it. Additionally, five comrades not involved will begin a death fast. During this period, we will not go for visits.

We are absolutely sitting on a powder keg.

As they have brought some ordinary prisoners here from the closed prison, who are opposite us, the sound of TV, radio, and cassette players is going 24 hours a day. It's giving us a headache. They've turned the place into a nightclub.

Block 8
10 November 1996

At around 02.30 in the morning, comrade Aziz, who was on watch, woke me up. He whispered that representative comrades were downstairs. I hurriedly dressed and went downstairs. Again, three comrades were there.

Apparently the authorities had summoned comrade Celalettin to ask him what we had decided. He replied, saying, "You have deliberately caused the action to drag on by not resolving our problems. You have chosen this prison as a pilot and want us to pay the price. Rather than be a bad example to other prisons, we are prepared to pay this price." They then told him that Amasya prison had ended its action. When the comrade refused to believe them, they called Amasya prison and let him speak to S. Korkmaz, one of our representatives there.

The authorities said they would accept the demands accepted in Amasya prison. These are: representatives will not go round the blocks. One will come from each block and meet in the governor's office. One of these will relay problems to the authorities. Two additional representatives will go to the visiting area. Once a week, a representative will go along the corridor and ask about problems in the blocks through the grilles. Once a fortnight, 20 people from different blocks can meet on the upper floors for three hours. Banned publications will be allowed inside for two or three days, then be taken back. In certain situations, lawyers will be permitted to see prisoners without a document.

We said, a basis has been established, let's take advantage of it. Comrade Sait and myself from the administration said agreement can be reached, but let's ask the opinion of the structure. We thought there's no need to die for these demands.

After the comrades had left, I was unable to get back to sleep for an hour, despite being tired.

Immediately after breakfast, we assembled in the block to consult. 30 people were in favour of continuing, while five wanted to end it. The number in favour of continuing surprised me.

On sending the outcome to the administration, I attached a note, saying, "Let's reach a decision along the lines of the view of the structure. We cannot end the action in spite of the majority view."

The 45th day of the action. We can feel and see here that comrades are walking step by step towards death. But we will act according to the majority view.

We are quietly, sadly waiting. Like a horrendous vice, it has clutched us and is crushing us.

Malatya and Elbistan prisons have ended the action. I assume there's a similar agreement.

Block 8
11 November 1996

I got up at 06.00 as I couldn't sleep. A note had arrived from comrade Celalettin. He writes that a delegation comprising the chair and members of the Contemporary Jurors' Association (CHD) has arrived. When, during the meeting, the governor acted insultingly, he had ended the meeting and returned to the block.

He said that we would not accept guard supervision of inter-block visits and if there was to be an agreement, a delegation from the families at the gate and representatives of other left organisations' prisoners needed to be present. As this demand had been rejected, the talks had stopped.

The cause of the obstruction is governor Kemal. During the meeting, he suddenly put a note in front of the prosecutor. He was blatantly imposing his will. He wants to break our will and impose his own conditions.

There has been an intense exchange of notes between our blocks.

I went as companion to block 7-15. The comrades in the first group are really thin. I helped some of them wash their hair.

Then comrade Saadi and I gave the place a good clean.

Blocks that are not involved in the action protested by rejecting the meal wagon at lunch and in the evening. Also today and tomorrow, slogans will continue to be shouted.

Block 2 has turned its action into an unlimited one.

Later, all blocks will participate in a two-day hunger strike.

Comrades Ethem, Faysal, and Rıdvan in block 7 have been taken ill. The authorities have been informed, but we did not allow them to be taken to hospital. We comrades will not accept being taken there and left in the basement.

Some comrades are proposing "stepping up the action."

When the meeting began last night, many comrades were eager to hear the outcome and some couldn't get to sleep until 04.00. As they tired themselves out today, some comrades have taken to their beds. Weariness has affected them, and there is also disappointment in the lack of an outcome.

When a person conditions himself to something, and the result is not as hoped, he may suffer breakdown. In order not to suffer this, it is necessary to have sound foresight and be politically grounded. Consequently, a sound perspective prevents a drift away from reality.

Block 8

12 November 1996

THE HUNGER STRIKE ENDS ON THE 47TH DAY

Comrade Celalettin was summoned, saying, "Let's resolve the problem." When we heard this, we were anxious, as yesterday their attitude was very different. We thought, "Something has definitely happened to one of the comrades in hospital."

When the comrade said, "First I must get the view of the comrades in hospital," they took him there. The comrades are apparently well. As A. Bor said, "I'll manage," he was continuing the action. We had told Sarıkaya, "If his condition worsens, use your initiative for comrade A. Bor."

All blocks have begun a two-day hunger strike. I was a bit annoyed this morning. It was 07.00 and the comrades were still trying to make tea. I told them angrily, "How long have you been in prison? It's about time you learned how to do these things." I didn't allow them to make tea, as our action was to start at 07.30, when the morning meal wagon arrives.

We were told that comrade N. Kartal had been taken on a stretcher to hospital. Lawyers were in the governor's office until the afternoon. Time passed slowly as we continued to wait.

After the exercise yard had been closed, the representatives came to the block. Apparently, two family members and representatives of other groups had also been brought along. They have accepted that the fortnightly internal visits can take place in the exercise yard of block 1. But they will also evacuate block 1.

Both demands were problematic. The most important point was that there are to be no guards present for the internal visits.

I made my opinion clear to the representatives, saying, "There is no longer any point in prolonging the action." After the representatives had gone, there was of course great activity. We all went down to the dining hall. Clusters began to form spontaneously.

At around 21.00, they began to take comrades from block 9-13 to the sick bay. This was followed by their asking us for canteen lists.

Representative comrades began to go round the blocks again in order to announce that the action had ended. We began to boil water in the large kettle to make rice soup for comrades who had been on hunger strike.

Both in the blocks and amongst our families outside, a feverish activity has begun. The families have collected money and deputed a person to buy milk for us. Even if the milk doesn't come, hearing about the effort is even more health-giving than milk.

Representatives of Turkish left groups have gone round the blocks involved in the hunger strike, exalting the action, and saying those who resist always have the final word. Emotional moments were experienced. They left the blocks to applause.

We later heard that some family members had cried with joy and embraced each other. There was apparently a festival atmosphere. There was a wedding taking place near the prison and they went there and performed halay. The band played "Prisoners of Freedom" to support us.

The ululations of families could be heard in the blocks. The sounds of joy were echoing from the walls of the prison. This was enough to make our eyes well up. We looked up at the sky and tried to feel them.

We believed that at that very time a guerrilla in the mountains was resting against a rock or tree, looking up at the sky, and sensing us and the ululations in the infinity of the universe...

There was an intense hustle and bustle until morning. An assistant was sent to block 8, which had ended its action. There were both comrades who were poorly and those with problems from falls caused by beginning to take on food again. Assistance was definitely needed, as 47 days is not a short time.

Block 8
13 November 1996

We learned early in the morning that there were around 400 family members at the prison gates. In order for all of them to visit, we needed to take precautions. We must thank them for their support. I went with assistants to block 7-15. The joy of success could be read in their eyes. We shook hands with them one by one. It was great to share this success and joy while congratulating them on their determined resistance.

Some comrades had been put on a drip, and others' blood pressure had been checked. Comrades had been brought from hospital.

Some particularly frail-looking comrades were having difficulty walking.

As far as possible, a diet programme has been implemented for our comrades. Milk, boiled potatoes, rice, yogurt, and crackers are the main things.

Cemal Günsel fell over in the toilet section this morning and cut his head in two places. Despite his wounds being dressed, the bleeding hasn't stopped.

Comrade Kasım has heart spasms.

As for comrade Cahit, he had fallen to his knees at the door of the toilet and hugged them to his chest. He was obviously in pain.

It is important to be very careful for three or four days after ending such a long hunger strike. If care is not taken, even fatalities may occur.

Although there are some who need it, no comrades have been put on a drip. They don't want comrades to get over it and feel comfortable. They're not saying it's not available, but delaying, and being evasive. In fact, it would not be expensive for them.

In the afternoon, M. Aydın and H. Vural were brought here from Buca prison. They have been put in block 4.

All the blocks took turns to go for visits. The visitors were in high spirits. We learned that three people had decided to set themselves alight in front of the prison were anyone to be martyred inside. They had even prepared the petrol. It's difficult to feel a coffin might come out at any moment. Many people who waited at the gate have gone down with colds. Despite that, they have remained with us. They considered our action to be theirs. They played a great part in its success. During the action, they were subjected to insults from soldiers, police, and guards on many occasions. Despite that, they remained at the gates.

The people and humanity once again took ownership of its children and came down on the side of humanity and those who are right.

Our pride is endless.

Block 8
14 November 1996

Towards noon, I went to the visiting area. It was crowded, although not as crowded as yesterday, when most of the active families came.

Some families were complaining that they couldn't have a proper visit. I perceived this to be more of a reflection of comrades' complaints.

Our little Mazlum woke in the middle of the night and said something like, "Mum, isn't the action over, when will my dad die?" For a five-year-old child, the effects of such things is serious. He also said, "Mum, take my syrup to the prison, tell them it's sweet, it will be a bit sour when they drink it, but it will make them better."

Even the children are exerting every effort for us. Just as we are waging a struggle for them…

We are experiencing a post-action syndrome. We are trying to ensure the comrades don't get ill through overeating. But this is sometimes difficult, as people are ravenous…

Comrade Acar, who fell ill after eating, has been taken to the sick bay. His pain had increased, but I think he still wasn't careful. In fact, he has experience from Adana. He was to have an operation there. He shouldn't have forgotten that.

I was shocked to learn while talking about this that there have been exceptional instances of guerrillas dying from overeating. The worst way for a guerrilla to die… Conditions are hard for guerrillas. There is constant fatigue and hunger, but when the opportunity presents itself, you mustn't lose control.

On one occasion in the Dersim region, when cutting down a wizened tree, they saw honey oozing out after a few blows with an axe. As the tree was hollow, bees had filled the trunk with honey. They took out the honey layer by layer and distributed it to the units.

Comrade Celal Barak was at first angry that a tree had been cut down, but laughed when he saw the honey. As they had run out of provisions, they ate honey morning and night. A comrade who was going to keep watch on a hilltop took honey with him and ate a lot of it there. He fell ill under the sun and they were unable to save him. I was shocked to hear about this incident.

Comrade Mümin mentioned a couple of other cases of food poisoning caused by honey.

A cause of death completely unbefitting to a guerrilla fighter.

Self-control is a problem everywhere.

Block 8
17 November 1996

Last night I didn't go to bed until after 04.00. While trying to get to sleep, I noticed my feet were freezing. I then dozed off. When I woke up, my feet were still cold.

These days, I'm having a lot of dreams…

Block 8
19 November 1996

For the first time since the action ended, comrade Nuri and I went around the blocks as "barbers." I went to blocks 1, 2, and 6. I took a few comrades out into the exercise yard and gave them a haircut where the guards could see. According to the agreement, four people can go around the blocks on two days a week as barbers.

In accordance to the agreement, the comrades in block 1 have been distributed around the other blocks. Extra bunks have been put in. Five comrades came to our block.

We now have one fewer block.

Block 8
20 November 1996

Comrade M. A. Kapar came from Ordu prison at 02.00 in the morning. They strip-searched him. After punching him a few times, they put him under observation. When morning came, he refused food and demanded to be taken to a block. As he explained things piecemeal, we were hesitant. We didn't react to the authorities, but informed the representative comrade. The authorities will be told we will not accept such things under any circumstances.

Block 8
22 November 1996

Comrades Necmettin Yıldız and Adil Morg arrived today from Buca. They went to blocks 6 and 14. I think the number of arrivals will increase in the coming days.

Block 8
27 November 1996

Today is Wednesday. As today is visiting day for several of our blocks, we have put off celebrating the party's founding until Saturday.

We just held a minute's silence and read out a statement at 09.00 and shouted a slogan:

"We are the Party, the Front, the Army Marching to Victory." It's the first time we have shouted this slogan.

After performing a brief halay in the exercise yard, we returned to the normal routine.

Comrades going for a visit will dwell on the meaning and importance of the day. On certain visiting days, we have an agenda that is given prominence.

Comrades will celebrate the day with their comrades and families, but will not go to excess. We do not want a problem with the authorities.

Block 8

3 December 1996

As today is our barber's day, Nuri and I went around the blocks. I spoke to lots of comrades until 16.00.

I observed that many comrades have become sensitive about quite basic issues.

Today, the situation of D. and İ. was handed over to the block structure. For the block structure to make a decision about them is both more democratic and more realistic.

The general view about the two of them is that they have nothing to offer our environment, and that they should be thrown out of our blocks so that they do not adversely affect the environment with their ideas.

The dominant view is that they have lost their beliefs. The reason for this is their practice. On several occasions, they have wished to leave the environment. Each time they have been persuaded to stay. But now, many people do not want to share the same block with them. The fact that people are saying, "We are ashamed to be in the same environment," indicates the gravity of the situation.

The administration will evaluate the view and proposal of the block and reach a decision.

In the afternoon, I heard that Öz and Burhan İlik had a punch-up yesterday and that it had been discussed in the block. The block structure proposed that the political relations of both be frozen. When I heard this, I realised that the issue went beyond a punch-up.

We heard that even before the administration had made a decision, Burhan had fled the block and taken refuge with the prison authorities. He had written a secret petition to the guards, pleading, "Get me out of this block before night." The authorities had said, "You have a parcel" and removed him from the block.

Once again, he has taken refuge with the enemy. It means he has not been able to kill the maggot of treachery inside him. The maggot has grown by the day and finally consumed him. His informer-personality has once again revived. I wonder whose heads he will "present on a silver platter" this time?

The comrades helped him get out of the swamp last time. This time, it will be hard for him to get out of that filth.

The general structure was immediately notified of the situation.

I assume this Burhan had different issues he did not want to be revealed. There was always an anxiety, an introverted atmosphere around him. The attitude of people like him that give them away is always observed, but people say, "Let's win them over." But sometimes this is pointless.

After fleeing, he asked for his belongings. The comrades didn't hand them over, saying, "Let the representative comrade speak to him, then we'll give them." The authorities did not accept this. We said there was no need to make such a demand over someone who has fled the environment.

We have been in Aydın for over seven years. This is the first time someone has fled like this. He has started a vile tradition in this way.

It has been raining for a few days, and now it has suddenly turned cold. There has been an outbreak of flu. We will have to be careful.

Block 8
6 December 1996

Comrades Abdullah Demir and İzzet Sain have been brought here from Konya.

Block 8
11 December 1996

This morning, Ramazan Tunç, Ender Kantaroğlu, and Davut Aslan have been sent away from our environment following the approval of a decision by the structure yesterday to remove them. As they went, the comrades did not pay any attention. No one showed any sign of sadness.

Individuals who have committed serious crimes against the people and the revolution in the past and are then given another chance, instead of embracing this opportunity, do the exact opposite and act as if they are taking revenge and try to destroy the environment and undermine comrades. Their very presence begins to become a problem. This then tests the boundaries of tolerance. Our structure goes out of its way to win people over, but after a certain point, it is intolerant towards those who damage the environment. It does not want people who do not recognise party life and rules, who oppose them and demoralise the environment.

Block 8
13 December 1996

Comrades that moved blocks on account of the action have returned to their old places. We also used the opportunity to make certain limited changes. The authorities made this difficult, despite having knowledge of it. When they saw we didn't accept this, they used the pretext of carrying out a search to take people out two at a time into the corridor and kept them there for hours, wanting to stress them out.

Deputy governors were also involved in the argument. At one point, the comrades returned to the block.

Nine new comrades have come to our block. There are some new faces. I have received a letter from my mother. She also sent photos of Numan and Nesimi. I couldn't work out where the photos were taken. Perhaps it was in small South [Rojava].

Block 8
15 December 1996

Today at 14.00 we held a general meeting. We haven't had such a meeting for a long time. I'm tired as I had to remain standing up for a long period.

The topics covered were in general things we have to be careful about in the new period, such as comradely relationships, understanding of responsibility, the risks of crude resistance, a revolutionary approach to the family, and the concept of enemy.

As the weather is cold, the water coming out of the tap is freezing.

It's been pouring with rain for 24 hours. I don't know how long it will go on.

This evening I had a chat with comrade İzzet Eker. When he talked about his village, I both laughed and was saddened. It's the first time I've heard such a thing.

They apparently use shoe polish on the plastic shoes they wear in the village. When they're told not to do it, they reply, "We polish them so that they don't take in water."

In a nearby village lives a sheikh [religious leader]. As the villagers are his followers, they go and clean his house. One day, there was heavy snow. A group set out to clear the sheikh's roof of snow. In front of the house was a savage dog that attacked them every time they tried to get to the house. When the villagers discussed how to get past the dog, the elder of two brothers said, "One can hold the dog while another hits it." The other replied:

"How are you going to hit the sheikh's dog?"

"Why?"

"It's a sin, you'll be struck down." So, come on, show me how you're going to hit it."

"You bark like a dog and I'll show you how I'll hit it."

As the conversation that began as a joke gets serious, the elder one says:

"Accept me as the dog," and the younger brother grabs a club and strikes his brother on the head with all his might. He falls to the ground.

This incident, at which we laughed, is a bitter reality for our people. There is blind loyalty shown to such religious leaders. These people, who present themselves as mediators, exploit people's devotion to religion and live a life of luxury.

Block 8

17 December 1996

Last night, owls hooting on the roof woke me up countless times. They made a racket all night.

I went to block 7-15. Soon after, a search began. Naturally, I remained there. Then I went to block 2. As there was a block meeting, I attended it. After the report was read out, it was the turn of individual reports. When I saw there was no criticism being made, I took the floor. This was both for morale and support.

We are all exceptionally weary.

I wrote a letter to my mother asking for money so that comrade Kenan can go to a dentist. We have a Laz amongst us, should he lose his teeth?

Yesterday, M. Bahattin Kavak came from Batman prison and Rauf Yıldız came from Niğde. Our number here is now 225.

Block 8

20 December 1996

We have begun our block meeting. Meanwhile, notes are arriving. In order not to be diverted, I had a quick look, then put them to one side. But one had "urgent" written on it, so I opened it. When I began to read it, my surprise increased.

When E. K. was arrested three years ago, the police pressurised him into cooperating with them.

Two days ago, the prison deputy governor summoned him from his block, saying he had a visitor and adding, "You made a promise at the police station, and they want you to do what you promised. I'm just a mediator." He replied, saying, "I agreed to it under torture. But I haven't done anything and I won't do it now. Don't disturb me again."

This proves that there are games being played with us. Apart from a general policy, they may be trying to drive the comrade and his family away from us. It also demonstrates that they are not able to get much intelligence about our internal structure. Or they may be trying to make the comrade a target for us, as he is not doing their bidding.

We have to take many possibilities into consideration and be careful. The information he has given us may also be incomplete.

At a time when we are gaining mass support in the big cities, there may be lots of people who have been made moles. The fact our people are frequently arrested may be because of this.

Today, I had sharp pains in my left kidney. It's probably infected again and is causing me problems. I think I've got a chill. The pain is affecting my back and my stomach.

Block 8
24 December 1996

Today, I went to blocks 7 and 15. There was an eight-page note written by As. B. to the administration. We needed to speak to him. On account of a natural change of surroundings, whatever had built up inside him, he spilled it out. His use of words in particular was contemptuous and insulting. We criticised him for feeling that people had treated him suspiciously, for seeing some things as cheap revolutionism, and his perception that looked down on the structure and comrades in the administration. We pointed out that he had made very different and mistaken evaluations.

As a result, he behaved in a self-critical way. He was pleased that we had taken him seriously and spoken to him.

He is a comrade who has not found it possible to rid himself of Kemalist characteristics.

At lunch time, I went to block 6. The comrades were whitewashing the block.

I had a chat with comrade Delil. We did mind exercises. Some topics are inevitably irksome. Obsessing over the most banal things, individualism, and selfishness blinds people.

Today, the situation of S. G. was addressed. His vulgarity in life and his becoming a problem in every minor incident is exhausting the block structure. At first, he didn't want to come to the platform. Despite his receiving education in prison for five or six years, and being amongst us, he has not changed a jot.

The structure did not take long, as he had nothing left to defend.

For a month, he will not be able to attend certain social activities in our environment. Perhaps he will think on this and reach a conclusion.

The structure has also approved our giving a break to philosophy and Kurdish classes. This was necessary so that preparations could begin for the prison conference.

Block 8
26 December 1996

We have been told that comrade Bahattin Şahin has been rushed to hospital. They said it might be abdominal bleeding. As he had been weakened, he was spending a lot of time in bed during the last month. The last time I saw him he laughed, saying, "They're going to take me to hospital, we may not be able to meet again."

Comrade Vehbi Koç has been taken to hospital in Izmir after being diagnosed with tuberculosis. It's strange that he caught this disease as he is still young and had not been here long.

Nazilli prison has begun an unlimited hunger strike.

Block 8
27 December 1996

Today, we whitewashed the entire block. Doing it in this month is not sensible, but we had to do it as we did not have a choice in the matter. They want to make us ill by having us do it at this time of year.

Eight to 10 of us worked all day. My kidney troubled me for a while on account of the cold and damp, but I didn't give up. Although comrades didn't want me to participate, I wanted to support them.

While we were working, they came to do a search at 3 p.m. We reacted and there was a discussion.

As I was very tired, I wanted to go to bed early, but before 23.00, *Siyaset Meydanı* began on the TV. As it was a programme in which only children participated, I watched it until 01.00. There were a few Kurdish children on it, too. Their comments and opinions of the world surprised us. We were also pleased. They expressed their awareness of social incidents very well.

It was obvious that most of the children who took part in the programme were from "elite" families.

Due to the whitewashing, the block is cold today. It'll be good if the comrades don't fall ill.

Block 8
28 December 1996

Today, our one-week speak Kurdish campaign has begun. We started the day by reading out a Kurdish announcement. For a week, no other language but Kurdish will be used in daily life.

Despite it being our mother tongue, most of us struggle when speaking Kurdish on account of not using it constantly.

Also today, our block were the hosts in block 1. Six comrades also came from the Turkish left. We discussed the general situation and issues specific to us.

Due to the whitewashing yesterday, I'm stiff all over. I can't move my arms. I'm thinking that were we to go out like this, we would have problems. Theory and practice are not the same thing. In our conversations every day, we climb up to the top of CUDI and come down again! The truth of the matter is very different.

Today, I read a two-page perspective article from the internal coordination. It mentioned what should be done before the conference and the issues to be borne in mind when selecting the new administration. An article also came from our fraternal party, DHP. They are making preparations for a new campaign in Turkey. I hope this time they will be successful. I know they have groups in some places. But they have suffered major problems on account of treachery and arrests at high levels.

Block 8
29 December 1996

We held a forum on the latest situation. It took place under two headings, internal and external developments. The number of participants wasn't bad.

Snow must have fallen nearby, as we're really feeling the cold.

To protest at the encircling of Atrush camp, all prisons are to start a three-day hunger strike. Everyone will take part, except those who are ill or who are near the end of their sentences.

The new editions of *Arjin* and *Özgür Halk* magazines have arrived. They have begun to be read in the evening sessions.

The article I wrote regarding comrade Zilan's action is in *Arjin*.

Block 8
1 January 1997

Yes, it's the first of January.

There are, undoubtedly, a lot of things that could be said on the first day of the year, but there's not a lot of point in using the usual customary expressions.

The most important fact is that we have grown a year older within these walls. Or perhaps it would be more correct to say we have grown up another year.

Yesterday evening, we completed our two-day action.

At night, we organised entertainment in the blocks. It began with conversation. There was a dessert prepared by comrades in addition to nuts, raisins, and fruit. There was a pleasant, different atmosphere. In the past, people would have watched TV until the morning. Now, it didn't occur to anyone. It seems meaningless to most of us.

Preferences change according to the subject on which you're concentrating and your lifestyle.

I wonder what comrades outside, in the mountains, are doing and feeling today?

Block 8
5 January 1997

We have finalised the preparation period of 40 days for the Aydın prison sixth internal conference. We will start it tomorrow. It will concentrate entirely on education. Until mid-February, we will read and debate the chosen sources.

Today, we read a statement of the representation. Meetings have been held with the prison authorities regarding certain issues, but the replies received were stalling, such as, "We'll see what we can do," or "We'll resolve it."

Today we wished to have a debate about C. S., who has been a problem for a long time, but he didn't take part, despite the fact he had been demanding a "platform" for some time. He should have written a self-criticism for the structure, but he has not done so, whereas if someone had done such a thing when he was in the administration, he would not have tolerated it. He does not respect himself as much as we respect his 20 years of work. He has surprised us.

A person shouldn't trample on their own work. First and foremost, he should take ownership of it.

The structure's proposal that his political relations be frozen was approved. In order for him not to be stressed out, a warning was issued to not debate this.

After a seminar on "What is debate?" we played volleyball. We hadn't exercised for ages. I noticed that straight away. After meetings involving five or six hours of sitting down, our most exciting and relaxing activities are also collective in the exercise yard. This can be football, volleyball, or halay. We also sometimes play table tennis in the dining hall downstairs. Some of these matches can be exciting with cheering.

The activities that excite us the most are those with the highest voluntary participation.

Block 8
9 January 1997

While throwing the message ball into block 6, it fell on the roof. This ball is the inner tube of a football. It is inflated to double the size, string tied around it, and then material sewn on to make it like an original ball. The only difference is that it has a pocket. We only use it for sending notes.

The comrades struggled for some time to try to retrieve it, but were unable to do so. It was wet and heavy and was right in the gutter. As the guards had seen us trying to retrieve it, one of them went up onto the roof and took it. Comrades in both exercise yards were shouting for them to throw it down, but that was never going to happen.

When the ball got stuck on the roof, my nerves were coming apart at the seams. Both because there was nothing we could do and because of the carelessness of the comrade responsible. There is only a 20 centimetre-wide wall between the two exercise yards. It's even more demoralising that it happened, in spite of a comrade alongside him warning him to be careful.

I'm also annoyed at myself. While composing the note, two comrades were with me. I was intending to give it to comrade Ömer, but when the comrade alongside him stretched out his hand, I had to pass it to him. To not give it would have been perceived as a lack of trust. In order not to provide a pretext for doubts and the unimaginable comments that were made in a past case, I gave him the note. But it is evident that, even if it gives rise to doubt and lack of trust, not everyone should be entrusted with throwing notes.

The note has led to four comrades having their cover blown. There was also a comrade's personal report inside the ball. He mentioned what happened when in police custody, information he had kept quiet about for two years. For the first time, he mentioned the five weapons he had revealed. Until now, he hadn't admitted this. There were also handwritten notes containing proposals made by three members of the administration under the report. It was also stated that the administration was to meet on Saturday. Hence, all this information has been provided to the prison authorities, and by us.

The prison authorities may use the pretext of this note to bring in new restrictions. And they could also cause us serious problems.

There's nothing worse than being absolutely helpless.

Tomorrow, Ramadan begins. Three comrades will be fasting in our block. We said let's not include these comrades on the rota for block duty for the month, but they said, "We won't accept this. We have to make even more effort during Ramadan." This was one of the rare attitudes that pleased me. For them to even think like this is great.

Following the visits, we gathered together the Med-TV news. The encouraging developments rub off well on us. On returning to the blocks, we centralise every piece of news we hear about.

Block 8
4 February 1997

Due to the preparatory work, it's been nearly a month since I've had the chance to write. Most days I've only just managed to reach my bunk.

The work is progressing in a mature way. Of course, from time to time, comrades' defensive attitudes lacking in self-criticism cast a cloud over it. Stating "I have a free personality" is neither realistic nor cuts any ice.

The draft for this year's individual self-criticism report is as follows:

1. What did you plan and set as a goal at last year's conference? How many of these goals did you achieve, and if you couldn't, why?
2. During the year, what concrete development and change took place in your personality?
3. What are the main lines of your personality and the main problems as regards becoming integrated in the party?
4. What are the goals you have set yourself for the coming period and what is the unhesitating, definite pledge you will make to achieve them.
5. Finally, your vow of loyalty…

Today, I went around the blocks. I stayed in block 7 for two hours. As the comrades were in a meeting, I chatted to comrade Sıdık for a while. I was pleased to see him for the first time so upbeat and enthusiastic.

I read the letter Mahmut Aktaş sent from Bursa prison. A. Karabacak has been transferred there from Eskişehir. At the moment, they are not in the comrades' blocks, but they are talking to them. This indicates that they will return to us. I was very sad when I heard they had fled from our environment.

He also wrote that Emin had withdrawn on account of his "distinctiveness." He is one of our veterans. Stay in the party environment for 20 years, survive much hardship, make such efforts, and then end up like this. It's a great pity.

When I moved on to 6 and 14, the comrades were preparing to play volleyball. Although I was reluctant, they insisted I play. It is good for both sides if someone from outside participates. Without going out, I went along the top corridor to block 4. These three blocks are accepted as a single block.

I know that uncle Xalef will be sad if I leave without seeing him. I found him, as usual, reading the Quran. I waited a while. When he came over to me, he expressed his joy, adding, "Sorry, but as it's a sin to get up when reading the Quran, I didn't come over straight away." He mentioned his recent illness. Since the comrades knew I would listen to him, they also listened and didn't intervene. Suddenly, he got up, saying, "Ah, I've got your sweet ration. Let me get it," and his short stocky frame shuffled off towards the stairs. And, of course, things such as us, the Quran, and sin went right out of his head. The comrades laughed, saying, "He's been saving the sweets for you, not giving them to anyone else. He has double standards." I replied, "If you dare, criticise uncle Xalef!" I know he wouldn't remain silent if criticised.

There's a dry cold. It's freezing at night. The ice on the clothes we hang out in the exercise yard has not melted by noon. It's the first time we've had such cold weather in the seven years I've been here. Last night, for the first time, I got up at 03.00 and put on thick socks. I must have warmed up a bit as I dozed off. During such weather, I don't want to think about our people who have been forced to sleep in nylon tents. No one deserves such a thing.

There is an outbreak of flu in our block. It's not good that it coincides with such weather. As the central heating doesn't work properly, it's certain we'll all go down with it. As the dining hall where we sit for collective education during the day is even colder, it will be hard. Despite this, we will try to ensure it doesn't disrupt our work.

Block 8
14 February 1997

Yesterday, I remained in the visiting area all day. As I was also on block duty, I only got to bed at 01.00.

Because I was exceptionally tired, I had a dream in which, as always, I was outside. There were also some comrades there from prison. We were on the concrete roof of a house. I was taking care not to fall off the roof. There were three or four iron bars embedded in the concrete, sticking out. I said to a comrade, in order to clean up, "Look how I'll break them," twisting them to left and right and breaking them off. The comrade intervened, saying, "They've been left there to go up another floor." At that moment, I remembered they were there for the girders. I left the iron there as if it wasn't broken. Looking down, I saw the family on the ground floor. To one side, I saw a metre-high briquette wall. A child about a year old was sitting on the wall. His tiny feet were swinging below him. I grasped him, thinking he would fall. I tried to ensure he wasn't frightened. Suddenly, there were lots of people around. There were about 20 comrades under the stairs in the blocks. We were waiting as if going to the bath house. The child was still on my arm. I asked the child, "Do you want to go to the village?" "No, no," he answered with a lisp and hand gestures. Then I said, "So, shall we send you to the city?" He responded happily with gestures meaning "yes." I said, "Look at that, he doesn't want to go to the village. Are you from Mardin?" As he responded positively, all the comrades burst out laughing. I, naturally, joined in.

I don't know, but perhaps I had this dream on account of the "pain-in-the-neck" children who came to visit. Present-day children are wonderful, intelligent, lively, but difficult to cope with.

Block 8
16 February 1997

Today, towards noon, while looking out of the window into the exercise yard, I saw a grasshopper on the iron bars. I picked it up with two fingertips without harming it and went downstairs. I tore a green leaf from the flowers (if they can be called flowers) and held it out. The grasshopper immediately gripped it with its legs and began to chew it. It attracted the interest of those in the exercise yard. I placed it amongst the corn we had sown in a bath-bowl, but it showed no interest. Comrade Zeki took the grasshopper and tried to put it on comrade Nevzat's neck. When Nevzat realised, he began to flee with his large 90 kilo body. On the other hand, he was also laughing. He looked like an elephant scared of a field mouse. As the chase continued in the kitchen, we expressed our annoyance, saying, "Is a two-centimetre long grasshopper going to eat you? Pick it up and overcome your fear." He stretched out his hand a few times, then withdrew it, making us laugh all the more. "Throw the grasshopper outside," I said, but after it had been thrown outside, it came back. A comrade was angry and said, "Is this what you call an action? If you fall on someone, you'll suffocate them." He replied, saying, "No, it's not that, it's just that I'm disgusted by them."

Everything went silent...

Meanwhile, I thought only hens ate small grasshoppers, but according to comrade Seferi from Şemdinli, they are fried and eaten with rice, or like dried fruits or nuts. I was really surprised when I heard this.

Today, the weather is quite warm. It's very nice...

Block 8
18 February 1997

In the morning, I went to blocks 4-6, and 14. A lot of people there have flu, too.

I passed on my belated Eid greetings to uncle Xalef. Of course, he had not forgotten my sweets.

While here, they called me to the sick bay. I had written an application regarding my kidneys and lungs. The doctor mentioned pharyngitis. I said, "Never mind." He wrote a prescription for medication.

From the sick bay, I went to block 7. There was a block meeting going on due to problems with three comrades. I participated. Following reciprocal criticisms, one comrade was persuaded, while the work of the other two was suspended until the conference. During this time, they will not take part in our activities, but concentrate on themselves.

A fire drill took place in the empty roof block above block 7-15. As they know about our conference process, they're doing it deliberately at this time.

Block 8
19 February 1997

At around 10.00, they came to do a search. They messed everything up and made a racket by banging clubs and iron bars on the floor.

We had begun to wash the block, thinking, "They won't come today because it's visiting day." They cut off the water on the pretext of the search. They supposedly want to catch us unawares in the event of an escape or a tunnel and want to irritate us further.

The weather has turned cold again. While many comrades have got over flu, if it recurs, we'll have problems during our conference.

Block 8
24 February 1997

We have started our annual prison conference. As we have completed all the preparations, we are planning to finish it in five or six days. A council has been elected for each block and there is also a central council. The council is responsible for administration and initiatives.

Block 8
3 March 1997
OUR ANNUAL CONFERENCE IS OVER

We had to sit down, all day, for six days. If there had been a little more careful preparation, it could have been shorter. Some evenings led to a loss of time.

Overall, 204 comrades in the prison took part. But the quality was not as high as last year. We saw this in all the sessions. Even on simple topics, we had to give explanations. The fact we even had to explain what a ballot paper is indicates that we still have a long way to go on the subject of democracy.

The biggest problem we had, like every year, was in the section dealing with the reading of individual reports and the taking of criticism. There were instances of refusal to accept criticism, misunderstandings, perceiving criticism as personal attack, taking offence at basic issues, and refusing to take notice of the council.

In our block, the reports of two comrades were not passed. Although it was difficult, they rewrote them. One comrade refused to listen to the council, got involved in a polemic, and tried to withdraw his report, leading to his not being admitted to a session.

As for the council, it was criticised, as always, both for being too flexible and, by others, for "not preventing inaccurate criticism on account of the council being obsessed with me."

The last item on the agenda was the election of our prison administration. I wanted young comrades who have been here for a long time but have not been on the administration to be chosen. Despite drawing attention to this as the council, only one new comrade was elected, with the other eight being "old." That is, those who've been in post for years, whereas we wanted at least half of the nine-person administration to be new.

This is the result of our conservatism and the lack of a culture of democracy.

When I see the same "old" comrades being elected, I recall the old men slumped in their chairs in the politburo of the classic Communist Parties.

We need to initiate this change from the top. We need to open the way for dedicated, honest, young comrades who are loyal to the party and that the structure can accept, and put them in place. Of course, for this to happen, the administration has to be on the same page.

The current period is one where decisions taken should be implemented in the swiftest way.

During the conference, there was no problem of security originating from us.

Comrades were particularly careful. But, however much repair work that needed to be done, the prison authorities squeezed it all into this last week. Welding the legs of the bunks, checking the bulbs, taps, and doors, whatever they had to do, they did it last week. They wanted to disrupt our conference, but despite the loss of time, we implemented our programme.

Block 8
6 March 1997

Comrades Y. Gülcan and F. Kolcu are being released.

For seven or eight months, we hadn't had any releases. Aydın prison was a virtual well. Anyone who fell in couldn't get out.

Y. Gülcan is a young comrade. He can make a contribution outside. His leaving will be an example. As it is visiting day, his elder brother and relatives are outside waiting for him.

As I write these lines, it is 03.00. I am at the table between the bunks. In his sleep, C. Ağcakaya mumbles, "These people who have money to burn should come in here." "His teeth are sharpened as if they've been on a lathe." I assume he's having a nightmare about urban activities.

Comrades are snoring in the silence of the night, as if they are replying to each other.

Block 8
7 March 1997

From time to time, news items appear in the Turkish press that please and honour us. 27 comrades have escaped after digging a tunnel in Iskenderun prison. Seven of them were captured soon afterwards. They were all our comrades, apart from four from the MLKP.

İ. Mantaroğlu, who went there from Aydın, is one of the 20. M. Gencer, M. Dirlik and M. Ali Yılmaz are unfortunately amongst those who've been recaptured. To escape through a tunnel after 17 years inside and then be recaptured immediately is difficult to accept. A really hard thing for these comrades…

Block 8
13 March 1997

For two days, Metin Gümüş's wisdom tooth has been aching. We pressurised the prison authorities, and he was taken to hospital. They removed his tooth. We were sad because he was in pain. He's one of the quietest people in our block. He looks very downtrodden. The fact that he is disabled in one leg accentuates his silence. Although he's only in his 20's, his movement is limited. He has put on weight as he can't exercise. He can only walk by dragging his leg. While he was a shepherd in the mountains, he ran into a special-forces team. As the team had suffered losses in the area, they shot comrade Metin as he was the first person they encountered. As the veins in his leg were severed, his leg lost its function.

He's been in prison for about three years. He was given a life sentence, although he had committed no crime and there was no evidence against him. As he doesn't speak Turkish, he was unable to express himself in court. He was brought here from Amasya.

He must have affected me a lot, as I saw him in my dream last night, although we were in Mersin prison.

The blocks are making intensive preparations for Newroz.

We have finished reading all the minutes and documents. From time to time we were quite vexed. The fact that people are thinking about things that are not on our minds makes you angry. Such a lack of trust makes one sad. This should not be the outcome after such efforts have been made. People should consult their consciences before deeming someone worthy of such treatment. Assessments such as, "They don't want to give up their positions" or "They are blocking the way of new comrades" regarding comrades who have been on the administration for many years upset me. On this point, they don't understand "old" comrades. It means that we don't understand comrades who make such evaluations. This must be what they mean by "generational conflict."

We are not enamoured by our position. On the contrary, we have tried to get younger comrades involved at every opportunity. We are always looking for "new" comrades. We have even been made to regret it when we have made the wrong choice and certain comrades have given us and the structure a hard time.

Distance lends enchantment. With us, as in every sphere, taking responsibility in prison means risk, self-sacrifice, and hard work. For years, I have not gone to bed at the time the general structure does. I don't remember a day of mine that has passed quietly.

But I must add that, of course, the general structure has not had this attitude. They won't hesitate to make self-sacrifices and defend us against danger. It is this attitude that sustains us.

Block 8
16 March 1997
WHEN REMEMBERING HALABJA

> *16 March,*
> *The day Kurds had their breath taken away.*
> *16 March 1988*
> *Iraqi planes in the skies over Halabja*
> *Today the sound of the planes is different*
> *Engines are screaming*
> *Just like Hiroshima*
> *Nagasaki*
> *Before the storm of Halabja*

Mustard gas
And other chemicals
Fell on the silence of Halabja
Cries for help rose up
The hearts
Brains
Of Kurdish people
Rose up once again in revolt.
Before opposing the enemy
They rebelled against themselves.
There were said to be 'five thousand'
In fact, ten thousand
Women
Children
And the elderly
Collapsed in the streets
Those who were about to say farewell to life
A baby who had only just said 'hello' to life
Shared the same fate
They fell breathless side by side
Embracing each other
One on top of the other…
There was no life for Halabja!
Nor for anyone from Kurdistan
History was repeating itself.
Let that day be remembered with pain.
So that history records it.
Yes, it recorded it.
Kurds
And humanity
Remember Halabja
In their hearts
Minds
Such a massacre
Which humanity did not deserve
Just like in Hiroshima

In Halabja
Humanity remained silent
For to remain silent
Was worse than Halabja
More traumatic
The old man in Halabja
Collapsed on a stone
Wailing a lament!
To Halabjas
To his children in the north
Turning towards the north
His children there
Part of him
Without forgetting Halabjas
Imprinting the future
In the valley of freedom
The old man wails a lament!
He knows his children won't wail a lament.
The wild gusts of the northerly winds
Halabja
It will prevent the laments
The old man is sure of this!
For his yearnings are blossoming in the north
Like snowdrops in the mountains

....

I wrote the above lines at 03.00 in the morning. After an appropriate beginning to a letter, I will send them to my mother.

Block 8
17 March 1997

MY DARK DAY

Today is the anniversary of my capture.

I have never forgotten that dark day, even for one day. The memory of that day, the moments of the clash, our capture, is still fresh.

I have been in jail for 16 years. But that day is just like yesterday…

They are days that need to be explained. But they are days that accentuate the sorrow.

The fact I haven't forgotten that date, that hour, is because that day is a historic turning point for me.

Darkness...

Torrential rain...

The harsh, but final journey...

Being frozen to the bone...

Young beautiful people...

Downtrodden people...

And the sound of gunfire echoing round the mountains...

Can it be forgotten?

CAN IT BE FORGOTTEN?

Block 8
19 March 1997

In order to avoid disrupting our Newroz celebrations and in case the guard who takes photos doesn't turn up, we took our photos today. Two photos each, and one group photo.

As always, poses were adopted that will be especially analysed.

Personalities and tendencies are inevitably reflected by the poses adopted.

It is being said that eight more of those who escaped from Iskenderun have been recaptured. That's terrible. If it's true, it shows they were unable to reach the guerrillas. If they are unable to do that, it is inevitable that they will be recaptured group by group.

The special war, as this is a matter of prestige, is desperately focusing on that area, the Amanos mountains.

Block 8
20 March 1997

As it is our visiting day, after reading a statement in the visiting area and holding a minute's silence, we exchanged festival greetings. We asked the families to get everyone to attend activities tomorrow in their home areas. We asked them to remind people who didn't come today. For it is of the utmost importance that Newroz celebrations are well attended, especially in Kurdistan. While we were in the visiting area, they came to do a search of the blocks. In fact, the last search was only ten days ago, so they were early. But we were expecting a search, as we are accustomed to searches in the prisons before Newroz and operations outside.

Block 8
21 March 1997
NEWROZ

This is the day when many comrades identify themselves as Newroz.

The day when personalities transformed into Newroz flow towards tomorrow.

A day we have celebrated as a people for 2,609 years.

When, at times, fires are lit amidst the mountain peaks.

And at other times, fires are lit behind closed doors, behind bars.

When at times, Newroz began to be forgotten.

At times, tens of thousands risked being shot and rushed to celebrate Newroz.

When Mazlum Doğan lit three matches in the savage conditions of Diyarbakır prison, tearing apart the darkness and inviting a return to the country.

When Zekiye Alkan said on the walls of Amed, "The Newroz fire doesn't burn best with twigs and branches, it burns best with the human body… This is a matter of choice," before turning herself into a flaming torch.

And when Rahşan Demirel, who rejected the depraved and fake life in the big city, did the same on the walls of Kadife Kale in Izmir.

And on the day when comrades Ronahi and Berivan turned themselves into flaming torches in Europe, unifying with Newroz. It was inevitable that we prisoners would celebrate today in the best way possible.

When we got up in the morning, there was a noticeable liveliness. Everyone was making his final preparations. Some were having a shave, others were taking out their best clothes, while others were rushing to prepare breakfast.

By 09.00, we were all ready and out in the exercise yard. A minute's silence, then our and the DHP statements were read, then "Ey Raqip" and the slogans:

"Long Live Newroz!"

"Long Live the PKK-ERNK-ARGK!"

"We have Accomplished the Awakening, Now for Liberation!"

"Long Live Leader Apo!"

The slogans rent the air at the same moment in all the blocks. We were sure the vibrant sound went in waves and reached the mountains.

As it was also barber day, when I went out into the main corridor, I noticed there were more guards than usual. We later learned that a fire engine was also stationed outside the prison gates.

I went to 6-14. They had yet to start their cultural activities. As it had begun to rain, they were moving the stage they had set up in the exercise yard into the dining hall. With things such as the reading of messages, choir, sketch, and folklore, they put on a colourful show. They had prepared better than other blocks.

When a break came for lunch, we heard that the prison governor and prosecutor were to enter the blocks. Although some "ultra" comrades suggested turning them away, this was not approved. It is not part of our culture to turn "guests" away at the door on such a day.

They had been sitting in the dining hall of block 6 for 10 minutes or so, when the sound of Nuri Dersimi's "vengeance" poem began to be heard from block 8-12. The entire block was loudly repeating the lines read by a comrade. The prosecutor was quietly looking around him. They finished their tea and left.

Towards 13.00, the sound of spoons prevailed, as chicken and rice prepared by the comrades was being devoured. It was a feast after the repetitive and monotonous food in the prison food wagon...

I then went to block 2. Short sketches were being performed. In order not to disturb them, I watched for a while from the dining hall door. Then I moved silently and joined the audience.

After a while, they called on me to recite a poem. I was going to read the poem I had prepared for block 8-12.

It was the poem martyr Mustafa GEZGÖR had written regarding Mazlum Doğan's action.

I started by saying, "If comrade Gezgör had been amongst us today, I'm sure he would have read this poem," and began to recite the poem. Many comrades were hearing it for the first time.

As there were not many in block 2, it was good that I was there. After staying there for an hour, I returned to my block. The comrades were holding a quiz in four separate groups. It was noisy and competitive. There were also jokes and banter between the groups. When the quiz was over, Selahattin said, "Let comrade Ali recite the poem he has prepared." I then recited the poem again. As they had spent some time with Gezgör, they listened in silence and applauded heartily.

Before the doors of the exercise yard closed, we all went out and performed halay under the gently falling rain. It was as if the raindrops were accompanying us. The rain ran off our hair and down our faces. We had become as one with the rain. Feeling nature, even on concrete, and being together as one, was enough for us.

We had sweated in the rain. The sweat and the rain had mingled. And we were happy about that. Was it Newroz, the halay, the rain, or being arm in arm with our comrades? It was hard to know, but we were as cheerful as children…

At night, each block was engaged in a conversation meeting. Of course, we also tucked into the cake our comrades had managed to conjure up.

They asked me to explain how Newroz used to be celebrated outside and in prison. I explained. But I couldn't believe it either. Comparing that time with the possibilities and mass gatherings in multiple places that happen now, it is like a revolution. The fact that tens of thousands of people gather for a celebration is evidence of this.

Block 8

22 March 1997

When we read *Demokrasi*, we saw how big the Newroz celebrations had been in provinces in Turkey and Kurdistan. Despite obstructions and bad weather, the fact that tens of thousands of people had gathered showed great resistance and determination. The best example of this was that 30 thousand people gathered in Mersin.

As today is Saturday, 25 of us met in block 1. We had also invited six people from the Turkish left. The folk dance group from block 6-14 also came. After a few dances, they also did a horon. It was greatly appreciated.

Comrades from DS accompanied them with songs from Grup Yorum. They were pleased we had invited them. We thanked them for participating on such a day.

We had food made for today.

Before leaving block 1, we learned that comrade Musa Turan (our Koçer) had been taken to hospital in Izmir. He had an X-ray taken here yesterday. He was taken to hospital as they suspect he may have throat cancer.

Recently, his voice had become very husky. It was said there was also bleeding from time to time.

If it's throat cancer, it will be bad, as such illnesses really mess you up in prison. I hope it's not that.

Due to tiredness after yesterday's celebrations, collective education did not take place before noon. Naturally, many comrades went back to bed.

They woke me up at 02.00 this morning, saying comrade İzzet was poorly. He's had an abdominal pain for several days. He had drawn his knees up to his elbows under his blanket. I gather they had given him milk, but the pain hadn't gone away. I gave him a tablet for the pain in his internal organs.

I told comrade Şehmus, "If the pain doesn't go away in half an hour, tell the guard that he should be taken to hospital." I went back to bed. I gather that the pain dissipated after 20 minutes.

When they told me in the morning, I was pleased, as he is the youngest comrade here. Previously, he's had an ulcer. I told him, "Go on a diet. If you are careful and eat small amounts at a time, you'll get over it. If the problem continues, it will go on troubling us."

Block 8

25 March 1997

All central entities, starting from below, have carried out internal regulation.

Some comrades have proposed not taking responsibilities, out of concerns over the reaction of the structure, or their own anxiety following the latest attacks. Normally, these comrades are demanding a post. It is saddening that such comrades emerge after all we've been through. It is better that such people don't have a post, but people still react.

Just before the exercise yard doors closed, we received a note from DS. "As a barricade was put up yesterday in Buca prison, we have built one here to support those comrades. We will not respond to the roll call or leave the exercise yard."

We were expecting such a move.

The authorities have summoned Arif for a transfer. They got him to sign a document saying, "I'm leaving the party environment." After returning to the block, he informed the comrades. I assume he told them himself as he thought they would find out.

We expressed our reaction through our representative. The governor replied, saying, "There is nothing complicated. If he wants to go to a district prison, he will sign to indicate that he is leaving your environment."

After some research, it emerged that Çeknaz and Sabri were behind it. After leaving our environment they had somehow got in touch with him and tempted him. He had asked us for permission to apply for a transfer and written a petition to the ministry. But due to this development, things have become confused. "Let's not give him permission. If he leaves, both he and his family will be in a difficult situation", I said.

They don't learn from the ignominy of others who've left. They later come back and cause us problems. The fact they come back as wrecks makes it difficult for us.

Block 8
28 March 1997

We held a block meeting with Sait hoca. Until noon, he presented a perspective on new and general topics. He explained what things need attention and care in the coming period.

In the afternoon, 41 comrades had their blocks changed. 11 left our block and 12 arrived.

Due to the new arrivals, we arranged entertainment in the evening. It went on until 11pm. Then we watched a bit of "Siyaset Meydanı" on TV.

Block 8
29 March 1997

Last night in my dream we were escaping.

Today we turned 472 million lira over to the central commune. This saving resulted mainly from the one-month giving up smoking campaign. We're more comfortable now.

Block 8
1 April 1997

Until noon, we consulted the structure on how to make lessons more productive, lively, and appealing.

We have started our first collective education work after the conference. From now on until lunchtime we will have collective education, while in the afternoon we will split into three separate groups.

In the morning, we will concentrate mainly on party analyses. This means I have to do more preparation for the morning sessions. It's necessary to find more creative methods.

Some comrades who have a mistaken approach to themselves are not happy about splitting up into groups in the afternoon. This is a very basic way of looking at things. Whatever group they are in, they will definitely learn things. Even the educator will learn things from his students.

We have 11 educators in our block.

Block 8
3 April 1997

Towards noon, I was called to the visiting area. Aziz P. had come... I had heard he'd been arrested at Newroz. Apparently, they released him after a few hours. He again complained about the apathy, complacency, irresponsibility, and degeneracy in the legal sphere. It is impossible not to agree with him in some respects.

I gather R. T. distorted the reasons he was thrown out of the environment when telling his family. A young relative of his came to visit. I explained to him at length the fact we had to throw him out. Apparently he is now in Muğla.

After the visit, I ate what was left over from the lunch time meal. After that, I listened one by one to the comrades who had had visitors. My head was throbbing. I sat down against the wall and kept going.

Comrade M. Yaldız had an operation today on a cyst that was on his ankle.

It is now midnight. The sound of Nevzat's snoring is coming from the lower bunk. Only five minutes ago he was awake. He's even worse than me. As soon as he puts his head on the pillow, he falls asleep. And the symphony begins immediately. Also, as he is overweight, his snores resemble old Massey-Ferguson tractors…

The ordinary prisoners who are in cells have turned up the volume on the TV to full and are listening to arabesque music. It reminds me of the open-air cinemas in Antep in the summer. We used to hear the sound from the cinemas on hills on the other side of the city. Sometimes the screen could be seen, too…

Block 8
4 April 1997

After the morning education was over I had lunch, then went to block 6-14. As the comrades were in session I chatted to the comrade on duty for a while. As he was new there, he explained his observations and impressions.

I went to see uncle Xalef. As usual, he offered me Eid sweets. "There's one for Kemal Aktaş and one for young İzzet, too," he said. He applies double standards, sending sweets to those he likes.

He is probably not keeping to his diet, as he doesn't look well. When I was in this block, I made sure he stuck to it. It means the comrades here are allowing their emotions to overcome their better judgement and letting him get away with it. I used to sometimes hide the salt in the kitchen so that he couldn't use it.

When I moved on to 7-15, the comrades were also in an education session. I went to see comrade Sadık, who was reading the Quran in the exercise yard. We had a short chat while pacing back and forth.

I then called comrade Recep outside, as I wanted to talk to him. It was more a matter of listening. He mentioned the practical goals he wanted to accomplish in the coming period. I expressed my pleasure on account of his wishing to contribute, because he is a comrade who has something to give. Like most "old" comrades, he is suffering a dilemma, weariness, and despair.

It is difficult talking to these comrades, as you are aware that they will know everything you are going to say.

Block 8
5 April 1997

When I woke up in the morning, it was only 06.00. As I felt tired, I decided to try to sleep for another hour. After half an hour, I was woken up by an alarm clock. After complaining, "Whose rooster is crowing at this hour?" I tried to get back to sleep.

At 09.00, we went to block 1 as guests. The administration had also come for a meeting. However, this is not a secure place for us to have a meeting. There is also no point in filling up the quota. It would also be better for morale if other comrades had come instead of us.

We discussed various topics on the agenda. The fact things we have been doing for years are being put on the agenda, as if they have just been discovered and time is being wasted, is irritating. Some things may seem easy for comrades who are not involved, but practical implementation is different.

When Delil again insisted on certain subjects, I had to respond. Being strict on certain points on which we should be flexible leads to reaction from the structure. Consequently, this administration will be blamed. Every administrator should be more constructive and have a closer dialogue with the structure.

There's no need for panic. There's no need to say, "Everything's gone" in the most minor situation. If we were like that outside, we would be a problem for the party. We would make a mess of everything.

We perceive centralisation to mean we should be doing everything.

As our meeting ended near noon, there was no time to talk to other comrades who had come. Naturally, there were some comrades who were put out.

When I returned to the block, I learned that some comrades had been oversensitive during morning education. It is not proper to debate every issue and to try to exert your power. It will also not help you.

Block 8
9 April 1997

This morning, comrade Cemal Kılıç went to the Izmir DGM. When he returned in the evening, we learned he was to be released. We were all delighted.

Our morning education was sabotaged. Officials from the prison authorities came. They were fitting video cables in the blocks. They're always finding pretexts to linger in the blocks.

Consequently, we sat down together in the afternoon. We read the leader's article regarding "The Antakya Popular Front." We obtained it from an old magazine.

This evening, we arranged entertainment for comrade Cemal's release. As he is older than us, it was good for his morale. We got him to sing a folk song. They called him about 7pm. In the exercise yard, he made a farewell speech in Kurdish, repeating that he would endeavour to be worthy of the struggle. He shook hands with us one by one and left. As he went into the corridor, he didn't dare to look back at us – his eyes were welling up…

Block 8
15 April 1997

After the announcement from Bursa, we also decided to start a warning three-day hunger strike to protest against repression in Erzurum, Giresun, and other prisons, and to support their protests. Also, we will not attend court while the protests in these prisons are continuing.

Today, our two-month giving up smoking campaign has begun. Once more, both the comrades' lungs will be cleansed (if only a little), and our economic situation will recover.

During Eid, the prison authorities want us to only have a half day of visits. After discussions amongst ourselves, we requested a full day. When they didn't accept our request, we said we wouldn't go for a half day, as visitors coming all the way from Kars or Hakkari, especially when you think of the time taken entering and exiting the prison, they would only have half the time. It would not be worth the expense and the time for the families.

Sait hoca came for the barbering. We discussed some issues on the agenda.

We dwelt in particular on some of the glitches in the collective morning education. The administration or block entities will remind educators of the issues they have to be aware of. Offending comrades and educators in the name of analysis or criticism, or people indulging their individuality and adversely affecting the education will not be permitted. This will only be possible if the educators are not nervous and use their initiative.

We heard on the TV news this morning that the HADEP members had been released.

The same special war is now preparing the most comprehensive attack on Kurdistan in history. All leave has been cancelled for soldiers, police, and all members of the security forces. From all over Turkey, military equipment and troops have been sent to various parts of Kurdistan during the last month. A complete mobilisation.

They may mount a major operation in South Kurdistan during the same period. They may try to frustrate the guerrillas' intensive preparations there. It seems things are going to warm up somewhat.

Today, we learned from the newspaper that İ. Mantaroğlu, who had escaped from Iskenderun prison, has been captured in a house in Adana. We were really disheartened. It's unacceptable that he could not be protected in a big city like Adana. It's such a waste of all that effort. Not to mention the fact he will be severely tortured.

Block 8
16 April 1997

Our warning hunger strike has begun. However, looking at the general assaults in the prisons, the course of support action could change at any moment. More comprehensive protests could come onto the agenda. Given such attacks, the detention centres must be supported with centralised and major actions. This is unavoidable, otherwise we will not be able to repulse the attacks. The detention centres are being especially targeted to break the will of those who have just been arrested and spread this to society as a whole. They have very broad goals.

Block 8
17 April 1997

> *TO THE KOÇERO OF BOTAN*
> *It was towards evening*
> *It was not yet dark*
> *A three-line note:*
> *"Koçero's cancer has been confirmed*
> *If he receives treatment, perhaps he will survive*
> *Shall we start a campaign?"*
> *My eyes are drawn to the word "perhaps."*
> *For a moment, the prison was silent.*
> *I felt the darkness before the evening set in.*
> *In front of my eyes*
> *With his silent and innocent glances,*
> *Koçer, his heart full of love for Cizre Botan*
> *He has always rebelled against the oppressor.*

First a "condemned man"
Years in the mountains
He considered the mountains,
A rifle,
And solitude…
To be freedom
They always called him a "bandit"!
He did not accept this,
They said he was 'condemned'.
The condemned man of those days,
Met heroes who loved freedom.
Those on the mountain
Their being rebels
Bearing arms
Pushed him towards real freedom.
He met Agit and Erdal in Botan.
With heroes he sharpened his heroism.
He memorised every stone on which he trod,
Every stream from which he drank water,
Every tree on which he leant,
Just like his struggle.
He witnessed resistance
And betrayal.
Later
Endless torture,
From between the corpses to prison
From 1985 to 1997,
Koçero was a captive,
Koçero has cancer!
He still loves Cudi, Kale Meme,
Gabbar.
And Fındık Kalesi
This is why he cannot accept prison
And the chains on his wrists.
Because he has faced bayonets on the walls of Dımdım Castle.

Block 8
19 April 1997

As we ended the hunger strike yesterday, we didn't have collective education this morning. Until noon, I was busy with the article I had to read.

Meanwhile, I have learnt that there is a total of 42 DHP comrades in all prisons. We have also received information regarding the situations of all of them, one by one.

While playing the first match of the ping-pong tournament we have organised, the prosecutor and governors came to offer Eid greetings. A short while later, they left. They then allowed five representative comrades to go round the blocks. Our refusal to accept the Eid visiting was effective in this. The prison authorities have supposedly made a goodwill gesture to us.

A brief note came from the coordination today. It mentions the possibility of a coup in Turkey and taking precautions. There is no point in making preparations for such an event. Prison components would be ripped to shreds. You couldn't even guess who would be transferred to which prison. The only thing to do is for everyone to speedily organise wherever they are, and not make any concessions. Our attitude to fascism and attacks is always clear. The enemy also knows this.

In case of possible developments, our fundamental publications have been written in tiny letters on tissue paper and hidden away. There's no guarantee, but we might be able to protect some of them. Some comrades have done amazing work — they have managed to fit sixty pages of a book onto one sheet of paper. It's incredible. We have dozens of fundamental works written in this way.

Block 8
20 April 1997

As I am the block look-out today, I did not attend the afternoon education. While waiting behind the door (meanwhile, listening in to all the conversations of the guards on the other side of the door), I read the "Guerrilla Diaries" in the March edition of *Özgür Halk* magazine. While making my way through the article, for a moment my thoughts went to the freedom valley and I revived my memory of the forested area there and the tempestuous stream. And of course, the solidarity of comrades in such harsh conditions...

Then I read a ten-page record of an incident in block 7-15. When I compared the two, the incident that occurred here disgusted and demoralised me. How quickly our people are affected by the corrosive life of the prison.

There was a fight between Direj and Seyit. Leaving everything else aside, how can someone set about 60-year-old Seyit? Is this acceptable? You can't claim as an excuse that he swore at comrades and the organisation. It's true that Seyit is a pain in the neck, but this is not a solution. He is reacting to the fact he is in prison and his son has joined the guerrillas. He is exacting a kind of revenge. His attitude is not that of a patriot. Despite this, Direj should have controlled himself. We have warned the block on countless occasions: "He's old, cope with him." Also, the fact that Direj has a post in the block and that the fight took place in the exercise yard, where guards could see it, and continued in the evening in the sleeping area is unacceptable. Lots of comrades also got involved in the incident. Those in the block are apparently shocked.

When we heard about the incident, we said, "Let the block entity evaluate it," as they are in the best position to know. Seyit was not admitted to the platform. He was not in a situation to deal with it. Direj's attitude was assessed. He was criticised severely. Various sanctions were proposed. As a precautionary measure, he was removed from his post temporarily, and his political relations were suspended.

Today Az. was thrown out of the environment. Despite being with us for three years, he has not been able to throw off the remnants of his bad habits. He has tried to maintain a relationship he established with a woman he met while active on our behalf in the Aegean region. When his practice outside was examined, it emerged he had been carrying on with a few others at the same time. Despite his saying he would abide by the decision taken by the structure, he did not behave sincerely. We couldn't remain silent, steps had to be taken. The besmirching of values created by lives, blood, and toil, and could not be ignored. Loyalty to the people's value judgements necessitates this.

It is a fundamental principle to do the right thing in the right place. In fact, it was necessary to take a stance earlier, but, as always, we said, "We can win him over, we can save him." Our approach to people whom we know will not change is nothing less than a waste of time and causes stress. This attitude of ours should be condemned. When some people are first seen, it is obvious they are hopeless cases… It is not possible for us to forcibly change someone who doesn't want to change…

Block 8
25 April 1997

Today Sait hoca was to go around the blocks, but he asked me to go. In the morning, I went to block 2. As I informed them I was coming, they had not sat down for education. After a brief chat with comrades, I sat with the administration. We dwelt mostly on matters relating to internal relations, understanding of duty, and harmonious work. The meeting lasted four hours.

I then went on to block 6-14.

The comrades had sat down for education, whereas the administration were in a meeting with comrade Mert. I joined the meeting. Comrades said he should correct his manner and attitude and that they expected him to make a contribution. As for him, he adopted a defensive attitude, seeing all problems as not being about him. In fact, the administration had supported him on account of his being new and young. And despite some comrades reacting, they had proposed he be given a post. When given a role, he had isolated himself by insisting, "My way is the correct one."

I made a short evaluation, noting there were duties that needed to be performed, and that he had fallen into the same position he had himself criticised previously, that this was shameful and that he, first and foremost, should not accept it.

He intensified his reaction by saying, "If you want, sever my organisational/political relations." Just like a baby. This is the outcome of his being treated with so much respect everywhere he's been, being given duties without making sufficient effort.

It means we haven't done well by the comrade. We are also guilty…

For when they throw themselves down, or have a serious problem, they always try to explain it with excuses, which leads to reactions from the structure.

Finally, we pointed out that he needed to correct his manner and accept that the organisation is his own.

I saw uncle Xalef and left the block.

Block 8
26 April 1997

Because he did not take part properly in the morning education and for close to insulting attitudes, I asked comrade E. Bekir to leave the session. That is, I threw him out. He was supposedly not listening to the lesson in order not to commit a sin and was constantly reciting prayers. We were only using a source on personality analysis. It's something that is done in every school.

What is interesting is that this comrade, who recites prayers, also sings folk songs while performing his ablutions. The tragicomic situation of the Kurd…

When he said he would not attend the afternoon group, we sat him down and talked to him. He said the education was too difficult for him to understand. We said, "Comrade, if that is the case, just tell us, rather than sabotaging the environment. And there was no need to find a religious cover for it." We will leave him to himself for a while.

As we need time to prepare for May Day, we will not have afternoon education for five days.

The block administration meeting we held lasted until the evening meal. It was comprehensive, but its length was down to our ponderousness…

Block 8
28 April 1997

We have sent a collective petition for Koçero to the President's office, the Prime Minister's office, and the Ministry of Justice. He needs to be released in order to receive treatment. I also wrote a literary article about him and sent it to the newspaper.

Block 8
30 April 1997

Despite three days having passed, a receipt to say the article was posted has not yet arrived. We asked the authorities, and they brought it back in the evening, saying it was "suspect." We refused to take it, saying, "If it's suspect, forward it to the prosecutor."

It's evident that, although there was no particular mention of Aydın prison, they took offence at the criticisms of general policies. It's arbitrary to not send it. Anyway, we will send it by our own methods. We had said we wouldn't send it illegally…

Block 8
1 May 1997

As today is also our visiting day, we will hold our May Day activities tomorrow. We just read out the joint statement prepared with other movements. All our blocks sang the May Day march and the Internationale in the exercise yards. And we shouted the slogans agreed. We wanted our voices, even those that are behind walls, to mingle with the cries of the toilers of the world.

It is the first time we have celebrated May Day in such a comprehensive way.

In the visiting area, after reading a short statement regarding the significance of the day, I invited everyone to stand for a minute's silence. I then wished them a happy May Day. In fact, the families are not familiar with this day, but they will become accustomed to it. There is no other way.

Comrade C. Kılıç had also come to visit. It was obvious that he was finding it hard to get used to the outside world. "Relationships outside are really fake. I don't miss the prison, but I already miss the comrades and the camaraderie here."

Of course, comradeship in the mountains and in prison are totally different. You cannot find them anywhere else.

Block 8

10 May 1997

We held a meeting on account of certain attitudes that contradicted our understanding during a football tournament we organised. In general, we were self-critical. Two comrades, who were involved in unsavoury incidents, have been banned from sporting activities for fifteen days. Six were criticised.

What occurred was not in keeping with the spirit of the tournament. It didn't look good, either. Although it was a game, street manners cannot be used.

What was really strange and unacceptable was that some educators were amongst those sanctioned. Is that how you're going to educate people? This is what is really demoralising about this.

Block 8

14 May 1997

Turkish military units have been massing on the border for months. According to official figures, 40,000 troops and 250 tanks crossed into South Kurdistan today. We all know that the true number is much higher.

Once again, they will suffer heavy losses. And when they want to withdraw, they won't be able to do that easily.

First the KDP and Barzani units attacked, then the Turkish units went into action on the pretext that they asked for assistance.

In short, the spear is once again being thrust from within.

It is certain there will be fierce clashes.

Block 8
20 May 1997

Today, just as we finished reading the analysis of M. Yıldız's leaving the environment, we heard that Art has been causing problems. He has gone off the rails. I said, let's ask him one last time what he is. Although he doesn't even meet the standards of being a patriot, our efforts have been designed to "transform" him. But he was trying to impose the life he knows on our environment. Was he doing this consciously or for some other purpose, I don't know. He apparently said, "As I am not a person who bends the knee, I will not accept any of the rules here." Yesterday, he told some comrades, "Here, people who resist are not respected." When we learned this, we realised we cannot expect anything from him.

It is clear that this is not his view, but we can't say anything. Is there anything more dishonourable than getting such wretches to advocate ideas you are unable to espouse? Can such people defend the ideas we know are right? Have we become that helpless?

As we cannot allow the environment which has been established over years through the toil and sacrifice of many comrades to be ruined, he was sent away. Let him go and try disobeying the rules of the prison authorities amongst the informers and deserters. Our humane way of life here is too much for some people.

I know very well that because I approach things in this way, the general prison administration will criticise me, or even ask for a report. But no matter what happens, the approach that insists on keeping people within the environment is not a correct policy. There is no point in forcibly keeping someone who does not accept your environment and does not adopt your way of life. Should we sacrifice 200 people for a few such characters?

Block 8
30 May 1997

When I went around the blocks today, I learned that Koçero had been brought back. I rushed to see him. His liver had been removed from two places in his right side. He'd had 26 stitches. They had burst and had to be re-stitched. He'd really suffered. He had lost a lot of weight and looked debilitated. There were around 50 comrades sitting with him, all of them silent. Beneath the silence was a seething rebellion.

We all knew that the Koçero of the mountains was not someone who would end up like this.

We also knew that, first and foremost, he wouldn't accept this.

And we knew that, if there had been an earlier intervention, he would not have been in this state. For months they told him there was "nothing wrong." At the last stage, they took him to hospital.

This morning, block 6-14 started a hunger strike. Every block will do a two-day hunger strike to protest at the massacre in the South.

Today M. Sarıkaya and I applied to be transferred to Maraş prison, us paying the expenses. We don't really expect a positive reply.

Block 8
30 June 1997

Today is the anniversary of comrade Zilan's self-sacrifice action. It's been a whole year, but it feels like it was only yesterday…

What keeps her relevant is her heroic action.

She is the initiator of a new tradition. Her followers are continuing to transform themselves into bombs from the north to the south. It is this which is devastating the enemy…

After a minute's silence at 09.00, they asked me to read out the statement. If my application for a transfer is approved, it will be the last statement I read out here. This was followed by all blocks shouting these slogans:

"Zilan is the Commander, We are her Troops!"
"We have accomplished the Revival, Now for Liberation!"
"South, North, East, Apo is the Leader of the Country!"
"Martyrs are Immortal!"
"Zilan-Hozan-Seyran are Marching towards Victory Kurdistan!"
"Long Live Leader Apo!"

We repeated these slogans five times until 23.00. But the most meaningful one was the one at 17.45, as that was the time comrade Zilan carried out her action.

We also read comrade Zilan's letter and an evaluation from the party leadership.

In the evening, I continued to read the *Serxwebun 1996* magazine. They have serialised an article I wrote together with comrades Tören and Nihat in 1995. In such times, the importance of peace processes is better understood.

Today, I read a statement by DS. They have made the same criticism of us that we made about them. They even used our wish to not take Az. back into our environment. They have developed a theory regarding taking into their blocks people we have thrown out, despite our warnings. We should have shown a stronger reaction on the first day they accepted him. Perhaps then it would have been better understood. In spite of everything, I hope they do not regret taking in the troubled characters who are unable to adapt to our environment.

They took comrade Vehbi to a hospital in Izmir for a computer scan. But after being kept waiting in the vehicle for 11 hours, he was given an appointment in two months' time. It's a policy to delay treatment. It's a different way of leaving people to die. Torturing people by leaving them to wait long periods in the transfer vehicle is a special type of torture.

Mesut Yılmaz has announced his cabinet. Sezgin is Defence Minister and Deputy PM, Sungurlu Justice Minister, and Ecevit Deputy PM... in short, a new war government... after the Refah Party, with the guidance of the army, they want to have such a government.

Block 8
7 July 1997

Finally, *Ülkede Gündem* has come out. As they only brought one copy to the prison, it has been around all the blocks. It arrived at our block this evening. We simply devoured it. After looking at its layout, we read a short assessment by the Leadership.

Block 8
14 July 1997

We held a fitting commemoration for those involved in the death fast resistance of 14 July.

We lived them again to the full.

As they live every one of our days.

Commemorating them in these circumstances makes us sad.

Those who best commemorate and understand them are our guerrillas.

Block 8
20 July 1997

They have begun to turn many E-Type prisons into a cell-based system. While on the one hand they are dividing up the blocks into cells, they are also putting barbed wire over the top of the exercise yards.

It is certain that in the coming period there will be a general attack on the prisons. Apart from the cell system, they envisage many changes with a new notice. In particular, they want to sever relations between blocks and with the outside world.

In the coming days, we will hold a forum to create awareness of this issue. We will discuss "what we can do" practically and organisationally.

Today S. Gür went from block 9-13 to a cell. After having a series of problems, he wanted to go to Manisa prison. We gave him permission, not wanting him to have an excuse, but the ministry did not allow him to go. When he wanted to get his family involved, we did not approve it. He used that as an excuse. He told comrades who tried to persuade him, "If you can stop it, stop it."

Apart from his indecision and refusal to attend the disciplinary council, a person should respect three or four years of effort and not reduce themselves to this.

Block 8
24 July 1997

The results of the X-rays and vaccination we insisted the prison authorities to do have come back. As six people in our blocks are in a critical condition, they have been taken to hospital. M. Ali Kapar was taken from our block. He is thin, has a poor appetite and, moreover, smokes.

They took comrade K. Bakay from block 2. The comrades learned by chance. He had apparently been coughing up blood for about a month. Despite this, he hadn't told the comrades. When I heard this, I got really angry. For a start, this is endangering the health of 20 comrades. How is it possible to be so thoughtless, so lacking in awareness?

M. Yıldız, who was under observation, has gone to block 9-13. According to those who came from there recently, he had reduced himself to a sorry state. They said, "He definitely won't come to our environment." I assume he has come on account of pressure from his family. Many families know very well how dishonourable life is outside our environment. And the consequences…

Knowing full well that they will have difficulties, we try to keep such people in our environment. Otherwise, the enemy will manipulate them, adversely affecting us and society.

Block 8
27 July 1997

We are watching with interest the TV news at 20.00, as always. Comrade H. Yağız comes into the dining hall of block 8 in a panic, saying, "Self-sacrifice action… woman comrade…," as we look on in surprise.

A few minutes later, there is a caption at the bottom of the screen. We wait in silence, curious as to what has happened.

In Bodrum district, a bomb has exploded in a woman comrade's hand at a public convenience. However, the explosives wrapped around her body didn't go off. According to the first announcement, her name is Kudret Denktaş, from Birecik, in Urfa province. She went to nursing college in Antep. (We subsequently learned that her name was Dıbıstan PERİŞAN and that her body was to be taken to her home town of Amed). What a coincidence. Comrade Zilan also went to nursing school.

It was hard seeing her shattered, blood-stained face on the TV screen. The bomb exploded prematurely. It caused panic, but it was unfortunate that it turned out this way.

At the moment in Bodrum there are tourists from all over the world. This action would have dealt a serious blow to tourism.

They are expecting self-sacrifice actions everywhere. They know after Zilan's action that every heart is a bomb.

Block 8
2 August 1997

Today is 2 August. It is the eighth anniversary of the martyrdom of comrades Eroğlu and Yalçınkaya. Tomorrow, we are entering the ninth year. What a long time. I remember them as if it was yesterday.

Our leaving Eskişehir, the journey, that never-ending journey that was turned into savagery, being held for hours on arrival here, and then being taken in two at a time…

Just like being taken into a monster's mouth that opens and closes… And what happened after that…

And that news we received while lying in the cells between the moans of wounded bodies. That news that we still cannot accept.

It was a journey, ours.

Towards morning, they brought us the news amongst our hunger and pain. For a moment, everything came to life…

On a journey, the ending of which was unknown, would we be able to see each other again? We couldn't know…

What we did know was that we trusted each other and ourselves. The rest was just a journey. But for those two, it was to be their last journey with us. They were to conclude their journey with us. I say with us, for they had been on a journey with us prior to that. That was a journey to the country they loved and for the sake of which they had devoted their lives, suffered torture for years, and run the risk of death…

They attained what they yearned for.

One day, we will accompany them on their last journey. We will express our longings and our yearnings with a childlike tenderness…

They will be sad when they see us, whereas we will be happy…

Let it be. Both feelings are comradely affection.

Yes, we were remembering them again. We stopped all the activities.

At 09.00 in the morning, we held a minute's silence. A statement was read out. At that moment, the exercise yard was too small for me. It was like an earthquake erupting inside me. It nearly carried me off. Then we shouted slogans:

"Hüseyin and Mehmet are immortal!"
"Down with the Special War!"
"Long Live Leader Apo!"

On account of yesterday's central statement, tomorrow we will begin a three-day protest hunger strike along with all political movements.

It is now 03.00 in the morning.

The night has silently evolved into day…

Block 8
5 August 1997

Today, after washing my dirty clothes and having a shower, I went around the blocks with comrade Nuri. The first thing that caught my attention in the corridor was that the guards did not open or close the doors before asking the head guard. This is a new procedure.

While in block 4, they somehow brought the *Gündem* newspaper. First I was uncle Xalef's guest.

Our action ended this evening. What I noticed in the blocks is that after only three days comrades were looking pale and thin. I wrote to the administration, saying they should take notice of this. Going on hunger strike frequently, if only for short periods, weakens the body's resistance.

The self-criticism written by comrade Yusuf was accepted by the general structure. For around a year, he has been outside organisational relations. For it to have gone on any longer would have adversely affected him. Although he's not entirely persuaded, he has addressed some fundamental issues regarding himself. He will be admitted to organisational relations but will not have the right to criticise for a period.

Most of the comrades who were active in the Izmir-Buca area have experienced similar problems when they came here. It's a result of their not having had a sufficient party education. Sometimes, they are the victim of their good intentions.

Block 8
14 August 1997

As tomorrow is August 15, we held a minute's silence in the visiting area today, followed by the reading of a message, after which comrades and families exchanged festival greetings. While reading out the message, an elderly man, despite being disabled, stepped forward and tried to stand opposite me. Although he had difficulty standing, he tried to make a victory salute. I noticed him at that moment and was delighted and deeply moved by his behaviour. He had come from Mardin to visit comrade H. Turgay. His eyes were sparkling, despite his 80 years. In such eyes you can see the liveliness and light of our guerrillas and of Kurdistan. His reassuring manner pleased us all. We chatted with him. His words were sparkling, just like the twinkle in his eye…

Block 8
15 August 1997

The 13th anniversary of the Glorious 15 August Launch. Preparations for the celebrations have been going on for days.

As it is one of the most important dates for us, all comrades were ready early in the morning. Everyone was as clean as a new pin.

Activities began after the "Ey Raqip" anthem, statement, and slogans.

Comrades had prepared five sketches, and they were embellished with a choir and a solo, etc.

It went off well. Our every moment was about the heroes who were involved in the firing of "the first shot."

We once again remember with respect and gratitude the legendary commander Agit and his comrades.

Block 8
19 August 1997

Up till now I.D. was not asked for on the way to hospital. For two weeks now, such a military measure has been introduced. The prison authorities claim it is not them.

Comrades are only giving their names at the moment. When this is not accepted, comrades return to the blocks and don't go to hospital. At the moment, only emergency cases are going. Representatives are going to discuss this with the prison authorities. If we don't react, there will be further measures.

Block 8
22 August 1997

We went around the blocks. We had a meeting in block 6 regarding some practical problems.

I don't know how it looks from outside, but we don't have an hour that passes idly by.

At lunch, the comrades treated us to peppers. For the first time this year, we had ample peppers on our table. They were pleasantly hot.

I returned after dropping in to blocks 9 and 2. Without even having time to rest or catch breath, an intensive bout of note traffic began.

A message from the leadership to the prisons dated 6 July 1997 had arrived. It has been decided how we will evaluate this. Alongside the message, an administration statement has been prepared.

While standing up reading out the leader's message, I couldn't still my excitement. On finishing, the applause went on for ages. There was an incredible atmosphere. Tears came to our eyes. We could hardly contain ourselves. Following the applause, I sat down and read the administration's statement. My tears were about to flow.

Following the statement, we all went out into the exercise yard and did a halay. This time we were greeting the Leader with a halay and our folk songs.

There was enthusiasm, excitement, and joy amongst all the comrades. The atmosphere in the block had suddenly changed. It was as if all the blocks had come to life. Morale was at a peak.

The leadership is announcing the good news that 1997 has been won in its first six months.

He was also pointing out the need for better organisation, as in some prisons there has been a drop off, and that the shortcomings in our education system are responsible for the failure of those being released to seek out the party.

From the sensitive tone used by the Leader, it is possible to understand the value he attaches to us.

He also reminded us of our duties. The rest is down to us.

The only solution to the attacks the enemy will develop in the coming period is to respond by representing the party.

Block 8

3 September 1997

Around a month ago, Kemal Aktaş wrote a petition asking to go to Konya. Today, he was summoned and told his request had been granted. He wasn't expecting a positive reply, as recently such requests have been turned down. It's a surprise that it was accepted.

Block 8
24 September 1997

It has been exactly a year since 10 of our comrades were brutally slaughtered. But it seems like it was yesterday that we heard about the attack in Amed prison…

Since that day, it has been those who were injured and died who have gone on trial, not the murderers. That is, the victims of this attack have been made the accused. That's Turkish justice for you…

Tens of thousands have started a hunger strike today to protest this incident. In all the prisons, we are protesting this arbitrary, low, inhuman measure with a day of hunger.

After the morning minute's silence and the reading out of a statement, we shouted slogans.

When the guards saw we had not taken in the meal wagon, they were surprised, then informed…

In the evening, we watched the film *Işıklar Sönmesin* (May the Lights Not Go Out) on TV. It was supposedly about the war in Kurdistan. It was entirely designed to obscure the image and manner of the guerrillas. And it was far from reflecting the reality of the war.

The fundamental message was of enemy forces becoming reconciled in the face of nature.

Despite that, seeing footage of nature in our homeland obviously affects you. If only for a moment, it takes you to those mountains, those snowy mountains.

It reminds you of the difficulties of life there and the importance of solidarity. Ah… ah…

Block 8
26 September 1997

I took part in a meeting in block 6-14 until noon. After lunch, I went to see uncle Xalef. He was sitting in the exercise yard of block 4, wrapped in a blanket reading the Quran. When he saw me, he hurriedly closed the Quran, as always, and we began to chat. After a short while, comrade Bayram came over and Xalef gave him a task. "There are a few pastries I squirrelled away two days ago. Bring them out." Bayram and I smiled at each other. Although I told him there was no need, uncle Xalef insisted. Bayram said, "Xalo, if you had told me when we made them, I would have saved a whole tray."

Xalo responded, "No, in that case, it would have been meaningless. These are my share. I won't take anyone else's."

Meanwhile, the prosecutor summoned Sait hoca. Apparently, the Ministry of Justice has requested Koçero's file. This is a good sign. They may release him. Not to lead to any expectations, he won't be told until it's certain.

As I was about to leave the block, Koçero said, "I suggested a transfer to another prison, but the comrades won't permit it." While shaking his hand, I looked him in the eye and said, "Don't insist, we will send you to Kurdistan." I don't know what he understood from that, but he just looked me in the eye. While he stared at me silently, I went into block 9-13.

Yesterday, they confirmed comrade Fuat Kav's transfer to Konya. He had immediately written a note. It was quite emotional. He asked us to write if we had something to say. He added that wherever and whatever happened, he would always act with concern for the party. He would be subject to the administration where he went and would not act self-importantly, etc.

When I first read his note, I couldn't help saying to myself, "vatan millet sakarya" [stale rhetoric].

As for comrade Şamil, he was to describe it, "Like the last words of a man going to be executed."

I'd wanted to see him today, as he could be called for transfer at any time. In fact, this transfer has shocked us all. We weren't expecting it. After ten years together in Eskişehir and the years here, his departure for another place will be hard for us. The same is true for comrade Kemal. It will be difficult to be separated from comrades with whom we have endured attacks on numerous occasions, taken part in many protest actions, attended countless meetings, shared both painful and joyful news, and been involved in many illegal activities together. They are also comrades who passed through the resistance to the brutality in Diyarbakır prison before coming here.

We have stayed with so many comrades. We have had such days that they were equal to a year. Together, we faced death on many occasions. We took the most risky decisions. From time to time, we had fierce debates. But our respect and affection for each other as comrades never wavered. The bond between us was based on trust and was strong.

Recent transfers indicate a change in ministry attitudes. I hope they will accept transfers to Kurdistan.

Zeki Karatay's transfer to Çankırı has also gone through.

I returned to my block at about 17.00. A short time later, the wall of block 6 was rapped and we were told that Koçero's release had been confirmed. On the one hand, I was pleased, but I was also suspicious. I couldn't help thinking, "If he hadn't been terminally ill, they wouldn't have released him." They have apparently released him on license to get treatment, and once he has recovered, they will recall him to prison. But most of those who have been released to receive treatment have died.

The campaign for the release of the comrade has had an effect. Our press also covered it well. I assume the doctors' reports were also influential.

In spite of everything, it will be good for him to go out. To live outside for ten days is better than ten years in prison. This is not sentimentalism, it is the reality…

At tea time, I went downstairs to the dining areas and told the comrades about Koçero's release. A storm of applause broke out. This was followed by more of the same from block 6…

Block 8
9 October 1997

Today, my brother Cemal came to visit me. He hadn't visited for two years. He explained that he had had a second operation and been in bed for six months. I find it difficult to understand him. More correctly, I get angry with him. A person should not allow himself to be reduced to such a pitiful state.

He passed on some news about the wider family. There is disorganisation and fragmentation. They cannot be said to be problem solvers. They have all become inured to the situation.

Block 8
10 October 1997

The DHP has taken a central decision, declaring 10 October to be martyrs' commemoration day.

We also held a minute's silence this morning and, after a statement was read out, shouted the following slogans in the exercise yard:

"Martyrs of the Revolution are Immortal!"

"The Mizgins and Yasins are Immortal!"

"Guerrillas strike, the Peoples of Anatolia become Free!"

"Long Live the United People's Front!"

"Long Live the DHP!"

"Long Live Leader Apo!"

Following the commemoration, we had just started on a 50-page article of the DHP, when they summoned me to the dentist.

He cut two of my teeth. After doing three teeth on one side, he will do five on the other. The way he threw the instruments he had used into the sink was repugnant.

Block 8
17 October 1997

Yesterday, during visiting, we heard the news that comrade Nuri Ekinci was to be released. The Court of Cassation apparently acquitted him. And during the search today, the prosecutor came into the exercise yard and told us the release decision had arrived. Hasty preparations began, as we were caught unawares. They said he should be ready to go in an hour. While making a speech, he said he would endeavour to be worthy of what he had experienced and of the values involved. As he went out the door, he said to me, "I don't have any particular preference, but I have some physical discomforts." For a moment, I found it strange. He shouldn't have felt the need to say that.

Today, we began our half yearly evaluation. After the general report had been read and views obtained, we moved on to assessing individual reports. We are intending to be in session all day to complete the task in three days. Apart from the election of a commission, it is like a semi-conference. The aim is to consider how many conference decisions have been implemented and to reduce the load of the annual conference at the end of the year.

Block 8
21 October 1997

At the midnight roll call, it was announced that comrade Kemal Aktaş was to be transferred. They wanted to leave it to the last minute to accomplish a fait accompli. We were watching the excitement in the block opposite. In the end, they didn't take him until the exercise yard door was opened at 06.00.

They hastily prepared a few breakfast things. The commune comrade joked, "You'll never have such a great breakfast again, comrade Kemal."

In order to see him off, we all lined up in the exercise yard. When I asked him to make a farewell speech, he said, "Comrade Ali, don't insist. I'm not being released, I'm just going to another prison. What can I say?"

I replied, "Perhaps you won't ever be able to see some of the comrades here again."

He made a short speech, pledging to endeavour to be worthy of the Kemals, Hayris, and Mazlums in the place he was going.

And he left, perhaps never to meet us again.

Fuat Kav, Salman Aktaş (going to Maraş), and Arif Ekrem (going to Midyat) were waiting in the corridor.

The main corridor swallowed them up. Like the darkness swallowing a weak light.

Comrade Kemal had sorted out some articles and interviews. He asked me to send them to Sait hoca. A 30-40 page article on the brutality in Diyarbakır caught my attention. When I looked carefully at the handwriting, I realised it belonged to comrade Mustafa Gezgör. Handwriting reveals identity just like a photo.

As always, the writings are precious. Unfortunately, sometimes they are all that remains of a person.

After the transfers, a letter came from block 9. Fuat Kav had written a three-page note to the comrades with whom he worked for years. Apart from the emotional aspect, it is possible to see honesty, self-sacrifice, determination, and loyalty to the revolution, people and party, and tolerance...

I will save the letter.

It is evident that we will really miss all the comrades.

It is our wish to meet in a free homeland.

Block 8
22 October 1997

Today they took Zeki Karatay for a transfer. He had written a petition to go to Çanakkale. When we request a transfer, we pay the travel costs. They took 20 million from Zeki.

We saw Zeki off like the transfers yesterday. Although he wanted to go, he looked reluctant to leave. I assume the fact his wife lives in that province influenced his decision. He was here for four years. At first, he found it very difficult, but later became accustomed to it here.

We gave him a few theoretical books so that he can benefit from reading them there.

Block 8
1 November 1997

Today, the "Let's analyse ourselves properly, let's make education part of life" campaign began. It will go on for a month. A statement was made to inform the entire structure.

As always, the preparations were only just completed in time. Some practical announcements were left to later.

The aim of this is for theoretical education to be practiced in personality and life. For a person to look into himself and see himself by confronting his own reality.

Block 8
4 November 1997

I got up at 6.40 in the morning. A few other comrades had also got up for exercise. As it's got colder, the number of comrades wanting to do exercise has dwindled.

I had also had a break from it, as washing with cold water in the mornings is not on. I was making up for it by playing football in the afternoons.

I visited block 9-13. As comrade Fuat has gone, I had to give the comrade there a general notification. After staying there for about an hour, I went to block 13 for lunch.

It is one of the blocks where I have stayed the longest, for years.

Consequently, it is a block where I have fond memories. There is no one else who has been here longer than me. A few comrades are in other prisons. Most of them have been released. Of course, some of them have been martyred. Mustafa GEZGÖR (Zaman), Derviş ÇELİK (Soro), Doğan KILIÇKAYA (Yasin) are the ones who were martyred. We don't know how many more comrades have fallen in the land they love.

Whichever wall, corner, bunk, or picture I look at in block 13, it will remind me of numerous things. Memories that are in the distant past feel as if they just happened yesterday…

Those memories, full of innocence, loyalty, honesty, and sincerity…

Those human-comradely memories, when trust was total…

I'm looking with the sadness of a person going into the past, at that silent and lonely place…

After lunch, we strode back and forth. Then, when comrade Sadi said his tea was ready, we sat down for tea. One of the most pleasant aspects of conversation is sipping well-steeped tea. I was asked about various comrades in other blocks. Meanwhile, some references we made led to laughter. It is possible to see comradeship, affection, respect, and yearning in all this curiosity and banter.

Bidding them farewell, I moved on to block 7. A smiling comrade, Ethem, was at the door. As the block was in education, I went to see the oldest person in block 7-15, comrade Sıdık. As I was aware of his sensitivity, I asked him about his health. He smiled and asked after the comrades. It was clear from the fact his sleeves were rolled up to his elbows that he had just performed his ablutions.

Moving on to block 15, I asked the comrades who were in an education session to have a short break so that I could inform them of recent developments. I then held a meeting with the block entity. I passed on the conclusions of the two long meetings we had held in block 1. I wanted them to be informed of the problems dealt with and people's attitude. When we heard the voices of comrades calling for a break, we also paused.

When I went down to the exercise yard, I shook hands with all the comrades. Everyone was interested in the "Şal-u Şepik" from the Hakkari region that I was wearing. Some comrades asked me jokingly, "Comrade Ali, are you on Cudi mountain?" Of course, I replied that these were our usual clothes, proudly recalling our "guerrilla" days.

When looking at the comrades who are full of life, the silence and downward glances of comrades with problems attract my attention. Is there any point in getting yourself into such a state? Can it justify depriving yourself of comrades' enthusiasm?

Comrade Recep suggests that "changing the blocks of some comrades who are under pressure may be useful, as they may be able to get themselves together." Comrade Recep joined in Antep, when the party was at the group stage. He is a Turk and is sometimes overemotional. He is a knowledgeable and valued comrade and one of the comrades we consult when necessary in all circumstances.

For two days now, they are causing problems for comrades going to the binding room.

Apart from a book-binder, there is also an iron and sewing machine there. Two comrades from our blocks take turns to go there. The needs of all blocks are met in this way.

Every time, they are obstructing in an arbitrary way. The prison authorities have intensified this recently. Most recently, they insulted two comrades during a search on the way to hospital. When they got to the hospital, they threw them in the basement while handcuffed. According to comrade Celalettin, they wanted to create a provocation.

Every restriction, every new measure they impose is a continuation of previous ones. None of them are coincidental. They are testing our patience and reactions. Similarly, they also harass our visitors in various ways.

Apart from our individual reactions, comrade Sarıkaya has also met with the prison governor to express our feelings.

Block 8
5 November 1997

Although I said three or four times this morning that I wanted to go to the dentist, they did not call me.

Although we pay to have our teeth done, they still mess us about by delaying treatment. It's been a month since the broken parts of the teeth were removed, but he still hasn't fitted the crowns. Meanwhile, the healthy teeth are also decaying. The guy enjoys causing us pain. He does the same thing to all the comrades. He's more of a money-grabber than a doctor. His name is Erhan, and he's been here for more than ten years.

Finally, I sent a message, saying, "For your information, I will speak to the governor and the prosecutor." Within ten minutes, he called me. But I wish I hadn't gone. Because the cement was like ice, the pain from the teeth reached my temples. The pain continued for two hours after returning to the block.

Today, Y. Turgut was thrown out of block 2. He was the most recent arrival. Both he and all his family members have been turned by the police. The police also used him outside. When this became known, comrades decided it was not appropriate either for him to remain in our blocks or for members of his family to be in the same visiting area as our family members. Before he left the block, comrades gave him eight million lira to meet his needs, as a humane gesture…

It appears that the police have targeted people from Muş and Siirt resident in the province of Aydın and the surrounding area, making some of them collaborators. Or "convinced" them to seek information.

A letter has arrived from comrade Kemal Aktaş. He apparently began to miss the comrades here even before he was released. He mentioned several topics we were curious about. Of course, some were troublesome. There are some who want to get married for a third time, like a Shah. It's a shameful thing. Apart from what you've been through, hasn't the education you received had any effect at all? Although these may be exceptions, they are still demoralising.

In comrade Kemal's letter, there are different emotions in every sentence.

In our volleyball tournament, our team lost 3-0. As it finished early, we played football for 30 minutes.

In the forum we held this evening, we discussed "Turkey-Greece relations." As the Cyprus issue has been prominent in the recent period, it was good to have a debate. There is tension between the two states. As Turkey does not want to divide its forces, it is not forcing the issue. It appears to be avoiding conflict. It doesn't want to broaden the front while involved in a war with the Kurds.

Block 8
7 November 1997

After the morning roll call, they summoned T. Özdemir to go to court. When the guards asked if he was going to go or not, we told him to go. He departed reluctantly. When they returned in the afternoon, we learned that he and M. Şirin Tekmenuray had been tortured in the vehicle and in the cell at the court.

Our representatives immediately became involved. If they don't receive a satisfactory answer, we will bang the doors and shout slogans. It is not possible for us to remain silent and passive in such situations.

As they sensed our stance is serious, they called comrade Sait to the office. They seem to have panicked. They said, "We will dwell on this and speak to the commander." But the attack was coordinated. The comrade expressed our reaction rigorously and came back.

While being assaulted in the vehicle, comrade Şirin said, "Why are you hitting us? This is indicative of your passing." When we heard this, we were both pleased and laughed.

In today's newspaper, there was an announcement made by all movements apart from DS. For now, an alternating, limitless hunger strike will commence, with people doing two days each. An accompanying warning adds that, if there is no positive response, more comprehensive actions will take place.

We were aware that a debate over a centralised action was going on regarding the cell system, but we weren't expecting two days each. It's limitless, but two days will be ineffective. At least ten days would have been better.

I have received a negative response to my request for a transfer to Maraş.

Block 8
8 November 1997

Immediately after sitting down for education in the morning, we were told that comrade A. H. Boztepe's father had been remanded in custody and brought to block 6-14. The fact he was remanded and put in the same block as his son is a clear message and warning to us and families.

Yesterday, the HADEP office in Aydın was raided. I gather 1998 calendars published by the *Özgür Halk* magazine were there, and they are illegal. A nonsensical pretext, but the police used it as a justification for a remand. But it is no coincidence that he was brought to Aydın prison.

Naturally, the arrest and imprisonment of a visitor we all know has upset and angered us.

Yesterday, they assaulted another comrade on his way to hospital. The authorities said they would resolve this problem. We know they're not sincere, but they are stringing us along. They are creating an expectation. To tell the truth, we also did not want things to get too tense or for the problems to get worse. But in spite of this, the authorities are intensifying the tension in all areas and are in attack mode.

It has been clarified that we will go on hunger strike tomorrow. Initially, it will be blocks 4, 6, and 14. Every block is ready and will take its turn.

In the afternoon, some of the comrades took their bedding out into the exercise yard. As they were shaking and beating their mattresses at the same time, the whole place was covered in dust.

Block 8

13 November 1997

We were intending to have education until lunchtime, but when visiting began early, we adjourned at around 10. Comrade Mazlum Doğan's elder sister, Serap, came to visit. She had last come with her mother to an open visit in 1990. She wanted to see the comrades. But she was disappointed that there are very few left whom she knows. Seeing comrades who were in Diyarbakır during the brutal era comforted her…

Because she saw Mazlum in them,

And the past,

And the intense suffering and great resistance.

Seeing them in every place cheered her up to some extent…

She saw in them a part of herself, and Mazlum, and Delil Doğan…

As the visiting families were to issue a press statement in front of the prison, we ushered them out at 13.00. About 150 family members gathered at the gates. TV companies filmed it, but they definitely won't broadcast it.

The statement was intended to create awareness about recent restrictions in prisons, the latest hunger strikes, the cell system, and incidents in Aydın – as well as to demonstrate their reaction to these issues.

Block 8

14 November 1997

While having lunch, we heard someone in the corridor shouting the slogan, "Torture Cannot Cow Us." We immediately asked the adjacent blocks. There was nothing in our blocks. We didn't understand what had happened.

Although we were expecting a search in the morning, they came in the afternoon. Though they know they won't find anything, they always carry out a search, as this is a war on our nerves.

Block 8
17 November 1997

In a notice published on behalf of S. Korkmaz in Amasya, amongst a list of martyrs is the name of comrade Metin Uluca. For a moment, my eyes were drawn to it. At the same moment, my memories of comrade Metin were taking shape in my thoughts…

We spent a long time together. Hard, painful days, when we tried to look out for each other. Resisting in the most arduous circumstances to within an inch of our lives…

As I had also known him outside, my pain and grief is more profound.

I first saw him (if my memory is not deceiving me) at the end of '78 or the beginning of '79 in the open air section of the "Nizip Café" on the Nizip road. It was a place frequented by workers.

He was sat at a table with flour workers and porters, as well as with Numan, who was then the head of the Antep group. Metin stood out amongst those there with his speech, attitude, and youth. His vivacity and warmth marked him out.

I was to get to know him well in the following years. We did not have a problem in our activities. The closest witnesses of this are comrades such as Nasır Göksungur, H. Şerik, A. Cerenbelli, and Sait Şimşek.

He was careful and meticulous in his relations.

After the 1980 military coup, Metin, who was then the head of the group in Antep, was arrested. He suffered severe torture. We were tried in the same case.

I got to know him better in prison. I recall the prisons to which we were sent, the incidents that occurred, the military courts to which we went frequently, and the defences we made in court, despite all the obstruction and torture…

After being released, he went straight to join the guerrillas. With his experience and knowledge, he came to the fore. But he was martyred too soon. He shouldn't have been parted from his comrades prematurely.

I can still hear his sincere, childlike laugh…

After the exercise yard doors closed, Sait hoca went around the grilles. He was returning from meeting the governor. The Aydın HADEP chair has been arrested and, despite coming here and wishing to be with us, he has not been placed in our blocks. I gather neither a positive nor negative answer has been received. Although Sait hoca was amongst the guards, he moved a little closer to the grilles and made the signal to "bang on the doors." This was because he had told the governor that, if the man was not allocated to our blocks within half an hour, he would not be responsible for what happened.

Shortly after Sait hoca had returned to his block, all the blocks began to bang their doors. We repeated it at 22.30.

Block 8
18 November 1997

Our two-day central alternating hunger strike has ended. But Erzurum and Batman have turned it into a limitless hunger strike. We don't know if there are other prisons involved.

Block 8
19 November 1997

Az. wanted to leave us and we didn't stop him, as the environment does not want to be in the same space as such depraved individuals. What was the meaning of his latest arrival? Did he want to do something with people amongst us? Of that we are not sure. But the truth will come out. His departure did not sadden us, but it did create question marks.

I have received a letter after 17 years from my step-brother Halil's wife. I was initially surprised, as it was a shock. It's a very strange feeling. After not writing a line for so many years, they suddenly write to me. They must have some problems. I hesitated whether I should write back, but as I know one shouldn't be resentful, I will write. I assume Cemal gave them my address over the phone.

Block 8
20 November 1997

They have taken HADEP members Osman Hoca and Duran Boztepe to Nazilli prison. They rushed them away yesterday after we made a fuss.

I gather they have been placed amongst comrades in Nazilli. Comrade Duran's wife came to visit today and passed on the news. Duran also said, "Staying in Aydın would have been a chance for me." It would also have been good for the family if he had stayed here.

Block 8
24 November 1997

As our morning education is on party analyses, it is natural that it predominantly involves criticism and self-criticism. At times, it becomes tense. It is more those comrades who consider themselves to be "sufficient" who are finding it difficult. While they are comfortable criticising others, when it comes to themselves, they erect verbal armour. When defending their own errors, they adopt an aggressive manner towards the comrades who criticise them. And when the language used begins to get out of hand, it becomes even more irritating.

There should not be this amount of lack of trust, suspicion, and prejudice towards comrades with whom they share a space and, when necessary, with whom they will face death.

Comrades who end up like this upset me. They should not become so pitiable.

Today, comrade Sarıkaya came to the grilles to inform us that 15 comrades were to change blocks. The authorities have been delaying things. We kept the list short.

I have been meaning to write a few letters for several days, but I can't seem to find the time. It's partly down to a lack of planning on my part.

As I haven't exercised today, I feel a lethargy in my body. Playing football occasionally makes you feel better. When I don't exercise, I get tired easily. It may be psychological, but what's important is physical activity, which makes you feel calm.

After I suggested it yesterday, my analysis was carried out. There was comprehensive and serious criticism. But it was all civilised, measured, and in accordance with our turn of phrase.

Block 8
27 November 1997

We have been preparing for this day for nearly a month. For us, 27 November is a significant day. We are duty bound to celebrate it in the best way possible. Conscious of this, all comrades took on duties in the preparation phase.

As on every day at 07.00, the dorm was awakened with the words, "Roj baş." As I worked until 03.00 in the morning, when I woke up, my temples were throbbing. I ignored it and hurriedly got dressed.

After getting ready and having breakfast, I read the statement again. At exactly nine o'clock, I invited the comrades to stand for a minute's silence in the exercise yard. Then we recited "Ey Raqip." For those who didn't know the words, we had written them in large letters on a blackboard and placed it on the opposite wall. Unfortunately, most of us don't know it by heart.

Although I had read the statement, I still faltered in places, as I was nervous. After the DHP comrade had read out their statement, we shook hands with each other in turn to mark our festival. After being given some eau de cologne and sweets, we dispersed, as our big celebration is tomorrow. But those blocks that do not have visiting will celebrate today.

At today's visit, children will be allowed inside. Consequently, it will be crowded, which works out well.

Just before the lunch interval in the visiting area, we halted the visit and comrade A. Kadir recited a poem in Kurdish. It was about greeting the visitors. The applause and ululating that broke out after the poem reverberated around the walls. I then read out a statement in Turkish. Every time I paused, there was clapping. When I invited people to participate in a minute's silence for martyrs, comrade A. Kadir recited another Kurdish poem in his strident voice. At the conclusion, I thanked everyone. Some family members made victory signs, others ululated, and others were overpowered by their tears.

We celebrated the day of all the families one by one. Their eyes gleamed and the rays of joy reflected on us. This wave of joy was not to be limited to this place. Of that we were sure.

While the message was being read out, a child of about three or four was probably frightened and began to cry. His elder sister, who was four or five years older, put her finger to his lips and indicated that he should be quiet. She looked embarrassed. It was obvious that she held herself responsible for her brother crying. This made her all the more appealing. In fact, there was no need for her to try to silence her brother, as his cry was a revolt against the prison and our captivity. The child's name was Mazlum. And coincidentally, his surname was DOĞAN.

MAZLUM DOĞAN…

This little Mazlum Doğan did not accept the prison either.

Sweets, eau de cologne, dessert, and cola were sent over to the visitors' side. Conversation began in small groups.

Enthusiasm, joy, and buoyancy continued until the end of visiting.

Meanwhile, we heard there had been an attack in Nazilli prison. They have apparently damaged comrades' belongings. As the comrades have only recently been remanded, measures are increasing every day. Comrades may engage in an action there at any moment. They are being forced into it.

Block 8
28 November 1997

The celebrations continued today. Until lunchtime we had choir, folklore, reading of messages, and the performing of sketches and poems.

Compared with previous celebrations, today was more colourful.

There were sketches that were both amusing and thought-provoking. The subjects covered ranged from the mentality of capitalist brand names to our internal and external problems.

The celebrations continued into the evening. At 22.30, as *Siyaset Meydanı* was live on ATV, we began to watch it. While thinking some issues could be on the programme, we saw that teachers and students from the Şırnak area had been selected for the show. Nearly all of them spoke from the special war handbook.

The girls spoke like caricatures of "businesswoman" Sema Küçüköz, known for manipulating the youth of Şırnak. Patriots know this woman well.

The teachers on the programme also mentioned where the soldiers were. This was proof of the importance the army attaches to assimilation.

The provincial governor was the character who finished off the programme. It was upsetting to see how far some young people in Şırnak have been distanced from their reality and degenerated…

I watched it until 02.00. The speakers were repeating themselves and, as I was tired, I went to bed. Most of the comrades continued to watch.

Although such programmes defame us, it is still possible to draw some conclusions.

Block 8
29 November 1997

After the morning roll call, those comrades who wished slept until noon.

After lunch, we continued the unfinished programme from yesterday. A play was staged in the exercise yard. The theme was the raid on tribal leader M. Celal Bucak in Siverek in 1979 and the announcement of the founding of the PKK. The comrades involved had prepared well. Comrade Kadir, in particular, played the role of Bucak exceptionally well. After the 90-minute long play, the competition prize was presented to comrade Doğan.

After everyone had lined up in the exercise yard, I recited Nuri Dersimi's address to Kurdish youth. All the comrades repeated loudly the word "vengeance" every time it occurred.

We followed this by doing a halay.

The joy and enthusiasm of a rebirth, not the sadness of November, echoed once more. And it spread in waves outside.

Those unbreakable waves carried us outside, to the mountains, to the vast free areas once more.

Because we knew that the same feelings, the same heartbeats, the same folk songs are being shared outside with us, with the prisons.

In the same way, there are comrades outside thinking of us in prison in every step they take, in the same way we, who are in the prisons, live them at every moment. We try to experience and feel their joy, their hunger, their weariness, their sleeping curled up on stony ground, their spirit of solidarity, their zest for life, and their resentment and anger for the enemy.

For we do not fear life. TENACITY, TENACITY, TENACITY…

Yes, we have celebrated another 27 November inside. In order to begin our normal lives tomorrow, we are sounding out tomorrow from today.

Block 8
30 November 1997

This morning, we collectively read a 15-page booklet consisting of the leader's articles regarding 27 November. The comrades followed this by going on to normal education. As for me, I began to read 50 pages of minutes and some articles. I have to state my opinion on every issue. In order to understand some topics, I had to carefully read every word. We have to express correct views regarding problems dealt with in narrow meetings in some blocks. Other subjects take up as much of our time as education.

As there is a general census taking place in Turkey today, we made a statement regarding how comrades should act. They came to our block at about 15.00. We saw they had missed out certain questions. We had an argument as they did not ask about "nationality." When they said, "These are our orders," we didn't answer the remaining questions. For we know the authorities will fill in the forms as they like. Our argument was fierce. When we said we didn't have to write down "Turkish Republic," that we were prepared to face execution for this, that it was a question of identity, and that we had also expressed this in the military courts, they left.

Block 8
5 December 1997

Today T. again proposed leaving our environment. He has done this four or five times in the last two months. He said, "I have been shown humanity in this environment, but I am not worthy of this. I don't deserve it, I am mentally ill. I am going to go to be put under observation, start a hunger strike, and try to go to Bursa or another prison."

Before sending him off, I spoke to him for a while in the exercise yard. I told him not to get in a worse situation and not to be an instrument of the enemy. He burst into tears. He said it was the first time he'd cried in seven years.

We gave him money, cigarettes, a spoon, and a plate. He promised not to allow himself to be used by the enemy and departed.

Although it was his wish to go, people are upset in such situations, but there's nothing you can do. He's gone to pot.

It's the first time I have encountered someone who insisted on leaving our environment and then cried.

According to a short item of news in *Gündem*, all forces in South Kurdistan, apart from the KDP, have gathered for a national congress conference. This development is the result of serious efforts that have been going on for a long time.

In the same newspaper, there is an item about the KDP, which said, "If it wasn't for us, the PKK would have declared an independent state here." This statement alone demonstrates just how serious the development is.

On the evening news, it was said 20 thousand Turkish troops have gone into the South once again. This is an attempt to prevent the national conference happening. But, once again, they are late…

Block 8
6 December 1997

The news has been clarified somewhat. The leader has sent a message to the conference. And it was greeted with resounding applause.

This news created great joy among comrades. It is a reflection of the advance outside. We greet in prison these values that have been created by the efforts of our people.

A short announcement was made saying we would celebrate this event in the whole prison tomorrow. Naturally, traffic has increased. Preparations began immediately.

Block 8
7 December 1997
THE BEAUTY OF TOMORROW

When we awoke in the morning, I saw that many comrades had shaved the previous night. The rest of us did it in the morning.

Although it was sudden, there was a noticeable change in all the blocks. Everyone was taking it seriously.

At 09.00, the comrade making an announcement regarding the meaning and significance of the day invited everyone to a one-minute silence for all martyrs. This was followed by the "Ey Raqip" anthem and a statement was read out. The poetic and flowing text was met by a wave of applause. At the same moment, slogans were shouted in the entire prison.

Sketches, solos, poems, and messages continued until lunchtime.

After lunch, there was a conversation meeting in every block. Apart from the significance of the day, emotions were shared. Sometimes, comrades found it difficult to express their feelings. Some had tears in their eyes. They were all a flood of emotions. In every word, there was a gem, a light, a bunch of flowers, and a flood of emotions.

Every word expressed a great yearning, sadness, longing and joy, and a belief in the future.

It flowed like water rushing through a dam, onto the dry and cracked soil…

It was as if it wanted to quench the aridness of centuries. It was like water being gulped down in the desert…

Eyes lit up as they witnessed a new history, or more precisely, the turning of the leaves of history. The glint of steel reflecting in eyes, transformed into a sad light. Sucking up the darkness, it flows to tomorrows. And it bears today the good tidings of the beauty of tomorrows.

This light, at times, turns into a halay, at others, into a slogan.

To flow from language to language, from heart to heart. To conquer the tomorrows. To begin constructing tomorrow, today… in such moments, a flood of emotions rips out the thick prison walls and the prison bars. It flows unhindered to unite with the hope of freedom.

> *Yes,*
> *Behind the prison bars,*
> *News of the national conference spreads.*
> *From ear to ear,*
> *From heart to heart,*
> *35 comrades chatting in block 8,*
> *In Aydın prison.*
> *First shining eyes,*
> *Emotions,*
> *Joy,*
> *From tongue to tongue,*
> *Every word like a poem.*
> *All of them a bouquet of light,*
> *A bouquet of flowers,*
> *The blooming of emotion,*
> *Every word a gem.*
> *A scene of pride emerged,*
> *We created today from our pain,*
> *"We moulded our pain with our blood",*
> *Yes, emotions are flowing like a poem,*
> *And also sadness.*

Block 8
15 December 1997

We have started an alternating two-day action in support of the hunger strike in Erzurum and Nazilli. Every block will take turns. Our block and 6-14 have started the action. Our stance will change according to developments.

Block 8
24 December 1997

Today all prisons have commenced a non-alternating, unlimited hunger strike in support of Erzurum and Nazilli. Our block started today.

From what we have read in the press, the situation of some comrades is critical. Our action is also a reaction to the ministry's lack of concern.

Block 8
25 December 1997

As I was writing this on a typewriter towards noon, I was called for a visit.

The noise, stuffiness, crowds, children, and other troubles wearied us, as always.

We received two pieces of heartening news.

Firstly, Nazilli has reached an agreement to end the action on the 34th day.

Secondly, Duran Boztepe and Osman Hoca have been released. Comrade Duran came to visit. "It was a great experience," he said.

His time in prison was brief. This process will either break his will and lead him to withdraw, or he will become more active than before.

His enthusiasm gave us hope. I hope we are not mistaken.

Block 8
28 December 1997

Despite it being our second day of hunger, we stayed in bed until 08.00.

By noon, I had finished reading an article I needed to read in *Özgür Halk* magazine. I then took notes on the characteristics of provincial personalities. The longest section was on the personalities of Amed and Dersim. This is an expression of the fact these personalities are more problematic.

According to the newspaper, Erzurum E-Type prison has ended its action. As for the Special Type, it is continuing. The state wants to pressure them to continue a bit longer to wear the comrades down.

Again, a news item that shocked us: in the Küçük Yamanlar district of Izmir, a patriot by the name of Mirza Mehmet Çimen set himself alight and was martyred in hospital. He was around 45 and has ten children. They had moved to Izmir from Erciş eight months ago.

He left behind a letter. He mentioned the burning of villages in Kurdistan. In particular, he wrote, "I am setting myself alight in support of the action in Erzurum prison and to protest at repression."

He went to the cemetery in order to prevent anyone intervening. He then took off his jacket, saying, "A poor person can wear it," poured a can of petrol over himself, and set himself alight. After his body had caught fire, he ran towards some houses, shouting slogans. He also said, "Don't put me or the fire out. I am burning myself in protest at human rights violations."

MIRZA, WHO LIT UP THE DARKNESS

Mirza shouted:
"Don't put me out!"
"I'm protesting the human rights violations in Kurdistan!"
And
He became a beacon of light.
The Four taught how to stoke the flames,
That Zekiye and Rahşan ignited.
In the fire in his body, it was colonialism that burned.
The place was Izmir,
His thoughts were in Kurdistan.
Seven arrests in the homeland and three in Izmir did not deter him.
His anger grew every time,
His yearning swelled,
Mirza's living flames
Firstly greeted Kadifekale,
Then the bastions of Amed,
For they had greeted the Four.
It was the same
Yearning for the homeland,
And comrades,
And endless anger at the enemy.
Today's Mirza,
A hero in a legend,
Its meaning was "emerging from darkness into light",
Facing death for others
To fight for the oppressed.

To overcome hardship,
To defeat the bad and the ugly,
It was like this
Legendary hero Mirza...
Again,
He chose the hardest action,
Intolerable death.
The summit of darkness,
Transforming himself into roaring flames.
Burning the enemy on his body
And
His greatest yearning:
To be able to say,
"BURY ME IN MY HOMELAND."

Block 8
30 December 1997

We've come to the end of another year. While this sometimes means a lot in our situation, sometimes it means nothing more than a change of numbers.

Even if feelings are complicated, it is certain that a new period is beginning. And that another year has been taken from our lives...

As years go by, it inevitably leads to sadness. And this is especially true in prison.

This year passed in a most active way for our people. Although they faced attacks in many spheres, serious steps were taken towards national unity. Incomparable developments were also made on the diplomatic front. Some governments have almost reached the stage of recognising our struggle. This is very important for us.

Block 8
31 December 1997

"EITHER WE SHOULD ENLIGHTEN OURSELVES BY SETTING THIS CITY ON FIRE, OR ENLIGHTEN THIS CITY BY SETTING OURSELVES ON FIRE"

As there was a morning roll call, all the comrades had already shaved and were waiting. At 08.45, we went out into the exercise yard and lined up. Comrade Selahattin invited us to a minute's silence for all martyrs of the revolution in the person of Mirza Mehmet Çimen. He then read the statement in a clear voice that filled the exercise yard.

As the statement both flowed and was poetic, we felt emotional in many places. The most striking emphasis was what a mother had shouted during a hunger strike in Amed:

"Either we should enlighten ourselves by setting this city on fire, or enlighten this city by setting ourselves on fire."

Perhaps this mother of ours was illiterate, but these words were really philosophical. Just like comrade Mirza's words, "Bury me in my homeland"…

Following the statement, everyone shouted slogans.

Comrades who went to the visiting area also held a commemoration with their families. They explained comrade Mirza's action.

At around 21.00, as we were holding our weekly forum, the prosecutor, governor, and guards came in. We concealed our displeasure. They said they had come to wish us Happy New Year. While asking, "Why are the blocks quiet?" they hinted that they knew about our activities. We paid no attention to them. After a few minutes, they left.

The subject of this week's forum was the significance and meaning of the action carried out by comrade Mirza. All blocks discussed the same topic. Hence, even if they have separated us with walls, what we talk about, our debate, and what we feel are very similar. This is how we achieve a unity of opinion.

I was up until 01.00. Although I didn't feel sleepy, I went to bed as it is visiting day tomorrow, and I don't want to feel tired.

Block 8
1 January 1998

The visiting area was really crowded. I invited everyone to stand for a minute's silence for comrade Mirza with a short statement. Comrade Selahattin read a short poem. Then, comrade H. Yağız initiated slogans. The participation of children in the slogan, "Long Live Leader Apo," was more lively and exciting. This delighted me.

We were really busy until 16.30. When I returned to the block, I had a quick glance at the accumulated notes.

After completing all the necessary tasks for the block, I realised I was very tired. I was swaying as I walked. I was virtually falling over. My head was aching severely from weariness.

Our journalist, comrade Hasan Özgün, was apparently brought back from the court in Istanbul as fast as he had been whisked away.

I only just managed to stay awake until 23.00.

Block 8
5 January 1998

The action in Erzurum E-Type is still continuing. The one in the Special type is in its 48th day, whereas in the E-Type, the comrades have restarted their action as the authorities did not abide by the agreement. As conditions are bad and as they have had to take action many times, they have been seriously weakened physically. Hence, it is at a critical stage.

Our alternating action is continuing, doing three days at a time.

Erzurum in particular is very important for us. The state is also experiencing a problem of prestige and is seeking vengeance.

Since 25 December, *Gündem* newspaper is not given to us on some days. They are using various justifications. They are both testing our reactions and trying to get us used to not having the newspaper. We will not get used to it. We will react. We cannot remain silent at such arbitrary measures. Firstly, our representatives will make contact.

Since we started our action to highlight Erzurum, we have shouted slogans three times a day.

Block 8
6 January 1998

Since the Erzurum action is continuing, today, all prisons turned the support action into an unlimited hunger strike. All comrades in Aydın wrote petitions to the ministry requesting a transfer to Erzurum. We have also informed the press.

Tomorrow morning, we are starting an unlimited action with a group of comrades in block 9-13. The other blocks will begin each week in turn. In each group, the numbers taking part will not exceed the number in the block.

They are testing the limits of comrades' endurance. If the problem in Erzurum is not resolved, more high level actions will come onto the agenda.

In Bayrampaşa prison, two guards were taken hostage for a short time in support of Erzurum.

Block 8
7 January 1998

KURDS ON THE ARARAT SHIP THAT RAN AGROUND ON THE SHORES OF ITALY

Today, comrades C. Bozkurt and H. İbrahim Turan were transferred to Bartın. They paid 75 million lira for the transfer.

Since the New Year, the drama of our people being forced from their homes and smuggled abroad has gripped the attention of the world. For years now, gangs have, with the encouragement and support of the Turkish state, virtually emptied our homeland by transporting our people to Europe in groups.

They also don't want our people to stay in the cities of Turkey. They fear the risk of an explosion if there are masses of Kurds there.

They both tear our people away from Kurdistan and fleece them for three to five thousand Marks each. They are emptying the country using special war methods. As, if it was not enough to burn down and destroy the villages, they also rob them of their belongings.

Most recently, the "Ararat," a floating wreck of a ship, has run aground with 800 people in Italy, arousing public reaction. These kinds of journeys are entirely designed to slaughter people.

Following extensive reactions, the special war regime tried to blame us. The "Mehmetçik Press" covered it in this way. But the whole world knows that it is not possible for the state to be unaware of hundreds of people being put on ships in the centre of Istanbul.

It was later understood that, when the ship ran aground, the crew abandoned the vessel and fled. The ship was one of those dismantled and taken apart in Istanbul. It's a ship that in normal circumstances would not be allowed out to sea, let alone carry passengers.

In this case, there has been a backlash. The ERNK has publicised this latest forced migration to the world. Most important of all, Italy has announced that, as these people are fleeing war, it will grant political asylum to those who apply for it.

This amounts to political recognition for us.

Since organisational activities began in Kurdistan, the state has opened the way for our people to go to Europe with a systematic policy of forced migration. This mass migration is troubling European countries, as they do not want organised masses. Also, Europeans are now a minority in many places in Europe…

Hundreds of people who have been packed into these ships for "journeys of hope" have either suffocated, died of hunger, or drowned in these rickety vessels. It is miraculous to stay alive in such inhumane conditions.

This is another war of annihilation being waged against Kurds.

But there is something they have forgotten. The more they kill, the more they throw in prison, the number of Kurds who resist increases. And will continue to increase…

Block 8
15 January 1998

As Erzurum ended its action yesterday, we ended our action today.

It lasted for 55 days. They forced the comrades to go on a long time to wear them down. There will definitely be permanent disabilities and illnesses. Throughout the action, the weather got colder and colder, to make matters worse. There were almost record cold temperatures. This was a great disadvantage for those on hunger strike.

Despite the adverse conditions, the comrades did not give in. This resolute stance was itself a success against the enemy.

The announcement regarding Asker shocked everyone. But those who had previously suspected him were not surprised, for his daily sectarian behaviour, his reactions to all officials, and his radical appearance on all issues roused suspicion. But most of us put that down to his "Kemalist characteristics."

The police know they cannot cause much damage with such people they infiltrate among us but, it is enough for them to cause harm at every opportunity, create an atmosphere of suspicion, and sow the seeds of distrust. The strange and bitter aspect of this is that Asker did all this in the name of "being a good party man."

His organisational ties have been frozen. The investigating commission will carry out a more detailed investigation and present its proposal to the structure.

Behaving in a radical, partisan manner on every issue can be used to conceal reality. But it doesn't work anymore. The enemy's ways have taught us this.

In all circumstances, we have to be cautious and political. Consequently, a lot of our activities and relationships are confined to a narrow circle in order to prevent them being exposed.

Block 8
23 January 1998

Last night, comrade H. Baraj Kılıç fell ill and was sent to hospital by the block opposite. A short time later, they brought him back. In the morning, we put pressure on the prison authorities, saying, "If anything happens to him, it will be on your heads." They panicked and took him back to the hospital. They kept him in, concerned that he might have a gall stone. I don't know if it's been the recent cold weather, but he was ill from time to time. He said, and we concurred, that he had an "intestinal ailment."

The prisons have rotted the comrades' insides.

Shame on those whose hearts are not thirsting for revenge.

Today, we received a fax from the comrades in Erzurum. The requests we all made to go there during the last days of the action had a morale-boosting effect. They say, "We will endeavour to be worthy of this regard and honour." Our request for a transfer was a gesture of support. It pleased us that it was appreciated. Once again, we have experienced the great feeling of solidarity between comrades in the most difficult times.

We were those who were there and they were us.

Those who resisted were us in Erzurum.

Block 8
27 January 1998

Comrades Muhittin Tacer and Şemsettin Gözcü were transferred early this morning to Burdur. Both had opted for paid transfers. As their families live in Antalya, they wanted to move to a closer place. But I'm sure they will miss being here, soon. They were comfortable here.

During the search yesterday, they took our message balls from blocks 9 and 7. It was immediately protested with slogans. We demanded they hand them back, but they said the prosecutor had them. These balls have been in the blocks for years and they know very well what we use them for. It is also deliberate that they only took them from two blocks. They are testing us out. If the reaction is muted, they will definitely take them from the other blocks.

They are determined to cut communication between the blocks. But they don't realise that necessity will find new ways. They can limit it, but definitely cannot prevent it. Even when there was widespread oppression during the military period, they were unable to entirely sever communications.

Block 8
30 January 1998
THE SAD NEWS OF HÜSEYIN AYTEMUR

As today is the second day of Eid, they didn't want to take us to the barber. They said the cabinet in which the products are kept was locked, and the key was with an absent guard. We summoned the duty head guard and said, "If you want, you can open the cabinet. This is Fazğıl's drawer, not a Swiss bank. Even if you don't open it, let us go there and we will shave the comrades with an electric razor." A short while later, they brought the equipment, saying, "We fortunately were able to open it."

While in 6-14 Sarıkaya, representatives of the Turkish left arrived. After lunch, the choir sang a few songs. Then a play was performed. Forced migration was the subject. It was presented lyrically.

Once more, we felt anger towards the enemy.

Once more, we felt sad for the cries of our people...

People returning from the visiting area passed on the news that Hüseyin Aytemur had been martyred.

To be honest, I don't know what to say or write. He had only gone to the camp a few months before. Being martyred so soon after spending 15 years in prison distresses us. It is difficult for us to bear. These comrades, with a legacy of 20 years, have much to offer the struggle.

While writing these lines, my pen has run out. Damnation. The pen doesn't want to relate such distressing news. It is as if it is rebelling. Against untimeliness, eternity, and also betrayal...

I gather the leader sent a special message to comrade Hüseyin's family. The family is resolute.

> *He was martyred on 15 October 1997.*
> *His departure from this prison seems like yesterday.*
> *He has attained eternity.*
> *One by one, they are reaching the sun,*
> *Without saying it is early*
> *Without looking at our sadness.*

Block 8
6 February 1998

I was very tired during yesterday's visit. Without recovering, we went off around the blocks. While striding back and forth in the exercise yard of block 6-14 in the afternoon with comrade Celal, the governor and guards suddenly came in. They said, "We have come here for a partial special search." Although we told them to inform our representatives, when we saw they were insistent, we said "OK."

I wanted to return to my block, but they refused, saying it was a search. At the same moment, we learned they had called comrade Şamil to see his lawyer. Calling us at this very moment and on a Friday raised our suspicions.

While the comrades took their "valuables" from the dorm, those in block 8-12 began to rap on the walls. They wanted to pass on some news. Although we did not respond on account of guards being present, they contined knocking insistently. I was annoyed because they hadn't guessed there might be something going on and because they were impatient.

While waiting in the exercise yard for the search to end, they began to bang on the doors in block 4. Sait hoca wanted to speak to the authorities to find out what was going on but received a negative answer. Naturally, all the blocks began to bang the doors. The governor came immediately and spoke to comrade Aşkın.

I think he was also unable to understand what was being said for all the noise. He mumbled something and departed.

Block 8
10 February 1998

Today, there was a general search. At around 16.00, there was the sound of doors being banged. This was followed by all blocks banging doors. I gather they took the despatch ball from block 4.

We delayed the closing of the exercise yard doors. When they entered, every block dragged things out, with all comrades arguing with the head guard. As such a reaction will naturally put them on the defensive, it is certain that they will be delayed by an hour or two before they have closed all the doors. They want to sabotage our education in this way, but they will never succeed in doing that.

At eight in the evening, we once again banged the doors. As I haven't done any exercise recently, I was out of breath by the end.

Block 8
23 February 1998

Today is our bath day. I was busy washing clothes and having my hair cut until noon.

In the afternoon, we all sat down together for a while. This was our final preparation meeting for our conference that will last for ten days. The framework has been completed. It may be said to have passed off successfully compared to previous years. However, despite this, the appropriate maturity has not yet been reached. We observed during debates that certain personal sensitivities have still to be overcome. A narrow perspective is obstructing a realistic approach.

Some comrades will just not accept the current situation. They also do not propose an alternative to replace it. In spite of all efforts, being subjected to the same criticisms every year and having to make self-criticisms on the same topics is damaging my self-respect. The perception that criticisms made are being disregarded really saddens me. In fact, there is nothing more that we can do. This is our capacity.

Fulfilling responsibilities is not just a matter of good intentions.

The strange thing is, when it comes to elections, the same people are preferred. This is the paradox. This has been repeated for years. Electing the same people that we don't like every year is, first and foremost, disrespecting yourself. It is not a good mental state. In this conference, we must definitely overcome this situation. Otherwise, we are wearing down the people we elect.

Although there are inadequacies in many spheres, it is pleasing that the comrades are able to make assessments on all subjects. Seeing the result of the education and the efforts made is the most important factor that reassures us.

Today, I completed the letter I started writing to Kemal Aktaş five days ago. It was long. We've had a bit of a heart-to-heart. I also sent him some news. I'll be sad if it doesn't reach him. I have toiled over it and also shared my feelings and opinions on many subjects. I want comrades to also share these.

For three or four days, I was reading the memoirs comrade Hamza wrote here. I didn't want them to end. He covered the era up to 1979. It took me back to the first period, to the first comrades, and those circumstances. And I was deeply saddened. Even though I am familiar with it, I was affected.

Everyone should read about how the first steps were taken in the creation of the extensive possibilities that exist today, how people were in need of a loaf of bread, a coin, a friend. And it is necessary for it to be known how Haki, Kemal, and countless comrades made efforts and self-sacrifice, and, most importantly, how they persevered despite all the hardship, and never once complained.

One of the most moving sections is about what took place at the cemetery and in the house in the days when comrade Haki's grave was being prepared. A real drama.

An awareness of yesterday is the key to being able to appreciate the value of today and living tomorrow in the right way.

I have read the 15-page article Kenan Şen wrote about comrade Doğan Kılıçkaya and sent it on to comrade Tören. I added a footnote in two places. The style of the writing was good.

Block 8
24 February 1998

When I went to block 7, I had a chat with M. Ayçiçek. He is to be transferred to Bartın. I gave him some information about the place. "I will do as much as possible to represent and will not embarrass the comrades," he said. He looked determined, which pleased me.

Today, I received a note from Az. He wants a swift reply. After saying he is ready to perform any duty here, he adds how we can get in contact with him. He says he has severed his relations with the "nonaligned" as the police are trying to use them.

It is striking that he should declare himself "ready for duty" after he has left us. In fact, T. Ö. there wrote adverse things about him.

One of them is trying to mess us about, but this will become clear in the future.

After tea at 22.00, comrades Kadir and Mümin were playing chess. Seven or eight comrades were watching them. Somehow comrade Kadir won. When he saw that I was writing, he came over to my bunk and said, opening his large eyes even wider, "write in your diary, say, 'Kadir beat Mümin.'"

Block 8
26 February 1998
EVERY SEPARATION COMES WITH SADNESS

Today was our visiting day. As children were brought inside, it was noisy.

In the visiting area, we learned that Sarıkaya and Kenan Şen's transfers to Giresun have come through. I was surprised. I have mixed feelings.

In one way, it will be good for comrades who have been here for a long time to go to another place. On the other hand, it will be very difficult for us to be separated from these comrades.

I have been in the same places as Sarıkaya for 12 years. A long time. We have worked together in many fields. We have lived through the most difficult times and periods of action together. We have shared reactions, joy, sadness, and all manner of hardship…

We have experienced the warmth of comradeship and sharing in the best way without calculating for our own advantage.

We had no problems getting on, comfortable in the knowledge that we knew each other well. As trust is fundamental in relationships, we never had a problem communicating.

We met in the days when Eskişehir had just opened.

Sarıkaya said, "Let me render my account at the conference, then I'll leave."

As I know he will never shirk accounting for himself to comrades and the party, I said, "There's no need to delay the transfer, as there's no guarantee it will happen. You can go and we will do the accounting in your place."

If there is to be a judgement, it will be with the administration.

He said, "I was intending to make a complaint about myself." However, he had not shirked any work or action all year.

As children were there, comrades took six or seven photos in the visiting area. They included Sarıkaya in every shot.

When I returned to the block, I summoned comrade Kenan from the wall of block 6. We chatted for a while. He said, "Since I've heard the news, I've been weak at the knees." He was added to our file from the Adana group.

1985-86-87. We went through lots of things in the trial process. As it was a military court, every hearing was a problem. In that period in Adana closed prison, they kept us mixed up with ordinary prisoners. As we didn't abide by rules like singing the national anthem, we were often placed in basement cells referred to as "wet," "fly-blown," or "shitty." They were intolerable in the hot, humid weather of Adana. After 15 days in those cells, there would be mould on our clothes and heat rashes all over our bodies.

After our trial had ended, they put the comrades who had received death sentences and life imprisonment in cells on the top floor that were called medium closed. There were three of us staying in one-man cells, but although the doors were always closed, we were more comfortable there than in the blocks. We were in two separate sections. I was in one near the entrance, whereas Kenan was in a cell at the end. He was our only Laz comrade, but he was more Kurdish than anyone. He was short, with a small paunch and a high-pitched voice. Everybody liked him. Over time, he became a member of the family. His family didn't come to visit him, but he wasn't worried about that, as all our families were his, too. Our families and mothers loved him, too.

He spared no effort in every block in which he stayed. We went through the same things from beginning to end in Adana, Eskişehir, and Aydın. He showed no weakness in any action.

As he received a life sentence, he has to serve 15 years.

While speaking to him from behind the wall, I swiftly recalled the past. We are going to miss him. But the most pleased about this will be R. Nur Cengiz, who is also going to Giresun. They will again be together.

From what we have heard, they ended the action in Giresun on the 50th day. But we have no information on the outcome.

There are intensive operations going on in Izmir and Antalya. 60 people have been arrested. One of these is an "intermediary" we know, which is very bad for us. I hope the operation doesn't extend to the rural areas.

Block 8
8 March 1998

Today, we finished the conference that we began on 2 March. We were thinking it would last four days, but it went on for five days due to certain hitches.

In general, compared to the past, it passed off relatively smoothly. It was our seventh conference in this prison. A long period of time.

In order to evaluate this year as one for education from my perspective, I have asked the administration that I should not be elected. The same people being on duty year after year creates reaction amongst some comrades. There's no point in persisting. I also pointed out that I was making this proposal recalling our higher organisation's instructions and perspectives. I added that this was necessary to demonstrate that we were not obstructing anyone.

However, it was the very comrades who complain most on this subject who were the most critical because I had made the proposal. I'm finding it difficult to understand this.

We suggested freshening up the administration a bit this year, but only one of the five comrades is new. The period is new, but the administration is "old."

It is striking that such an outcome emerged despite the instructions. Basically, the structure does not want it. There are various reasons for this lack of change.

The continuing presence of the "oldies" makes them feel secure. This is because they will live comfortably, things will be flexible, and there will be no uncertainty. Thus, there is a reluctance to have change. This makes it difficult for those of us who have been in post for years. Doing the same tasks for years wears you out.

After the reading of the closing statement, we sang "Ey Raqip." And, after going out into the exercise yard and shouting slogans, we did a halay.

We hadn't had a halay for about a month. At the same moment, the sound of halay folksongs rose from every block. The authorities must have wondered what was going on and made lots of different comments while trying to figure it out.

Generally speaking, comrades were enthusiastic and joyful. A few still looked hurt on account of the criticisms directed at them. This will pass. Individual sensitivity should not be on this level. It's unacceptable that, when it is personal, they are over sensitive; but when it's general, they are comfortable. This demonstrates how distant they are from the concept of feeling as one with the party. Furthermore, it demonstrates their immaturity.

Today is also International Women's Day. The police attacked our people marching in Istanbul and Amed. The TV broadcast a lot of footage.

This is the cry of women in cities becoming liberated along with our struggle. In particular, the way the women in Taksim Square in Istanbul fought off the police was amazing. It was like an uprising amidst a sea of yellow, red, and green. Just like in the towns and cities of Kurdistan a few years ago…

Just as on every important day, the powers that be want to degrade it and empty it of meaning. But first and foremost, Kurdish women are setting forth their presence in the most radical way. Liberated women are crying out the fact that they are no longer enslaved and, most important of all, that they are able to make decisions about the future despite all the attacks.

Women are creating their real freedom themselves, within our struggle. While liberating the country by overcoming all manner of hardship, they are also freeing themselves.

Happy 8 March, International Women's Day.

Block 8
10 March 1998

Today, I went around the blocks with comrade Doğan.

I went to see comrade Celal in block 7-15. He will be released in eight days' time. We chatted about an educational compilation he has prepared. Comrades who have read it, liked it. He was trying to finish typing it up. We discussed how he would get it out.

He was concerned about going outside after 16 years of incarceration. It's only natural. He will be stepping into a new world.

Thinking we may not meet again, our conversation was quite emotional. From time to time, we have been annoyed with each other or not understood one another, but our positive sides have come out on top. We said we would always remember these times wistfully, and that, whatever we did, it was with good intentions…

He was also affected. He said, "In my practice outside, I will both make self-criticism and criticism, and endeavour to be worthy of the values entrusted in me."

After lunch, I went to 6-14. They have bought a plastic table and four chairs. They looked rather strange in the corner of the exercise yard. For a moment, they recalled a seaside resort. The fact they are white makes them all the more conspicuous. These things are completely alien to us.

When the comrades sat down to education, we took the table and chairs to block 4. I sat and chatted to Kenan, uncle Xalef, and three other comrades for a while. When the search sound was heard, the comrades began to prepare. Shoelaces were securely tied and valuables like pens and watches were put in pockets.

After the search was over, I observed the comrades sat at the plastic table and the general scene. Everyone was angrily straightening out the things that had been thrown about. Uncle Xalef was insistently trying to present me with a pair of trousers he had been given. I refused to accept them. When he persisted, I said, "Xalo, these trousers are civilian; I only wear guerrilla gear." He then threw the trousers on his bunk. Comrades began to laugh.

We went down to the dining hall for watery, milky coffee the comrades had prepared. People were sitting and conversing pleasantly over their coffee. When the conversation touched on changes of block, a few comrades asked me, "Ali, aren't you coming to our block?" They were those who wanted to come to the block I wanted to stay in.

Comrade Mesut asked, "Are you going to pop in to block 9-13?"

"Yes, who do you have a message for?..."

Before leaving the block, I said farewell to comrade Kenan Şen. They are to leave tomorrow morning. I wished him success with feelings all over the place.

Today I have bid farewell to four comrades. We have been together for years. Their departures have already begun to hurt.

Perhaps we will never be able to see each other again.

Perhaps some of them will strike out towards eternity and become immortal.

As for those who remain, they will yearn the most beautiful days of comradeship like yearning for eternity.

This is what is hard…

Block 8
17 March 1998

LIKE YESTERDAY

Again it is 17 March.
It has been exactly 17 years
But it seems like yesterday
It is vivid in my memory
The pitch black nights
The pouring rain
Walking from the mountain to the meadow
Just three of us
Three willowy youths
Yet serious like a mass
In the meeting place of comrades
Yearning for Newroz and comrades
Then
The sound of military vehicles tearing up the dawn
Once again towards the mountains

The mountain rising as if it was cut by a knife
The whiteness of the snow
And the blue of the sky
Glaring into one's eyes
Then
Where the mountain ended
Greenery
Poplar trees
And a Kurdish youth
Worried
Timid
And endearing
An ambush of betrayal
The Kısık stream, flowing obliviously
The calm before the storm
Nature is sad
It will witness new lives falling to the soil
And
Like life being torn apart
Shouts of "surrender"
And the bangs of guns
BULLETS coming down like rain
Reverberating bitterly around the mountains
The sound of G-3s
Smothers the sound of our light weapons
One heart is bare
Blood mixed with the melting snow
Silent and motionless
Martyrdom
Then
Hundreds of shivering creatures
All of it
But all of it like yesterday
Again I am in prison
Surrounded on all four sides by walls
Like on that first 17 March

Cold
And silent
And the day is hot
Only four days to Newroz!
I remember them!
As I do every day
As my sadness grows
My affection for them grows.

Block 8
21 March 1998

RAIN GREETS US AT EVERY NEWROZ

We are experiencing the excitement of Newroz.

The excitement of the fires lit in squares and on mountains that expresses freedom and rebellion.

We have put on our best clothes and are like drops in a colourful sea of people.

We are like children doing halay around the fire of freedom, or like children marching towards armoured cars with stones in their hands.

The best Newroz fire is that which burns amongst the peaks of our mountains, stretching out towards the sky. Or that which is at the front of a mass of people flooding into the centre of a city from the outlying districts. The Newroz fire can only be expressed in this enthusiasm.

We would like to celebrate this day of renewal, that brings good tidings of the future, outside in a free environment. But we cannot ignore the fact that our reality does not permit this.

With this awareness, we have tried to celebrate today in the best way possible, given our circumstances.

When we awoke early in the morning, we realised it was raining. We were all angry, for yesterday was fine and sunny. Rain will adversely affect attendance at celebrations outside in the cities. And it also means we will have our celebration in the dining hall, rather than in the exercise yard.

All comrades had a shave and put on their best clothes. Everyone was cheerful and smart.

Following the minute's silence at 09.00, "Ey Raqip" was sung, then comrade Mümin read out our statement, and I read out the DHP's message before everyone shook hands to celebrate our festival. And we shouted our slogans.

The falling rain ran down from our hair onto our faces, as if accompanying our slogans. It was like being in the mountains when it rains.

We had just moved into the dining hall for the cultural activities when they summoned those who were going to block 1 as guests. Yusuf Aydın and I went from our block.

Three each came from Dev-Sol and the TDKP, while one came from Rızgari. We had invited them.

After a short conversation in the exercise yard, comrade Tören made a quiet but very good speech. After generous applause, the messages of other groups were read out.

Then a play prepared by comrades in block 6-14 was put on. Comrades Mahmut and A. Rıza were captivated.

The theme of the play concerned the guerrillas' first entry to the Black Sea region, and their first contact with the people. After the play ended, the same cast came back onto the stage as a choir. The folk songs composed by comrades here were particularly well received.

We had lunch there, too.

When we returned to our block, we joined in our own activities here. It continued until five, then went on in the dorms in the evening…

From what we gleaned from the TV coverage, the day was celebrated in mass gatherings, enthusiastically, in the cities of Kurdistan and Turkey, despite attempts by the police to obstruct them, and attacks by the police. The most radical slogans were shouted in the big cities of Turkey. Our flags and banners were unfurled. This really pleased us.

As they wanted to cast a shadow over this day, which our people have been celebrating enthusiastically for 2,610 years, a day that has become more meaningful and contemporary on account of our struggle, the TV news announced that Şemdin Sakık had surrendered to the KDP. It was a dastardly move, deliberately done to coincide with today.

It's a very difficult situation to accept. Be actively involved in fighting for 18 years, then surrender. It's not possible. You can't do this unless you have lost your mind.

We would like this to be made-up news, but it seems to be true.

The special war will do whatever it can to make use of this situation against our struggle and our people. If he is brought to Turkey, it is certain they will step up the psychological war. From this perspective it is essential that he is prevented from falling into their hands.

There were apparently five "protectors" with him. If one of them had been honourable and honest, he would have finished him off there and then. They must also be guilty types.

Block 8
24 March 1998

Comrade Necmi Akgün, who was transferred here from Çankırı, was brought straight to our block. We argued with the guards at the door. The situation became charged. We told them we didn't accept this. The fact this was done to a comrade of 60 made it worse.

Block 8
25 March 1998

Today, comrades Sarıkaya, Nur Cengiz, and K. Şen were transferred to Giresun, while comrade Ayçiçek was taken to Bartın. We didn't understand why there was such a delay. In recent days, we were all subks once more to say farewell through the grilles.

Block 8
26 March 1998

LIVE NEWROZ TORCHES IN THE PRISONS: SEMA AND FIKRI

Comrade Fikri Baygeldi, who set himself on fire in Çanakkale prison on 23 March, has been martyred. Receiving this news only two days after the shock of comrade Sema Yüce setting herself alight on 21 March was hard to take and affected us profoundly.

Comrade Sema was taken into intensive care in Istanbul and had an operation. It is said she has lost her sight. Her condition is critical. If the situation is as reflected in the press, then she will become a martyr, too.

Both told doctors on being taken to hospital, "I set myself on fire to protest at the state's brutality in Kurdistan and in the prisons."

Comrade Fikri said, "Don't treat me, just give me an injection."

I respect the actions of both comrades, but I am sad as both are young, and they did it under current circumstances. Was this really necessary today?

Undoubtedly, this is the most difficult type of action. It requires great self-sacrifice and determination. The agony they will have experienced for every second after setting themselves on fire is indescribable. A human being will die a thousand deaths every second. At that moment, death will seem very easy. A person cannot sit down, cannot sleep, cannot lie down, and every movement will involve great pain. The worst agonies are experienced in such moments.

At this moment, I can feel the pain and groans of comrade Sema. And I feel the pain of being unable to help her in my heart and brain.

I appreciate these comrades who carried out such a difficult action and bow low in respect for the Newroz action they decided on themselves.

Block 8
29 March 1998
WHO'S CLEVER, WHO'S CRAZY?

At 9.00, we held a commemoration for comrade Fikri. Comrade Selahattin read out the statement.

Since the statement was combined nicely with Newroz, it was a flowing text. We then shouted slogans. We will repeat them in the afternoon and evening.

When we sat down for education, comrades' attention was drawn to the fact that some comrades' hands were clenched during the minute's silence. This was criticised and it was pointed out that comrades should behave appropriately.

Until noon, we read the interview Mahir Sayın had carried out with the leader regarding *Erkeği Öldürmek* [To Kill the Man].

We also did this…

There is a lot that can be said about the book. It was fulfilling and flowing for us. If it is widely read, it will be of benefit to many groups of people in Turkey.

In the afternoon, we read the March issue of *Özgür Halk*. We read the remaining articles between eight and 10 in the evening. The theoretical articles by comrades Fuat and Can covered crucial questions that concern us.

We also read a section from comrade Harun's guerrilla journal. He explained his preparation and Zagros journey. He explained, in poetic language, the beauty of life and setting foot in the nature of Kurdistan. I read it in one breath. We felt the rain, cold, and melted snow here in Aydın. We felt ourselves in that guerrilla group. We felt as if we were shivering with them, and walking with them.

Wherever he went, comrade Harun waged a relentless battle against the insufficiencies of personality. This aspect is the first thing one notices about him. In addition to assisting his comrades and understanding them, he listens carefully to the news. He stays in Iran, but follows every development in Turkey. He even heard about the verdicts in our court case. He expressed his anger about 25 death sentences in his journal.

The fact he continued to write his journal on a daily basis, in all circumstances, is a separate self-sacrifice.

For years, we have yearned to be guerrillas. And if one day we become guerrillas, I will write every day.

While reading comrade Harun's journal, I saw myself there. He has put down in writing what I have felt for years.

I vow, my freedom-loving comrade, that when one day we set foot in those mountains, I will continue that journal you so loved. Like a continuing quarrel, your journal will continue to be written. It will never cease, for you have not put an end to it yet... It will continue in every sphere of life.

In the newspaper, there is a statement by the leader on agent Şemdin. He compares him to the comrades who set themselves alight in Çanakkale. While he expresses his anger at those who put their own personality before the party understanding, he is very emotional regarding the comrades who burnt themselves. "Me included, do not bind yourselves to anyone, only bind yourselves to martyrs and heroes," he adds.

While thinking about agent Şemdin, Kadir in our block caught my eye. I've known him since Nizip in '79, before he was arrested. He was younger than most of us. He was a militant activist. Although, after being arrested, he was tried in the same case as me, we spent as much as ten years in different prisons.

Nazilli prison was emptied and most of the prisoners were brought here, to Aydın. Around 20 comrades were placed in block 2. When we were informed by the authorities, they said, "Apart from one, we're going to put them all in your blocks." I responded, "Let me speak to the comrades, and then we'll take them," and I immediately went to block 2. After I had become acquainted with the comrades, I asked who was in a cell A. Karabacak replied, "We don't know him. He was alone in a cell. He'll stay apart from us here. There's no need for us to take him in."

"What's this person's name?"

"Kadir Yıldırım."

"Kadir?"

"Yes. He's said to be crazy. He's also battered and bruised."

"Call Kadir here."

When Kadir, who had been waiting in the exercise yard, came in, he was as thin as a rake, and his body was covered in scars. He was cowering in an "S" shape and was in no condition to recognise me. To see him like this distressed me, and I was angry. "He is a veteran activist and a comrade of ours. He was just like us when he was arrested. Is there any guarantee we won't be like him one day?" I said. When 40 of us were transferred from Mersin to Antep E-Type prison in 1984, Kadir was with us. The ordinary prisoners there used to call the guards "uncle." It must have remained in his subconscious, as Kadir addressed everyone as "uncle." After telling him he would stay with us, that he should have a shower and throw away his clothes, I added:

"Look Kadir, you're going to stay with the comrades, but you will do whatever they say. OK? Whatever you need, tell them, and they will provide it."

Bent double with his hands clenched in front of him, Kadir replied, "OK, uncle."

When comrades fall ill, if we don't look after them, who will?

I subsequently heard that every time the door of block 2 opened, Kadir, with his thin but agile frame, would bound down the stairs and say, "Uncle Ali is coming."

Every time I dropped into the block, he would come and sit next to me. Once, when I saw he was constantly asking comrades for cigarettes, I said, "Why don't you put a packet in his pocket?" to which they replied, "We do, but he forgets it's there."

After a while, I arranged for Kadir to come to our block. He had rallied round. He played football more than we did. He would attend our meetings when he wished and leave whenever he wanted. Although he was thin, he would grab the metal bar and swing himself up to the upper bunk in one move.

We didn't have him in our education sessions, but allocated him an educator so that he wouldn't do different things. M. Akbaş made two copies of the same book. While he read from one out loud, Kadir would follow with the other. Once, he said, laughing, "Kadir reads so fast, I can't keep up with him."

Kadir's one weakness was that he smoked too much.

One morning, when I got up, they said that Kadir had given up smoking. I didn't believe it, but it was true. Kadir had sat up all night with three or four comrades. When he asked for cigarettes again and again, comrade Acar made Kadir sit at the table and put three of four packets in front of him, saying, "I'm warning you. You're going to smoke the lot, one after the other, otherwise…" Apparently, Kadir enjoyed it at first but was eventually disgusted. Even though it happened like that, I was pleased.

(Kadir remained in our block until he was released. I don't know how he perceived the prison, but he was happy with us. When he went out, his family took him back to Nizip. I gather it was very difficult for him to be outside after 20 years. I guess it must have been hard for his mother.)

While looking at Kadir, I thought that, despite what had happened to him, he hadn't left us, hadn't betrayed his people, and never insulted us.

Whereas, although the party provided agent Şemdin with such opportunities, he went over to the enemy. So, now, who's clever and who's crazy?

Block 8
31 March 1998

Today, we remember with respect Mahir Çayan and his 10 comrades who were slaughtered at Kızıldere in 1972. Their resistance is now living in today's struggle of the people of Kurdistan.

Since arriving from Çankırı, comrade Necmi has been coughing constantly. When he coughed up blood yesterday, we thought he might have TB, so we summoned the guards and made them take him to the sick bay. They've referred him to the dispensary, but we don't know how many days later he will be taken there.

When I woke up at one in the morning, I saw he had again coughed up blood. He was sat on his bunk trying to stop coughing. For three days now, neither he nor the rest of us in the dorm have been able to sleep. He is also upset about that.

We once again went to the door in the middle of the night and demanded they take him to hospital. An hour later, they took him away.

I was still awake when a guard came at 04.00 and told me, "They've taken your friend to hospital."

Despite comrade Necmi being both ill and 60 years old, he still smokes a packet of cigarettes every day. I'm annoyed about this, but I don't believe he will give up.

I am both angry and sad that comrades openly cram themselves full of cigarettes and tobacco. It's demoralising to witness such a lack of willpower and a state of addiction. It's paradoxical that the same person can risk death facing the enemy and can be a slave to an addiction like cigarettes.

In prisons such as Buca, Ankara, Bayrampaşa, Ümraniye, and Bergama, protests continue in the form of boycotting roll call and taking guards hostage, with the demand for the return of ten people who were transferred from Buca.

There shouldn't be such large scale protests over the transfer of ten people, as they could have adverse effects. It is not possible to prevent transfers in prison. The important thing is to resist everywhere and act in an organised manner.

A banner displayed in Ulucanlar read, "Come if you dare." To make such a claim in prison, behind bars, is to forget where you are. It is to fall into the grip of the enemy and not see these realities.

The transfers could not be prevented, but when the ten people were taken to prisons nearer to where their families lived, the actions were ended.

Block 8

3 April 1998

It was necessary for us to go around the blocks to do barbering. When there was a delay, we realised something unusual was going on.

Although it isn't a search week, we realised they had gone into the DS block. It was busy in the corridor. After staying there for four hours, they came into our block at 14.00.

Head guard Yolcu Yıldırım, who was on duty when two comrades were murdered on coming to the prison and for years has been involved in shady business, a man who incites the prisoners, acts arbitrarily, and is always eager to attack, had entered the opposite block. Comrades there said, "If this guy is in our block, we won't accept a search." The governor then had him removed. He was apparently like a fish out of water.

Comrade Şehmus Koyun has come here from Nazilli prison. He has been on remand since 1996. He asked for a transfer here.

Comrade Necmi has come back from hospital. As soon as he stepped into the exercise yard, he reproached us, "for not sending him his belongings." When we told him we had tried to send him his things for two days and that, eventually after arguments, they had taken them, he said, "Despite this, they didn't give them to me. The only solution to this is through the barrel of a gun." At which, we all laughed.

They had given him 12 phials of drips. He still had one attached to his arm. They're going to give him more.

I spoke to him, saying that it would be a good idea for him to take a plate and spoon and isolate himself. Normally, the prison authorities should put him in quarantine. But here they don't care. In fact, they want others to be infected. They do whatever is necessary for this in an underhand way.

He accepted it in a very mature way. "It would be better for the comrades not to be harmed," he said. It pleased me that he didn't react in the easily offended way that young comrades do.

As we prepared to play football in the evening, I was summoned to the office for a parcel. My mother had sent a pair of shoes, three pairs of slippers, two pairs of trousers, and three pairs of socks. One pair of slippers had the name Kenan on it, and another had comrade Celalettin's name. They also count as her sons…

It's a nice gesture. Reminding us that she hasn't forgotten her sons.

Block 13
14 April 1998

I washed my parka that comrade Sincar had repaired thoroughly and hung it out to dry in the exercise yard. I will put it away and wear it again in the winter.

Before going to the blocks, I made preparations for a search. Comrade Şenol send a message asking me to go to 6-14 first. They have matches and they want me to play.

When I went to 6, the volleyball team was ready. After visiting uncle Xalef, our match commenced.

It was a competitive game, between those who are to leave the block and those who will stay. They put me in the leavers' team. We narrowly won.

This was followed by the young comrades' football match. They included me. It wouldn't do to say no to the youngsters. After a short time, it started to rain, and we halted the match.

The departing comrades were preparing frantically.

Meanwhile, comrade Celalettin got a crick in his back after having a cold shower following the volleyball match. When we were talking about this, Sait hoca said he had also got a crick in the back, but "was reluctant to say so." Comrade Celalettin asked me whether I intended to move, to which I said it didn't matter either way, but that I would prefer not to be in 7-15. This must have seemed a good idea to Sait hoca, as I was told I was to go to 9-13.

When I returned to my block, those who were here were ready, too. The prepared packages had been piled up in the middle of the dorm.

When I announced I was going, while some comrades were sad, others said it would be for the best. I've stayed here with lots of different people, but I think the most colourful was Kadir…

A general warning was issued to the effect that no one should make an individual stand during the search to take place at the changes, and that everyone should behave in an organised way.

I hurriedly prepared my things. As I was the last to be added to the list, I was the last to get ready. Some comrades said, "Since you're late, let's keep you here, comrade."

The day and night shift guards speedily started the changes together. The governor and Sait hoca were observers.

After a three-year absence, I was back in block 9-13. Apart from a few comrades, the structure had been entirely renewed. I recalled the 1990 composition. Who was left from that time, what had happened here? If only the walls had tongues and could tell what had gone on here, I thought. That lively structure that assessed the world, debated the smallest development for days and weeks, and the many comrades who were martyred…

I recalled that structure with yearning and sadness.

In the reorganisation, I was allocated to block 13. I settled down on the bunk I'd had in 1990. Eight years later, I was in the same bunk! This is an indication of what a supporter of the status quo I am. When I told the comrades, they found it amusing.

For the first time in this prison, 90 people changed blocks at the same time without any objections. We were in suspense until the last moment.

In the evening, we had a festival of conversation and folk singing in the blocks. In a sketch, they portrayed comrade E. Bekir. When he first came here, he had said during a conversation, "I'm fifty-nine and a half." Three years later, on being asked how old he was, he had given the same answer. When he was told "Xalo, you still haven't got to 60," his burly body shook with laughter. One day, Madonna had a concert in Izmir. It was live on TV and comrades were watching it downstairs. A few of us were upstairs reading a book. When I saw E. Bekir fidgeting, I asked him, "What's up?" After hesitating, he said, "I think I'll go downstairs. Madonna's not important, but our children have gone to the concert, so perhaps I'll catch sight of them." Once he had gone, we laughed for several minutes.

Comrade Sakıp Hazman recalled that moment for us in his comic style.

Block 13
17 April 1998

On being told, "There's a photo in the 16 April edition of *Yeni Yüzyıl* newspaper concerning the operation in the rural areas of Antalya province," I went to the block.

Comrade A. Cerenbelli was in the picture next to several others. He had had an outline put around him, but it was not clear from the article what had happened. Had he been one of those martyred? It wasn't clear. If that is the case, it is too early.

After he had left with comrade Hüseyin Aytemur, we hadn't been able to get any news from him. It is now apparent that he has been in the "Mediterranean province."

I don't even want to think about him being amongst comrades buried in the "cemetery of the nameless." I was going to write to his mother to tell her to look at the pictures, but I changed my mind. I don't want his family to panic and to cause worse things. I can't do that to mother Fatma. Poor woman.

It is also not acceptable to die within two years after 15 years in jail. On seeing his picture in the newspaper, I remembered the time he went to school, our close acquaintance, our activities, the difficult period after the military coup of 12 September '80, prison, and, of course, his family. My memory swiftly recalled all of these.

Memories... Memories... Memories...

Block 13
1 May 1998

Last night at 01.00, comrade Esat woke me up, saying, "Greece has officially recognised us." I was excited. As the seriousness of a state officially recognising us occurred to me, I asked, "Who made the announcement?" When he replied, "A Turkish channel," I didn't take it too seriously and went back to sleep.

We learned the details in the morning. The PKK's first official office (PKK Balkan Office) has been opened in Greece. A reception was held to mark the occasion, attended by lots of MPs, at which a message from the leader was read out. That's why the Turkish media is up in arms.

Today, we celebrated May Day. After the morning roll call, the day began with comrade Mümin reading the statement in the exercise yard.

Pictures of martyrs had been brought out and placed on a table.

Our activity went on until 17.00.

There were mass celebrations in the big cities. However, in Istanbul, there were many attacks by the police. It was very painful to watch. It's unacceptable to brutally attack defenceless, innocent, peaceful protesters. Being malicious at every opportunity has been made into a culture. But in spite of this, they will not be able to cow the resisting masses. They will again be mistaken. And when they see they are mistaken, they will become even more aggressive.

Today, a central announcement was made. Tomorrow, all prisons will stage a three-day hunger strike in protest at the special war using agent Şemdin's confessions to step up the psychological propaganda, lies, and the inhuman measures being implemented in Kurdistan.

A DAY WITHOUT A DATE

Shall I consider that today has not been lived?

Around ten years ago, after being held in a hot vehicle for hours, I was taken into Aydın E-Type prison, suffering severe torture on the way in. Now, once again, I am handcuffed to a comrade and leaving the prison.

Should I be sad or happy? Is today a gain or a loss?

We lived through tumultuous times. Although the comrades with whom we shared both joyous and bitter news are in different places, this place, this heap of concrete, has had a profound effect on our lives.

Despite experiencing very painful and difficult days here, we had become accustomed to the place. To the extent that even when we went to hospital, we looked forward to returning as soon as possible.

A tragic and paradoxical situation. Just like the storms in our souls, which even if they disrupt everything, are still an existing reality.

We are leaving this place for the last time, a place where we saw many of our relatives and friends for the last time, in handcuffs. And I know I will not come back here.

And I'm leaving without looking back.

After saying farewell to the comrades one by one, we remained in profound silence. Since I stepped into the corridor, I feel empty.

I'm on my way to Antep Special Type prison, along with comrade Kasım Karataş.

We are both in a deep silence. Once in a while, we mention the incidents that took place over the years and the comrades.

After my death sentence was ratified by the Court of Cassation and my file was in parliament, I was ready for execution at any moment. The red t-shirt I intended to wear on the gallows was like a sacred object in my cupboard. When writing our letters and having our picture taken, the comrades avoided looking us in the eyes. We also behaved as if nothing had happened. We were trying to ensure our comrades were not upset. To live like this is a very different feeling, but it becomes natural here. A person adapts to even the worst conditions in a few days.

From a position of awaiting execution at any moment, a provision introduced in May 1991 meant death sentences were commuted to life sentences.

For comrades from the Turkish Left, who were experiencing the same conditions as us and had received death sentences in the same period, it was said they would serve 10 years before being released, while we had to serve 20 years.

Once again, a different law applied to the Kurds. But we didn't care.

We are talking about missing comrades who were expecting a death sentence, were released, and burst into tears as they went out the door.

I don't know how long we were on the road. It was both a long time and a short time.

At a service station, where we halted, they boosted our morale. After the soldiers had checked things out, they allowed us to get out of the vehicle and go directly to the WC. People were looking at us strangely. We were also looking around, out of curiosity. When we went into the WC, our handcuffs were loosened. The soldiers waited at the door opening into the corridor. When I came out of the cubicle, I looked for soap and a tap. There wasn't any. I didn't want to ask the soldier. Meanwhile, comrade Kasım came out. He whispered to me, "Comrade Ali, just do what I do." He put his hand into a cavity in the wall and soap flowed out. He moved to the side and washed his hands with the water that spurted out. I did the same thing, putting on a bold face.

When I had been arrested 18 years earlier, no such thing existed. Comrade Kasım took care that I wouldn't be embarrassed. He had come from Switzerland to Izmir seven or eight years before to get involved in activities. His family lived in Antep. This transfer was going to be good for him and his family.

As we arrive at the Antep Special Type prison, we talk about what may happen and clarify the stance we need to take.

After 15 years, I am once again breathing the air of Antep.

The city of my dreams. But in the prison at the military brigade HQ.

While being processed on entering the prison, the guards clustered around us. We were wary of possible attacks. An elderly head guard approached us and looked at me.

"Ali Poyraz, is it you?"

"Yes, it's me."

"Hey! Are you still inside? We're about to retire and you're still inside?"

"Yes, unfortunately."

"Which year was it when you came to the E-Type prison?"

"November 1984."

"What the heck!"

The chief guard was stunned. He was the head guard in '84, when 40 comrades were transferred from Mersin to Antep E-Type prison. And he was one of the infamous torturers.

They had tried to force us to sing the national anthem, and when we refused, they tortured us severely. After being beaten on the soles of the feet with shovel handles, our feet were black and blue for months afterwards. Despite being in military custody for 105 days in Pazarcık, Maraş, and Antep after being captured, I hadn't been tortured as badly as here. In spite of that, we did not accept their rules. They put us in twos and threes in blocks with ordinary prisoners and fascists. They didn't give us any peace in the blocks either. In fact, we too weren't "quiet." Many times, we were put in cells for fighting with fascists. But after comrades Ömer and H. Şerik set themselves alight, a line was drawn in front of repression.

One of the head guards who were the leading actors in that period was now standing in front of me, 15 years later.

It was apparent that he, too, like me, had meditated on the past. He said:
"Where would you like to go?"
"Any block with comrades."
He turned to the guards:
"Search the guys and then take them to the representatives' block."

Kasım was looking at me questioningly. I whispered to him, "I will explain later." He merely smiled.

We passed down the corridor of the Special Type prison. After passing the canteen, we hear noises coming from the blocks. The long main corridor did not seem unfamiliar. We took sure steps towards our comrades.

As we reached the block door, we saw that the comrades had massed behind the bars. It was clear that they had heard of our arrival and were waiting for us. When the door opened, we embraced as comrades sharing the same feelings and circumstances. They did not know us, but they hugged us as if we had been in the same place for years. We were like them.

After asking whether we had any problems on arrival, mutual friends were asked after. Questions and answers followed.

I am once again in a prison. I am once again amongst comrades.

ANTEP SPECIAL TYPE PRISON

13 November 1998 / E-3

THE NEWS FROM ROME THAT SHOCKED US

Just as all over the world, the news hit us like a bomb. It literally shocked us.

I had gone as a guest to block E-1. I was with comrades Galip, İsmet, and Hakkı in a cell, busy marking the short stories competing in the 27 November competition…

A comrade came in saying, "The leader has been arrested in Rome." We couldn't believe our ears. It was something that seemed impossible to us. We knew he was in Europe. Hence, we didn't think it was possible for him to be arrested.

After we had recovered from the shock, we began to speculate regarding the reasons for the arrest. Our first comments (if the news was true) were:

A step towards our political recognition.

It may be part of an international conspiracy.

In the afternoon, at 14.00, we gathered around the television set. All the comrades were waiting in silence. Those who'd been playing football came in sweating. As they were out of breath, at every inhalation, their chests went up and down.

Every channel we tried featured the leader's capture.

While striding back and forth in the lower corridor, our sadness, anger, and guesses of possible outcomes were intertwined. Bedrettin said that, because of this, "There might be emotional reactions like people setting themselves alight. Let's be on our guard until we understand the matter properly and prevent such things." After our conversation continued in the same vein, I went back to my block. Comrades were clearly demoralised. Their emotional state could be seen in their eyes. They were all like bombs about to go off. It's difficult to describe these feelings.

We tried to watch the news every hour. The special war media was trying to portray the event as a "victory."

In the evening, a meeting was held in the block at which an announcement was made calling on people not to act emotionally.

14 November 1998 / E-3

The special war regime is putting endless programmes on TV in order to use this development to cover the government crisis and to prevent any potential benefits for us.

In particular, the aggressive tone of P.M. Mesut Yılmaz is a result of this.

Towards evening we heard that the leader had started a hunger strike. At a press conference, Kani Yılmaz said, "Until this matter is resolved, no PKK member should even breathe, let alone eat and drink." It is now unthinkable that we wouldn't take action. After a brief exchange of messages, our structure decided to go on an unlimited hunger strike. Kani's statement demonstrates that we are faced with a serious situation. In particular, his mention of a Damascus-Russia-Greece plot is an indication of that.

While speaking to comrade Nizam, I said I would remove adhesives and eau de cologne from the block. When he said they could remain with him on the ground floor, I smelt a rat. I said I would lock them up on the top floor. When I asked him to handover the existing adhesives, he said, "They're needed downstairs so there's only one left." However, I had seen five or six a short time earlier. When he said he had sent them to other blocks, I desisted.

A few minutes later, I noticed he was going upstairs. I followed him and stopped him. When I saw a bulge in the front of his jacket, I called him over to the cell, where we keep communal things and told him, "Hand over the stuff you've got on you." He looked at me sheepishly and denied he had anything. When I persisted, he handed over one tube of adhesive. When I looked him in the eyes and continued to wait, he gave me another one.

I gripped him by the arm and said, "Don't do it. There's a lot of uncertainty at the moment. There's no need to behave emotionally. It's not clear what's going to happen." He then handed over four more.

I subsequently learned that this was something that had been organised by a few comrades.

15 November 1998 / E-3

The first day of the hunger strike. We sent 11 joint petitions to some embassies and ministries informing them that 222 comrades had started a hunger strike.

From visitors, we learned that thousands of people are flocking to Rome.

They told us that the leader has actually commenced his hunger strike today.

Also, self-immolations have begun, the first taking place in Çanakkale.

Nadir has fled our environment.

16 November 1998 / E-3

The second day.

The tone used by the special war is changing by the hour. As developments move in our favour, they become more aggressive.

But we know very well that many of the things in full view are misleading.

We are following with great apprehension.

When, in the evening, the sound of banging doors came from the section of the E-Type where women comrades are held, comrade Bedrettin went to the prison administration. They told him there was no such thing on the E-Type side and that the radiators were being repaired.

17 November 1998

THE PRISONS AND OUTSIDE HAVE BEEN TURNED UPSIDE DOWN

The third day.

At around 02.00 in the morning, comrade Ekrem woke me up. When he said, "There's a martyr," I dashed into the corridor. I had heard the scream but had not comprehended it in my drowsy state. The slogan, "Long live leader Apo" had been shouted.

We learned that ZİHNİ ARAT, who was in block D-3, had set himself on fire. The smell of burning was evident. Perhaps it was a result of our helplessness that it seemed like that. There was nothing we could do. We were angry, despairing, but we didn't just want to wait.

We spent the night tense, as if sitting on a powder keg.

A statement by the Italian government comforted us. It was expressed clearly that in absolutely no circumstances would there be an extradition to Turkey. The fact that the Italian Prime Minister used extracts from leader Apo's fax at a press conference infuriated the Turkish special war regime.

It was also announced on the news that some comrades had spoken to the leader in hospital. The TV channels reacted, saying, "He is being treated as a guest rather than a prisoner."

Tens of thousands of people have flocked to Rome. People are continuing to go from many countries.

I saw my mother in the footage on the news. She caught my attention straight away with a yellow, red, and green band around her head. To see her six years later, if only on the screen, and at such an important action, delighted me/us. For days I have been saying to myself, "She won't be able to stop herself, she'll have gone to Rome."

In addition to slogans expressing loyalty to leader Apo, there were also internationalist slogans shouted about Italy. Thousands of our flags were fluttering in the squares of Rome.

Even on the Turkish news, they had to admit, "It was an enthusiastic demonstration."

We listened to the leader's message on our radio. He stressed that every one of our people has long-term responsibilities. And that they were ready to start a peace process. Listening to this news/message comforted us.

We watched live on TV, as two young men first poured petrol over themselves in front of parliament in Red Square, Moscow. Then one of them left a letter on the pavement before bringing out a lighter. Suddenly, they were both immersed in a huge fireball. The camera shot was clear. They shouted, "Long live leader Apo." Seeing those comrades shouting amidst the flames, feeling it, made our hair stand on end.

There is no reason why a people prepared to sacrifice themselves for the leader cannot win.

Again, the resisters will have the last word.

A woman comrade in Yüksekova, Hakkari, blew herself up amidst a military convoy.

The Turkish TV channels are continuing to broadcast contradictory news. The police and the fascists savagely attacked our families at a demonstration in Istanbul. Women, the elderly, and young people were beaten and arrested in an Italian church where they had taken refuge. Seeing the mothers being kicked as they were dragged down stairs on the TV screen increased our anger.

They are trying to compensate for their helplessness with these attacks. But let them not forget that our resisting people will not be cowed. The chauvinistic fascist attacks will do no more than adversely affect the special war. The weapon they are using will backfire on them.

18 November 1998/E-3
THE AGONY OF THOSE WHO SET THEMSELVES ON FIRE IS A STORM INSIDE ME

The fourth day.

Just as I was setting out to go around the blocks with A. Oruç, they rushed into the blocks to carry out a search. They went into all the blocks at the same moment. They scattered things around and left.

While tidying things up in our block, I noticed they had torn a photo. It was a picture of two sisters the state had murdered in Adana, Berivan and Dilan. They can't even tolerate a photo of our two-year-old martyrs. These fears will, day by day, bury them deeper in the swamp. As they feel this, they are becoming more savage.

We sent the torn photo to the prison administration, saying, "Tell your governor we do not accept this."

After the search, we first went to D-3. The comrades were quiet. Comrade Zihni's self-immolation had worsened the situation.

This impact will have a meaning in the event that personalities are reviewed, negative aspects overcome, and ownership of life taken.

Being worthy of our values in life, which was the reason for them setting themselves on fire, will help us understand these actions. Otherwise, they will have no more than a fleeting emotional effect. Taking ownership of these actions necessitates this. The persistence of those who remain will bring with it immortality.

There was a visible liveliness in all the blocks we visited. We went to all the blocks, not dallying long in any of them.

We also visited comrade Müslüm Muhammed. He was in the same position he has lain in for days. When I lifted his mosquito net to look at him, I felt an indescribable pain. His abdominal and chest area looks like a bubbling pot after it was burnt. Blood and a yellow liquid oozes out as the body forms scabs and then cracks. It is as if the internal organs are exposed. As scabs begin to form, they cut the drying areas with scissors so that there is not too much constriction. This is apparently how it is treated. Naturally, this is very painful.

He has difficulty speaking. Even breathing causes him pain. On seeing him like this, I react deep down to the fact that comrades extinguished him when he set himself alight. Rather than being beneficial, it did him harm. But, of course, you cannot tolerate seeing a comrade burn furiously alongside you. You can't stop yourself acting. However, when you see the pain he is in during the treatment, you can't help but say to yourself, "If only there hadn't been an intervention, then he wouldn't be in such agony." These actions are entirely individual decisions. Despite this, precautions must be taken to prevent such self-immolation but, in the event they take place, it would be better not to intervene.

Although two comrades are constantly on hand to look after comrade Müslüm Muhammed, this doesn't reduce his pain. They are not enough to end his moaning.

The comrades are unhesitatingly doing whatever they can for Müslüm.

Despite all his pain, his morale was good. This demonstrates that his will power and resolution are strong.

When we dropped into F-3, we started to listen to comrade Şerif. Since he's the oldest comrade in the block at 60, we started with him to boost his morale. Since he is comfortable with us, he began to complain about other comrades while alongside them. "They don't listen to education, they don't know themselves or the enemy," he said. The comrades around him smiled without interfering.

As he is constantly complaining in this way, one day, they put him on the council for collective education. He threw out, one by one, those who didn't answer his questions. Of 20 people, only seven remained. He said, "These seven people didn't give full answers, but I managed." Of course, the comrades added that the questions had nothing to do with the subject of education.

Even if that is the case, his enthusiasm is pleasing. Such comrades are appreciated everywhere. They are a source of morale in a block.

When I asked the comrade responsible for the commune, "Do you give comrade Şerif extra sugar?" Şerif butted in, saying, "If that were the case, comradeship would be harmed. Everyone gets what they are entitled to…" Without giving me the chance to reply, he added, "Don't forget to send sugar to our block." This must have amused the comrades, as they started laughing.

As we left the block, he shouted out to us, "If there's a complaint about me, come and take my statement, OK?" He doesn't neglect to safeguard his own position.

In the afternoon, I edited some short stories that were considered the best in a competition. They will be typed up.

Comrade Mümin sent a card. He had sent the interview we did about comrade Doğan Kılıçkaya to a competition in Çanakkale, and it won first prize. I didn't know that. I was pleased. It's a pleasant feeling for one's efforts to be appreciated.

In this way, I have found out that comrade Mümin is still in Aydın.

The bourgeois media is up in arms about events in Rome. The special war officials who until yesterday were bristling and making grand speeches have now lowered their heads and begun to swear at Italy. They are repeating time after time that the leader is not in detention, saying, "They are deceiving Turkey."

They have mobilised fascists in Turkish cities. When arresting our people who have started hunger strikes in HADEP buildings, they allow them to be attacked by fascists they themselves have provoked. They are encouraging others to do the same by repeatedly showing the footage on TV. They may step up such attacks in the coming days and even hold rallies.

The special war is trying to imitate the demonstrations in Rome.

Fascists have set fire to some of our offices in Brussels.

The slogan, "THE LEADER IN ROMA, TURKEY IN A COMA," is just one example of our people's creativity. Our people are amazing at responding according to circumstances and needs.

With every passing hour, developments are moving in our favour. On seeing this, the special war regime becomes all the more aggressive. This is why Mesut Yılmaz is threatening Italy.

The answer of the Italian Prime Minster, "We will not give in to any blackmail or threat" is sufficient for them.

Due to these developments, most of the comrades are still not feeling hungry. Tension, vigilance, and these developments in our favour are keeping our minds off hunger.

We gather that the petitions we sent on the day we started the hunger strike have still not been delivered. We demanded a meeting with the prison authorities, but we have not received a reply.

19 November 1998/E-3
"IF YOU ACCEPT ME AS COMMANDER, DON'T BURN YOURSELVES"

The fifth day.

The turbulent period continues without a let up. As long as there is no sharp turn, the developments are notably in our favour.

Today, all the speeches made in the European Parliament were directed at the threats made by the special war regime. Europe is slowly beginning to demonstrate an approach that supports the Italian stance.

It is said the leader has been moved to a house in Rome. Turkish TV says he has moved to a "villa."

After a comrade set himself on fire in Rome, the leader said, "If you accept me as commander, don't burn yourselves."

Hamit Çakır, who was one of those arrested while on hunger strike in Diyarbakır HADEP, was murdered in a police station.

In Bursa, a young man was seriously injured.

There is an intensive campaign against HADEP. Murat Bozlak and hundreds of party members have been arrested. All HADEP buildings are being attacked and damaged, either by the police, or by fascists under the supervision of the police.

Chauvinism and racism are being incited in Turkish cities every day. They want to provoke clashes between Turks and Kurds.

Today, we spoke to the governor. The 21 comrades to be transferred have been confirmed. In a few days, 15 of them will go to Kürkçüler and the rest to various other places. We were told that a canopy would be placed above our windows on the top floor. They don't want us to see anything of the outside world. We won't accept it and tomorrow we will write a petition to the prosecutor.

20 November 1998/E-3

The sixth day.

For days now we have been in a haze. For the first time, we have relaxed. All the comrades' eyes are smiling. The leader will now stay in a house. But he will apparently be subjected to a period of mandatory residence.

Germany has withdrawn its extradition request. The Italian appeal court made its decision after the Pope made a positive statement.

After moving into the house, the leader published a message thanking the people for coming to Rome. And he asked them to return home. As I was writing these lines, comrade Kadri came over and said, "As always, we have won, comrade Ali," clenching his fist and waving it in the air.

I have given comrades the key to the cupboard where I locked up the eau de cologne and adhesives. There is no need for them to be locked away any longer. In the early days in particular, we had to make several announcements regarding this. We later learned that lots of comrades had gone as far as fixing a time for setting themselves on fire. Some in our block and in E-1 had even reached an agreement, saying, "Let's have a mass self-immolation."

After handing over the key, comrade Nizam said, "I had other adhesives. I hid them." I smiled, saying, "I know. Do you think you are the only smartass here?" He laughed as he walked away.

21 November 1998/E-3

The seventh day.

We learned during the visit today that retired teacher, 46-year-old Metin Yurtsever, one of those detained in Izmit, has been murdered.

There were some interesting items of news.

Our people in Rome received a lot of support from the people of Italy and the Red Cross.

We heard about comrade Kani and Avreş's statements.

In general, there is enthusiasm, and this is continuing. Hunger strikes outside have been turned into three-day alternating actions.

If there is no change in the situation, we shall review our action and update it.

Comrades on hunger strike are, generally speaking, well. Just those on hunger strike for the first time have concerns, naturally. Although they don't mention this, we understand.

Attacks are continuing on our people in HADEP buildings. In spite of mass arrests, our people are continuing to commence hunger strikes in groups. This is by itself an expression of resistance and resolution. Emin Yılmaz came for a visit. He said that my mother appeared on a TV programme in Rome, summarizing what she has been through since I was arrested, and expressing her yearnings.

22 November 1998/E-3

Towards evening, we ended our hunger strike. From now on, it will continue in the form of a three-day alternating limitless action.

The square in Rome has still not been vacated entirely. While some people have left, others are apparently on the way. My mother has returned to Germany. I gather that today she rang acquaintances here and sent 300 Marks.

They passed on our European representative's message. "Let them stop self-immolation. They upset the leader. Let them conceal flammable materials. They should keep watch in the blocks in twos." I remember the turn of expression used by Kani from Eskişehir prison.

They asked those who are to be transferred to Adana and other places to be ready by the morning. Tomorrow, our number will go down by 20. But this won't make much of a difference. One reason for prisoners making this choice is that they were unable to adapt to this place. Nevertheless, as an administration, there is an approach and implementations that should be reviewed, as such a number of comrades have opted to leave. First and foremost, ways of doing things, methods, adaptation, and self-presentation should be placed under the microscope. If some comrades are "fleeing" from here, this is primarily a problem for the administration. It's not realistic to just link it to individuals. If they are having difficulties, this is also a problem for the administration.

Preparations are continuing in all blocks for the 27 November celebrations.

The leader has written a letter to the Pope asking for his support in finding a solution to the Kurdistan question. Even this enraged the Turkish media. The special war is like ice rapidly melting under our sun. This ice that has turned to stone over 600 years is now swiftly thawing. And while melting, it wants to flood some places. But it is futile…

23 November 1998/E-3
ROTINDA

Yes, Rotinda. If only you knew how hard it is to understand you. We were unable to comprehend you smiling as you knew your comrades were dashing towards you as a fireball.

I have such admiration for those who know their final smile will be as they become immortal by going up in flames.

We will pay homage to those who feel your warmth in their hearts and pay homage to you, Rotinda, for ever more. For in our struggle, there will always be you and new Rotindas.

ROTINDA

In the struggle you will always be our comrade. While running from position to position, you will always be with us. We will race ahead with the joy of knowing this. In our most difficult moments, you will be our guide.

You will protect us from the freezing cold of the Zagros mountains and the searing heat of the desert sun. With the pride of knowing this, we will aim for victory. And news of that victory will be heralded by the glint in our eyes.

Don't forget, comrade, that our Rotinda is in Moscow, in Rome and ... Rotindas are now uncountable. Just like her. Can the rays of the sun be counted?

Yes, she cannot be deemed a sunbeam.

Millions of Rotindas.

Wherever there is life, there is a Rotinda. Every heart and every brain is a Rotinda.

Every one of our souls spread all over the world is a Rotinda.

Every one of our souls in prison is a Rotinda.

From seven to seventy Rotindas...

Because they are the future. They are us.

Rotinda, you live everywhere. But the most beautiful place, which rouses envy, is the mountains for which you yearned. It is the guerrilla life, those wonderful moments where the young "portable" and the elderly guerrilla fight in a comradely way for freedom.

Ah, Rotinda, ah!...

If you could only know how many wildly beating hearts there are that long to reach the heat of your flames...

To live, yet with one condition, understanding Rotinda...

We understand, Rotinda. For your smile, that freedom-spreading smile, is always in front of our eyes...

Our Rotindas are amongst the peaks of all our mountains, in all our capital cities and in every heartbeat...

24 November 1998/E-3

Despite not going to bed until 02.00 last night, I awoke at 06.00. I was unable to get back to sleep and got up without waiting for the "Rojbaş" at 07.00.

After the roll call, we gave the whole place a thorough cleaning as part of preparations for 27 November. We even cleaned the iron doors. But most of the comrades suffered stomach upsets as a result of being barefoot in cold water for a long time.

Towards noon, Mehmet Ay, Ömer Üzüm, Fudayl Calp, Hasan Yağız, Esat Turan, and Hamdin Demirkıran arrived from Aydın. As I knew these six comrades from Aydın, we immediately accepted them in our block. One person also arrived from Burdur. He had been on trial from DS, but when he said, "As a human being, I want to stay in your blocks," we couldn't refuse him. Such people stay in our environments in lots of prisons. Whatever organisation they are from, as long as there is not a situation of betrayal, collaboration, etc., we see no problem in them sharing our environment.

After 20 comrades were transferred from here, the administration discussed this development at its meeting.

Although they left of their own volition, we still need to examine certain things. The administration cannot exempt itself from this. However much some comrades may not accept this, making "radical" comments, this is our reality. Issues discussed included the need to act sensitively, the importance of administrators adopting measures themselves, adhering to collectivism, being empathetic by putting themselves in the shoes of comrades, being constructive when implementing rules, ensuring former modes of administration are abandoned, using the language of the organisation when imposing a system and discipline, involving the structure in decision-making and, most important of all, understanding that an administrator must be accepted by the structure. From time to time, there was tension, it cannot be denied.

Being an administrator in a prison brings with it various difficulties and risks. And administering our people is particularly difficult. Although we sometimes joke about it, there is a reality we occasionally voice:

1. The administrative type who irritates the structure, and
2. The type who irritates the administrator

Unfortunately, both types are our reality. No one can abstract themselves from this.

The easiest way to resolve any problem is for the administrator to begin with himself.

27 November 1998/E-3
WE CELEBRATE OUR TWENTIETH YEAR

On account of the serious situation in which we find ourselves, we have been unable to prepare properly for today. We did most of it in the last few days.

When we got up in the morning, all the comrades had a shave. After the roll call, we had a minute's silence, anthem, and reading of a statement; then all comrades exchanged greetings. Guests had come from other blocks. After chatting in the exercise yard for a while, comrade Bedrettin said, "Let us, as representatives, go to the other blocks to wish the comrades a happy festival for an hour." As it is not a usual day, we got special permission, naturally surprising the comrades.

In all the blocks, there was visible joy and enthusiasm.

In the 20 years since the party was founded, there have been many tumultuous periods. Today is the result of all those stormy times. There has been resistance to death outside and in the prisons. From the time the party was withdrawing to the Middle East in 1979, reorganising and participating in the Israel war in Palestine, to the struggle developed within the country, first and foremost the resistance in Diyarbakır prison, developing the party into a front and army organisation, great, unimaginable progress has been made. During this period, unfortunately, many leading cadre were immortalised and became guides in the struggle. Most important of all, the party has reached millions amongst the people and, by organising in the form of a women's army, achieved an effective position in the struggle unprecedented in history.

In this way, the party is a movement that has succeeded in raising its struggle to a higher level, as a "party of martyrs," as the leader has said, from its initial founding. Our joy today in prison is an expression of this.

I was able to have conversations with the six comrades who came from Aydın. They passed on the criticisms and expectations of comrades there. They are right that I should have written, but I had a problem of time due to the intensity of work. Despite this, it is no justification.

In the evening, a fax came from comrade Mahmut Aktaş. He said the action had been ended. We understood this was a decision of the internal coordination. Naturally, we also have to end the action.

We immediately passed on the news to the women comrades in the adjacent prison.

We informed the comrades in E-1, and they ended their action. We then informed the comrades in all the blocks we visited.

Our activities continued between 17.00 and 20.00.

Today I feel tired. Being on my feet all day and doing a halay have caused this.

28 November 1998/E-3

I gather the leader again made a speech last night. He thanked friends who had offered support and our people. He sent special greetings to those who had set themselves on fire and are now groaning in their beds.

Another item of news I heard today shocked me. An eleven-year-old girl in East Kurdistan (Rojhilat) set herself alight. She said, "I am protesting at the silence of Kurds in Iran, their lack of participation, and attacks on the leader."

It's impossible to explain such determination, such an action from someone so young. The new period is creating new acts of heroism…

I don't know the name of our 11-year-old comrade, but I know she is a hero…

1 December 1998/E-3

Towards noon, four comrades were brought here from Kızıltepe prison. Three of them had joined recently and were arrested en route. And one of them is the brother-in-law of comrade Menaf Osman, who is here alongside us.

Three of them are between the ages of 14 and 19. When I learned that Mevlüt Batır, who has been placed in our block, is 14, I was really surprised. I am really sorry they were arrested. They travelled all the way from Istanbul to Kızıltepe with the loveliest dreams and were captured there. What a let down. These young comrades are open to positive and negative things. It is now down to the comrades here to make sure they grow acquainted with good ideas and life.

Some of the Kurdish youth who want to join the struggle in Kurdistan, from the big cities in particular, are either being arrested on the road and thrown into prison, or slaughtered while unarmed and defenceless in the mountains. The effect of such developments is unfortunately quite severe.

It is either due to a lack of care or infiltration that allows the enemy to hear of such new recruits.

Apparently one of the items on the agenda of the MGK (National Security Council) concerned the prisons. It is calculated and insidious for it to be on their agenda at this time. We will need to be even more on our guard.

2 December 1998/E-3

I went round the blocks with comrade Bedrettin. While in E-1, the photographer arrived. Photographs are to be taken in every block on the occasion of 27 November. We didn't want to pose, as it would mean changing our plans, but the comrades insisted. As always, the atmosphere changed instantly. Everyone was enjoying posing for photos.

While speaking to Yusuf Bozan, who arrived from Kızıltepe yesterday, Oruç came in. As he's had a pain in his kidney for a week, he had tied a head scarf around his waist. He had pulled his white woollen socks up over his trousers. With his socks up to his knees, he looked as though he was going out to walk in a metre of snow.

He asked Yusuf, "Are you getting used to it here?"

"So-so."

Oruç replied, "Look, I got used to it here straight away, in five months. You'll get used to it soon."

Yusuf pointed at him, saying, "He's lived his life."

Comrades Selahattin and İsmet laughed, quietly.

Yusuf continued, "When I look at him, he reminds me of a militia man in our village."

I replied, "He was a militia man, but they arrested him and brought him here."

Yusuf looked at him, shaking his head, "You rascals, you. You have destroyed Turkey. You were constantly bringing in fighters."

Meanwhile, A. Oruç was smiling.

In spite of being only 18, Yusuf has been smoking for five years. I told him, "There are comrades who gave up smoking in here after 30 years of doing it. You should give up, too. It's bad for you."

He replied, haughtily, "Let me smoke for 30 years, then we'll see."

From his manner of speech, it is apparent he is quite shrewd and also a bit arrogant. But given the society he comes from, this is to be expected. Despite this, I believe that after education and practice, these comrades will be real activists.

As we left the block, I whispered in Yusuf's ear, "He's an old comrade, he was pulling your leg." He went red in the face. When one day he learns all about him, his face will redden even more.

In fact, such young and dynamic comrades always enliven the environment.

Today, I completed the letter I am sending to M. Gülmez and block 9-13 in Aydın. I hope they receive it.

12 December 1998/E-3

We have learned the name of the young hero in Rojhilat – Zehra RIZGAR.

She was only eleven. The fact she timed her action to coincide with 27 November proves she was more mature than her age.

Heroism has no age limit.

And heroes are immortal.

They become perpetual due to their action.

ZEHRA is one of these.

We learned her name while reading the *Yurtsever Gençlik* (Patriotic Youth) magazine.

Still a child.

But unfortunately, like her peers in Kurdistan, unable to live her childhood.

Through their actions, they have surpassed themselves and time.

Further exacerbating the load on our shoulders…

Once again opening the deep wounds in our hearts…

14 December 1998/E-3

Hunger strikes have been started again in Europe and in all the prisons. Until the leader's situation becomes clear, they will continue in an alternating five-day limitless form. D1 and D3 have started the first shift.

19 December 1998/E-3

This morning, we in E-3 and E-1 started a hunger strike. Judging from the latest fax we received from Bursa, the action may be prolonged. "We should prepare ourselves for intensified actions according to external developments" is an expression of this.

According to what we were told by visitors, a call has gone out all over Europe to attend a mass rally in Bonn today. Our people are travelling there from all over Europe. The participation of those in Germany is expected to be particularly high.

23 December 1998/E-3

While going round the blocks with comrade Bedrettin, we saw that everyone was making preparations. While the D blocks were in education, the E blocks are preparing to end their hunger strike and the F blocks are preparing to start a hunger strike tomorrow. There was a separate excitement in all of them.

We received a fax from Bursa in the afternoon. It stated that the hunger strikes in prisons were ending and that court hearings would be attended from 5 January 1999.

We sent a message to the prison administration informing them that the F blocks would not be starting a hunger strike tomorrow.

As is the case in such situations, there was naturally a traffic of notes between blocks.

Despite the fact that public opinion is in our favour, the special war's calmness concerns us. Such periods of calm have always been followed by dangerous developments. Hence, we will have to be on our guard.

3 January 1999/E-3

THE AGONISING NEWS ABOUT RAHŞAN IS A SPEAR IN MY SIDE

New developments await us in the New Year. Although there are things that concern us, we believe that those who are good, resist, and not bow their heads will prevail.

Today was our visiting day. From now on, we will have visitors on Wednesdays instead of Sundays.

Comrade Kasım's elder sister came and mentioned our Rahşan. She asked whether she had been martyred. I found it odd, but said I had no information. Although I added, "If you've heard anything, say so." "I've heard nothing," she replied.

On returning to the block, I asked comrade Kasım.

My dark, curly-haired little sister, who visited me in the most difficult times, my comrade and confidant RAHŞAN, has been martyred.

The last I heard, she was apparently on Cudi mountain. But I'm not sure she went there.

They didn't know where or when she had been martyred [years later, between the cold walls of a prison, I was to learn that she had died with a comrade in September 1996 in a clash near Dersim city].

When you receive such painful news, the uncertainty causes even more pain. It makes you feel even more helpless. You freeze, as if all your cells have turned to ice. You once again rebel at the darkness and cold of prison and the way it eats away at your nerves. But this rebellion becomes an erupting volcano in your silent world.

When I was captured, she was only six or seven years old. She wasn't even able to spend her childhood with us. After we were arrested, the family's poverty worsened. Despite this, she never abandoned us. Rahşan, like many of our relatives, grew up at prison gates. As if it was their destiny, they were unable to enjoy their childhoods or experience the child's world, and before knowing themselves, they became acquainted with the painful reality of thick prison walls. They became acquainted with gendarmes, prison guards, and insults.

She was detained and tortured countless times.

Every time they exiled us, those outside were also subjected to exile. Despite being exposed to cold in winter, heat in summer, and most importantly, having to struggle to survive in grinding poverty, they never complained or mentioned what they were going through. But we were aware of it. But their self-sacrifice took our bonds and love to another realm beyond that of siblings.

My feelings are difficult to describe. Prison walls are like a vice, squeezing you as they contract. I am feeling the pain deep in my heart. But there is nothing I can do. There is unfortunately nothing I can do to change what has happened.

As every moment of our lives is woven with pain and anguish, news of death becomes "normal." Even if this is stated simply, we shall not get used to it. We won't accept this as destiny.

Every comrade who falls in the war for freedom is precious. But the martyrdom of a comrade who has been a guerrilla for six or seven years and has had two sessions of education at the academy has a more profound effect.

The end after such effort, toil, experience, education, and practice shouldn't be like this.

The open visit in May 1990 in Aydın was our last meeting.

Our youngest sister, Handan, her, and I weren't silent for a moment during the visit. We chatted the whole time. I passed on my concerns, experience, and suggestions. She was all ears. Her decision was final. She had prepared herself months before. No one, including our mother, knew.

Near the end of the visit, when the three of us were strolling slowly up and down in the exercise yard, we were saying our farewells. We both knew very well that this might be our last meeting and that these might be the last words we said to each other. But we refrained from expressing this, as if we had agreed not to do so. We didn't want to say it. [I couldn't have imagined that I would use a photo we had taken that day at a commemoration years later].

As we parted, we hugged each other fiercely, telling each other to take care, and wishing each other success.

We were both happy and sad. But no one around us could comprehend how difficult this separation was.

From here, she went straight to the Mahsum Korkmaz Academy in the Bekaa Valley.

I can still see her white sweater, plump body, and curly hair.

Her last innocent and wistful glance is still in front of my eyes.

I don't even want to think about my poor mother at this time. If she has heard, she'll be distraught.

Maybe my mother and sister Fatoş haven't heard, or they haven't let on.

Rahşan was a good friend to both of them...

I will carry her in my heart with its wound that will not close.

Her last glances will remain imprinted in my eyes.

May the stars be your comrades, my curly dark-haired middle sister, and comrade...

14 February 1999 E-3

Those who went for visits yesterday found out. Our prison coordination's statement was broadcast on MED-TV. From 14 February, all the prisons will start a five-day alternating hunger strike in protest at the conspiracy against the leader.

Although since the leader left Rome it has not been officially announced where he is, the attacks continue. Hence our people's protests will be intensive everywhere, particularly in Europe. Statements issued everywhere have been decisive and angry.

Rahşan Poyraz (Dicle)

Our people outside and in prisons will not hesitate to make any sacrifice. The special war regime and the imperialists also know this.

This morning F-1, F-2, F-3, and F-4 blocks started a hunger strike. They will be followed by the other blocks. The stance will change according to developments.

Today, we received an 11-page instruction-perspective from our internal coordination. After a hectic exchange of notes, we made our plans accordingly. The sources to be read have been identified. Special education will be arranged for a week. The instruction and a short explanation that accompanied it were read out to the structure in the blocks.

16 February 1999 E-3

Yesterday and today will be remembered as a dark day in the history of the people of Kurdistan. I dread having to write about this dark day. However, in spite of everything, we cannot ignore what has taken place.

Yes, a dark day…

The news shocked us. All Turkish TV channels had the news that leader Apo had been brought to Turkey by plane at around 03.00 in the morning.

Comrade İsmet dashed in, panicked, while we were sitting on the top floor, and relayed the news to us. We immediately went downstairs. Prime Minister Bülent Ecevit was making a statement on the TV.

I heard a few comrades sob. They couldn't help themselves. Some comrades' chests were heaving. One could hear the breathing in the silence. If you touched any comrade, they would explode.

From the corridor came the sound of someone colliding with the wall. When we ran out into the corridor, we saw Mustafa Gökdemir lying in the middle on the floor. He had butted the sharp corner of the column like a ram. Hair and skin was stuck on the stone. A deep V-shaped wound had opened on his forehead. A whiteness was visible inside. For a moment, we were so shocked we didn't know what to do. He had gone out and smashed his head against the column while no one was there. As the corner of the column had struck the middle of his head, a terrible sight confronted us. It was as if he had been struck with an axe, leaving a straight wound. It was the first time we had seen anything like this. We immediately brought a clean towel and bound his head. He hadn't fainted, but was unable to speak. Either from concussion or the shock, he couldn't speak.

We sent him to the sick bay. We then made an announcement to all the comrades gathering in the corridor to the effect that they should be calm, refrain from emotional reactions, and that the fundamental task started now. We then returned to our blocks.

All blocks were galvanised, but there was such a silence – it was as if, were you to whisper, the whole prison would hear.

The prison administration withdrew all the guards from the corridors. It was obvious that they were having a meeting. They doubled the number of guards on duty five to 10 minutes later. They had taken emergency measures.

We discussed amongst ourselves what we could do.

The people of Kurdistan had once again been stabbed in the back…

17 February 1999 E-3

Our people are on their feet all over the world, first and foremost in Europe. Greek embassies have been occupied in 28 countries. Greece sold us out in bringing the leader from Kenya to Turkey. Of course, behind the scenes are the US and Israel.

Death fasts have begun to be discussed in the prisons.

The people of Kurdistan are acting in a more organised way than ever before. It is as if there is a general uprising with a kind of mobilisation…

Our people are demonstrating their loyalty unhesitatingly. Everywhere is on fire…

Kenya has temporarily closed its embassies all over the world. It has been announced that its ambassadors and staff have been recalled.

In Germany, five of our people were martyred and 14 wounded when staff at an Israeli consulate opened fire. Israel then recalled its ambassadors in Europe. This is something that doesn't usually happen even during wars.

They broadcast footage of the leader during the flight for the first time. He was blindfolded and in handcuffs. They had drugged him before putting him on the plane. The fact they removed the blindfold and put cameras on him before he had fully woken up caused rage in all the comrades and an indescribable sadness.

We will never forget these images…

18 February 1999 E-3

Today, comrades Selahattin Kılıç, Yılmaz Yürek, Bülent Direk, Metin Toprak, and H. Hüseyin Ebem have begun a death fast here. They explained their reasons in a long petition.

We read the petition in all the blocks.

Many comrades wanted to join the action, but comrades prevented them from doing so. Alternating actions will continue alongside the death fast.

19 February 1999 E-3

Our block has begun a five-day alternating hunger strike. Every five days, another block will take its turn.

There is a clear lethargy amongst all the comrades. It is a difficult situation to bear. However, there is also an awareness that we have to assume responsibility more than ever. The best response to the international conspiracy will be for people to look at themselves and add their strength to that of the organisation and its action.

We now have to learn how to fight and live without the leader, to manage to do this. Genuine loyalty and real militancy will be seen from now on.

For every Kurd to turn himself into an Apo, a force, a flood of anger, is something the leader has endeavoured to create from the very beginning.

Being over-emotional will lead us to defeat. Whereas being organised and calm will lead us to victory…

20 February 1999 E-3

There was a large crowd of visitors this morning. They came because they thought we might be demoralised and behave emotionally. With a few exceptions, their morale was better than ours.

In many provinces, there is a new wave of uprisings. Actions are continuing all over Kurdistan. And in the large cities of Turkey, there are demonstrations and the burning of buildings. In Istanbul, more than 20 workplaces and 50 vehicles have been burnt after illegal demonstrations.

The bourgeois press is ignoring the protests in the cities, but the foreign press is publishing long articles.

The protests continuing all over the world have surprised even Europe and the US. Secretary of State Madeleine Albright commented, saying, "We weren't expecting such a reaction."

It is apparent that such support for the leader was not expected, hence even the Americans are surprised.

On the international stage, it was Gaddafi who demonstrated the most pro-Kurdish stance, saying, "If Turkey thinks it is going to resolve the Kurdish question by capturing Öcalan, it is mistaken."

The special war is trying to demoralise Kurdish society by distributing new photographs. Methods such as blindfolding and handcuffing him, emptying the island of İmralı and declaring it a forbidden zone are an expression of this. At this moment, the leader is being held alone on İmralı. Access to the island by air or sea has been banned. It has been declared a military zone.

According to news from the Internal Coordination, there will be a limitless hunger strike alongside the death fast.

Consequently, 223 of us have written petitions to embark on a limitless hunger strike. Tomorrow, we will send them to foreign consulates and the ministry.

We have not included the new arrivals from HADEP, some of whom are ill, but several of them have said, "In practice, we will join in." As for Müslüm Muhammed and Mürşit Aslan, they wrote notes stating, "If you don't include me in the action, I will start it myself." We hadn't written their names down as they are ill. When we were unable to dissuade them from taking part, we added them to the list.

After the visits, a HADEP member called Yadin fled from D-3. He went at a very bad time...

On the TV news we saw yellow-jacketed Kurdish Zeynep. As demonstrators clashed with police, she was hitting the police with a flag in her hand. We smiled as we realised she was hitting them with the slender flag pole. We were also pleased to see my mother in the front line of the protesters.

3 March 1999 E-3

The thirteenth day.

Our limitless hunger strike involving 225 comrades was brought to an end on the 13th day. Ten comrades will join those on the death fast. They are:

Sinan Türkmen

Şükrü Yurt

Adnan Çelebi

Yaşar Kırmızı

Ali Koç

Fuat Bor

Hakkı Aygün

Kasım Karataş

Tacettin Turan

Fendi Tekin

We don't know the total number of people who have joined in other prisons, but we will find out.

As the action ended in the evening, there was naturally a lot of activity. But as many comrades did not go on the death fast, they are experiencing a certain resentment.

Today, the TV channels mentioned agent Zeki (Şemdin Sakık) being tried and facing a death sentence. It is no coincidence that it is happening now. There is definitely an insidious plot against the leader afoot. As it is a sensitive period, they want to create confusion. They want to take advantage of the hiatus because of the forthcoming election.

We have put the comrades in our block who are involved in the death fast in the last cell on the top floor. Comrade Kutlucan will stay with them and be of assistance.

I have mixed feelings, like a lot of comrades. With every passing day, our burden is increasing. Having to act with seriousness makes us experience a variety of emotions.

14 March 1999 E-3

Since there has been a central reorganisation, the comrades on the death fast ended their action today on the 24th day. In line with the general state of action, the hunger strike will continue in the form of fifteen-person groups doing twenty days each. As for the structure, it will offer support by doing three days each. As long as the action lasts, every block will take turns to do a three-day action.

Today, the following comrades started the second round:
Yaşar Cinbaş
Ali Kaya
Muhittin Pirinççioğlu
Umut Beyaz
Çaçan Topçu
Halil Süren
Murat Emek
Ruşen Tutku
Ekrem Akman
Resul Baltacı
Mehmet Polat
Hakkı Dursun
Hüseyin Duman
Fırat Dicle
Gani Yalçın

17 March 1999 E-3

Today is the anniversary of my capture. Not a day goes by without me remembering them.

This time I won't write anything. However, I remember them as I do every day with respect and gratitude.

Memories of them will live in our struggle…

29 March 1999 E-3

After receiving a fax from comrade Nimet in Bursa prison, we have ended the unlimited hunger strike.

3 April 1999 E-3
MOMENTS WHEN WE ARE HELPLESS

Last night, I had only just dropped off, when comrade İsmet woke me up. When he said, "Kasım is poorly," I quickly went to his cell. At the same time, I was trying to wake up properly. Kasım was lying in front of the radiator. There were beads of sweat on his face. When I knelt down and asked him what was up, he said he didn't know. He was very pale and was having difficulty speaking. As he felt hot, he said, "Take off my clothes." We did that immediately. His sweat was like ice. I checked his pulse. It was weak. I hastily summoned the guard and told him the comrade needed to be taken to hospital, urgently. Then, I went back to Kasım. When he said, "Take me to the toilet," İsmet and I managed it with some difficulty. He was in a bad way. He was knelt on the floor, trying to vomit. But he couldn't bring anything up. As there was no room, we were unable to be of much help. Suddenly, congealed, black blood came out of his mouth. It had a strong odour. It was hard to bear. İsmet was trying to stop himself throwing up. I was angry and told him to go outside. I shouted at comrade Kutsi, who was waiting in the corridor, telling him to come in.

About half a kilo of blood flowed out. It looked more like crude oil than blood. The smell was really awful. But we had to try to help.

He then said he needed a number two. As comrade Sami had arrived, I went out into the corridor and told the guard he was suffering gastric bleeding. When the guard began asking meaningless questions, I lost it and shouted as loudly as I could, "The comrade has internal bleeding and is about to die, and you're asking if it's serious or not!" Then other comrades on the floor ran out into the corridor.

Meanwhile, comrade Kutsi and Sami's efforts to help caught my attention. This is what is meant by unlimited support for a comrade.

We changed Kasım's clothes, as they were in a real mess. We couldn't have sent him to hospital like that. We were in such a panic, I don't know what we dressed him in. It must have been insufficient, as comrade Bahri took off his tracksuit top and put it on Kasım, who was shivering. Despite this, he seemed to be better after throwing up blood. He was conscious. When he said he was cold, we put on a jerkin and a jacket as well.

I asked the guards to bring a stretcher. When they said they didn't have one, we wrapped Kasım in a blanket to save time and carried him out to the main corridor. The guards in the corridor said, "Okay, leave him here, let the guards carry him," whereupon I noticed comrade H. Çepik was reluctant to let go of the blanket. He looked me in the eyes as if to say the blanket was like a comrade. I put a hand on his shoulder, saying, "Comrade, they won't allow it. Let's go inside so that they take him to hospital as soon as possible," at which he let go of the blanket.

It took about an hour from the time they woke me up to the time they took him to hospital. Just in case, I noted the time he was put out in the corridor. After about 10-15 minutes, we heard the siren of the ambulance. We weren't really expecting them to take him out of the prison so quickly. It means they deemed it to be serious.

All the comrades were waiting in the corridor in their pyjamas. They were all demoralised and not one of them spoke. After telling them to go back to bed, as there was nothing more we could do, I told comrade Kadri, who was on watch, to inform comrade Bedrettin. I then went back to my bunk, but I couldn't get back to sleep. I had noticed that after the initial panic, some comrades had gone back to bed. I was most put out by this while we were trying to get the comrade sent to hospital. How can you sleep when there is such a racket going on?

An Apocu should not be able to sleep so easily. It means that even if the enemy were to attack at that moment, they still wouldn't wake up. Such a lack of concern is saddening. One should never be so insensitive in prison.

I had just got off to sleep, when I was woken up again at 03.00. They wanted us to pay for some medication they were unable to get hold of because of the holiday. Normally, it is necessary for the hospital to meet this expense. But as the situation is critical, and as they have not yet been able to treat comrade Kasım, we gave the guard 20 million and sent him off. We had to pay up, even if it was only to prevent an accusation like, "It happened because his comrades didn't pay for his medication." The bastards have got us by the throat. It's not a problem to pay for comrades, but the prison administration is acting opportunistically and pettily.

Kasım has had internal bleeding before in previous years. During the last hunger strike, he said, "I've got a bit of a stomach ache, I need to go on a diet, but I won't accept it, as it's hard to eat separately from the comrades." Despite our insistence, he refused.

In the first days of the religious holiday, he had a toothache. They didn't take him to the sick bay on account of the holiday. One night, when he was poorly, we summoned a deputy governor by the name of Ogün and demanded Kasım be taken to hospital. But he refused to do so, saying, "There's no duty dentist there." Naturally, Kasım had taken lots of painkillers and antibiotics to suppress the pain. As far as we know, on the night he suffered the gastric bleeding, he had said, "The dental medication decreased the pain. If I take a couple of Apranax tablets, I'll have a decent night's sleep after how many days." But as a result, he suffered a serious internal bleeding.

After the morning roll call, we sent him some things he might need and some money.

At the visit, none of his relatives came. However, we gave other families the address of his elder sister, Fatma, and told them to go there. Because, if no one goes to the hospital, they won't look after him properly. His sister has a heart problem. I hope there isn't an issue, but I'm worried.

Towards noon, the guards came and took another nine million to pay for medication. They said he was well and had been put on a drip.

Comrades who witnessed what happened were demoralised for the whole day.

When the children were allowed inside during the visit, there was a moment when the families panicked. When there were cries of, "He's fainted, he's fainted," we asked them to calm down. Comrade Mustafa Çepik's elder brother had had an epileptic fit. When he saw comrade Çepik hug his nephews and nieces, he collapsed. When he came round a short time later, he said, sheepishly, "When I saw him hug them, my heart gave out."

9 April 1999 E-3

At around noon, while a guest in D-1, we heard that comrade Kasım had been brought back from hospital. When I went back to the block, I went to his cell. He looked very thin. I wanted to find out what had happened at the hospital.

The only light in his colourless eyes was down to the joy he felt at being back among comrades.

10 April 1999 E-3

I have received a letter from comrade M. Tören, the first letter he has sent since going to Burdur. Reading every sentence took me back into the past. He was again swimming in a sea of emotions. He expressed his rebellion, pain, and yearnings. He put into words his revolt against the system and those who want to bring the world crashing around the Kurdish people's heads.

I gather he has posted to his mother the section of the diary I had completed and given to him.

24 April 1999 E-3

We began our annual conference today after some delay. Apart from certain particular aspects, it began like previous ones. Undoubtedly, every year is important, but this year, being the first conference since the capture of the leader, makes it all the more significant. It is imperative that we act with this in mind.

27 April 1999 E-3

We have finished the conference. We were thinking it would last about a week, but it only took four days. It progressed rapidly and, apart from a few shortcomings, went off well. There were no surprising changes in the election of the administration. Here, too, the structure doesn't offer much opportunity for innovation.

22 May 1999 E-3

As the leader's trial is approaching, a three-day alternating hunger strike began in all prisons on 19 May. As news of this reached us late, we began on 21 May. Yesterday, D-1 started.

Attitudes will become clear on the first day of the trial. As it becomes clearer, stances will be adopted.

Although indirectly, we do receive news. Inevitably, certain things affect us profoundly. Such as in the last letter from Bursa, where the leader was quoted as saying, "I am sad because my connections with you and the people have been severed," and, "My pain is on account of my affection for you"…

Excessive emotion is not good, but there is nothing we can do about it. This is what makes our captivity even more unbearable. In spite of this, we are trying to restrain our obstinacy and anger.

Today, we read the letter from Bayrampaşa together. It was in the form of two letters written in response to the women and men comrades. His feelings were reflected. At some points, he provides information we were not aware of. He points out that Britain was behind the affair.

Looking at the sensitivity expressed in the letter to the women comrades, it is evident that the women comrades wrote better letters. In the reply to a male comrade, he wrote, "You could have written in a more refined way."

I don't know about the content of the letters, but I do know that comrades have found it very difficult to write to the leader on account of being unable to express their feelings.

24 May 1999 E-3

On receiving the news, the prison was revitalised. In Amsterdam, the Kurdistan National Congress assembled with 189 delegates. Delegates and observers came from all over the world. 33 organisations and parties were involved. The congress is planned to continue until the 26th. The Burkay, Talabani, and Barzani parties did not attend. The fact they did not take part in this gathering under a national framework demonstrates that they have certain expectations and await for benefits from the imperialists. The fact they are persisting with their treachery after all these developments shows how much they have become accustomed to the swamp.

Just as in all the blocks, a surge went through our block, too. Comrades' eyes were smiling. Half an hour before the doors closed, everyone was out enthusiastically doing a halay. Comrades were soaked in sweat. After going inside, most of us had a shower and washed our clothes.

This is a historic opportunity for the people of Kurdistan.

How the people of Kurdistan have longed for today…

30 May 1999 E-3

The first day.

The tenth day of our protest hunger strike and the first day of our block's hunger strike. Consequently, we didn't have collective education today. We had free work.

A 12-person voluntary education group which we have considered for some time has come into being. We sat down and established method and sources. As this is extra, apart from the general education, these 12 people will naturally sit down more.

Tomorrow is an important day. The trial of the century will begin. The special war has focused fully on this. We are also waiting.

Tomorrow, clues will emerge as to the current state of affairs.

The "Mehmetçik press" have begun their salvoes. The press has been given a special duty. Some images of the leader will profoundly shake many comrades. It is not hard to see this already…

31 May 1999 E-3

The TVs have shown certain images dozens of times. The sight of the leader being brought into the courtroom in handcuffs will never be expunged from our memories.

He apologised to the families of soldiers who have died on account of his political responsibility. The media repeatedly dwelt on this.

In a glass cage…

Our people put in a glass cage. Us. Come to that, it was humanity…

29 June 1999 E-3

Today was verdict day in court. They handed down a death sentence. But they didn't break the pen. Although it may not be that significant, it is a tradition to snap the pen. The fact it wasn't broken sends a different message. This will become apparent in the future. But this is definitely not a matter of forgetfulness, or of it being up to the judge.

The death sentence indicates that they are not at the moment interested in a solution. The leader continued his approach of seeking a solution. As he left the courtroom, he conveyed a message by waving to the lawyers.

This was the ninth session. I gather there will be two at the Court of Cassation. 11 in all. This is not a coincidence. Kurdish leader Sheikh Said received a death sentence after 11 sessions. And on 29 June. The same number of sessions and the same date is the result of a "deep" decision. The date he went to the gallows was 4 September 1925.

It was also timed to take place the day before the anniversary of comrade Zilan blowing herself up amongst Turkish soldiers in Dersim city in 1996.

All these calculations demonstrate the insistence on harsh, brutal policies of denial. A continuation of İttihatçi [Committee of Union and Progress] Turkish nationalism.

When the words death sentence were heard, there was a moment of silence in the block. Even though the possibility of a death sentence had been discussed, it was still not possible to remain unmoved.

For two days now, I have been reading the leader's defence (manifesto), which has been published as a book. The book is 167 pages and has been distributed everywhere outside. Mem publications. It is the third time I am reading it and I am trying to understand the new methodology, for we are having difficulty in understanding and explaining it.

17 July 1999 E-3

The first day.

We have started a three-day hunger strike calling for a response to the leader's proposals for a solution. All prisons are taking action simultaneously.

18 July 1999 E-3

The second day.

Hunger strikes are an opportunity to do more reading. Many comrades are reading. In two days, I have read 450 pages of *İçindeki Devi Uyandır* [Awaken the Giant Inside You]. As it's a heavy tome, I am finding it a bit of a struggle. Tomorrow, I will take notes from the points I have highlighted.

19 August 1999 E-3
MARMARA EARTHQUAKE

We finished the action early in the evening.

The quietest time in our environment is when we are involved in actions. While many comrades concentrate on reading, and some try to write, others prefer to sleep (sleep is their favourite pastime). It's as if the place has been abandoned.

Last night, I was woken up by the sound of the E-Type generator. Everywhere was pitch black. I managed with difficulty to see that it was just after 03.00. In addition to the power cut, such a wind was blowing it felt as if it would rip up the darkness. The tin eaves on the roof were rattling.

In the morning, we heard what had happened.

At 03.02 in the morning, an earthquake measuring 7.4 occurred in the Marmara region. The power cut in the middle of the night was down to this. They cut off the power all over Turkey.

In particular, Izmit, Yalova, and Sakarya suffered serious damage. Thousands of houses were flattened like playing cards.

Heart-rending images.

Screams, entreaties, and silent yet sad faces…

Impossible to forget…

20 August 1999 E-3

For the region affected by the earthquake, there are some erroneous views, even if they are the exception. I reacted to opinions expressed such as, "While Kurdistan is being blasted to smithereens every day, the people there remain silent…" First and foremost, one must look at things humanely. There are also lots of Kurds in those areas. Even if there weren't, there are thousands of ordinary people and workers who are victims.

The general structure has been reminded of the need to be careful over the manner of speech used.

21 August 1999 E-3

We have sent a petition containing 250 signatures to the Ministry of Justice, stating we are willing to donate blood to those who need it as a result of the earthquake.

There is an amazing solidarity campaign going on outside. It is a very positive thing that HADEP municipalities and Kurdish institutions are expending efforts in this regard.

5 September 1999 E-3

According to official figures, more than 15 thousand people have died in the region affected by the earthquake, and there are more than 24 thousand injured. I'm sure the real figure is much higher.

This is horrendous and heart-breaking.

The earthquake zone has been turned into an area of devastation.

Yes, people there are weeping. Both for those they have lost and for those that remain, that is, themselves…

Aftershocks are continuing. They are not as bad as the first quake, but what fear they cause …

There have been 2,362 aftershocks since 18 August.

Because of this, people are sitting on a powder keg. Naturally, this upsets people's mental state.

22 October 1999 E-3

This morning, a three-day alternating hunger strike began. In all prisons, blocks will take their turn. A central announcement has been made regarding the demands. Among the demands are calls for the "partial amnesty" under consideration to be turned into a general amnesty, for a response to the steps taken toward peace, and for the creation of humane conditions for the leader by ending his isolation. We heard it will continue for 20 days.

A collective petition was written containing the names of 260 comrades.

If an action demanding an amnesty had been on the agenda before, I would have laughed and found it pointless. This is the first time we are taking action for such a demand.

Moreover, for the first time in an announcement made on behalf of the prisons, no name was used. "On behalf of PKK and DHP members in all prisons" is the term used. It is apparent that this happened after M. Can and Meral left.

If there is no obstacle during the hunger strike, I will write to Fatoş, Hamza, Sait hoca, comrade Mesut, and Balıkesir prison. I'm feeling embarrassed because I have not written to them for some time.

Comrade Celalettin wrote recently. He mentioned comrades Mümin Ağaçkaya and Mahmut Aktaş being released. They did exactly 20 years inside. They had been in jail since 1979. Both of them had aged. Comrade Mümin, although quite lively, had lost his hair and some of his veins were gone. Despite this, he was still more dynamic than many "young people."

I wonder what they're doing now outside. They're both resolute and honest.

They have taken steps towards the life they had dreamed about for years, but there's no doubt that after so many years, they will have encountered a world they never expected.

Along with both comrades, I witnessed many incidents in different prisons. Together, we squared up to many difficulties and tried to support each other. On many occasions we courted death. At this moment, it is as if they are close to me, and also far away...

Did we live through all that? Those harsh conditions, lack of things, helplessness, torture, actions and the years that passed by...

10 November 1999 E-3

Our hunger strike is over. Our block had the last turn. Now, the support hunger strikes in all prisons have ended. Some prisons did 20 days, others 25.

Frequent hunger strikes wear out the body. Even if you only do a two-day strike four times in a month, the body is wrecked. As nutrition is already insufficient, the damage is worse...

18 November 1999 E-3

THE AGONISING NEWS THAT TOOK ME THROUGH A TIME TUNNEL TO THE PAST IS A SECOND SPEAR IN MY LEFT SIDE

There are days that bring the walls of the prison closer together. They make the grave in which you are living even smaller. You take deeper breaths so that you continue to live and your body is not crushed between the damn concrete walls that draw closer. The air you draw into your lungs, as if to bursting point, you blast out like a volcano. And the walls retreat. You see the clear sky in the space that emerges between the fragments blown away by the force of the volcano.

In prison, you look at the blue of the sky, the caressing rays of the sun, and sometimes the stars shining in the sky and winking at you, between the stacks of concrete and iron. As you gaze, you think both how far away the universe is, and how close. You feel as though, if you stretch out your hand, you will touch it. But at one moment you will see an eternity that you cannot reach.

In spite of this, you embrace life even more tightly and look to the future. You don't allow an opportunity for hope and the future to be dampened...

When I was captured, she was still just four years old. She was a sweet, talkative little girl. As she was the youngest in the family, she naturally received a lot of attention. This spoilt her somewhat. The fact that we were involved in revolutionary activities at the time meant our approach to her was more careful and appropriate. Our serious attitude and interest led to her becoming more attached to us than anyone else. In her calico dress, she looked as if she was adorned with flowers. A pretty wild flower among a bunch of house plants...

Her short, unruly hair gave her an air of champing at the bit. Her glowing, bright black eyes made her even more likeable.

As our captivity went on, she grew up. It was easy to understand her initial silence when she first visited. She was frightened by the long rows of rusty iron bars. It was not hard to understand this from her wide open eyes.

As she grew older, she gradually overcame her fear and became a more regular visitor.

In time, she became our friend and our little "mother" outside who was having a hard time.

As she got a bit older, she began to identify her path and direction. She began to abandon her spoilt, loveable child, and take on a more mature personality.

Our HANDAN... her mother's "little bird"...

Although she grew taller than her mother, she was always her mother's little bird.

They told me the news of her, that is, Handan, today...

It is not clear where, how, or when she fell. This uncertainty is gnawing away at me.

The news of her came suddenly, like that of her elder sister, Rahşan.

When I had an intuition, I avoided going into it, as I didn't want to hear heart-wrenching news.

Every time we hear about dozens of our souls falling, our feelings surge. But we know we cannot avoid hearing this.

I was sad when I heard about Handan. I was sorry to hear about her untimely martyrdom. A comrade of ours, our youngest, should not have fallen in the land she loves at this time. I should not have heard this now.

If only such an incident had not occurred and if only I could always think of her in Zap, in Behdinan, in Cudi, in Ali Boğazı, in the liberated areas of Kurdistan...

If only I had heard of her successes in the life which she insisted on due to the harsh circumstances in which she found herself.

Fighters are those who chart the way. They are always prepared for death, permanent disablement, and capture. Hunger, thirst, the burning heat of the desert, or the freezing cold of the Zagros mountains, these are all a part of their lives. In this respect, as they overcome their fears, their routines and their weaknesses, they decide that, in spite of everything, life is something wonderful that is worth embracing wholeheartedly.

As a hungry person overcomes their fear, they become free…

A fighter who once shoulders their weapon is prepared for death at any moment. For them, fear of death is meaningless. They become accustomed to death. And death to them…

To fighters, death is not strange or hard. For it is ever-present around their necks like a necklace.

However, some deaths are hard for those who remain. On being remembered, they also give pain. The reason for this is their untimely nature.

Just think of the death that strikes when warfare is being ended. After millions of bullets have been fired and at the last moment a step is being taken towards peace, you meet the last bullet fired and reach eternity…

The last deaths are the hardest to take for those who remain. Particularly for a mother, the anguish is hard to bear…

Untimely grievous deaths are always tragic. And every time they are recalled, resentment is created.

For a mother, a child's death is always a hard thing to accept. This is inevitable, even if the child becomes a comrade of the mother. Maternal feeling predominates. And, crying a lament deep down inside, recreates the child and the comrade. With the pain of the lament, she makes the child the more precious. And expanding her love, she rediscovers the child's inaccessible beauty and bravery.

Perhaps, at first, they concealed the final news of her favourite child, but they will have said, "It's heart-breaking, let her share her hope and loneliness."

The number of us who have fallen is now not known…

Even within four walls, we have become accustomed to it. In that case, are we going to get used to you, my youngest, dark-eyed baby? It is so hard, if only you knew, my sister.

Since the beginning we have had to get used to so many losses of life that we no longer feel the need to hide it even from each other. Even though it's painful, it is now our reality. The deep trauma of our society, of its heart-wrenching grief. The unrelieved heart-breaking shriek of our mothers…

25 November 1999 E-3

For a few days now, we have been waiting with curiosity and concern. The president of the Court of Cassation announced the court's decision this morning at 9.20. It ratified the death sentence. There was a moment of profound silence in all comrades. Colour and morale changed in a moment.

Our normal daily life continued. But it was different in the exercise yard. No one felt like doing any exercise.

Handan Poyraz

There is great anger. And great sadness.

In two days' time, all prisons will start five-day hunger strikes to protest the verdict.

2 February 2000 E-3
YOU TOO, UNCLE XALEF?

I was examining the articles I have. I wanted to edit them before lunch. Correcting some comrades' articles is more difficult than rewriting them. It also takes a long time.

When I had lost myself in an article, comrade Hüsamettin appeared at the door and said sadly, "In *Özgür Bakış* newspaper, it says that uncle Xalef has been martyred." I was riveted to the spot. For a moment, I was back in Aydın with uncle Xalef.

Sad, sometimes absurd memories came flooding back. I again felt the pain and anger of the comrades there. In particular, I thought of how much some comrades will have been affected. I don't know, perhaps I wanted to see them affected as much as me.

I sat silently for a while. I couldn't work, but I couldn't get up either. Once I had calmed down, I went upstairs. Comrade Recep was reading out the newspaper headlines to a few comrades. He handed the paper to me on account of the news about uncle Xalef. I turned the pages silently. I don't know how the comrades felt, but they left the cell.

They had published the photo we had taken in block four of Aydın prison. He had pulled a knee up and was partly stretched out, resting his back on the wall… I remembered having this photo taken. One day, when the photographer was in the exercise yard, I had said to the guard, "When I sit down next to uncle Xalef, take a photo without letting on." I sat down next to him and the guard crept over and suddenly took a snap. At first, uncle Xalef was surprised, then said, "Take one of me on my own." It was one of the poses where he put his index finger and middle finger together on his cheek. The newspaper enlarged this nice pose and published it. And it published an article about the statement made by comrades in Aydın. Between the lines, I could understand the anger of comrades.

Despite reading the article in silence, I gulped and was out of breath.

20 days ago, uncle Necmi was not treated in Aydın and left to die. Before I had forgotten the pain of him, the pain of uncle Xalef has been added.

Uncle Xalef was 70 or 73. Even if he was sometimes bedridden, at times he was livelier than the young people.

We were in the same blocks for a long time. When he was healthy, he was like a rubber ball bouncing down the stairs with his plump 1.50 metre body.

He would tease the younger comrades by showing off his dynamism. Everyone who witnessed it would laugh.

Although he was old, it is hard to accept his passing. Believe me, this kind of parting has nothing to do with age. Just like two young friends who do not want to split up, or two old buddies who lose each other for ever, the news of his passing hit us hard.

It is also unacceptable that he should die 40-45 days before he was due to be released. The state deliberately sent him to his death. Firstly, they punished him twice for the same "crime," which is contrary to existing law. And then, they gave a negative answer to the campaign for his release to receive treatment as his illness worsened. By doing this, the state wanted to both make him suffer and to intimidate his circle. The message is clear.

"Losing" is undoubtedly a relative concept. But we would prefer for him to be with us in person, rather than in spirit.

Like all human beings, he too never wanted to die.

I know that because, as his vital functions slowed down, he was trying to reinforce his connections to life. But, once the body has started to weaken, there is nothing that can revitalise it. He too knew that very well, but people cannot live without hope…

One day, I will write about his situation in prison and what he said about his past. Yes, one day…

I wrote my feelings to comrade Celalettin in Aydın so that he could share them with comrades there. I know they will expect that from me.

Although the comrades here did not know uncle Xalef, they had some feeling for him from what we had told them. As they also knew the effect he had on me, many comrades expressed their sadness to me…

15 February 2000 E-3

In general, life in the damned prison is monotonous. It is a case of the same things being repeated. Since I don't want to be boring or repetitive, I don't write every day.

Today, in the newspaper, I read about the death of our Koçero (Musa Turan). He died on 13 February in Tarsus. In accordance with his will, he was buried in Cizre. A thousand people attended the funeral.

Cizre-Botan has embraced another of its children.

He was another of those who fell ill in Aydın. Although, following a campaign, he was released in 1997, it was very late for treatment. They didn't release him before he had lost a lung.

When he came to visit us, he said, "I've been released, but a part of me has stayed here. Outside, I long for the friendships here."

There was yearning in that comment, reproach and anger with himself.

As today is the first anniversary of 15 February, we have started a two-day protest hunger strike in all prisons.

It's been a year. It has been the hardest year in the history of our struggle. For those of us in prison, it has been the most unbearable of years.

It was a really hard year…

16 February 2000 E-3

I am now frightened to read the newspaper. Every day, it seems there is news of a comrade…

The comrades made a statement regarding Ömer ERDEM. They mention that his health is critical and that, in addition to chronic allergic asthma, he also has lung cancer. They say that if he is not released in order to receive treatment, we will lose him, too.

At the moment, he is in Adıyaman prison. He has been taken to hospital four times in a month. I think he was arrested in 1993.

Apart from this news, it is mentioned that around ten comrades in Aydın have serious illnesses. This naturally raises different questions. I wonder if they infected us with something in Aydın by stringing things out?

In some of our blocks in Aydın, if someone was taken ill, it would last for two or three months. They could never make a firm diagnosis. They insisted on not making one. The administration brazened it out every time, but we were never persuaded. For even when there was an emergency, a sick person would be kept waiting two or three hours before being taken to hospital.

This practice reflected an attitude of, "By then, he will either die or get better."

In ten years in Aydın prison, we lost seven comrades.

It is not known whose turn will be next…

Today I received a letter from comrades Ö. Akıncı and E. Teker in Burdur prison. I was very pleased. They say, "You've forgotten us, but we were very influenced by you." But, just because I haven't written, does it mean I've forgotten them? I will write to them as soon as possible.

I also received a long letter from my mother. She sent the last photo I had taken together with Rahşan and Handan.

There was a lot of emotion in her lines. She also didn't neglect to include some criticism,

Her morale appears to be good.

Ali Poyraz and Halef Özer (Xalo Xalef)

14 April 2000 E-3

They are planning to open F-type prisons once their construction is completed. They have prepared public opinion for the opening of five of them in May. The construction of cells in all E-Types is also almost complete.

Within a year, they will begin the process of putting inmates in cells. They consider this to be imperative, particularly to obstruct organised life. Essentially, they want to alienate us from ourselves by isolating us. Putting people in cells at this stage will bring many problems, however we look at it. Whether we like it or not, it's going to happen. But, after all that has gone on, what are we going to abandon in cells? They are trying to take revenge, but they know very well that we will never abandon our principles.

In order to raise public awareness about cells and to express our opposition, we will start a ten-day alternating hunger strike in all prisons on 15 April.

We have written petitions on behalf of all comrades and sent them to various places.

The prison administration has said it will no longer provide us with detergent, soap, brushes, etc. Our representatives immediately got involved to convey our reaction, as we have to have these items for hygiene, and if we have to buy them in the canteen, where the prices are high, we cannot fund it.

After a short while, the deputy governor summoned our representatives and told them, "There has been a misunderstanding. There will just be a one-month delay."

15 April 2000 E-3

I have felt gloomy for a few days now. I want to connect it to certain practical problems, not to the diagnosis a few days ago that I am a carrier of hepatitis B. Not that…

Gloom and tiredness. In spite of this, I am trying not to let myself go. I am trying to remain faithful to my vow not to abandon myself inside these accursed four walls.

My gloom is more connected to my feelings regarding the outside world. I hope I do not encounter another piece of bad news…

16 April 2000 E-3

Today, I wrote a long letter to comrades Celalettin and Mesut. I also wrote long cards to Mazlum Şendur, Yusuf Kocabey, İdris Batur, and Ali Şendur.

I feel weary now, as we played football today.

1 May 2000 E-3

At 09.00, we held a minute's silence before commencing Mayday celebrations. After singing the Mayday march and the reading of messages, we exchanged greetings and had a short break. Meanwhile, the stage was assembled.

The sketches were topical and aroused interest. The most gripping was the one about attitudes following the changeover to F-Types, where people will be in cells. Comrade Bülent played the role of a person in self-denial. It was fascinating, as he was dressed like someone on the beach, with a white shirt, shorts, and sunglasses, although the space he was in measured only two square metres.

5 May 2000 E-3

As he is being released tomorrow, comrade Salih Sezgin went around the blocks saying goodbye. He was trying to hold back the tears. "I've made a promise to myself not to cry", he said.

I think that after 20 years inside, the outside will seem very different. He will find it very difficult at the beginning, for sure. I can guess this pretty much from his emotional state.

6 May 2000 E-3

Today is the anniversary of the execution of Deniz, Yusuf, and Hüseyin. Their spirit of resistance, and their memories, live on in our struggle.

Towards noon, comrade Salih passed us in the visiting area on his way out. It was as if his knees were knocking together. He had a strange look on his face – a mixture of excitement, worry, and joy. I was pleased to see him leave, but was sorry to see him in that state.

As for us, we are pleased that he is going out.

All power to your elbow, Salih Sezgin…

27 May 2000 E-3

It was the opposite block's visiting day. I think comrade Tören sent his nephew. I gather he has been released and is now in Osmaniye. It's difficult to imagine him outside after 20 years. When I think of him encountering that new world with his unique gestures and bewilderment, I both laugh and feel sad.

I gather that, if he can manage it, he will come to visit us himself.

I know he will have new problems to deal with, which will be tough, but I believe he will persevere and overcome them.

We've lived through almost everything together since 1979. In a way, we have sent another part of ourselves outside. In several prisons, we were in unbelievable conditions and suffered unthinkable attacks. Numerous times, we were close to death...

In 1988 we were in Eskişehir special type prison, and a prison uniform was imposed. We refused to wear it and soldiers and guards attacked us, trying to isolate us in cells. When we linked arms, the truncheon blows began to rain down on us. Tören and I were in the front row, so that the first blows came down on our heads. At the same time, they were trying to separate us. At that moment, I saw comrade Tören shout, "Hit me, hit me! I won't die easily!" Amidst the confusion, he recited a poem by Ahmet Arif. I think this example is sufficient to explain comrade Tören.

My old friend. I wish you all the best in your new life, in the new period. More power to your elbow.

31 May 2000 E-3

It's been more than a year
He is still on that island
Still all by himself
He is being deliberately isolated from the world, from human beings, from his comrades.

I gather he has been ill for the last two months. The damp climate there is affecting him particularly badly. All prisons have begun a one-month alternating hunger strike to demand that he be treated and transferred to another prison. Every block will take turns to do three days each, until a month is completed.

3 June 2000 E-3

Today we began a hunger strike.

Until 11.00, I wrote on a typewriter. It was one from a state office. It's an old, mechanical one, but I like it.

Towards noon, I was called to the visiting area. Former prisoner Ş. Göktaş had sent someone to defend his untidy practice. I explained our position and tried to persuade him, but when he insisted on speaking like Göktaş and began defaming our structure, I sent him on his way.

18 June 2000 E-3

Our hunger strike is continuing. Today, our block started for the second time. The first time we excluded seven comrades who were ill, but as there are some problems amongst them in their daily lives, we are all involved in this second action, except from two comrades with ulcers.

For 15 days now, we have been busy painting the block. While normally it is up to the authorities to do this, we're having to do it ourselves. If it were left to them, they would try to bury us in filth. Even though it's a prison, we have to protect our living space and keep it clean.

Many comrades have been working hard for 15 days. The upper floor was finished today. It will be left empty for two days to allow the paint to dry and for the smell to go. All the cracks were scraped and filled with plaster. The governor said, "It has been 16 years since this prison was opened, and it's never seen repairs like this." During the repairs, they came to check on it almost every day. Once the prosecutor came too.

For two weeks, we have all stayed on the lower floor. We will move to the upper floor when the lower floor is being fixed.

Yesterday, they gave us information about the comrade who came from Midyat prison. Küçük Başurlu was amongst informers for two years. He apparently wrote a petition to take advantage of the Penitence law. Despite this, he said, "I'm not an informer. I just applied to take advantage of the law." Do you laugh or cry?

Moreover, while in the rural areas, presumably to avoid participating in an action, he shot himself. Now, he limps. To avoid enduring a moment of difficulty, shoot yourself and be disabled for life. It's incredible. If that's the case, why did you become a guerrilla? Unfortunately, such peculiar incidents do happen.

A. Oruç's novel about the prophet Abraham is finished. We've sent a copy to the publishing committee. Sinan, Hüseyin Yılmaz, and I have begun to examine it. It consists of 200 large pages. Because we are editing it as we go, it is taking time. We only read 53 pages in a whole day. Fortunately, it had already been edited twice and rewritten before it came to us. It would have been really difficult without those comrades' efforts. We are planning to finish it during the hunger strike. Let's see.

20 June 2000 E-3

Comrade Bedrettin came to our block. Our conversation was mainly about his transfer to Çankırı prison. There have been problems there, and the structure there is weak. For this reason, the internal coordination asked him to go there. Comrades Sinan, Yakup, and Musa have also written petitions asking to be transferred there. But we are not that optimistic about the outcome.

As for Midyat prison, comrades Hakkı and Nizam have written petitions to go there. It will be good for both places if these transfers take place.

Hanifi Aslan was in hospital. They operated on him. As it was a serious operation, they gave him a blood transfusion. Since the hospital where the operation took place supposedly did not have an agreement with the prison, they asked us to pay 32 million. We had to pay up, both due to a concern that they wouldn't look after him, and to prevent a bad outcome in case of an emergency.

We have continued to read and examine the novel about Abraham. As we continued to 22.00, it wore us out. We've almost finished. And with the effects of the hunger strike, I have a bad headache. Despite this, we said let's finish it. We've made lots of corrections.

Although the construct is good, its literary element is weak. It has also been rushed. It needs to be rewritten, taking into account the criticisms and proposals made. If this is done, it will attract attention as the subject matter is topical. I don't think ours will publish it, but perhaps Yurt Publishing will, as they have published historical and mythological novels recently.

Today, once again, the name of my old friend Tören was mentioned. Since our visit last week, he has frequently been on our agenda. While stroking a puppy in Osmaniye, the dog bit him on the hand. The animal then turned out to have rabies. They began to give comrade Tören rabies vaccinations. At the moment, there is a shortage of rabies vaccinations in Turkey, and what does exist is often out of date. I hope nothing happens to him. Stay 20 years in prison, survive lots of things, get released, and you're bitten by a rabid dog. You couldn't make it up!

When I think about it, I am angry, and sad, and then I laugh. I imagine comrade Tören at that moment. For certain, as the dog approached him, he will have said, "What a cute puppy" and encouraged it. And when it bit him, he will have laughed at himself. And when people suggested going to hospital, he will have said, "There's no need for that. It's just a little dog." And when he realised the seriousness of it, he will have exclaimed, "Wow!"

The comrades washed the upper floor with lots of water.

During the morning roll call, comrade Mahmut Muhammed had an epileptic fit. As there were a lot of guards present, we were late getting a dried onion to his nose. Towards evening, he fell down again. It took him quite a long time to come round. He frequently collapses. And he doesn't listen to us. When we tell him to take it easy, he moves around more than ever.

Once, when comrade Şendur was making lentil soup in a large pot in the cell we have turned into a kitchen, M. Muhammed was popping in and out. The pot was boiling in the narrow cell, but comrade Şendur didn't want to tell him to get out. Just when he had gone outside, Muhammed had a fit and fell into the narrow space between the concrete wall and the pot. His arm was on the side of the pot. When Şendur came back and saw what had happened, he was shocked. He shouted for help to the comrades, while also saying, "Just as well the boiling soup wasn't spilt, otherwise it would have scalded Muhammed."

His arm was stuck against the side of the pot up to his elbow. He suffered pain for months afterwards. There is still a scar on his arm.

21 June 2000 E-3

As with all hunger strikes, when I woke up in the morning, my mouth felt like mud. It was 07.00. After washing my face, I brushed my teeth. Feeling slightly refreshed, I went out into the exercise yard and sat at the far end, where the sun's rays were falling. It had been a cold night and there was a tremendous storm. Once, when I woke up, I wondered if it was an earthquake. That's why the sun was so appealing.

In the morning, the upper floor was washed again. In the afternoon, we began to move in. It was as if we had moved into a new house.

I stood by the door into the corridor on the lower floor and looked for a long time. If you told folk outside that people live here, they wouldn't believe it. It becomes noticeable when it is emptied. It is just like a derelict building. It looks like a building awaiting demolition. Just living in a place like this rots people.

I often say, "Prison is a damnable place." Looking at the lower floor, it is not possible to disagree. However, when you're living here, it's more difficult to tell.

We finished our hunger strike at 16.00.

Comrade Mahmut had another epileptic fit this morning. He's had more because he didn't take his medication during the hunger strike. We tried to persuade him not to take part, but were unable to do so. He insisted on taking part in the action. The moments when he insisted were worthy of a sketch.

26 July 2000 E-3
"AFTER ALL, THEY ALWAYS SAY THEY ARE WELL"

Think of a guerrilla.

In the most difficult conditions, never forgetting their comrades in prison, using the injustices inside and the yearnings, anger and helplessness as steps that motivate them to overcome trials and tribulations…

While sitting at the summit of a mountain, sadly observing the stars and saying, "Even in prison, we watched the stars from behind bars. Now they too are also watching," I want share the wonder of infinity…

And think of them when they are hungry and thirsty, saying, "Keep going comrades, don't forget Hayri, Kemal, and the others," reminding them of the superhuman resolution demonstrated in Diyarbakır prison to counter the brutal measures that were as harsh as the desert of Karbala, wishing to encourage and motivate those whose knees are weak and who are hesitant.

They know very well that those inside strive to overcome the hardest moments by thinking of their comrades in the mountains. They see them as the strongest leverage.

Someone who had left prison and knew well those inside – a guerrilla, a comrade, an elder brother – said, when told that we had said we were well, "After all, they always say that they are well."

Although it may seem strange to some, guerrillas are the most emotional of people, in spite of their life amongst cold, gun barrels. The incidents that are difficult to contemplate propel them into a profound state of emotion. And it is for this reason that they better understand the language of eyes and soul…

Today, I was visited by my sister Fatoş after a gap of 12 years, although I don't remember precisely. As soon as I entered the visiting cabin, she recognised me and shouted out. She had come with her three children. When I left home, she was herself a child. She had been accompanied by aunt Aley, but our aunt was not allowed in. She was going to wait outside until the visit was over. She helped us a lot and was a good friend to my mother.

As it was the last visit of the month, they allowed children inside. I waited for Helin and Hande at the gate and picked them up. They were both wearing clothes of the same colour. Their hair was black and their clothes the colour of chicks.

The eldest daughter, Hatice, is between eight and 10, and naturally perceives the reality of the place I'm in better. When she hugs me, she begins to sob. When my young sister saw me for the first time from the other side of the cabin with her children, she also wept in silence. Still, I managed to stop both of them crying, quickly.

Hande and Helin both looked about three. They know me from photos. But despite that, they didn't want to stay with me for very long. I think they found the atmosphere strange. I would like to have known what they thought.

Although I said that Helin "looks like Granny Zayne" because of her plumpness, she actually reminds me of her aunt Rahşan as a child. As for Hande, with her slender figure, she looks just like her aunt Handan.

I kept confusing their names. Every time, Fatoş corrected me, saying, "She's etc."

We sent Hande and Helin back early. Hatice stayed with us. As she had grown up in London and was at school there, she was not familiar with Kurdishness. Also, although she could speak Turkish, she couldn't write it. She said, "Uncle, learn English, then let's write to each other." Little witch! She doesn't say, I'll learn Turkish, but is going to teach me English at my age!

They came back in the afternoon. We requested that they be allowed in again, saying, "They've come a long way." And we again took Hatice and Hande inside. I gave Hatice a pencil. She didn't want to take it, but Fatoş insisted.

I found Fatoş more mature than I had expected. Also sad, of course…

She had been to the house where we grew up in Antep. I realised from her voice that it had been very difficult for her. "Chatting to you, I feel I'm back in the old days, as if the bad days hadn't happened," she added.

We talked about a lot of people we knew. We kept coming back to our siblings, Rahşan and Handan. She mentioned what she had heard about their martyrdom. She was most anguished about the fact that the elected representative of our village had not accepted Rahşan's body for burial, saying, "There are none of her relatives here." Of course, at that time, she and our mother did not know about it. They were right to be angry about it.

I sent her an album with 75 photos in it for her to keep.

Naturally, one of the people we talked about most was our mother. Sometimes we laughed, other times, we felt sad.

I think I understood her. To some extent, I find her expectations normal.

My mother has calculated exactly what remains of my sentence, including my additional sentence.

Prior to the visit, she called Fatoş and explained her latest "perspectives." She is always on her guard. She's right to do that. She has experience in these things.

Fatoş and the children will come again next week. Then, I assume, they will return to Britain. I wonder whether they will leave having had a pleasant time.

They visited our village, Bozhöyük, and really liked it. They said it was "So green." I asked Hatice, "Which is better?" and she didn't hesitate, saying, "Britain is better."

Out of the hearing of the children, I asked Fatoş, "There's a rumour that my elder brother has been martyred. Is it true?"

"No, that's not the case," said Fatoş. "Whenever he gets the chance, he calls us. In fact, the last time he called, he asked about you and the people inside.

When I said 'They say in their letters that they are well,' he replied, 'After all, they always say that they are well.'"

Fatoş explained this so convincingly that my doubts vanished. What he said about us inside also pleased me a lot.

Comrade Salih Sezgin also came to visit. It was strange. He was lively and excitable, but also reproachful. It was obvious that he was pleased to see us again.

"When I enter a room outside, I feel suffocated. I hate prison, but when I see the relationships outside, I miss the relationships in prison and yearn for the friendship here," he said.

This means that we, too, will find it hard going outside. We get the message.

A. Aktaş has been arrested while trying to leave the country with a forged I.D. They say he will serve a few months in prison. Even though it's a short time, it will be really tough to be back in prison after doing 20 years. It would crush you. I hope he's not in custody for long.

When we returned to the block, H. Yağız said, jokingly, "You know, your Helin thought I was her uncle." He persisted. "She didn't recognise you." "What are you on about?" I replied. "She recognised me from photos. You're trying to take credit for it," I said, laughing.

10 August 2000 E-3

As soon as I opened my eyes at 06.00, I was told that ten comrades had been transferred here from Aydın. For a moment, I was flabbergasted. It wasn't normal for ten people from Aydın to go to the same place. Most importantly, who were these people? While these questions occupied my mind, I dressed hurriedly and went downstairs.

Apparently, they are on their way to other prisons and have just stopped off here. At the moment, they are at the gate. When they asked to stay in our blocks, the prison governor told comrade Bedrettin, "As long as you let us have them back in one piece, we'll let them in." The comrade didn't hesitate in saying yes.

This is the first time such a stopover has taken place. If it has happened before, they would have been put in cells.

They put all of them in D-3. I immediately asked for their names. Soon, a note arrived. One of the arrivals, Sakıp Hazman, had written it. Before even saying hello, he had started with the jibes. Surprised, I both read the note and laughed. Those who had come were Sakıp Hazman, Kahraman Oktay, Baki Akbay, Cevdet Demiroğlu, Mehmet Eryılmaz, Şükrü Topkan, Nurettin Topkan, Özcan Erdem, Osman Demir, Kenan Bakay, and Mahsun Tekin.

He had also added a note, "Apparently, you are on duty in the kitchen. Since we didn't want to go hungry, we didn't come to your block. Revolutionary greetings. Sakıp."

As it happens, today, Hasan Yağız and I are on duty. It is evident that he found this out immediately and used it for banter.

Before the roll call, we chatted through the window. I wanted immediate answers to all my questions.

I gather that in Aydın, the prison authorities wanted to empty block four, so 11 comrades agreed to be transferred to Batman, Midyat, and Siirt.

The journey from Aydın to Antep took 20 hours. They had sweated so much in the vehicle that their clothes had white patches on them. The sweat had dried, turned into salt, and formed shapes. They were obviously tired, but were in good spirits. Their eyes were sparkling, as they were all going where they wanted to go.

In spite of our insistence, none of them had a shower. "Within 10 minutes in the vehicle, we'll be soaked in sweat," they said.

From here, Hüseyin Gezer is to be transferred to Beşiri. We asked the authorities to take him with these comrades and they agreed. We reminded them of the things to be careful about in the places they were going.

They provided lots of information about Aydın. The negative attitude shown to comrades Delil and Salih particularly pained me. I gather they were treated as scapegoats. Criticism and the stance taken should not have breached the boundaries of respect. Both these comrades were veterans who had demonstrated the utmost self-sacrifice in all circumstances. They had never turned their backs on any of our values.

They also mentioned uncle Xalef. I was very sad when I heard about his final days. After uncle Necmettin died, he had apparently often said, "It's my turn next." He had let himself go and paid no attention to his diet. This had naturally shattered his resistance. He had sent me a card in his last days. I am very sorry that I never received it. When they reminded me that he was due to be released 45 days later, I was devastated once again. It's so unfortunate and really makes you angry.

I once again remember him with respect and gratitude.

Being martyred in prison after the age of 70 is an honour.

Uncle Xalef, you will live forever in our hearts.

28 August 2000 E-3

Many pages that are written in prison turn into a sea of sadness and separation on account of what takes place.

Even though we are in a small space, we've seen off many comrades at different times. And sometimes we have set out on the road.

In prison, people generally go out on "internal journeys." But, despite all the lack of opportunity, sometimes external journeys do take place. And these deeply affect both those who stay and those who go.

We've just had another of these. Comrades Bedrettin Kavak, Yakup Soylu, Sinan Türkmen, and Musa Altun left the blocks at 05.30 this morning to board the transfer vehicle. We heard the vehicle move off at 05.50. The sound of the vehicle reached us in those early hours.

Despite their having paid the transport costs a month ago, they were being kept waiting. Finally, on Friday, they were told that they would leave on Monday. We are not used to being told the day and time.

Yesterday, the four comrades went around the blocks saying their farewells. When they came to our block, they treated us to some black grapes as we were chatting. They said, "A crate of grapes came during our last visit. From Amara village, from the leader's family." Naturally, the conversation moved from Amara to İmralı.

All the comrades gathered in the exercise yard. Comrade Bedrettin made the farewell speech. In general, he talked about the importance of taking ownership of life, the organisation, and comradeship. He mentioned the past, with its good and not so good days. While indirectly telling those with problems to pull themselves together, he also called on other comrades to provide them with more support.

When he spoke to the structure, he asked me for my mother's phone number, which I gave him.

As Sinan is in our block, we held a meeting between eight and 10 in the evening. When he was given the floor, he said, "I have many things I want to say, but I can't express them. When comrades from the main case were exiled to Amed in 1993, comrade Süleyman made a speech and was hard put to speak. I didn't understand then, but now I understand him well." He became more emotional, saying, "In getting to know myself, the contribution of comrades here has been immense. I will endeavour to be worthy of this everywhere I go."

Then, some comrades sang folk songs, and others recited poems. There were impressions, those of Sinan being the most amusing. I hope our commune managers won't be offended, but the snacks they distributed were a kind of a cocktail. As the amounts of raisins, roasted chickpeas, sunflower seeds, and hazelnuts were meagre, they were all mixed together and handed out a bit at a time. Still, for us, it was a luxury and pleasing to see.

I met comrade Bedrettin in Aydın in 1991. He was one of those taken to Amed for the court case.

1991 was a very important year for us. Along with the prison resistance conference that took place outside, also in prisons, everything began to be put on the table and reorganised. This naturally led to a conflict of ideas and methodology. As in Aydın, we had central comrades from many prisons, and the meetings were lively and prolonged. Our debate platform in '91 went on for close to three months.

Let me give a few examples to help with comprehension.

The following were some of the experienced comrades who were in Aydın prison at that time:

Hamili Yıldırım
Kemal Aktaş
Mustafa Sarıkaya
Fuat Kav
M. Sait Üçlü
Şamil Batmaz
Mehmet Tören
Mustafa Gezgör
Yusuf Onat
Hüsnü Altun
Faruk Altun
Metin Aslan
İrfan Babaoğlu
Hüseyin Acar
Kenan Şen
Celal Salgut
Mümin Ağcakaya
Hasan Şerik
Doğan Kılıçkaya
Celalettin Delibaş
Erdoğan Sönmez
Ali Aksoy
Nimet Sevim
M. Ali Yılmaz
Cesim Soylu
Nesimi Kiliç

As much as it was an advantage to have such competent, popular personalities from many prisons together in one place, it also had its disadvantages.

Although during this period comrade Bedrettin was not in Aydın, he was aware of all developments.

When I saw him seven years later, he was more active, resolute, and aware. I was pleased to see this.

Who knows when and where our paths will cross again. He has actually done his 20 years but is being kept waiting by additional sentences. If these sentences are dropped, he could be released at any time.

As comrade Bedrettin has gone, today I went around the blocks with comrade Yaşar Cinbaş as representative. There was a marked flatness in all the blocks. This was most evident in the block Bedrettin had been in, D-3. There was banter such as, "Don't neglect us, don't let us notice his absence."

29 August 2000 E-3

Last night I put on a tracksuit top for the first time in months as there was a sudden drop in temperature. As everything is concrete, the cold is felt more. Since I am not using a blanket yet, I felt the cold under a quilt.

After the roll call at 08.00, we took out the blankets and winter clothes from the first cell (blind cell) at the entrance to the block. As those on night duty had filled up all the bins, buckets, and bowls with water, we began to wash them in turn. In each batch, there were two cells. The second group was us and comrade Kutlucan's comrades from the opposite cell. As the blankets were heavy because they were wet, it was difficult to carry them and wring them out. We washed them in a corner of the exercise yard that had been cleaned. Although lots of comrades offered to help, we didn't allow anyone except comrade Kasım to assist us.

All 11 cells finished their washing. It was good to get them out of the corner. As moth balls had been placed there to prevent vermin and mice, we need to spread out the winter clothes in the exercise yard. We can't use them until they have been well aired.

As we will have a one-day hunger strike to mark "1 September," we have circulated petitions for signing in all blocks. A total of 12 pages. 238 people will take part. We omitted the 11 comrades who have less than a year left to serve.

The petition was in the form of a call, noting that the lands of Anatolia and Mesopotamia are where the philosophy of peace developed, and urging all segments of society to be receptive to the leader's step toward peace, so that it receives the response it deserves.

Last night, I wrote a seven-page letter to my mother. I hadn't written for a long time. I am sure that, when she receives it, she will be both happy and weep. I mentioned the visit by Hatice and her family. And of course, her. I also enclosed a photo, an article about F-Types, and an article titled "Historical and General Organisational Awareness amongst the Kurds." The envelope was quite heavy. I hope it arrives complete.

Today, comrade A. Karatay was transferred to Cizre prison. As he only has seven or eight months of his sentence to serve, they agreed to the transfer. He won't find a more comfortable place than this one. We approved the transfer due to his age and because his family is there.

Despite today being our bath day, they didn't give us hot water. As always, in every prison, apparently the "central heating is broken."

I assume they didn't give us hot water because of the fortnightly search…

1 September 2000 E-3

We started a hunger strike today to create awareness of peace, unfortunately, in the region where it was first expounded in history.

To spite those who benefit from warfare, we have offered our bread, our food for peace.

21 September 2000 E-3

On seeing comrade Mehmet Tören's name on an envelope when the letters arrived, I opened it eagerly. He had sent a photo, a panorama. At first glance, I realised it was Nizip. It was obvious from the view and the colour of the soil.

A few months before he was released, I had sent him a couple of Nizip postcards as a joke. He had replied, saying, "When I'm released, I'll show you how photographs are sent." Three months later, he has retaliated.

It took me back to 1979 because it's impossible for us not to be affected by a few lines he has written. In his characteristic left-handed handwriting, he says, "Ali, it's so difficult writing to you from outside. But not writing is even more difficult… It's a real dilemma. I'm sending you photos of the streets/places where we started to pursue our dreams and began to run. It's unbearable to walk these streets without you. There, I would run into such-and-such a friend, here another. Especially you, Yaşar, Bozan, villager Sait… It's unacceptable, but I cried like a child. About everything. I embrace and kiss you and all the comrades. Your brother."

The sentences, feelings, and yearnings took me back to the old days and those souls. Once again, I was alongside them. In those days, when we had nothing, when there were shortages of everything, there was little complaint and everyone worked hard for the ideals. There was a lively awareness…

Undoubtedly, we didn't have the knowledge and culture on many topics that we do now, but conviction and loyalty were strong, and we had yet to encounter certain adversities.

I understand how much comrade Tören yearned for those days and those comrades while he was writing these lines. When comparing them with today's people and relationships, it is unthinkable that he shouldn't yearn them.

Yes, I understand well why comrade Tören was unable to stem his tears while walking the streets of Nizip. Also, his loneliness in the crowds there. But, in spite of everything, it is real, real, real…

I also want to see the comradeship, warmth, loyalty, effort, trust and, most important of all, resistance of those days. But you, too, know that the character and people of every period are different.

We have never lost touch with those days and those comrades. We will always remember them with yearning. We will wait patiently and with hope that the red dawn will always expect them.

The letter was posted in Aksaray, Istanbul on 13 September 2000. I'm sure that our Tören will have been overwhelmed by the big city. But I believe he will have managed. And I wish him all success in this new period.

23 September 2000 E-3

We have started a three-day hunger strike in protest at the attack launched by the PUK in the South, and for it to be halted. 237 comrades are involved. All prisons started on the same day. It is designed to create awareness and arouse public opinion.

There is a lot of reaction outside to this attack. They weren't expecting this from Jalal Talabani and the PUK. It seems, unfortunately, that they are no different to Barzani and the KDP…

17 November 2000 E-3

All prisons have started a six-day hunger strike. 234 of us are involved here. The demands are political. The aim is to create awareness about the leader's hearing at the European Court of Human Rights, and to call for a general amnesty and the abandoning of the F-Type prisons.

While I was thinking I would read a book during the hunger strike, I had to go to F-3 today. And as tomorrow is a visiting day, I will be busy all day.

7 December 2000 E-3

The death fast and limitless hunger strike launched by the Turkish Left is continuing. It has been more than 40 days since it started. In these conditions, this is a critical point. Consequently, we have started a limitless, alternating hunger strike in all prisons. Each group will do two days. I don't know how long it will go on. In the morning, I went to hospital. I had my eyes tested on a computer. My left eye is 1.25, the right one 1.00. Although I sometimes have an ache in my eyes, I didn't consider it serious. But I was surprised by the degree. Still, it's not bad. I will have to wear glasses all the time.

In the afternoon, I dropped in to blocks D-1, E-1, and F-1. As comrade Yaşar Cinbaş is on hunger strike, I went on my own.

19 December 2000 E-3

Comrades in other prisons have turned the action into a limitless one. We have also turned our alternating action into a limitless one. At the moment, 20 comrades are on a limitless hunger strike.

20 December 2000 E-3

I really don't have the heart to write about the savagery that has taken place. Yesterday morning in 20 prisons, where death fasts were going on, there were simultaneous operations. In all these places, the inmates responded by putting up barricades.

Just when it seemed agreement was about to be reached to end the protests, when public opinion was expecting this, they suddenly attacked…

We don't yet know the extent of the attacks. We are anxious!

24 December 2000 E-3

They couldn't get into some prisons for four days. They had to smash down the walls to get in. It is not known how many inmates were killed by flame throwers and live bullets. According to official figures, there are 30 dead and many wounded.

For days, we have been watching the images in fright and anger. We will not forget the resisters who set themselves alight when attacked and stood firm despite all the pain.

The issue should have been resolved without it coming to this. Intellectuals had been getting involved through mediation, and serious talks were taking place. We don't fully understand why there was deadlock. But whatever the reason, there is no denying that there was a heroic resistance.

Hundreds of prisoners have been forcibly taken to F-Type prisons. On the way in, they suffered torture as rules were imposed.

It's really hard to explain. The measures used against people who had been on hunger strike for 60 days are unacceptable. 3,500 tear gas shells were fired into a single prison. We watched the footage. As flame throwers were used to force entry, even the plaster on the walls burst. It was as if the iron bunks melted.

If we consider that even the eyes and nostrils of reporters filming two kilometres away were affected, think about the effects of those shells on those inside the prison.

31 December 2000 E-3

Today, there were visits on both sides. We have heard that the limitless hunger strike has been ended and turned into an alternating one. Naturally, we too will continue like this, as our stance is a central one. Our blocks will continue doing three days each.

6 January 2001 E-3

We didn't use to be too bothered and were not that affected. Our generation is getting old, I reckon. Actions are now becoming hard for us. Despite this, I didn't sleep for three days while on hunger strike, as I consider time spent in bed a waste of time. It is more meaningful to spend time on articles, books, or work that needs to be done. In fact, I couldn't relax even if I wanted to. If I stop, they won't let me rest…

10 January 2001 E-3

On the way back from the visit, comrades Kasım and Kutlucan at the door of the opposite block gave me good news. A letter and four photos have come from comrade Şamil. He says he is going to be released on the 29th of this month. We thought he had another 15 months to do. It's a surprise for us, but we're delighted.

As though he was writing his last letter, the emotion-laden sentences both saddened and pleased us. As always, his humbleness was evident.

I wrote him a letter until midnight and enclosed a photo.

Comrade H. Yağız also hurriedly prepared two photos. We will send it registered and will be happy if he receives it before he is released.

15 January 2001 E-3

For some reason, I didn't sleep well last night. I woke up several times and tried to get back to sleep. Then I was angry, as not being able to sleep is irritating.

We got up at 06.15 for exercise. As comrades Tacettin and Karatepe in our cell also got up, our cell was up in its entirety. I only occasionally miss a session.

After having the morning soup, I wrote a short letter to Fatoş before roll call. I included a note to send the interview I did regarding comrade Doğan Kılıçkaya (Yasin). I sent it registered, as I want to turn it into a book.

As the hole in the downstairs shower is blocked, water has been building up for three days. They cleared it. We watched them do it for 15 to 20 minutes.

Until noon, we continued to read H. Kissinger's *History of Diplomacy*. As they are new topics, it is going slowly.

In the afternoon, we went round the blocks. We ran into comrades Şükrü Yurt and Memduh Kolona, who were going round the blocks, in D-1. One is being released tomorrow and the other the day after. We chatted to both of them for a while. They were both excited. Comrade Şükrü made a speech to the block structure on behalf of the two of them. His address was short, fluent, and orderly. I told him, "It was a good speech. You'd prepared well." He answered with a smile. When I asked him what he was thinking about, he hesitated, then said, "I've only got a day left, but I'm saying to myself that it's enough. I don't even want to think about comrades who are doing long sentences." I didn't say anything, because he was right.

I had a look at the latest paintings done by comrade Menaf Osman. He is one of the most productive of those arrested after 1990. His new paintings are really good. The harmony of colour is especially striking.

I was called to see the doctor after having a blood test. He said, "Unfortunately, you haven't got over the illness. You have the hepatitis B virus in your blood. At the moment, there's no problem. You're a carrier, but if you get run down, it can become active. You need to be careful and look after yourself." It's at a level of 36. Once again, he referred me to the hospital for a check-up.

In the prison, I made a request for a general check-up, and the doctor said, "I'm trying to persuade the administration."

Tomorrow, I will send an urgent telegram to Aydın prison, urging them to put pressure on the prison authorities to test the blood of all inmates. For it was said that it had not been possible to make a firm diagnosis of some comrades who were with us and were permanently ill. This is not at all credible. I thought about this after being diagnosed with hepatitis B. I think lots of the comrades in Aydın have this condition. The prison authorities are deliberately spreading it.

Comrade Sıdık in D-3 was ill. There is once again an outbreak of flu in our blocks and there is no way we can protect ourselves by taking precautions.

Between 16.00 and 18.00, we continued reading the diplomacy book. Between 20.00 and 23.00 in the evening, I carried on reading Vedat Türkali's novel, *Güven* [Trust].

6 May 2001 E-3

Today is the anniversary of the execution of Deniz and his comrades. At this moment, I can see Deniz's innocent face. His bearing and dynamism continue to arouse admiration in all those who see him.

We once again bow our heads in respect for their memories.

Death fasts are continuing in many prisons. They are nearing 200 days. There have been 20 deaths, including four of family members involved in support outside. It is only a matter of time before there are mass fatalities. Despite this, the ministry has not taken any steps towards resolving the issue. The murderers don't care, although around 100 prisoners are at death's door.

Those who are preventing a solution are doing Turkey a great disservice. They are only thinking of their own positions.

For six months now, our comrades in all prisons have carried out countless support actions in the form of alternating and unlimited hunger strikes. At the moment there are 20 comrades here on a limitless hunger strike. They are:

İsmet Aslan
Bayer Uğurlu
Naci Kanak
Bülent Direk
Tacdin Turan
Rıfat Kaya
Kemal Tüzün
Cafer Savaşan
Asım Demir
Taner Kahraman
Mevlan Bala
Mehmet Kanıt
Sedat Gönenç
Taylan Çintay
Fırat Arzu
Ekrem Solhan
İsmet Yüzügüldü
Fendi Tekin
Metin Dalan
Abdullah Aksu

Just like outside, and with the guerrillas, dozens of comrades step forward. But we have to be organised and controlled. Although they know this, comrades may feel demoralised when they are left out.

A letter has arrived from Aydın prison. With great difficulty, they managed to persuade the authorities to give them blood tests. In the block where I stayed, 12 comrades were diagnosed with hepatitis B and one with hepatitis C. They deliberately kept this comrade with us to spread the illness to everyone. If someone has hepatitis C, they should be quarantined and treated. The comrade didn't even know he had it. This is one of the ways to kill people in prison. This is a central, planned measure used in all prisons.

5 June 2001 E-3

The action that lasted 30 days ended today in the afternoon. All the comrades are well.

Throughout the action, I found it difficult emotionally. If I had been involved, perhaps it wouldn't have been so bad. Comrades were on hunger strike, and I also lost weight with them as the days went by.

The death fasts are continuing. In these conditions, we could not have offered more support. During the last six or seven months, we have been on hunger strike half the time. We couldn't have weakened the comrades any more than we have. Also, as we need to be prepared for anything, comrades have to be able to recover.

We have, of course, not had any disagreement with the groups carrying out the protests.

We have done all we can to support them in all prisons.

In spite of everything, we pay respect to their actions.

20 November 2001 E-3

This evening, like an unexpected guest, snow began to fall. As it was dark, when you looked at the projectors in the exercise yard, you could see the small snowflakes swirling around aimlessly. Seeing these white dots fluttering left and right surprised us. Even though it's very cold, we weren't expecting snow.

The cold is going right into our bones. As the radiators are not on, our cells are like refrigerators. On such cold nights, I wash my feet with cold water before going to bed. At first your feet freeze, but when they warm up a while later, you drop off to sleep without knowing it.

My right kidney is not feeling well. I will wear a corset as a precaution before going to bed. I don't want it to get worse, because the pain can be very bad.

21 November 2001 E-3

The freezing cold made itself felt this morning, too. As on Wednesday and today, it is visiting day, and I'm concerned for the families. Travelling in this weather and waiting for hours at the prison gates is really hard. At such times, if we tell them not to come, they definitely won't accept it. They endure sun, rain, wind, and snow, all hardships, without complaint and always come. They calm down and calm us down as well.

The dry cold continued until noon, but then it began to snow. And with big flakes. By 15.00, there was ten centimetres of it on the roofs. If it goes on like this, it'll be really deep.

They still haven't put on the radiators.

Despite feeling the cold on our skin and in our internal organs, it's nice to watch the snow fall. Strange and varied feelings follow one another.

Of course, everyone is affected in different ways, but when it snows, people are generally taken back to their childhood. Sometimes to shocking incidents in the past. As the snow descends, the flakes never touch each other. Even if the snow becomes heavy, you can feel the flakes landing softly. At that moment, you're absorbed in it. It's as if your thoughts take you away.

Snow mostly sustains sadness and joy in company. When people dash out into the street with the initial excitement and start to make snowballs, they perhaps don't think about the consequences, but as problems occur, they become apparent.

When comrades first become aware it is snowing, they make strange noises as they express their surprise. Most are naturally words of joy.

Watching it snow in prison makes one sad. I don't know how many times I've witnessed snow inside, but it is becoming hard to endure seeing those white flakes descend.

Seeing the snow carpeting the ground, I thought, "What are homeless people outside doing?"

When darkness fell, there was a power cut. It got even colder. You can't do anything in the dark. For a while, I thought about people I knew outside. I imagined chatting to them. It's joyful, but bitter-sweet. Perhaps because it won't be long before I'm released, I'm thinking more about the outside.

According to what I hear during visits and from letters, the people who are fond of us are becoming impatient. They're entitled to be.

There has also been a power cut in the city. In addition to the snow, there is a stiff wind blowing. When you listen, it is evident that the snow and the cold have taken control. There is no noise apart from that of the wind. It's as if I can hear our family and friends telling us, "Make sure you wrap up warm!"

Despite going to bed at 01.00, I couldn't get to sleep. I dropped off at about 03.00, then woke up again at 05.00. I then remained in bed until 07.00 in the same state of mind.

Thoughts about the future and certain ambiguities are fluttering around in my head like snowflakes.

My wish is to go to the liberated areas when I am released. However, the comrades there want me to remain in the city. From my point of view, it doesn't appear possible for me to remain in the city.

My belief that everything will turn out well is firm. I trust those who love and value us. But possible outcomes that might develop beyond our control obviously worry us.

I have corrected a poem and given it a final shape. And while whispering it to myself, I felt as if the people I love were listening. The fact they liked it also made me happy.

This is the effect that poetry, imagery, has...

BİRECİK/URFA PRISON

12 July 2002

LEAVING PRISON

It's the first day I've been outside a prison without handcuffs.

It's a lovely, sunny day.

I came out of Birecik prison, where I was transferred six months ago, after 21 years and four months in various prisons, without handcuffs or a soldier on my arm, walking. As this is a district prison, it is smaller than the others. As I strode around the courtyard, I sensed a profound silence. I said farewell to my prison friends Abdurrahman, Ali, İsmail, and the others, and as I stepped outside, a group of 40 to 50 people applauded and ululated. I couldn't work out exactly who was there, but most of them were relatives who had visited us over the years.

As the applause and ululations floated into the sky, I felt strange. I embraced those I knew, and shook hands with everyone, one by one.

I was outside, but the applause and ululation reminded me of the atmosphere in the Adana military court at the moment when 25 of us received death sentences on 8 August 1986.

When the names of those sentenced to death were read out and the judge broke his pen, all those in the gallery began to ululate and applaud. The slogans we shouted at the top of our voices shocked the judges and they scurried away. We and our relatives were standing up and shouting as loudly as we could.

The soldiers were surprised as it was the first time they had witnessed such a thing, but when they recovered, their truncheons began to descend on us, leading to the slogans and applause growing even louder.

This was young Kurdish prisoners once again challenging the death penalty.

It was an expression of continuing the honour of those heroes in history who shouted on the gallows.

It was the resisting Kurd throwing down the gauntlet to colonialism.

It was doing the immortal Kurdish heroes proud.

Those who resist have never feared, and will never fear, death.

It was showing how to stand up to the enemy's unjust, invidious trials and the death sentence.

It was the historic and topical trial of the judges.

The continuing applause and ululations at the prison gate when I was released brought me back to the present.

The delight of those who had come was evident in their eyes. They had all put on clean clothes.

In order for it not to go on too long, I addressed them:

"I thank you for meeting me at the gate on such a day and once again for not abandoning me. To be together with you after so many years is wonderful. But I am leaving part of myself inside. That is, I am experiencing both joy and sorrow at the same time. It is difficult to express this. There is no point in waiting here any longer. Let's continue on our way."

I looked strange in my baggy trousers and check shirt.

As people got into the vehicles, my sister Fatoş's daughter, Hatice, said, "Mum, give one of the phones to my uncle."

Fatoş extended her hand, holding two Nokia phones she had brought from Britain.

"We bought both of them. One is for you, the other is for Hatice. Take whichever one you like."

"No, let Hatice choose."

I wanted to give Hatice first choice. It was to be her first telephone.

When Hatice refused, I chose the small phone, as wide as two fingers.

Hatice whispered in surprise to her mother, "My uncle understands telephones."

I laughed, but didn't get involved.

I hugged four-year-old Helin and Hande multiple times.

Birsel, who had been released two days previously, was also there. He smiled, saying, "Didn't I tell you I'd definitely be released before you and meet you at the gate?"

Fatoş, her daughters, and Birsel's family got in the same vehicle. Seven or eight vehicles moved off.

The vehicle I was in was in the middle of the convoy. I looked around curiously.

Years later, I was seeing the outside without barbed wire and prison bars. My feelings were confused on seeing street traders, shops, and pedestrians on the pavement as if for the first time.

As we headed towards Antep, the road sloped down towards the bridge. The first thing I noticed were the tables and chairs on the banks of the Euphrates. I felt the beauty of sitting opposite the water and losing oneself in one's thoughts. The buildings above, made of white stone, caught my attention. These images reflected history.

As we approached the bridge, I said to the driver, "Could you stop in the middle. I want to walk. Wait for me on the other side. I'll get back in there."

The other occupants looked at each other, baffled. So that they would relax, I explained, "When I was in prison, I promised myself I would walk across the Euphrates on this bridge."

After I had told Cevdet to give me his phone, I told them to continue. They left me and moved off.

As I approached the railings of the bridge, Fatoş, Birsel, and his sister, who had got out of the minibus in front, came running towards me. I shouted, "Don't come, wait!" and waved at them to wait, but they ran towards me, shouting, "Don't do it." At first, I didn't understand what was going on. They insisted on coming over to me. As they neared me, Fatoş said,

"Why did you get out?"

"Go back to the vehicle, I'm coming."

"Why did you get out here?"

The noise of the traffic and the wind made it difficult to hear. I shouted,

"I just want to walk across the bridge."

"We misunderstood you," they said.

I was silent. I pretended not to understand. I didn't want to upset them. I'm not that helpless and weak as to throw myself off this bridge after 21 years of standing up to all manner of pain, suffering, and brutality. Our motto in all circumstances was, "Resistance is Life." It was this spirit that sustained us in the most trying conditions, when repression was at its worst and seemed unbearable at times.

When they returned to their vehicle, I looked at the water and drifted into the distance. The flow of the water was such that in the middle of the bridge even looking at the Euphrates was scary.

Historically, who knows what the Euphrates has witnessed. What pain, exile, and massacres has it witnessed? How many times has it flowed red with blood…?

Perhaps its feisty flow was a reaction and rebellion against that…

I phoned my mother in Germany. She was expecting me to call as she knew I was coming out today. I had promised I would call.

"I'm out, Mum. How are you?"

Trying to control herself, she replied in a tearful, feeble voice:

"I'm fine, son. It's over at last. How are you?"

"I'm fine, don't worry. I've just got out. At the moment, I'm over the river Euphrates. First, I've rung you, and I'm watching the Euphrates for you."

The wind was buffeting my face. I could just about hear my mother's voice.

She talked about my sisters Rahşan and Handan who were immortalised in the struggle for freedom. And she said something about my elder brother, Hüseyin, who joined the guerrillas after eight years in prison. My long-suffering mother was crying with the pain of not hearing his voice for 11 years.

She was sobbing because she hadn't been able to come today.

As I listened to her I, too, began to cry.

The two of us wept, comfortable in the knowledge we were alone.

My quiet, large tears spilled into the Euphrates.

The river Euphrates was weeping once again.

It was crying as if it was carrying the pain and joy of history to the present and future. The river was keeping us company with our weeping.

I don't know how long I was on the phone to my mother and how long we cried together with the Euphrates.

As I walked over the bridge, the cool air I breathed in deeply helped me compose myself.

Those who were waiting for me on the other side of the bridge looked at me silently. But I noticed that Fatoş avoided looking me in the eyes.

We quickly got in the vehicles and moved off.

I had opened the window. No one was talking. I was alone with my silence. The trees on the side of the road were speeding by. I was able to distinguish pistachio and olive trees amongst them.

I wanted to touch the earth, to walk barefoot. I wanted to feel the softness of the red soil on the soles of my feet, to feel every lump of earth.

I didn't know where the road flowing under the vehicle was taking me and what I would encounter.

I was setting sail for the future like a boat going out to sea.

But one thing I was sure about. The comrades I had left inside would be with me everywhere and in all circumstances.

Freedom was relative.

"HELLO" to new tomorrows…

ILLUSTRATIONS

Cumhuriyet newspaper, 3 August, 1989.

(*Top, left to right*) Mehmet Gencer, Omer Gelici. (*Bottom, left to right*) Hasan Merdan, Ali Poyraz (Maraş Closed Prison, 20 July 1981).

October 1984 - (Mersin E-Type Prison).

Hasan Şerik (*l*) and Ali Poyraz (*r*) (Adana Closed Prison, 1986).

Handan Poyraz (*l*), Ali Poyraz (*m*), Mother Zeynep (*r*)
(Mersin E-Type Prison, 7 September 1984).

Author: Ali Poyraz,
(Antep, E-Type Prison, 1984).

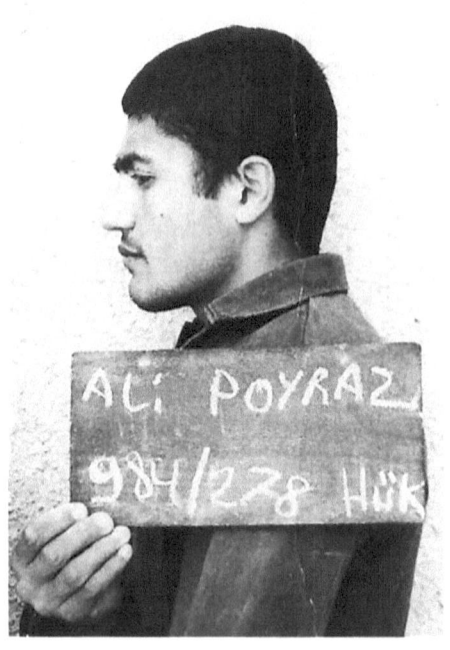

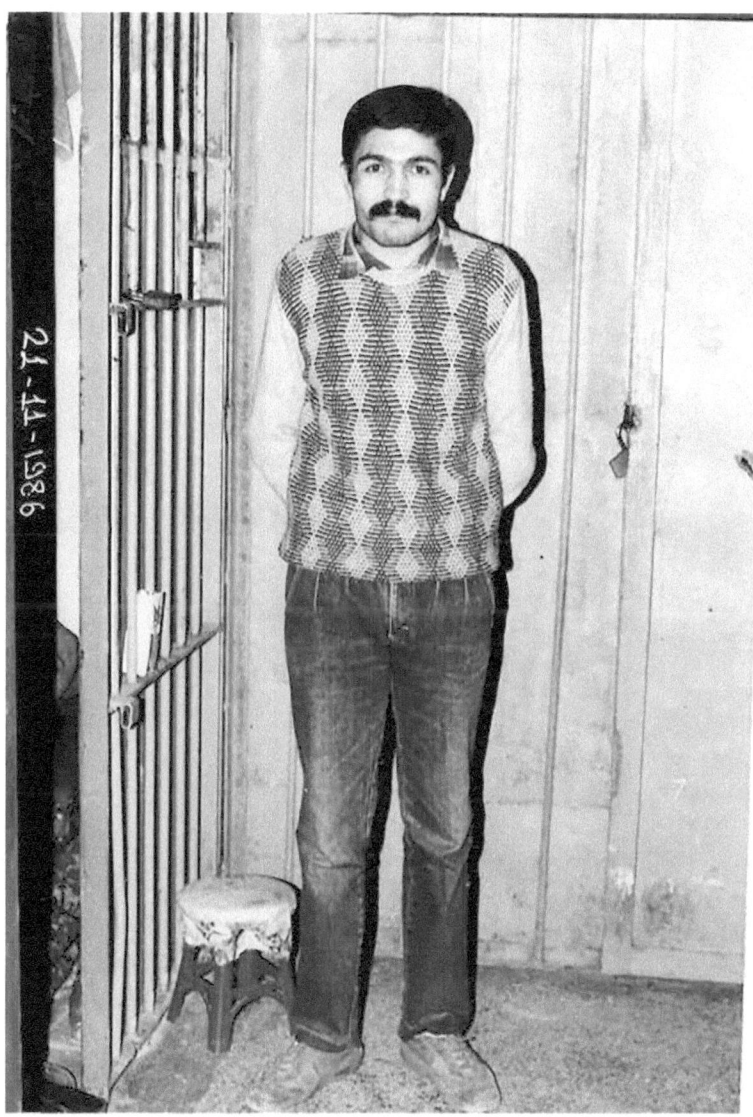

Adana Closed Prison, 21 November 1986.

Eskişehir L-Type Prison, 28 November 1988.

Eskişehir Prison, 1988.

Illustrations 355

(*Left to right*) Rahşan Poyraz, Ali Poyraz, Handan Poyraz, Aydın E-Type Prison, 1990.

Aydın, 18 August 1990.

Aydın E-Type Prison, 9-13 Ward, 1990.

(*Top row, left to right*) Mahmut Bolca, A.Rahman Solmaz, Metin Aslan, Mustafa Keser, Abdullah Uzun, Hamit Kandal, İlhami Adıyaman, M.Sait Üçlü, Mümin Ağcakaya, Mehmet Özkan.

(*Standing, middle, left to right*) Nurdoğan Köroğlu, Haluk Gül, A.Selam Apaydın, Hasan Özen, Ali Kastalmış, Aladdin Aktaş, Ahmet Yavuz, Ali Aksoy, A. Cabbar Gezici, Şükrü Göktaş, Ali Poyraz, Hamili Yıldırım.

(*Sitting, upper, left to right*) Remzi Karakaş, Hüsnü Altun, Şamil Batmaz, Yusuf Onay, Erdoğan Sönmez, Mustafa Çelik, Ahmet Cerenbeli, Mehdi Gökçe, Mustafa Gezgör.

(*Sitting, bottom, left to right*) Kazım Kılıç, Mahmut Aslan, İskan Açıkça, Kemal Aktaş, Mehmet Doymaz(Küçük), Muharrem Karabulut, Fuat Kav, Hasan Şerik, Doğan Kılıçkaya (Yasin).

Antep Special Type Prison E-Type, August 1999.

Also from the Gomidas Institute

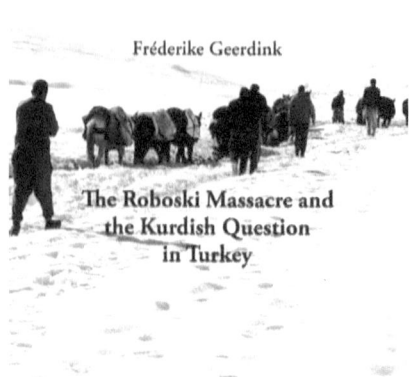

* İsmail Beşikçi, *International Colony Kurdistan* with a new foreword by Ismail Beşikçi, (2005), ISBN 9781909382206.

* Ahmet Kahraman, *Uprising, Suppression, Retribution: The Kurdish Struggle in Turkey in the Twentieth Century,* (2010), ISBN 9781903656747.

* Fréderike Geerdink, *The Boys Are Dead: The Roboski Massacre and the Kurdish Question in Turkey* (2015), ISBN 9781909382190.

www.ingramcontent.com/pod-product-compliance
Lightning Source LLC
Chambersburg PA
CBHW021134230426
43667CB00005B/115